Light on Tantra in Kashmir Shaivism

Abhinavagupta's Tantrāloka

Chapter Four

Revealed by

Swami Lakshmanjoo

WITH ORIGINAL AUDIO

Viresh Hughes, Editor

Lakshmanjoo Academy

Published by Lakshmanjoo Academy

First printing 2023

Printed in the United States of America

For information, address:
Lakshmanjoo Academy
www.lakshmanjooacademy.org

ISBN 978-1-947241-13-8 (hardcover)
ISBN 978-1-947241-14-5 (paperback)
ISBN 978-1-947241-15-2 (ebook)

This sacred text is dedicated to Swami Lakshmanjoo,
our beloved teacher and spiritual father
who has given us everything.
Glory be to Thee!

Table of Contents

Tantrāloka
Fourth Chapter (Āhnika) – Śāktopāya

Appendix

Topics according to Tantrāloka 1 index

In *śāktopāya*, nine subjects will be discussed:

a) *Vikalpa saṁskriya*: how *vikalpa* (thought) is refined from differentiated to undifferentiated thought (one-pointedness).*

b) *Tarkatattvaṁ*: what is the essence of *tarka*, pure logic. How you can get entry in God consciousness with pure logic.

c) *Gurusatattvakam*: what is the essence of the master, and who can be a master in this system.

d) *Yogāṅgānupayogitvam*: the eight limbs of Patañjali's Yoga are not useful in this system.

e) *Kalpitā arcā anādaraḥ*: outward worship is also discarded.

f) *Saṁvit cakrodaya*: the rise of the twelve Kālīs in creation, protection and destruction, with regards to the states of *prameya*, *pramāṇa*, *pramātṛ* and *anākhya*.

g) *Mantra-vīrya*: the power of all *mantras*, what recitation really is. *Mantra-vīrya* means, whatever you say, it must become *mantra-vīrya*. In *śāmbhavopāya*, there is only '*ahaṁ*' (I-ness), that is the thought-less process. In *mantra-vīrya*, there are thoughts, it is a thought process.

h) *Japyādi vāstavam*: what is meant by *japa*, real recitation.

i) *Niṣedha vidhi tulyatvaṁ*: nothing is right and nothing is wrong.

---

* Lit., the impression (*saṁskāra*) of a thought (*vikalpa*). In terms of practice, it refers to the continual one-pointed impression or awareness of a single thought.

Guide to Pronunciation

The following English words exemplify the pronunciation of selected Saṅskṛit vowels and consonants. The Romanized Saṅskṛit vowel or consonant is first listed and then an English word is given to aid you in its proper pronunciation.

a	as	a in ***A***merica.
ā	as	a in f***a***ther.
i	as	i in f***i***ll, l***i***ly.
ī	as	i in pol***i***ce.
u	as	u in f***u***ll.
ū	as	u in r***u***de.
ṛi	as	ri in mer***ri***ly.
ṛī	as	ri in ma***ri***ne.
e	as	e in pr***e***y.
ai	as	ai in ***ai***sle.
o	as	o in st***o***ne.
au	as	ou in h***ou***se.
ś	as	s in ***s***ure.
ṣ	as	sh in ***sh***un, bu***sh***.
s	as	s in ***s***aint, ***s***un.

Swami Ram and Swami Lakshmanjoo with Swamiji's Parents

Foreword

In December of 1958, Swami Lakshmanjoo took his usual winter seclusion, during which time he meditated on the twelve verses of the *Kramastotra*. These hymns form a poetic eulogy to the twelve Kālīs as depicted in Kashmir Shaivism. Over a period of two and a half months Swamiji contemplated on the essential meaning of each of these mystical verses. On the following birthday (20th May 1959), as a gift from Swamiji to his devotees, a small booklet was published in Sanskrit and Hindi, titled, *Shri Kramanaya Pradīpikā.*

As the twelve Kālīs form an important part of this present publication – Chapter 4 of Abhinavagupta's *Tantrāloka* (vol III of the LJA *Tantrāloka* series) – numerous footnotes from Swamiji's *Kramanaya Pradīpikā* have been added to give the reader a deeper insight into the mysterious workings of these twelve Goddesses who form 'the main connecting rod between individuality and universality'.

In his rendering of this chapter – which forms volume III of the Lakshmanjoo Academy *Tantrāloka* series – Swamiji has used the Kashmir Series of Text and Studies, Number XXX, vol III (1921).

Introduction

In the previous *āhnika**, Abhinavagupta revealed the practice (*upāya*) of *śāmbhavopāya* (the supreme means), which is also known as *īcchopāya* (the means pertaining to the energy of will), for the direct attainment of universal God consciousness. For practitioners who are incapable of grasping *śāmbhavopāya*, Abhinavagupta reveals, here in the fourth *āhnika* of his *Tantrāloka*, the practice of *śāktopāya*, which is also known as *jñānopāya* (the means pertaining to the energy of knowledge or cognition). Whereas *śāmbhavopāya* operated in the field of pre-discursive thought (*nirvikalpa*, thought-lessness), *śāktopāya* operates in the field of discursive thought (*vikalpa*) with the intent of leading the *sādhaka* (practitioner) towards the thought-less state of universal God consciousness (*śāmbhavāvasthā*). Abhinavagupta will describe the mechanics involved in this formidable, though accessible, practice.

According to the *Śiva Sūtras* (2.1), the essence of *śāktopāya* is *cittaṁ mantraḥ* (mind is *mantra*), and so Abhinavagupta begins his discourse by explaining the foundation of this practice: *vikalpa saṁskāra* (the one-pointed/purified impression of a thought). Whereas the practitioner of *śāmbhavopāya* maintains perpetual awareness of the initial thought-less moment (*prathamābhāsa*) in the rise of a thought, the practitioner of *śāktopāya* maintains perpetual awareness of the the risen thought itself. Abhinavagupta tells us: "Anyone who wants to get entry in that nature of God consciousness should associate in continuity his thought, just to keep that one thought in continuation so that it does not get diluted or it does not get astray; and rapidly (*añjasā*), without a break, without a break you should put again and again that thought, just to associate that with the previous thought." The slightest degradation or change from the original impression of the chosen thought in the proceeding impressions of that thought will disable this practice. Every succeeding thought must not only be a mirror image of the original thought, but a progressive intensification in its clarity in order for *śāktopāya* to prove successful. Swamiji tells us:

---

* Lit., what may be read on one day.

"The first *vikalpa*, the first *saṁskāra*, is residing in the field of *asphuṭa bhāva* (not vivid), the next *saṁskāra* is vivid (*sphuṭa*), the next *saṁskāra* is more vivid (*sphuṭatāra*), the fourth *saṁskāra* is most vivid (*sphuṭatama*). And in the fourth *śloka*, he explains that there is another *saṁskāra* manifested in-between these. There is one *saṁskāra*, *asphuṭa*, and between *asphuṭa* and *sphuṭa* there is another *saṁskāra*; in-between *sphuṭa* and *sphuṭatara* there is another *saṁskāra*; in-between *sphuṭatāra* and *sphuṭatama* there is another *saṁskāra* to be held, you have to see. So, it means that the travel of these impressions should be so filled with awareness that you must observe all these *saṁskāra*s."

Abhinavagupta then goes on to explain the means by which the *sādhaka* gains the wherewithal to practice *śāktopāya–tarka* (or *sattarka*). Swamiji translates *tarka* as "discriminating transcendental logic" by which the practitioner understands "what is to be left aside and what is to be owned. Differentiated perception is to be thrown out and the undifferentiated reality of Being is to be owned." Having intellectually discerned the difference between Lord Śiva and ignorance, the aspirant is made capable of experiencing said reality without any doubt or hindrance. But how does one attain to *tarka*? Swamiji tells us: "He has to travel first from a master, to the *śāstra*s (scriptures), and [then] to [his] own experience, and then travel again from [his] own experience, to the *śāstra*s, and the master. This is the way of our thinking. This is the way for attaining knowledge of God consciousness." The aspirant must, therefore, be able to discern the right masters from the wrong masters, and the right scriptures from the wrong scriptures. And so, Abhinavagupta will describe the hierarchy of masters and scriptures. But as ones own experience is the predominant factor in ones journey, he says:

"*Tattva jñāna* (knowledge of reality) is the main point to be achieved. That is *sādhya*, that is to be achieved. *Yatra yatraiva dṛśyate*, wherever it is achieved, wherever it is perceived, that is the master, that you must confirm in your knowledge that it is the master. When your experience, your inner experience, believes that your master has told you the exact thing, then you should believe in the words of your master. When your *śāstra*s have [explained to] you according to your experience, then you should believe those *śāstra*s. Because *svatantram svato mānam*, this *māna* (*māna* means, *śāstra* and guru), *śāstra* and the guru are not independent, that independently they will thrust in your experience.

This [knowledge] must be digested in your experience. If it is not digested in your experience, there is still the need of a master, there is still the need of *śāstra*, some other *śāstra*. If not that [master, then] some other master; if not that [*śāstra*, then] some other *śāstra*."

Abhinavagupta then contextualizes the role of *tarka* (transcendental logic) in terms of Patañjali's limbs of Yoga (*yogāṅga*), which are designed to lead the aspirant to *citta vṛtti nirodhaḥ* (thought-lessness), the state of *yoga-samādhi* (union of the contemplator with the object of contemplation). Just as we find in the *Maitrāyaṇīya Upaniṣad*, however, Kashmir Shaivism recognizes only six limbs of Yoga rather than the eight limbs of Patañjali's system. These six limbs are *prāṇāyāma* (breath control), *dhāraṇā* (concentration) *pratyāhāra* (sense withdrawal), *dhyāna* (meditation), *tarka* (transcendental logic), and *samādhi* (union). The *yama*s (moral restraints), *niyama*s (positive duties or observances), and asanas (postures) are omitted, and *tarka* is added. In the practice of *śāktopāya*, however, only one limb is required for the achievement of universal God consciousness: *tarka*. The *sādhaka* who is capable of *śāktopāya* stands at the summit of the yogic limbs, thus rendering them useless. Abhinavagupta says:

"All these limbs of Yoga are explained only *sva pūrva pūrva upāyatvāt*, because they become the means of their previous limbs. For the *yama*s, the *yama*s are the means to get entry in the *niyama*s; the *niyama*s become the means to get entry in *āsana*; *āsana* becomes the means to get entry in *pratyāhāra*, and so on–*svapūrva pūrva upāyatvāt*. *Antya tarka upayogataḥ*, and in the end, all these limbs are meant to get entry in *tarka*. *Tarka* is the final state and the supreme state of yoga."

Established in *tarka*, the practitioner is fit to undertake *śāktopāya*, the practice of which is equated to the act of internal worship (*pūjā*). Unlike the external worship that is observed in *āṇavopāya* (the means pertaining to the energy of action) where the preceding yogic limbs are necessary, in the internal worship of *śāktopāya*, Abhinavagupta tells us, "*Iha sarvātmake kasmāt tat vidhi pratiṣedhane*, there is no *vidhi* (injunction), there is no *pratiṣedha* (prohibition)" because the practitioner's awareness, being firmly grounded is *tarka*, is beyond such requirements. Abhinavagupta continues:

"This *sāmagrī* (offering) of *pūjā* (worship) is to be sought first. I mean, the things by which you will adore/worship Lord Śiva, that is, flowers, *chandana* (sandalwood), scent, essence, all these things you have to collect first before you adore Him. And that collection is to be done from where? Not from the garden, not from flowers, [but from] yat *kiñcit mānasāhlādi*, whatever is digested in your brain, whatever is digested peacefully in your brain, happily, joyfully in your brain."

Whatever thought the practitioner's mind is naturally and enthusiastically drawn to, that is to be used as the *sāmagrī* (offering) in *śāktopāya* practice/worship. In fact, it is considered illogical to utilize anything other than what pleases the worshipper provided that it enables him/her to maintain one-pointedness (viz., *vikalpa saṁskāra*). "Wherever your consciousness moves," Swamiji tells us, "it may move to the five senses or pleasures or the daily routine of life, there you will find the real *pūjā* existing because your individual consciousness is totally united with God consciousness there–if you have developed awareness, not otherwise." The *sādhaka* performs this worship and achieves this union by meditating upon the "wheel of consciousness" (*saṁvit cakra*), the twelve Kālīs (cognitions), which arise in rapid succession in any given thought-perception. "The twelve Kālīs," Swamiji tells us, "are the main connecting rod between individuality and universality." These twelve cognitions (*pramāṇas*) are the links by which God consciousness descends to become individual consciousness and individual consciousness ascends to become God consciousness. In the third *āhnika*, Abhinavagupta discussed how this is so by defining the verbal root of Kālī, "*kāla*". He says:

"*Parāmarśātmakatvena*, '*kāla*' means who puts *parāmarśa* (awareness) of I-consciousness, when there is *parāmarśa* of I-being. *Visarga ākṣepa yogataḥ*, when there is flow of creation, that is *kāla*, that is the meaning of *kāla*–to flow in creation. I-consciousness flows in creation, creative being, and *ākṣepa*, it gets expansion externally. When you are expanded externally, that is the meaning of *kāla*. *Iyattākalanat*, after getting expanded in the universe, you get shrunk, this is the meaning of *kāla*; *iyattākalana*, get entry from unlimited nature into limitation, this is the way of Kālī. And [*kāla* is] *jñānāt*, and to know again, afresh, your own nature, again get entry in your own God consciousness."

The practice of *śāktopāya* operates within the field of differentiation and time–time, which is another meaning of "*kāla*". Consequently, Abhinavagupta notes that *śāktopāya* "is the means of *māyā*, the means of illusion." Nevertheless, Swamiji tells us, *śāktopāya* is considered to be "the highest process because this process is more stable" than *śāmbhavopāya* as it removes the threat of differentiated perception for good by infusing it with undifferentiated awareness. Unlike *śāmbhavopāya*, where the practitioner immediately experiences the differentiated world through the lens of undifferentiated and timeless perception of *unmīlanā* (extroverted) *samādhi*, the *śāktopāya* yogi must first strive to rapidly wind up time (*kālakarṣiṇī*) and differentiated perception through *nimīlanā* (introverted) *samādhi* in order to achieve the undifferentiated timelessness of *unmīlanā samādhi* within the world of differentiation. "This," Swamiji tells us, "is the essence of these twelve Kālīs: this going up and coming in *nimīlanā*, and then coming down in *unmīlanā*." Abhinavagupta will detail the name and function of each of the twelvefold Kālīs in this process.

Once the practitioner succeeds in holding a single thought in perpetuity (viz., *vikalpa saṁskāra*), he must then observe the rapidly successive fluctuations that arise in the course of that thought, each of which are delineated by the twelve Kālīs. Whereas *śāmbhavopāya* functions only at the initial thought-less moment just prior to the actual creation of a thought-perception, *śāktopāya* operates within the flux of its creation (*sṛṣṭi*), preservation (*sthiti*), and destruction (*saṁhāra*) in its *prameya* (objectivity), *pramāṇa* (cognition), and *pramātṛ* (subjectivity), with the intent of observing the unspeakable void (*anākhya*) of *pramiti bhāva* (pure thought-less/object-less subjectivity) between each fluctuation and ultimately throughout the entire phenomenal process. "And the purpose of twelve Kālīs," Swamiji tells us, "is to find that state in each and every state. In *sṛṣṭi* (creation) also, you have to find *anākhya*. These twelve Kālīs are the explanation of *anākhya cakra* only. It is not the explanation of objectivity or cognitivity or subjectivity. You have to find that real transcendental state of nothingness in each and every act."

Having wound up the flux of differentiated perception through the internal process (*nimīlanā samādhi*) of the twelve Kālīs into *anākhya*, the twelve Kālīs of *anākhya* then flash forth externally through *unmīlanā samādhi* (viz., *śāmbhavopāya*), and everything that the yogi perceives is now endowed with the power of *mantra* (*mantra vīrya*), and so every thought becomes his *japa* (recitation). "Whatever he does," Abhinavagupta tells us, "whatever he creates externally or internally–[internally] in the formation of pleasure, pain, joy, sorrow; externally in pots, jugs, everything, [all] external objects–*tadevāsya dhyānam syāt*, that is, in the real sense, the meditation center for him." Every perception sentences his mind towards the pure knowledge (*śuddhavidyā*) of universal God consciousness, and so he lives in a world where "*nisedha vidhi tulyatvaṁ*, nothing is right and nothing is wrong" because he experiences both the good and the bad, pleasure and pain, purity and impurity, to be filled with the glory of God, the glory of his own Self (*ahaṁ parāmarśa*).

This introduction by no means captures the entirety of Abhinavagupta's description of *śaktopāya* in this fourth *āhnika*. It is intended only to prepare one's mind and intellect for the journey ahead. Let us begin, then, to read and listen to Swamiji's translation of the fourth *āhnika* of Abhinavagupta's *Tantrāloka*.

Acknowledgements

First of all, I would like to thank our associate editors: John Hughes, George Barselaar, and Denise Hughes. They took the raw unedited audio transcript and transformed it into a polished document ready for publication. Being closely attuned to Swamiji's vision, they were able to lightly edit the manuscript without tarnishing the flow of the narrative. Recognizing that these revelations were meant to aid the student in gaining a deeper understanding of Trika philosophy and the practices of Kashmir Shaivism, comprehensive footnotes and an exhaustive appendix have been added to facilitate this quest. Lastly, I would like to thank Michael Van Winkle, our audio engineer who enhanced the original audio, Claudia Dose, our creative director who was responsible for the creation of the overall design of this book, and Shanna Hughes who coordinated this project.

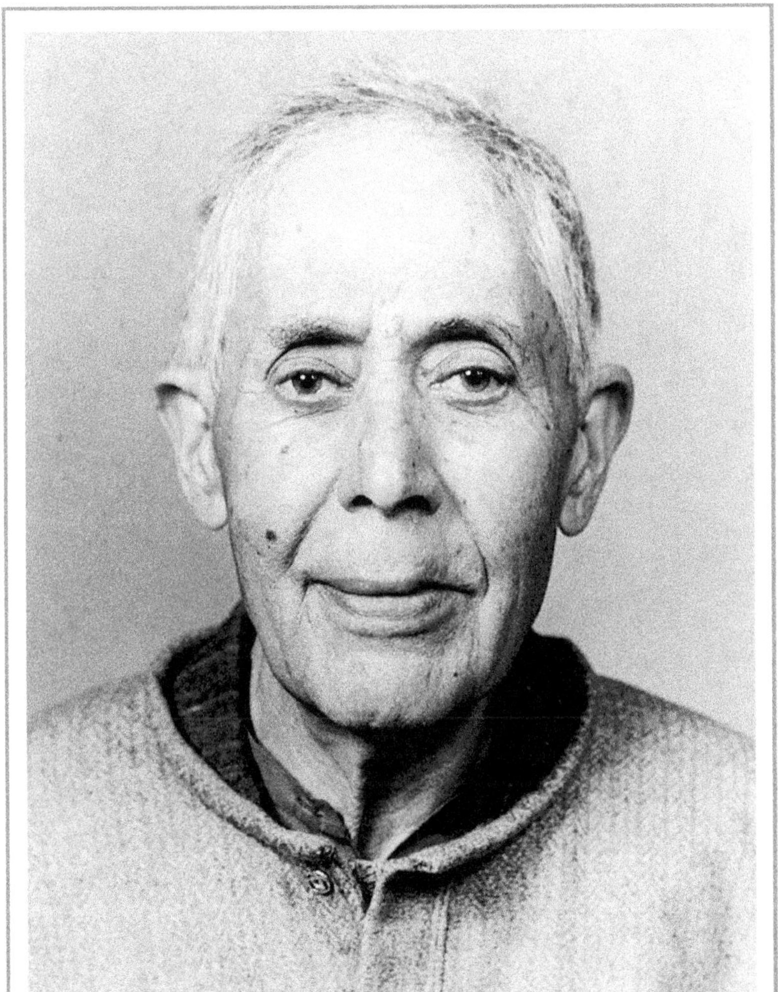

Swami Lakshmanjoo

Swami Lakshmanjoo

Swami Lakshmanjoo was born in Srinagar, Kashmir, on May 9, 1907. He was the most recent and the greatest of the long line of saints and masters of the Kashmir Shaiva tradition. From a young age, Swami Lakshmanjoo spent his life studying and practicing the teachings of this unique and sacred tradition. Having a complete intellectual and spiritual understanding of the philosophy and practice of Kashmir Shaivism, he was a true master in every respect.

Being born with a photographic memory, learning was always easy for him. In addition to possessing a complete knowledge of Kashmir Shaivism, he had a vast knowledge of the traditional religious and philo-sophical schools and texts of India. Swamiji would freely draw upon other texts to clarify, expand, and substantiate his lectures. He could recall an entire text by simply remembering the first few words of a verse.

In time, his reputation as a learned philosopher and spiritual adept spread. Spiritual leaders and scholars journeyed from all over the world to receive his blessings and to ask questions about various aspects of Kashmir Shaiva philosophy. He gained renown as a humble devotee of Lord Shiva and as an accomplished master (*siddha*) of the non-dual tradition of Kashmir Shaivism.

Throughout his life, Swamiji taught his disciples and devotees the ways of devotion and awareness. He shunned fame and all forms of recognition. He knew Kashmir Shaivism was the most precious jewel and that, by God's grace, those who desired supreme knowledge would be attracted to its teachings. He taught freely, never asking anything in return, except that his students, young and old, should do their utmost to assimilate the teachings of his cherished tradition. His earnest wish was for Kashmir Shaivism to be preserved and made available to all human-kind.

On the 27th of September, 1991, Swami Lakshmanjoo left his physical body and attained *mahāsamādhi*, the great liberation.

Swami Lakshmanjoo

Śrī Tantrāloka of Abhinavagupta

Chapter (Āhnika) Four – Śaktopāya

Revealed by His holiness, Swami Lakshmanjoo
Ishwar Ashram, Srinagar,
Kashmir, 1974

SWAMIJI: Now the *Tantrāloka* of the fourth *āhnika* (chapter).

अथ शाक्तमुपायमण्डलं कथयामः परमात्मसंविदे ॥ १ ॥

atha śāktamupāyamaṇḍalaṁ kathayāmaḥ paramātmasaṁvide //1//

Now, the group of *upāyas*, the group of the means concerned with *śāktopāya* will be explained just to realize God consciousness.

Vikalpa Saṁskāra – The Purification of a Thought

LJA TA04A (00:32)

अनन्तराह्निकोक्तेऽस्मिन्स्वभावे पारमेश्वरे ।
प्रविविक्षुर्विकल्पस्य कुर्यात्संस्कारमञ्जसा ॥ २ ॥

anantarāhnikokte'sminsvabhāve pārameśvare /
praviviksurvikalpasya kuryātsaṁskāramañjasā //2//

The nature of Parameśvara,[1] which is already defined in the previous *āhnika* (*śāmbhavopāya*), anyone who wants to get entry in that nature of God consciousness should associate in continuity his thought, just to keep that one thought in continuation so that it does not get diluted or it does not get astray; and rapidly (*añjasā*), without a break, without a break you should put again and again that thought, just to associate that with the previous thought. For instance, this thought is to be functioned, a thought of *śāktopāya*. There is no breathing exercise, just pointing out. For instance, point out the junction [between each] breath; point out while walking one step and then another step, in between, point out that gap; point out that, "I am Lord Śiva myself," this inner consciousness, this awareness of inner consciousness. Take any thought of these, don't take all these thoughts. Take only one thought amongst these and then associate another new thought on it.

SCHOLAR: The same thought but with more intensity.

SWAMIJI: The same thought, a similar thought, with great power, greater power [of awareness]. Otherwise, it will get impured, that thought will get impurity and the *śāktopāya* [practice] will be ruined, the function of *śāktopāya* won't exist. So you have to put again and again the same similar thought on it. For instance, you are keeping awareness on that one point between the two breaths. Keep that awareness afresh again and again, so that that awareness remains bright in each and every moment.

---

1. The supreme Lord.

SCHOLAR: So that awareness in the centering is *ahaṁ* (I-ness).

SWAMIJI: It is *śāktopāya.*

SCHOLAR: Self-awareness in that point.

SWAMIJI: Let it be *ahaṁ*,[2] let it be the center between two movements. That is also *śāktopāya.* But *ahaṁ* is not to be repeated, *ahaṁ* is not to be recited.

SCHOLAR: But in awareness.

SWAMIJI: Awareness, that is *ahaṁ.* The junction of these two breaths, where you find that junction, that is *ahaṁ.*

JOHN: In other words, to maintain your awareness in these junctions, in these points.

SWAMIJI: On any junction! Take one junction, one point, or take this awareness that, "I am Lord Śiva myself". Put again and again this thought, adjust it again and again, so that this thought does not become, does not get, destroyed by [other thoughts].

JOHN: But isn't that *dhyāna*?

SWAMIJI: What?

JOHN: Isn't keeping the thought, "I am Lord Śiva myself," isn't that *āṇavopāya–dhyāna*? Isn't that contemplation?

SWAMIJI: It is not *dhyāna*, no. It is not *dhyāna*. There is no place for it. It is just awareness on that point. Nowhere in the body…neither in the body nor in the universe.[3] Just put awareness on that point.

SCHOLAR: Swamiji, when the *vikalpa* (thought) is, "I am all this power," etcetera, does that also require some point of centering? Does the yogi maintain that awareness between the breath, or between steps, or in the sexual act? Is there a point needed as well?

SWAMIJI: There is a point, yes, needed.

SCHOLAR: But then there would be *sthāna*. Wouldn't that be *sthāna*? Wouldn't that bring…?

SWAMIJI: Not a point. You have not to…Leave that point. [It is] just to realize, for the time being, realize the point and leave the *sthāna* away, and then keep awareness on that point.

---

2. The thought that "I am Lord Śiva".

3. Viz., the *āṇavopāya* practice of *sthāna*, concentrating on a particular place in the body (the heart, navel, etcetera), or *dhyāna*, concentrating on a particular point in the objective world.

JOHN: So, in other words, you are moving from the point of, say, one step or one breath, you have your awareness on the breath, and then all of a sudden …

SWAMIJI: Not the breath! The junction of the breath, the center of the breath.

JOHN: But you start with the breath and then move to the junction.

SWAMIJI: Yes, move to the junction and…

JOHN: So, you have *sthāna* at the beginning and then you move from that *sthāna* to …

SWAMIJI: Yes. It is just to make it vivid.

Praviviksu, the one, the *sādhaka* (aspirant), who wants to get entry in that God consciousness, which is already explained in the previous *āhnika*, should associate his [one] thought in awareness again and again and without a break, *añjasā/śīghraṁ* (instantly). For instance, this thought between the two breaths is an *asphuṭa* point, this is not vivid. It must come to that point where it is most vividly shining. That point, when it is most vividly shining, will become *samādhi*, that is *samādhi*, that is entry in your God consciousness. But now, in the beginning, it is *asphuṭa*, it is not vivid. So, just to make it most vivid, to make it shine vividly, this practice is adopted.

JOHN: So this "without break," does this mean that between every breath you have that?

SWAMIJI: Or between every thought!

JOHN: But you don't stop, you don't miss a breath.

SWAMIJI: No, no, no, you have not to breathe.

JOHN: No, not to breathe, but, in other words, you said to maintain this, does that mean between every step?

SWAMIJI: Not between every step. [It is] just to recognize that point once and for all and hold it. Leave those steps aside, forget those steps, forget this breathing function.

SCHOLAR: So, in some sweet sound or sensation also, that point is found?

SWAMIJI: Yes, that point is found …

SCHOLAR: And then …

SWAMIJI: … hold it! Hold it with awareness, and once you recognize that in a not-vivid way, adjust that point again with it. Adjust again and again so it is refreshed.

JOHN: In other words, you don't miss that adjusting.

SWAMIJI: You have not to miss [adjusting at] first, yes.

JOHN: That is the point you are saying, that's what you mean. You don't miss a step or lose or go into some other thought. In other words, you said if it doesn't become clear that time, then you adjust again.

SWAMIJI: No, just to put thought on that point again and again. That thought, not the step, not the breathing.

JOHN: Not on the step, not on the breathing, in the gap between.

SWAMIJI: Yes, once you have to realize that gap, realize it again, realize it again, again and again in continuity, just like…

SCHOLAR: But not in the rhythm of the breath, that would be *āṇavopāya*.

SWAMIJI: No, no. That will become *āṇavopāya* then.

JOHN: But what do you mean "again and again"? At every point that there…

SWAMIJI: You have to observe that point again and again.

JOHN: Every time.

SWAMIJI: Every time, every moment in continuity.

SCHOLAR: There seems to be a misunderstanding. John seems to be thinking that when each time that breath moves, you hold your awareness on that point.

SWAMIJI: No, no, no.

JOHN: No, not on that…

SCHOLAR: When you hold that you hold it in continuity.

JOHN: No, but he says, "If you miss it, then you adjust it on the next point."

SWAMIJI: Go to that point only! No, if you…

JOHN: Miss it…

SWAMIJI: Not "miss", missing is not the point. It is there, it is there.

JOHN: If it is not clear.

SWAMIJI: It becomes old, it becomes old, after another second it becomes old. It has not so much strength then. It loses that strength. Just to inject another strength over it, you have to…

JOHN: But not in the same point.

SWAMIJI: The same point, yes.

JOHN: I mean, it's in the same point but…

SCHOLAR: The point is inside, so…

JOHN: Say you are walking and you are adjusting your awareness between steps, not in the steps, not in the walking, but between steps.

Well, once that becomes old, you have already moved to another step.

SWAMIJI: No, no, no, you have not to move to another step. Just to realize it once for all. Realize the point once for all, first. Once you have realized that point, keep awareness again and again on it. Awareness should be refreshed.

SCHOLAR: It's by force of awareness that that continues.

SWAMIJI: Yes, that should continue.

SCHOLAR: There's nothing to be done like in the gross way in *āṇavopāya.*

SWAMIJI: No (affirmative).

SCHOLAR: It just finds itself in that point and then flows from there.

JOHN: I can understand finding yourself in the point, but I can't understand refreshing it, adjusting it again and again. It seems that if you miss it once, then it is gone.

SWAMIJI: No. Once you have perceived these specks, you know that this is [a pair of] specks. [Now] see it again and again in consciousness.

SCHOLAR: But without *viccheda* (break).

SWAMIJI: If you keep it only observed once for all, that won't do. You have to put awareness again and again. That is [*vikalpa*] *saṁskāra.*

SCHOLAR: But if it were again and again in the sense of one after another, that would not be a continuity.

SWAMIJI: No, again on that very point.

SCHOLAR: In continuity.

SWAMIJI: You have to observe the same point again! Observe the same point again!

SCHOLAR: It is explained in the next verse.

SWAMIJI: Yes.

LJA TA04A (10:52)

विकल्पः संस्कृतः सूते विकल्पं स्वात्मसंस्कृतम् ।
स्वतुल्यं सोऽपि सोऽप्यन्यं सोऽप्यन्यं सदृशात्मकम् ॥ ३ ॥

vikalpaḥ saṁskṛtaḥ sūte vikalpaṁ svātmasaṁskṛtaṁ /
svatulyaṁ so'pi so'pyanyaṁ so'pyanyaṁ sadṛśātmakam //3//

Now he clears this thought. For instance, there is one thought that, "I am Lord Śiva," or this point [of awareness] is between two breaths, [and] you have realized it once. When you have put awareness [on it], it means you have put a *saṁskāra* on it.

SCHOLAR: Impression.

SWAMIJI: Impression on it, an impression on that thought. But this is the nature of thought that it will create another thought, another similar thought, but with some foreign thought also.

SCHOLAR: It is a connection, but it moves.

SWAMIJI: For instance, "These are specks", this is one thought. Again it comes, "These are specks. Denise's specks are more fine than these." This [other] thought is also adjusted. Don't let that [other] thought be adjusted there! Only "[These] specks," and that's all. Don't let it go ahead.

JOHN: In something else.

SWAMIJI: In something else. But it will go, it goes ...

JOHN: Automatically.

SWAMIJI: ... it goes automatically in something else concerned with this same thought. For instance, "This is a bed cover. This is a fine bed cover." Another thought will come, "This is a fine bed cover. Sharikaji has not this bed cover." So, that thought is polluted, that thought has become impure. Don't let that other adjusting thought come in-between. Put again the same fresh thought that, "This is a bed cover," then again the same fresh thought, "This is a bed cover." Don't let any other adjustment take place with this thought. Because this is the nature of thought that it will adjust another foreign matter also with it. For instance, "*Oṁ namaḥ śivāya, oṁ namaḥ śivāya*", I am reciting, "*Oṁ namaḥ śivāya, Oṁ namaḥ śivāya, Oṁ namaḥ śivāya*" in continuity, at the same time it becomes, another thought comes, "*Oṁ namaḥ śivāya* is very sweet." Don't let that thought be adjusted there. Only "*Oṁ namaḥ śivāya*!" In the same way, only one thought should get awareness in continuity. That is *vikalpa saṁskāra*.

JOHN: So, what is this, how does this work for maintaining awareness between breaths, in that point, in that junction?

SWAMIJI: For instance, you breathe in and out and mark that point [between the breaths]. Leave aside this breath. Mark that point, mark that point again and again. Don't let it go away in another similar thought, another similar point. So, refresh it again and again with the same thought, with the same-similar thought.

JOHN: So, if it went away, would that mean you would go into, say, the outgoing breath?

SWAMIJI: It will, in the course of time, reach [the thought of] Amirakadal.[4] For instance, "These are specks. Denise also has specks. She had gone to Amirakadal yesterday. Now Amirakadal is like this." So, that [initial] thought has gone astray at once. Don't let it happen. You have to put awareness only on the very first thought again and again so that that thought gets awareness in continuity. So, you have to refresh it. [*Vikalpa*] *saṁskāra* is to put the impression of the same thought, in the same manner, without any other adjustment, any other foreign adjustment. It may be a very subtle adjustment. [For instance], "These are specks", just [then] there is a foreign adjustment, "This is glass. This is glass." *Bas*, a foreign adjustment has begun to leak in. That should not take place. This is *vikalpa saṁskāra*.

SCHOLAR: Can you explain how it is different from *dhāraṇā* (contemplation) in *āṇavopāya*, or in Pātañjali Yoga where you have continuity of *ekatānatāra*[5] of a thought?

SWAMIJI: *Dhāraṇā* is also in its [own] way to maintain awareness in continuity.

SCHOLAR: But it's lower.

SWAMIJI: That's lower.

SCHOLAR: Because there is some object of perception, there's not just awareness.

SWAMIJI: Yes, in *dhāraṇā* there is a point, there is a point to be fixed.

SCHOLAR: So your example of the specks is only an analogy. That would fall into *āṇavopāya*.

SWAMIJI: Yes, it is just to make you understand. It is just to make you understand. Take one thought, that one point of God consciousness, and put the impression again and again, the same similar impression again and again in continuity!

JOHN: In other words, don't slip away from that.

SWAMIJI: You should not slip away in any way, in any other foreign world, foreign matter.

---

4. Amirakadal is an area in Srinagar.

5. Attention fixed upon one thing only.

JOHN: Now, in this maintaining of awareness in that gap between breaths, in the gap, there is no *sthāna* in the gap.

SWAMIJI: No (affirmative).

JOHN: There is just a gap. Falling away would mean falling into outgoing breath or in-going? Would that be falling?

SWAMIJI: That is also falling.

JOHN: Is that what…? In that way, would…?

SWAMIJI: That is also falling. That should not take place.

JOHN: And if you do fall away, then what do you do? In the next gap…

SWAMIJI: Then *śāktopāya* is over, there is no *śāktopāya*, the functioning of *śāktopāya* is finished.

SCHOLAR: One is not qualified.

JOHN: So, in other words, the *sādhaka* (aspirant) who can function *śāktopāya*, he has that capacity where he won't fall away.

SWAMIJI: He must not fall away, then he is an aspirant of *śāktopāya*. Otherwise, he is functioning *āṇavopāya*.

LJA TA04A (17:02)

Vikalpaḥ saṁskṛtaḥ sūte vikalpaṁ svātmasaṁskṛtaṁ, because this thought again puts another impression of the same-similar thought.

SCHOLAR: Gives rise.

SWAMIJI: Just similar (*svatulyaṁ*). *So'pi so'pyanyaṁ*, and that, another thought, creates another thought similar to that thought.

SCHOLAR: "Similar" means, almost the same, but this means, exactly the same.

SWAMIJI: Almost the same.

SCHOLAR: Almost or exactly?

SWAMIJI: Almost the same; no, almost.

SCHOLAR: If almost, there will be some falling away?

SWAMIJI: It is falling away, yes.

SCHOLAR: But this is the process of *vikalpa saṁskāra*, the process of intensification of the same.

SWAMIJI: You hear first. It produces the same thought, almost the same thought, again and again. *So'pi so'pyanyaṁ, so'pyanyaṁ sadṛśātmakam*, and that also, that other thought, creates another thought almost similar. This is the way of *vikalpa*s, the functioning of *vikalpa*s.

JOHN: And this carries you away.

SWAMIJI: And now, what you have to do is put this thought afresh, always. Don't let it go in all these other thoughts. And when, in that way, when you put awareness on that one thought, another bright thought will come of the same point. This is *vikalpa saṁskāra*–a brighter thought.

JOHN: In other words, an intensification of the same thing, it just carries you right in…

SWAMIJI: And when you put your awareness in continuity on that thought, it will create another thought of the same level…

JOHN: Exactly the same, but more…

SWAMIJI:…but more brighter, more brighter.

JOHN: So, in other words, awareness becomes, this gap becomes, clearer and clearer, intensifies.

SWAMIJI: Yes. So from *asphuṭa* (non-vivid) it will take the step of *sphuṭa* (vivid, *sphuṭībhāva*), then from that it will take the step of *sphuṭatara bhāva* (more vivid), then in the end it will take the place of *sphuṭatama bhāva* (most vivid). No sooner the *sphuṭatama bhāva* of this thought has appeared, you get the trance in *śāktopāya*.

SCHOLAR: You experience *śakticakra*.[6]

SWAMIJI: Yes.

BRUCE: Swamiji, does the movement where one finds the gap go on?

SWAMIJI: No, it does not go on.

BRUCE: So, if you are walking, what then? You just fall down?

SWAMIJI: What?

BRUCE: If you are walking and you find that point…

SWAMIJI: Sit!

BRUCE: You just sit.

SWAMIJI: Sit and concentrate on that.

BRUCE: But you must think to sit!

SWAMIJI: It doesn't matter. You may stand. You have not to walk again and again.

DENISE: You won't fall?

BRUCE: But if walking is the movement that is going on, to change that in any way you must think…

SWAMIJI: But that walking is meant for those who have got greater

---

6. The wheel (*cakra*) of energies (*śaktis*).

capacity. Take only this point of breath in the beginning. While walking also, you can observe *śāktopāya*.

JOHN: That is more difficult.

SWAMIJI: That is more difficult. You must have greater ability and capacity for doing that.

SCHOLAR: So, only really when one is in *śāmbhavopāya* can one operate with awareness in all movements without…

SWAMIJI: Then there is *śāṁ[bhavopāya]*. It is above all, yes.

SCHOLAR: In walking, you go on walking, stop walking.

JOHN: So, in other words, in this breath, if one catches that gap between the breath, his breathing can go on, it can go on to…

SWAMIJI: Let it go. He has to ignore breathing.

JOHN: But he's into awareness then.

SWAMIJI: Yes.

JOHN: And the breath that he's taken that…let breath go.

SWAMIJI: Let the breath go or stay or whatever it is, but you have not to put your consciousness on that [breathing].

SCHOLAR: It automatically stops when that reaches its full clarity?

SWAMIJI: What?

SCHOLAR: When that thought reaches it's full fact…

SWAMIJI: Clarity, *sphuṭatama bhāva*, yes.

SCHOLAR: … and *mātṛ maṇḍala saṁbodha*[7] takes place, then the breath is stopped anyway–*cit kuṇḍalinī*.

SWAMIJI: The breath, the function of the body also stops, everything stops, you get entry in *samādhi*, *śākta samādhi*, *śakti cakra*. What to speak of breath? Breath is only inferior.

JOHN: So, in the space of time, when you first begin to clarify that void…

SWAMIJI: It is just to recognize that. Stepping [or breathing] is only just to recognize that.

JOHN: No, I know that.

SWAMIJI: You have not to step again and again.

JOHN: No, there is no more stepping. But in terms of time, is it just in a moment that you go from having that first awareness to that clarification?

---

7. In verses 57b and 58, Swamiji explains the two ways of *mātṛ maṇḍala saṁbodha*.

SWAMIJI: If you maintain that awareness in continuity of the same similar thought–then.

JOHN: It goes very quickly.

SWAMIJI: Then, otherwise not. If another adjustment is being done there, finished, the *śāktopāya* process is over. So, it is why he says "*añjasā*", you must take the chance rapidly, without any break, hurriedly.

SCHOLAR: So, once that *vikalpa saṁskāra* starts, it goes fast.

SWAMIJI: Yes.

SCHOLAR: It's not like *dhyāna* going on a long time.

SWAMIJI: Because here, the Buddhists are well informed in these *saṁskāras*. Only they have understood how *vikalpa* travels rapidly. *Vikalpa* travels rapidly. From [the thought of] specks it will go to another [thought of] specks, [then] from another [thought of] specks it will go to another [thought of] specks with some adjustment, and then, at the end, that *vikalpa* will reach [the thought of] Amirakadal, and there is no possibility of [the thought of the] specks, there is no thought of the specks in the end. This is the strength of *vikalpas*. So, you have to maintain…you have to withdraw this strength of *vikalpas*. Once you withdraw it and put awareness on the same similar thought again and again, refresh it, refresh it, refresh it, go on refreshing it again and again, then vividness will be transformed into…*asphuṭa bhāva* (non-vivid) will be transformed in *sphuṭa bhāva* (vivid), and then *sphuṭatara bhāva* (more vivid), and in the end into *sphuṭatama bhāva* (most vivid). Not only that! There is another gap in-between *asphuṭa* (non-vivid) and *sphuṭa* (vivid):

LJA TA04A (23:05)

चतुर्ष्वेव विकल्पेषु यः संस्कारः क्रमादसौ ।
अस्फुटः स्फुटताभावी प्रस्फुटन्स्फुटितात्मकः ॥४॥

caturṣveva vikalpeṣu yaḥ saṁskāraḥ kramādasau /
asphuṭaḥ sphuṭatābhāvī prasphuṭansphuṭitātmakaḥ //4//
(not recited)

Caturṣveva vikalpeṣu, these *vikalpa*s have been explained in four ways. The first *vikalpa*, the first *saṁskāra*, is residing in the field of *asphuṭa bhāva* (not vivid), the next *saṁskāra* is vivid, the next *saṁskāra* is more vivid, the fourth *saṁskāra* is most vivid. And in the fourth *śloka*, he explains that there is another *saṁskāra* manifested in-between these. There is one *saṁskāra*, *asphuṭa*, and between *asphuṭa* and *sphuṭa* there is another *saṁskāra*; in-between *sphuṭa* and *sphuṭatara* there is another *saṁskāra*; in-between *sphuṭatāra* and *sphuṭatama* there is another *saṁskāra* to be held, you have to see. So, it means that the travel of these impressions should be so filled with awareness that you must observe all these *saṁskāra*s, that it has gone from *asphuṭa* to *sphuṭatābhāvī*, and then *sphuṭanayogya*, then *prasphuṭana*, *udgacchat sphuṭata*, *sphuṭita-ātmakaḥ*, *siddhasphuṭatva*.

SCHOLAR: So, unclear, about to come into clarity, becoming clear, and then clarified.

SWAMIJI: Clarified, yes.

SCHOLAR: And then clearer and clearest.

SWAMIJI: Clearer and then clearest.

SCHOLAR: But he could use any because actually the divisions are infinite.

SWAMIJI: Divisions are infinite, but you have to put awareness. This is the process of *śāktopāya*, how to maintain awareness in continuity so that *vikalpa*s don't go astray.

JOHN: What *vikalpa* is there in that gap between breath? What is that *vikalpa*?

SWAMIJI: No, when there is one point, you have to observe one point between two breaths–observe it. Don't go to this thought that, "I am observing these breaths", "Shanna is not observing", "After three years she will observe." All these adjustments should be vanished, should be kept away.

SCHOLAR: So when awareness is held in a point like that, the *parāmarśa* is automatically there …

SWAMIJI: *Parāmarśa* (awareness).

SCHOLAR: … it is not thought by *vikalpa*.

SWAMIJI: No (affirmative).

SCHOLAR: So, *ahaṁ parāmarśa* is …

SWAMIJI: *Ahaṁ parāmarśa* (Self-awareness) is there …

SCHOLAR: … automatically established.

SWAMIJI: … because that point is *ahaṁ parāmarśa* itself.[8]

SCHOLAR: So this *vikalpa* is not "I am all this power" in a discursive way.

SWAMIJI: No, not in a discursive way.

SCHOLAR: It's not, and he thinks that more and more, "I am eternal, I am eternal."

SWAMIJI: It is only *parāmarśa*. No, it is only consciousness.

SCHOLAR: Can he use those…? It says in book one [of the *Tantrāloka*] that he can contemplate upon the various aspects of God, [e.g.,] His eternal nature, His all-pervading-ness, so…

SWAMIJI: Yes, in the beginning.

SCHOLAR: So, [can he think] "*Nityo ahaṁ*, I am all-pervading, my consciousness is everywhere"?

SWAMIJI: In the beginning, but put that thought again and again, refresh it again and again.

SCHOLAR: But without a point, it's not *śāktopāya*.

SWAMIJI: No, without a point it's not *śāktopāya*.

SCHOLAR: But can the point of awareness emerge through *vikalpa saṁskāra* as he describes it in book one, contemplating that you are eternal in your nature, that you are *Deva* (God)?

SWAMIJI: Yes, it is for the time-being to make you understand. But you have to do it this way.

SCHOLAR: So, that is not really *vikalpa saṁskāra*.

SWAMIJI: No, that is not really *vikalpa saṁskāra*. It is just to make you capable of this thought.

SCHOLAR: So why does he say in book one that, in *śāktopāya*, one may enter into…

SWAMIJI: Any thought!

SCHOLAR: … Śiva *sadbhāva* through any pure thought?

SWAMIJI: It does not mean… you can observe only a thought of this *sari* (garment) also in *śāktopāya*. Put the thought of this *sari*, or this shirt, again and again, again and again, [the thought of] the same shirt, the same shirt, the same shirt [in the] same mood, again and again, and you will get entry in *śāktopāya*.

SCHOLAR: That's *dhāraṇā*.

---

8. For a complete understanding of *parāmarśa*, see Appendix 1, p. 385.

SWAMIJI: That is not *dhāraṇā*. That is *saṁskāra, saṁskāra* of this thought.

SCHOLAR: But that's *prameya* (objectivity) there?

JOHN: But it is like *dhāraṇā* because you have the thought of a shirt. It is almost like *mantra*, you are thinking ...

SWAMIJI: Yes. It is not *mantra uccāra*[9], it is awareness.

JOHN: Only awareness.

SCHOLAR: So, it is not like *dhāraṇā*. There is no *prameya* (objectivity) there.

SWAMIJI: There is no *prameya*.

SCHOLAR: You empty your senses.

SWAMIJI: Just empty your consciousness of that formation and think of this shirt again and again.

SCHOLAR: "Think of this shirt"... when you have emptied yourself of it.

SWAMIJI: Put awareness on that consciousness.

SCHOLAR: But not think of the shirt again and again.

SWAMIJI: No (affirmative).

SCHOLAR: But that would be just like *dhāraṇā*.

JOHN: No, in other words, you could put your thought on that perception.

SCHOLAR: In the *pramāṇa* (cognitive) way.

SWAMIJI: Yes. It is just to make you understand. But generally the aspirants of *śāktopāya* put awareness on that point, the center.

JOHN: So, in other words, the practices in *āṇavopāya* help you learn to maintain awareness in continuity.

SWAMIJI: It is why *āṇavopāya* also will carry you to *śāktopāya*, and *śāktopāya* will carry you to *śāmbhavopāya* in the end. *Āṇavopāya* is the foundation for *śāktopāya*. When you breathe in and out, breathe in and out, contemplate on that center again and again with each and every breath, it means you are going to make yourself capable of entry in *śāktopāya* in the end. The point is to be observed, and that point is at present *asphuṭa* (not vivid). As soon as this point will [become] clearest in the *sphuṭatama* state, then you will get entry in *śāktopāya*.

---

9. The outward utterance (*uccāra*) of *mantra*.

SCHOLAR: So that point of Self-awareness, which appears through *āṇavopāya*, begins to appear spontaneously in the creative field.

SWAMIJI: Yes, the creative field. But it has the adjustment of breathing also in that.

SCHOLAR: Yes. But the point that is realized, this point, the center, which is realized outside in *śāktopāya*, is really that point of *mantra vīrya*, *ahaṁ*, which you realize through *āṇavopāya.*

SWAMIJI: Yes, that is *ahaṁ*, yes.

LJA TA04A (29:20)

ततः स्फुटतरो यावदन्ते स्फुटतमो भवेत् ।

tataḥ sphuṭataro yāvadante sphuṭatamo bhavet /5a

And in the end, that thought becomes *sphuṭatara* (more vivid), and in the end, it will become most vivid.

SCHOLAR: *Sākṣātkāra* (direct perception).

SWAMIJI:

असफुटादौ विकल्पे च भेदोऽप्यस्त्यान्तरालिकः ॥५॥

asphuṭādau vikalpe ca bhedo'pyastyāntarālikaḥ //5//

In these *asphuṭa vikalpa*s (*asphuṭa*, *sphuṭa*, *sphuṭatara*, and *sphuṭatama*), there are some stages in-between also found by those who put awareness on those *saṁskāra*s. Because it appears…it does not take too much time, for a *śāktopāya* aspirant it does not take too much time, to get entry in God consciousness. Just five minutes, in five minutes he must enter in God consciousness. But the only thing is, the important point is, to maintain that strength of awareness in continuity. If it is done in five minutes time, you will get entry in God consciousness.

SCHOLAR: Five minutes time.

SWAMIJI: Five minutes. It won't take more than five minutes. This is the strength of *śāktopāya*. And then, in the end:

LJA TA04A (30:39)

ततः स्फुटतमोदारताद्रूप्यपरिवृंहिता ।
संविदभ्येति विमलामविकल्पस्वरूपताम् ॥ ६ ॥

tataḥ sphuṭatamodāra tādrūpyaparivṛṁhitā /
saṁvidabhyeti vimalām avikalpasvarūpatām //6//

Then this thoughtful consciousness, which is put in the field of awareness in continuity, it gets strengthened by *tādrūpya*, by being adjusted with that *sphuṭatamī bhāva* (*sphuṭatama bhava*), the state of the most vivid state of that thought. When it becomes one with that state, this thought, this thoughtful consciousness, gets entry in supreme purified thought-less consciousness in the end.

SCHOLAR: *Nirvikalpa.*

SWAMIJI: *Nirvikalpa.*

SCHOLAR: So, up to that point, it is *vikalpa*.

SWAMIJI: That is *vikalpa saṁskāra*. *Vikalpa saṁskāra*, the journey of *vikalpa saṁskāra*, ends there. The journey of *vikalpa saṁskāra* will end as soon as you get entry in the thought-less state of God consciousness.

SCHOLAR: So, you start from a *vikalpa*, a proposition.

SWAMIJI: You have to start from *vikalpa* just to observe it. You must be acquainted with that *vikalpa*, what *vikalpa* we have to maintain. So, just to get an observation and acquaintance of that *vikalpa*, you have to put these two breaths in the very beginning, just to observe it in fullness, in its fullness. Once you have observed it in fullness, then you have to put awareness on the same point, the same point, again and again, just to make it refreshed. Don't make it old.

JOHN: If it gets old, you have gone from that.

SWAMIJI: Yes (laughs), if it gets old.

JOHN: Then you are into another thought, another breath.

SWAMIJI: Because another similar thought will be adjusted with it. That should not take place.

SCHOLAR: So, *ahaṁ* starts out as *vikalpa*.

SWAMIJI: *Ahaṁ* also is *vikalpa*.

SCHOLAR: But it becomes *nirvikalpa.*

SWAMIJI: In the end when awareness is maintained on it in continuity, otherwise not, otherwise *ahaṁ* will be just like *vikalpa.*

JOHN: It's *ahaṁkāra* (ego) in the beginning, is it? That *ahaṁ*?

SWAMIJI: Not *ahaṁkāra, ahaṁ* is *vikalpa* then.

JOHN: That's what I mean. In the beginning, when you start, you're limited ego.

SWAMIJI: That is limited ego, yes.

JOHN: So you start in that state of the limited ego…

SWAMIJI: It is why he has said it is *asphuṭa* (non-vivid), it is the *asphuṭa* state.

JOHN: And when you realize the state of *sphuṭatama* (most vivid),…

SWAMIJI: *Sphuṭatama*, then this is the real…

JOHN: … then you have gone to the universal state and individuality…

SWAMIJI: Then individuality is digested [in] that universal God consciousness.

JOHN: So this *vikalpa saṁskāra* is the purification of individual into universal?

SWAMIJI: Yes.

SCHOLAR: So, when in *śāktopāya* it is said that the *siddha* and the *yoginī* should contemplate *śivaśaktyātmakaṁ rūpaṁ*[10] …

SWAMIJI: …

LJA TA04A (33:37)

शिवशक्त्यात्मकं रूपं भवयेच्च परस्परम् ।
न कुर्यात् मानवीं बुद्धिं रागमोहादिसम्युताम् ॥

śivaśaktyātmakaṁ rūpaṁ bhavayecca parasparam /
na kuryāt mānavīṁ buddhiṁ rāgamohādisaṁyutām //[11]

10. The unified formation (*rūpa*) of Śiva and Śakti.

11. "You must not think that you are mating with your wife or you are mating with your husband. You should not think like that. You should think that, 'My husband is Śiva and I am Pārvatī and we are mating like that.' It is divine mating." *Stava Cintāmaṇi of Bhaṭṭanārāyaṇa*, translation and commentary by Swami Lakshmanjoo (original audio

SCHOLAR: That is in *śāktopāya. Vikalpa* is there.

SWAMIJI: That is also in *śāktopāya*, not in the beginning! Not in the beginning! In the beginning it is not *śāktopāya*, but in the end it will get…

SCHOLAR: In the beginning it is *āṇavopāya.*

SWAMIJI: In the beginning, when there is the sexual function, it is *āṇavopāya*, but when awareness is maintained…

SCHOLAR: But there is no *mantra* there?

SWAMIJI: No *mantra* there.

SCHOLAR: But why is it *āṇavopāya*?

SWAMIJI: Because there are two objects.

JOHN: Just like two breaths.

SWAMIJI: Yes, just like two breaths.

SCHOLAR: So what is that *bhāvanā* (meditation) there when they contemplate Śiva-Śakti there? Is that *vikalpa saṁskāra*?

SWAMIJI: That will rise along [with] the rise of *kuṇḍalinī* at that time.

SCHOLAR: But at the beginning of that act?

SWAMIJI: It is *āṇavopāya*, it will be *āṇavopāya.*

SCHOLAR: But there is *vikalpa saṁskāra* in that act if it is *śāktopāya.*

SWAMIJI: You have to put *vikalpa saṁskāra.*

SCHOLAR: Is this *pīṭhika bandhaṁ* here?

SWAMIJI: Yes, *pīṭhika bandha*, the foundation [of the bond].

SCHOLAR: So he has to develop that thought.

SWAMIJI: Yes, you have to develop again and again, again and again.

SCHOLAR: But it starts from *vikalpa*, the level of *vikalpa.*

SWAMIJI: Yes, everything starts from *vikalpa.* In *śāmbhavopāya* state also you put the adjustment of *vikalpa* in the beginning.

SCHOLAR: But it's immediately abandoned.

SWAMIJI: And once you have entered in the kingdom of *śāmbhavopāya*, then there is no adjustment needed. When you are residing in the kingdom of *śāmbhavopāya*, finished, you don't need *vikalpa*s. You just hold it and you are there.

JOHN: You just hold.

SWAMIJI: Yes.

---

recording, LJA archive, 1980–81). Verse is also quoted in Jayaratha's commentary for *Tantrāloka* 1.1. See also verse 136, p. 197 for a further discussion of this quote.

LJA TA04A (35:13)

अतश्च भैरवीयं यत्तेजः संवित्स्वभावकम् ।
भूयो भूयो विमृशतां जायते तत्स्फुटात्मता ॥७॥

ataśca bhairavīyaṁ yattejaḥ saṁvitsvabhāvakam /
bhūyo bhūyo vimṛśatāṁ jāyate tatsphuṭātmatā //7//

So, the one who is putting his awareness in the state of the consciousness of Bhairava again and again, then the most vivid state of that Bhairava takes place (*jāyate tat sphuṭātmatā*).

SCHOLAR: Can I ask one point which seems important?

SWAMIJI: Yes.

SCHOLAR: The commentator explaining "*vimṛśatāṁ*" says: *tīvra tīvra śaktipātavatāṁ mahātmanām.*

SWAMIJI: Yes.

SCHOLAR: Why is this only *tīvra-tīvra śaktipāta*?

SWAMIJI: Because they are carried to that point by His grace. Your effort [won't work].

SCHOLAR: Yes, *śaktipāta* I understand. Why *tīvra-tīvra śaktipāta* here?

SWAMIJI: Because this is *tīvra-tīvra.*

SCHOLAR: *Tīvra-tīvra* is the highest form of *śaktipāta.*

SWAMIJI: Highest form of *śaktipāta.*

SCHOLAR: And this is in *śāktopāya.*

SWAMIJI: Yes, in *śāktopāya* and *śāmbhavopāya* also.

SCHOLAR: And what about *āṇavopāya*?

SWAMIJI: That is *manda* (inferior) *śaktipāta.*

SCHOLAR: Now, yes, so why is there suddenly *manda* and now *tīvra-tīvra*? Why is there no in-between?

SWAMIJI: In-between also there are. There are twenty-seven ways of *śaktipāta* explained in the *Tantrāloka* in the thirteenth *āhnika* (chapter).

SCHOLAR: So, why does he say only *tīvra-tīvra śaktipāta vataṁ mahātmanām* here?

SWAMIJI: Not *tīvra-tīvra-tīvra*, not triple *tīvra.* When there is the triple *tīvra* way of *śaktipāta*, then you die, you shatter, you shake, this physical body also, at once. You can't adjust that state in this physical frame. So the physical frame is to be discarded away and you are dead, your body is finished. That is in *tīvra-tīvra-tīvra śaktipāta*. But *tīvra-tīvra śaktipāta*, in that you can maintain the body. Although that body is also filled with that blissful fountain, but still you maintain it for some time. But in the *tīvra-tīvra-tīvra* state, you can't maintain this body, you can't accept it, you become one with God. God cannot maintain a body – nostrils, a mouth, that filth inside, going to the bathroom (laughs). All these things are put aside – hunger, thirst.

Now he puts a question on this subject:

LJA TA04A (37:57)

ननु संवित्परामृष्ट्री परामर्शमयी स्वतः ।
परामृश्या कथं ताथारूप्यसृष्टौ तु सा जडा ॥८॥

nanu saṁvitparāmraṣṭrī parāmarśamayī svataḥ /
parāmṛśyā kathaṁ tāthārūpyasṛṣṭau tu sā jaḍā //8//

The question is, this consciousness, God consciousness, is really *parāmraṣṭrī*, is in the real sense *parāmraṣṭrī*, not *parāmṛśyā*. That state of God consciousness is the observer, it can't be observed, it won't take the position of being the object of anybody.

SCHOLAR: *Saṁvit parāmraṣṭrī parāmarśamayī …*

SWAMIJI: *Parāmarśamayī svataḥ*, this consciousness is, by itself, filled with the *parāmarśa* of Her own nature. *Parāmaṛśyā kathaṁ*, how can it be contemplated [upon]? How can you put consciousness on that thought, the thought of that point? That point is the observer, it can't be observed. *Tāthārūpya sṛṣṭau tu*, if you force that point and carry that point to the level of objectivity (what you have said already, that you have to put your consciousness on that thought), *tu sā jaḍa*, that will become *jaḍa*.

SCHOLAR: Unconscious.

SWAMIJI: Unconscious.[12] So, that nature of God consciousness,

12. That is, an object.

how can that nature of God consciousness be observed by *sādhakas* (by aspirants)? It is impossible. This is a question. *Ucyate*, for that he explains the answer:

LJA TA04A (39:44)

उच्यते स्वात्मसंवित्तिः स्वभावादेव निर्भरा ।
नास्यामपास्यं नाधेयं किञ्चिदित्युदितं पुरा ॥९॥

ucyate svātmasaṁvittiḥ svabhāvādeva nirbharā /
nāsyāmapāsyaṁ nādheyaṁ kiñcidityuditaṁ purā //9//

The answer to this objection is that *svātma saṁvittiḥ*, the nature of your own consciousness is already full, already complete by nature. *Nāsyām apāsyaṁ*, in that state, there is nothing to be carried away and there is nothing to be put inside. *Iti uditam purā*, it is already explained in *anupāya āhnika*, in the second *āhnika*. That state is explained in the second *āhnika*, where there is nothing to be done.

LJA TA04A (40:33)

किं तु दुर्घटकारित्वात्स्वाच्छन्द्यान्निर्मलादसौ ।
स्वात्मप्रच्छादनक्रीडापण्डितः परमेश्वरः ॥१०॥

kiṁ tu durghaṭakāritvātsvācchandyānnirmalādasau /
svātmapracchādanakrīḍāpaṇḍitaḥ parameśvaraḥ //10//

But here, you see that Lord Śiva is very clever in hiding his own nature just for fun. He hides his nature just for fun, *durghaṭakāritvāt svācchandyāt*, by his free independent energy which is always pure. By that energy of *svātantrya śakti*, he is clever in hiding his nature. When he has hidden his nature, then you have to put this *saṁskāra*, *vikalpa saṁskāra*, again and again to get entry in it in fullness.

SCHOLAR: *Durghaṭakāritvāt*, because he can affect the impossible, which is to hide his own nature, to become unconsciousness.

SWAMIJI: No. *Durghaṭakāritvāt* means that hiding his nature is impossible. He can't hide his nature, but he makes it hidden!

SCHOLAR: Whose objection was this? Murti. What did Professor Murti say about this?

JOHN: He said that, "How could Śiva consciously become unconsciousness?"

SWAMIJI: He can't, but he has got this independent *svātantrya śakti* [by which] he makes it unconsciousness.

SCHOLAR: But that's the same question: How can he do that?

SWAMIJI: By *svātantrya*, by his …

DENISE: He makes it appear to be unconsciousness.

SWAMIJI: He makes it appear to be what is not possible! He makes the impossible possible. Just you see, you have become an individual. You couldn't become an individual and you *have* become an individual. This is his *svātantrya śakti*, how Lord Śiva becomes [an individual]. From universality, it travels to the individual state.

JOHN: This is *visarga*. Huh? From one point of view, he hasn't limited himself at all. From his point of view, from Śiva's point of view …

SWAMIJI: No, it is only a play. It is only a play because he is consciousness! He is filled with consciousness!

JOHN: There is no place that is unconscious to him.

SWAMIJI: No (affirmative).

JOHN: But it is only from the point of view …

SWAMIJI: Of play, *krīḍa*.

JOHN: … of that power which he plays with that it becomes unconsciousness from that point.

SWAMIJI: It is just to reveal the drama of the universe.

LJA TA04A (43:02)

अनावृत्ते स्वरूपेऽपि यदात्माच्छादनं विभोः ।
सैव माया यतो भेद एतावान्विश्ववृत्तिकः ॥ ११ ॥

anāvṛtte svarūpe'pi yadātmācchādanaṁ vibhoḥ /
saiva māyā yato bheda etāvānviśvavṛttikaḥ //11//

Although his nature of God consciousness is never hidden, is never covered by any power in the earth, not by his own power also …*

He can't cover it because no sooner he covers his nature with some covering, that covering will also be revealed in God consciousness, that covering also will take the place of God consciousness. That covering by which you cover it, that covering will also shine in the God conscious state. So, you can't conceal him, but he makes it concealed by his will.

JOHN: To you, for us, for us.

SWAMIJI: *… and this way of acting to conceal it, is called *māyā*, is called the energy of illusion. That energy of *svātantrya śakti* is transformed in the energy of illusion there. *Yato bheda etāvān viśva vṛttikaḥ*, and it is from that energy of *māyā*, the illusive energy of Lord Śiva, from which this whole differentiated world has appeared.

LJA TA04A (44:26)

तथाभासनमेवास्य द्वैतमुक्तं महेशितुः ।
तद्द्वयापासनेनायं परामर्शोऽभिधीयते ॥ १२ ॥

tathābhāsanamevāsya dvaitamuktaṁ maheśituḥ /
taddvayāpāsanenāyaṁ parāmarśo'bhidhīyate //12//

And to appear in the worldly state, to appear in the sphere of the objective world, that Lord Śiva has appeared in the world of objectivity, that is the differentiated state of Lord Śiva. That is, he holds the differentiated state of himself. *Tat-dvyāpāsanenā*, just to remove that differentiated state of Lord Śiva, this *parāmarśa* (awareness) of *śāktopāya* is being explained.

LJA TA04A (45:18)

दुर्भेदपादपस्यास्य मूलं कृन्तन्ति कोविदाः ।
धारारूढेन सत्तर्ककुठारेणेति निश्चयः ॥ १३ ॥

durbhedapādapasyāsya mūlaṁ kṛntanti kovidāḥ /
dhārārūḍhena sattarkakuṭhāreṇeti niścayaḥ //13//

This is another subject. We will do it tomorrow.[13]

DEVOTEE: What is *dhārārūḍha*?

SWAMIJI: *Dhārārūḍhena*, you have not done it. *Dhārā* is *parā kāṣṭhā*.[14]

DEVOTEE: *Pārampāra*.

SWAMIJI: *Parākāṣṭha*!

[Questions pertaining to the *upāyas*]

SCHOLAR: So although *siddha-yoginī krama* starts and operates in *āṇavopāya* because of the predominance of *kriyā śakti*, ...

SWAMIJI: Yes.

SCHOLAR: ... unless it bears fruits of *śāktopāya*, it bears no fruit.

SWAMIJI: But that traveling in that way, in Vāma *mārga* or in Kaula *prakriyā*, the way of Kaula *prakriyā* is a fast journey, just like a jet aeroplane, just [like] traveling in a jet aeroplane. From *āṇavopāya*, in two seconds you get entry in *śāktopāya*, and in two seconds you get entry in the *śāmbhava* state, while doing that act. Just you have to observe this lady, observe yourself as Lord Śiva, observe that lady as Pārvatī, and being...

SCHOLAR: But not in an objective way.

SWAMIJI: Not in an objective way – no.

SCHOLAR: Not in imagination, but in awareness.

SWAMIJI: In divinity. In divinity, and you are traveling from *āṇavopāya* to *śāktopāya* in seconds, and from *śāktopāya* you'll get entry in the *śāmbhava* state in the end.

SCHOLAR: So when this *bāhya* (external) *pūjā*, etcetera, *bahir ārcanam* (external worship) and all that takes place, he is realizing that *mantra vīrya* in that.

---

13. This is the first verse on the subject of *sattarka* (logic).

14. The highest summit.

SWAMIJI: It is why the twenty-ninth chapter and all these chapters are explained in the section of *āṇavopāya*. Aren't they explained in the section of…?

SCHOLAR: Because of *sthāna*, *maṇḍala*, etcetera.

SWAMIJI: Yes, all these.

LJA TA04A (47:09)

इत्येष प्रभृतेशाः जीवन्मुक्तिर्विचार्यति

ityeṣa prabhṛteśāḥ jīvanmuktirvicāryati [15]

Jīvanmukti (liberation) is explained from the fifth *āhnika* in variations. All those *āhnika*s are remaining in the level of *āṇavopāya*–in the beginning. The foundation is *āṇavopāya* there.

SCHOLAR: But they are not pure *āṇavopāya* …

SWAMIJI: They are not …

SCHOLAR: … because they lead into the *śākta* state.

SWAMIJI: At once, rapidly.

SCHOLAR: But they start with the support of *maṇḍala* and those things.

SWAMIJI: Yes.

SCHOLAR: But *maṇḍala* can be included or excluded, depends upon the awareness of the master.

SWAMIJI: No, *maṇḍala* is included first, then no sooner you get entry in that state, finished, *mandala* is… [16]

---

15. "The lecture on *jīvan mukti* ends here in *śāmbhavopāya*–this book. *Iti eṣa prabhṛti*, from this point onwards, *jīvan mukti* (liberation) will be explained in various ways." *Tantrāloka* 3.272ab (LJA archive).

16. In *Tantrāloka* 5.3, Abhinavagupta mentions the eleven external meditating centers: "*Maṇḍala* means this circular (diagram) where you adopt that sacrificial fire. *Sthaṇḍalam* is a small levelled and squared place for a *havan*, that sacrificial fire. *Pātram* is the sacrificial vessel used for putting water, ghee and everything. *Akṣa sūtram* is a garland of beads. *Sapustakam*, a spiritual book. *Liṅgam*, some image of God made by stones. *Tūraṁ* is some image of God engraved on some metal or on some wall. *Paṭa* is the (painted) image of God on some cloth. *Pustaṁ*

SCHOLAR: But it says in the beginning of twenty-nine that *maṇḍala*, *kuṇḍa*, etcetera…

SWAMIJI: Is not necessary.

SCHOLAR: *Kṛtaṁ vā khaṇḍanāya no.*

SWAMIJI: Yes (laughs), *kṛtaṁ api khaṇḍanāya no*, if you adjust that *maṇḍala* also, no harm.

SCHOLAR: But then he goes on to make them necessary. He explains this *bahir ārcana*, this *argapātra*, etcetera.

SWAMIJI: Yes, it is *āṇavopāya.*

SCHOLAR: But for *śākta sādhaka*s.

SWAMIJI: For *śākta sādhaka*s.

SCHOLAR: *Āṇavopāya* in *śāktopāya.*

SWAMIJI: Yes.

SCHOLAR: Not *śāktopāya* in *āṇavopāya*. I see.

SWAMIJI: And there are *āṇavopāya*s also.

SCHOLAR: But in predominance it is really *jñāna*[17] that is in predominance there, because as he does *tarpānaṁ*, etcetera?

SWAMIJI: Not in all *āhnika*s. In some.

SCHOLAR: But in that process, that *śākta* process, *śākta krama* …

SWAMIJI: In that process, yes.

SCHOLAR: … when he performs that *argapātra*, etcetera, he contemplates those deities …

SWAMIJI: That is *śāktopāya*, traveling to *śāktopāya* from the *āṇava* state.

SCHOLAR: … he maintains that *vikalpa saṁskāra* all the time.

SWAMIJI: Yes.

SCHOLAR: So, that is why it says, "This is *snānam* (a bath), this is *pūjā* (worship), this is …", not that outer [bath/*pūjā*].

SWAMIJI: No (affirmative).

SCHOLAR: But he is still doing that outer *pūjā.*

SWAMIJI: You have to do.

SCHOLAR: Even though he is in *śāktopāya.*

---

is an image of God made by painting on a wall or by clay. *Pratimā* is the image of God on a gold plate. *Mūrti* is the image of the master in front of you and you meditate on it." *Tantrāloka* 5.3 (LJA archive).

17. Knowledge, cognition.

SWAMIJI: Doesn't matter.
SCHOLAR: So also in Krama System there is elaborate rituals.
SWAMIJI: Have you not…?

LJA TA04A (49:05)

यावानुपायो बाह्यः स्यादान्तरो वापि कश्चन ।

yāvānupāyo bāhyāḥ syādāntaro vāpi kaścana / TĀ 2.11[18]

Yadanyadapi kiñcana, etāvatī mahādevī rudraśaktiranargalā, this is all …[19]

SCHOLAR: All outer means, anything is all *rudra śakti* unimpeded (*anargalā*).

SWAMIJI: Yes. Once you have established your consciousness in the *śāmbhava* state, *śākta* also becomes *śāmbhava* for you, *āṇavopāya* also become *śāmbhava* for you.

SCHOLAR: So, when you are in the *śākta* state, *āṇava* is *śākta*.

SWAMIJI: *Śākta* also.

SCHOLAR: That is why there can be this *cakra pūjā*, etcetera, with outer things without falling from the *śākta* [state].

SWAMIJI: Yes. You can do your daily routine of life and be in God consciousness in the *śākta* way if you are established once in *śāktopāya*.

---

18. "*Yāvānupāyo bāhyaḥ syāt*, whatever means we would suggest for entry in the *anupāya* state, it may be outward means or internal means (*bāhyaḥ syāt, āntaro vāpi kaścana*), those two-fold means are all *tanmukha prekṣī*, are dependent to that *anupāya saṁvitti*." *Light on Tantra in Kashmir Shaivism, Vol. Two, Abhinavagupta's Tantrāloka, Chapters Two and Three* (with original audio), Swami Lakshmanjoo, ed. John Hughes (Lakshmanjoo Academy, Los Angeles, 2021), 2.11ab, p. 12.

19. *Tantrāloka* 1.194 commentary."This is the kingdom of Lord Śiva's energy, *svātantrya śakti* (Mahādevī). This is not other than that kingdom from our point of view. So it can be *śāmbhava samāveśa*, this elementary *samāveśa*." *Light on Tantra in Kashmir Shaivism, Vol. One, Abhinavagupta's Tantrāloka Chapter One* (with original audio), Swami Lakshmanjoo, ed. John Hughes (Lakshmanjoo Academy, Los Angeles, 2017), 1.194cd, p. 213.

SCHOLAR: So, that is why *vikalpa saṁskāra* is so important.

SWAMIJI: Yes. [For example], when you get chloroform, when I put that smelling dust on your face just to breathe, you breathe it – I will give you a double dose; for instance, I give you a double dose – you breathe it and you remain unconscious for four hours, five hours. Afterwards, when your consciousness rises, comes again, after a few seconds you become unconscious again, and after a few seconds you become unconscious again. This is the force of that dose.

SCHOLAR: You come up a bit and then you go back and ...

SWAMIJI: [In the same way], when you are once established in the *śāmbhava* state, you go to the *śāmbhava* state while doing breathing exercise also. You get entry.

JOHN: You said this Kaula practice is very quick like a jet plane.

SWAMIJI: Yes.

JOHN: Is it the same as Kula? [Are] Kula and Kaula the same thing?

SWAMIJI: Kula is also the same, [but] not to that extent.

SCHOLAR: But when you say Kula, you mean, by predominance with emphasis on these *bahir ārcanam* (external worship) and...

SWAMIJI: *Bahir ārcana*, yes.

SCHOLAR: ... these eight *kula*s, etcetera, this *puṣpapaṭa* (flowered cloth), all these things, that's the Kula system. Kaula is just in awareness.

SWAMIJI: Kaula is adjusted in *śāktopāya* and *śāmbhavopāya*.

SCHOLAR: There is no trace of *āṇavopāya* there.

SWAMIJI: No (affirmative).

SCHOLAR: So Trika is the highest stage of Kaula.

SWAMIJI: No. Trika is... all this is Trika, everything is Trika combined.

JOHN: Kula and Kaula?

SWAMIJI: Kula, Kaula, everything is Trika.

JOHN: But you told Denise one day that there is difference between Kaula and Kula.

SWAMIJI: Yes. There is a difference. There is difference, but in Trika there is no difference. When you are adjusted in the Trika system of this thought, everything becomes Trika for you.

SCHOLAR: But from the point of view of practice, you are the highest sort of Kaula *sādhaka*.

SWAMIJI: Practice, they are separate, they are separate, they are separate. From the point of view of practice, they are separate, but once you get entry in God consciousness in the way of the *śāmbhava* state, you are always in the *śāmbhava* state.

JOHN: No matter what.

SWAMIJI: No matter if you breathe, if you do *japa*, or a *havan*, you are in the *śāmbhava* state.

JOHN: Can you tell me what the difference is from the point of view of practice between Kula and Kaula?

DENISE: What you said before was that, "Kula was the attempt and the Kaula was the entry."

SWAMIJI: Yes.

DENISE: The actual rise of (inaudible).

SWAMIJI: That is quite true. Kula is in the beginning.

SCHOLAR: So this Trika Kula *krama* that is explained in book twenty-nine is called the Kula System, Kula *prakriyā*, because it involves a form of *upāsanā* (worship).

SWAMIJI: Yes.

SCHOLAR: There is a *prakriyā* to be adopted, …

SWAMIJI: *Prakriyā*, yes.

SCHOLAR: … a program.

SWAMIJI: Just to get entry in Kaula, and in the end …

SCHOLAR: But it rests in Kaula because it's in the *Tantrāloka*, …

SWAMIJI: Yes.

SCHOLAR: … not in some Kula text. And Kaula is spontaneously *sahaja saṁvittiḥ*[20], …

SWAMIJI: Spontaneous *sahaja saṁvittiḥ* on that.

SCHOLAR: … pure *śāktopāya*.

SWAMIJI: Yes.

SCHOLAR: And also in *śāmbhavopāya*, in last book, we had the explanation of this *haṭha pāka krama*.[21]

SWAMIJI: Yes.

SCHOLAR: That is also this process, this Kaula process.

---

20. Natural or un-artificial (*sahaja*) consciousness (*saṁvitti*).

21. "*Haṭhapākapraśama* is: don't leave [your practice] until you meet Him." Swamiji agreed that the Buddha must have had this conviction when he said, "He'll sit under that tree and either realize God or leave his body." *Light on Tantra in Kashmir Shaivism, Tantrāloka, Vol. Two*, 3.260, p. 405.

SWAMIJI: Yes. This is a very wonderful book. Nine points are to be explained in this book–nine subjects. *Vikalpa saṁskāra* is the first. *Tarka tattvam*, the reality of logic, what is the reality of logic, this is the second. What is the reality of the master (the third subject).

SCHOLAR: The nature of the guru.

SWAMIJI: *Gurusatattvakam. Yogāṅgānuprayuktam*, why these limbs of Yoga are not useful here–to maintain the limbs of Yoga (*yogāṅga*). And outward worship is also negated (*kalpita ārcā anādara*).

SCHOLAR: So it is negated, it's not lifted onto another level–it's negated.

SWAMIJI: No, it is negated here.

SCHOLAR: Like in the Kula System–he should not do these.

SWAMIJI: *Kalpitārcā*. And real *ārcā* he will explain–what is real worship.

SCHOLAR: What is real *snāna* (bath), what is real *pūjā* (worship), etcetera.

SWAMIJI: Yes. *Kalpitārcā*. And *saṁvit cakrodaya*, …

SCHOLAR: The twelve Kālīs.

SWAMIJI: … the rise of the twelve centers of consciousness. *Mantra vīrya*, what is the power of *mantra*, what is the real power of *mantra*. And what is real *japa* (recitation), real *pūjā* (real worship). And in the end, he explains, nothing is right and nothing is wrong.

LJA TA04A (55:00)

SWAMIJI: Another subject from nine subjects. One subject is over. Which subject?

JOHN: This *vikalpa saṁskāra*.

SWAMIJI: *Vikalpa saṁskāra*.

Tarka Tattvam – The Reality of Logic

Now *tarka tattvam*, the reality of *tarka* will be explained, the reality of logic, what logic really is. Logic is not discussing things with each other, but it is something else. That he will explain in this [section]. The thirteenth [*śloka*]:

LJA TA04A (55:45)

दुर्भेदपादपस्यास्य मूलं कृन्तन्ति कोविदाः ।
धारारूढेन सत्तर्ककुठारेणेति निश्चयः ॥ १३ ॥

durbhedapādapasyāsya mūlaṁ kṛntanti kovidāḥ /
dhārārūḍhena sattarka-kuṭhāreṇeti niścayaḥ //13//

Kovidāḥ, those who are recognized persons, recognized souls, yogis, first-class yogis, they cut into pieces the root of that tree that creates differentiated perceptions in this universe. So these realized souls cut into pieces the root of that tree which creates differentiated perceptions in this universe. The root of that tree is cut by those realized souls by the *dhārārūḍhena*, by the sharp-edged hammer of…

SCHOLAR: Axe.

SWAMIJI: … the sharp-edged axe of *sattarka*, of actual logic.

SCHOLAR: *Dhārārūḍhena*?

SWAMIJI: *Dhārārūḍhena*.

SCHOLAR: *Parākāṣṭhāprāptena*?

SWAMIJI: *Parākāṣṭhāprāptena, athavā niṣedhadhārāyuktena*, with sharp blades, they cut the root of that tree with a sharp-bladed axe, and that axe is only logic, the axe of logic. *Iti niścayaḥ*, this is our *siddhānta*, this is our conclusion, for this logic, what logic really is.

LJA TA04A (57:52)

तामेनां भावनामाहुः सर्वकामदुघां बुधाः ।
स्फुटयेद्वस्तु यापेतं मनोरथपदादपि ॥ १४ ॥

tāmenāṁ bhāvanāmāhuḥ sarvakāmadughāṁ budhāḥ /
sphuṭayedvastu yāpetaṁ manorathapadādapi //14//

And those realized souls nominate that *sattarka* as that supreme contemplated state of consciousness (*bhāvanām-āhuḥ*), …

SCHOLAR: Contemplative state.

SWAMIJI: … contemplative state, and which is *sarva kāma dughām*, which is the bestower of boons in every way–*sarva kāma dughām.* And that *bhāvanā*, that contemplative state, which is no other than this *sattarka*, clears (*sphuṭayet*), makes clear that object which has gone above man's imagination–you cannot imagine. And that object is cleared by this *bhāvanām*, by this contemplative state of that *sattarka.*

SCHOLAR: *Manoratha pādadapi*, it is beyond his wildest dreams.

SWAMIJI: *Manoratha pāda api*, which is beyond your imagination also. You can't imagine that it will happen, but it happens.

SCHOLAR: Goes beyond his desire. It is more than he could have possibly have desired.

SWAMIJI: This *bhāvanā* makes it happen into consciousness.

LJA TA04A (59:27)

श्रीपूर्वशास्त्रे तत्प्रोक्तं तर्को योगाङ्गमुत्तमम् ।
हेयाद्यालोचनात्तस्मात्तत्र यत्नः प्रशस्यते ॥ १५ ॥

śrīpūrvaśāstre tatproktaṁ tarko yogāṅgamuttamam /
heyādyālocanāttasmāt-tatra yatnaḥ praśasyate //15//

It is also explained in the *Mālinīvijaya Tantra* (*śrīpūrva śāstre tat proktam*) that *tarko yogāṅgam uttamam*,[22] this *tarka*, this point of logic, is the supreme state of the limbs of Yoga as explained in Śaivism. In Śaivism, the limbs of Yoga are explained in six ways. There are only six limbs of Yoga explained in Śaivism, not the eight limbs of Yoga as it is explained by Patañjali in his Yoga *Darśana*. There are not eight limbs, there are only six limbs, and those limbs are *prāṇāyāma*, *dhyāna*, *pratyāhāra*, *dhāraṇā*, *tarka*, and *samādhi*. *Prāṇāyāma* is the first limb of Yoga, *dhyāna* is the second limb of Yoga, and *pratyāhāra* is the third limb, and *dhāraṇā* is the fourth limb, and *tarka* is the fifth limb, and ultimately the last [is *samādhi*].[23]

LJA TA04A (1:00:52)
LJA TA04B (00:00)

[This *tarka*], it is not outward reasoning, not the reasoning from books. It is reasoning from your own consciousness, contemplative state. Because this reasoning he has nominated as the contemplative state of [*sattarka*]-*bhāvanā*. So, *heyadyolocanāt*, because it clarifies what is to be left aside and what is to be owned. It clarifies that thing in awareness, what is to be owned and what is to be thrown out. What is to be thrown out? Differentiated perception is to be thrown out and the undifferentiated reality of Being is to be owned.

Now, this is the *śloka* of the *Mālinīvijaya Tantra*, and in the next *śloka*, this next *śloka* is the commentry of this *śloka*, the previous *śloka*. No, this is also the *śloka* of the *Mālinīvijaya Tantra*:

---

22. yogāṅgatve samāne'pi tarko yogāṅgam uttamam |
heyādyālocanāt tasmāt tatra yatnaḥ praśasyate ||

"*Dhāraṇā*s and *tarka* (logic) are equally parts of yoga. Of them logic is the best as it clarifies what is to be avoided. Therefore, effort in this direction deserves appreciation." *Mālinīvijaya Tantra*, 17.18, English translation by Vishnu Datt Shastri, 1956.

23. The Yogic limbs of the *yama*s (moral disciplines), *niyama*s (positive observances), and *asana*s (postures) are omitted in Śaivism for reasons that will be discussed later on in this chapter.

LJA TA04B (01:21)

मार्गे चेतः स्थिरीभूतं हेयेऽपि विषयेच्छया ।
प्रेर्य तेन नयेत्तावद्यावत्पदमनामयम् ॥ १६ ॥

mārge cetaḥ sthirībhūtaṁ heye'pi viṣayecchayā /
prerya tena nayettāvad-yāvatpadamanāmayam //16//[24]

Mārge, on the path, if on the path *cetaḥ sthirībhūtaṁ*, your mind is established on the path which is to be owned, which is to be perceived, which is to be realized, *heye'pi viṣayecchayā*, although that path, although it is *heya*, although it is to be discarded, to be thrown away, that path, …*

It means, the wrong path. The wrong path is Vedānta and all other systems with the exception of Śaivism. Only Śaivism is the right path.

*… so, anyone whose mind is established on the path, on the wrong path, because of *viṣayecchayā*, because of [the lure of] its so called yogic powers or other things (they achieve those yogic powers by treading on that path, on that wrong path), if although his mind is established on that path, *prerya tena*, this internal logic (*tarka*) is the only way, the only means, to take your mind out from that path (*prerya tena*), *nayet*, and it must be sentenced to that point, *yāvat padam anāmayam*, until you are carried to that state which is *anāmaya*, where there is no …

SCHOLAR: Time, space. No change, no …

JOHN: Differentiation.

SWAMIJI: *Āmaya* means, *roga*.[25] *Anāmaya* means where there is no worry, a worry-less state, that is the state of transcendental Lord Śiva.

Now he commentates, now he gives you the explanation of these two *śloka*s, because these two *śloka*s are from the *Mālinīvijaya Tantra* [that] he has quoted here.

---

24. *Mālinīvijaya Tantra* 17.19.

25. Lit., *āmaya* and *roga* mean sickness and disease. *Anāmaya* means the absence of these afflictions.

LJA TA04B (03:39)

मार्गोऽत्र मोक्षोपायः स हेयः शास्त्रान्तरोदितः ।
विषिणोति निबध्नाति येच्छा नियतिसङ्गतम् ॥ १७॥
रागतत्त्वं तयोक्तं यत् तेन तत्रानुरज्यते ।

mārgo'tra mokṣopāyaḥ sa heyaḥ śāstrāntaroditaḥ /
viṣiṇoti nibadhnāti yecchā niyatisaṅgatam //17//
rāgatattvaṁ tayoktaṁ yat tena tatrānurajyate /
(not recited)

Mārgo'tra mokṣopāyaḥ sa, this path which has already been explained in the verse of the *Mālinīvijaya Tantra*, that the one who is treading on the path, that path is called *mokṣopāya*, just the way to get liberated, but that way to get liberated is false. Although you are liberated in that way, you are not liberated from the Śaiva point of view.

SCHOLAR: *Amokṣa, amokṣalipsayā.*

SWAMIJI: *Śāstrāntaroditaḥ*, because that path is explained by other systems of *śāstras* (scriptures), not by Śaivism. So that path will not liberate you. On the contrary, *viṣiṇoti*, it will bind you to that point. *Nibadhnati yecchā*, and that [bondage] is desire, the desire for achieving the goal of Vedānta, the desire for achieving the goal of Sāṁkhya, and other systems other than Śaivism. And that desire is *niyati saṅgatam rāga tattvam*, that desire is, in other words, called attachment (*rāga*). Because you are attached to Vedānta, so you love Vedānta. You must be detached from Vedānta. This love will entangle you in that shrunken path.

SCHOLAR: *Amokṣa* (non-liberation).

SWAMIJI: *Rāgatattvaṁ tayoktaṁ yat tena tatrānurajyate*, this is why he gets attachment towards that wrong path.

SCHOLAR: *Niyati saṅgatam*?

SWAMIJI: *Niyati saṅgatam rāga tattvam*, [he feels], "But this is my goal, only Vedānta is the right path for me", without understanding what is the right path. The right path is the Trika System. And when you understand that Vedānta is the only right path for you, it is the function of your *rāga* attached with *niyati* (*niyati* means, [attachment for] only this, not another).

LJA TA04B (05:51)

यथा साम्राज्यसम्भोगं दृष्ट्वाऽदृष्ट्वाथवाधमे ॥१८॥
भोगे रज्येत दुर्बुद्धिस्तद्वन्मोक्षेऽपि रागतः ।

yathā sāmrājyasambhogaṁ dṛṣṭvādṛṣṭvāthavādhame //18//
bhoge rajyeta durbuddhistadvanmokṣe'pi rāgataḥ /

He gives now an example. Although that path was wrong on which he was treading, why was he treading on the wrong path? What was the reason he stepped on that wrong path? There was the right path also at the same time available for him. Why did he tread on the wrong path? He says an example for this: *Yathā sāmrājyasambhogaṁ dṛṣṭvādṛṣṭvāthavādhame bhoge rajyeta durbuddhi*, just like *durbuddhi*, having an inferior intellect, an inferior understanding, a person having an inferior understanding, he does not like the universal kingdom (*sāmrājya sambhogaṁ*, the joy of the universal kingdom he hates), and *dṛṣṭvādṛṣṭvā*, although he perceives the joy of that universal kingdom (I mean, the worldly kingdom), but *athavā adhame bhoge rajyeta durbuddhiḥ*, but he is attached to *adhama bhoga*,[26] e.g., he is attached to his own house, he does not [want to] go to America and find the ultimate perfect joy there. He wants to live in Ishber, in the four walls of Ishber. This is a shrunken state of your mind. *Tadvat mokṣe'pi rāgataḥ*, in the same way, by this attachment, people are attached to that wrong path also by this *rāga* (attachment), and they don't like that supreme *mokṣa* (liberation) of the Trika System.

26. Lit., the lowest (*adhama*) enjoyment (*bhoga*).

LJA TA04B (07:56)

स एवांशक इत्युक्तः स्वभावाख्यः स तु स्फुटम् ॥ १९ ॥
सिध्यङ्गमिति मोक्षाय प्रत्यूह इति कोविदाः ।

sa evāṁśaka ityuktaḥ svabhāvākhyaḥ sa tu sphuṭam //19//
siddhyaṅgamiti mokṣāya pratyūha iti kovidāḥ /

Kovidaḥ, great realized souls say that, *sa evāṁśaka ityuktaḥ*, this is *aṁśaka*,[27] this is the state of *aṁśaka* that carries you, that makes you abandon the right path and carries you on the wrong path. This is the state of *aṁśaka*, being *aṁśaka* in you. Because, [for example], I am a Śiva *aṁśa*.[28] If you are an *aṁśa* of Brahmā, you will like Vedānta.

JOHN: *Aṁśa* means exactly?

SWAMIJI: *Aṁśaka* means, you are part of that, you are a ray of that being, a ray of that Brahmā, and it is your nature that you will like Vedānta, you won't like Śaivism, as that Jankinātha Kavi likes Vedānta. You know Jankinātha Kavi who used to attend lessons of Śaivism. But still, even after hearing lessons of Śaivism, he is attached to Vedānta because he is an *aṁśaka* of Brahmā, he is not an *aṁśaka* of Śiva. I am an *aṁśaka* of Śiva. [Even] if I am thrusted in the atmosphere of Vedānta, I will never be caught in that system.

JOHN: What are the Buddhists an *aṁśaka* of?

SWAMIJI: Of the Buddha.

Sa eva aṁśaka ityuktaḥ, that is *aṁśaka*, he is called an *aṁśaka*, which is his *svabhāvākhya*, which is his nature, by nature he is that *aṁśa*.

JOHN: This means he tends to see the world this way, is it?

SWAMIJI: Yes. *Sa tu sphuṭam siddhyaṅgam*, although he gets the power, the yogic power out of that system, out of that wrong path, he gets and achieves the yogic power also, *mokṣāya pratyūha*, but that is a hindrance in the real *mokṣa* (liberation) of Śaivism. *Iti kovidāḥ*, this is explained by our great masters.

---

27. Lit., a forming part, a share.

28. A ray (*aṁśa*) of Śiva.

LJA TA04B (10:23)

स्थान्युपनिमन्त्रणे सङ्गस्मयाकरणं पुनरनिष्टप्रसङ्गात् ।

sthānyupanimantraṇe saṅgasmayākaraṇaṁ punaraniṣṭaprasaṅgāt /
(*Yoga Sūtra* 3.51)

In the Yoga *Darśana* also, Patañjali has said: When you are established in *samādhi*, when you are entering on the sixth state of *samādhi*[29] – it is said in Patañjali – then what you feel, what you experience in *samādhi*, is *sthāni upanimantraṇe*, *sthāni-devata*s (gods) invite you to their abodes [and say], "*Bho iha ramyatām*, this is your seat, sir; *iha āsyātām*, you must enjoy our place; *kamanīyo ayam bhogaḥ*, this is a very joyous pleasure for you; *kamanīyo ayam kanyā*, this is the most beautiful lady for you, for your use; *sarvamidam upārjitam bhavatā*, this you have gained by conducting your yoga, so it is your own wealth, you enjoy it." To that he says (Patañjali): *Sthāni-upanimantraṇe*, although they invite you this way, *saṅgasmayākaraṇam*, you must not be attached to that invitation and you must not get yourself overjoyed that I have reached that highest state. This is *sthāni-upanimantraṇe*. *Saṅgasmayā-karaṇam*, you must not be attached to that invitation or you must not be alarmed by this invitation from the deities, the lords from heaven. [The feeling] that, "I have gained so much", this ego must not appear in you. *Punar-aniṣṭaprаṅgāṭ*, if this happens, *punar-aniṣṭaprаṅgāṭ*, you will fall again. This is said by Patañjali also.

LJA TA04B (12:28)

शिवशासनमाहात्म्यं विदन्नप्यत एव हि ॥२०॥
वैष्णवाद्येषु रज्येत मूढो रागेण रञ्जितः ।

śivaśāsanamāhātmyaṁ vidannapyata eva hi //20//
vaiṣṇavādyeṣu rajyeta mūḍho rāgeṇa rañjitaḥ /

29. The sixth state according to Śaivism, the eight state according to Patañjali.

That fool (*mūḍha*), that ignorant person who is absolutely a fool and attached with that *rāga*, attached with that wrong path, *śiva śāsana māhātmyaṁ vidannapi*, although he experiences and realizes the greatness of Śaivism, but even then, *vaiṣṇavādyeṣu rajyeta*, he is attached to Vedānta, just like our Jankinātha. He goes to that Śivālaya Mandir to study Vedānta. After hearing the divine lectures of Śaivism, he is again diverted towards that. *Vaiṣṇavādyeṣu rajyeta*, he is attached to that other system because he is *rāgeṇa rañjitaḥ*, he is attached with the *rāga* of that particular point.

But what is the cause of that? How could that be? For that he explains the next *śloka*. *Yatastāvati sā*…do you understand?

JOHN: Yes.

SWAMIJI: Do you understand (laughter)?

LJA TA04B (13:49)

यतस्तावति सा तस्य वामाख्या शक्तिरैश्वरी ॥२१॥
पाञ्चरात्रिकवैरिञ्च सौगतादेर्विजृम्भते ।

yatastāvati sā tasya vāmākhyā śaktiraiśvarī //21//
pāñcarātrikavairiñca-saugatādervijṛmbhate /

Because this energy of Lord Śiva in the formation of Vāma, the Vāma energy of Lord Śiva, is ruling on them.

JOHN: What is Vāma in this?

SWAMIJI: Vāma is that energy of Lord Śiva that carries you away from the consciousness of Lord Śiva.[30]

SCHOLAR: *Saṁsāra vāmanāt.*[31]

---

30. "There are two energies of Lord Śiva. One is the Vāma energy and another is the Jyeṣṭha energy. Vāmā energies are those energies which kick you down in hell, and Jyeṣṭha energy makes you rise in God consciousness." *Tantrāloka* 15b.422 (LJA archive).

31. The left-handed (*vāma*) energy that keeps you in the cycle of repeated births and deaths (*saṁsāra*).

SWAMIJI: Yes. *Yatastāvati sā tasya vāmākhyā śaktir-aiśvarī*, and that kingdom shines on the Pāñcarātra system; *vairiñca*, the Vedānta system; *saugatāder*, and the Buddhists – that Vāma energy of Lord Śiva.

SCHOLAR: Pañcarātrika is this Tantric Vaiṣṇavism.

SWAMIJI: So, it is obvious that they are attached to other systems and they ignore the real system and the right path. *Dṛṣṭvā sāmrājyasambha-*... but how could it be possible when he experiences that the Trika System is the topmost system [among] all the schools of thought? For that he explains the next *śloka*.

LJA TA04B (15:07)

दृष्टाः साम्राज्यसम्भोगं निन्दन्तः केऽपि बालिशाः ॥२२॥
न तु सन्तोषतः स्वेषु भोगेष्वाशीः प्रवर्तनात् ।

dṛṣṭāḥ sāmrājyasambhogaṁ nindantaḥ ke'pi bāliśāḥ //22//
na tu santoṣataḥ sveṣu bhogeṣvāśīḥ pravartanāt /

Dṛṣṭā, we have experienced these things in this universe (*dṛṣṭāḥ, asmābhiḥ dṛṣṭā*, we have experienced these things happening in this universe), that, *sāmrājya sambhogaṁ nindanta ke'pi bāliśaḥ*, there are those classes of fools, we have seen in this universe that those classes of fools give bad names to *sāmrājya sambhogaṁ*, the joy of, the glory of, *sāmrājya*. *Sāmrājya* means, ...

SCHOLAR: Empire.

SWAMIJI: ... being the emperor of the universe. If they are the emperor of the universe, if they are asked, if they are invited, to be the emperor of the universe, they won't agree to that. They will say, "No, we don't like it." We have seen such people who do not like that kingdom of joy. *Na tu santoṣataḥ*, not by contentment, they are not contented [by *sāmrājya*], because *sveṣu bhogeṣu āśīḥ pravartanāt*, they like to remain in their rags, in their small cottage, in their small huts with their poor wives and poor children without clothes. They like [that]. They like [that] and they dislike that kingdom [of joy]. We have seen such examples in this universe. So this happens like that. They leave that right path aside and are attached to that wrong path.

LJA TA04B (17:01)

एवञ्चिद्भैरवावेशनिन्दातत्परमानसाः ॥२३॥
भवन्त्यतिसुघोराभिः शक्तिभिः पातिता यतः ।

evañcidbhairavāveśa-nindātatparamānasāḥ //23//
bhavantyatisughorābhiḥ śaktibhiḥ pātitā yataḥ /

This is the effect, this is the after-effect of the energies of Lord Śiva in the formation of the *ghoratarī* energies. The *ghoratarī* energies function this way on these human beings, because these *ghoratarī* energies of Lord Śiva make one fall from the right path, because they are *cidbhairava āveśa nindātat paramānasaḥ*, they always discuss that, "This Śaivism is only imagination, there is nothing in it, there is no substance in it." *Cidbhairava āveśa nindātat paramānasāḥ*, you must understand that those people who give bad names to this system of Śaivism, they have been trodden down by those *ghoratarī* energies of Lord Śiva.[32]

SCHOLAR: *Cidbhairavāveśā*?

SWAMIJI: *Cidbhairavāveśa* is Śaivism. *Cidbhairava āveśa*, the entry in *cid*-Bhairava, the entry in Bhairava, who is all-conscious, full of consciousness.

32. "There are three classes of energies of Lord Śiva: one class is that of the *aghora śaktis* (*aghora* energies), another class is of the *ghora* energies, and the third class is the *ghoratarī* energies. *Aghora* energies are those energies which carry you to the topmost elevated state. And the function handled by *ghora* energies is just keep you in that [standstill] position, neither rise nor fall. *Ghoratarī* energies are those energies which make you fall down." *Light on Tantra in Kashmir Shaivism, Tantrāloka, Vol. Two*, 3.72ab, p. 124.

LJA TA04B (18:27)

तेन शांभवमाहात्म्यं जानन्यः शासनान्तरे ॥२४॥
आश्वस्तो नोत्तरीतव्यं तेन भेदमहार्णवात् ।

tena śāṁbhavamāhātmyaṁ jānanyaḥ śāsanāntare //24//
āśvasto nottarītavyaṁ tena bhedamahārṇavāt /

So, the conclusion is that *śāṁbhava māhātmyaṁ jānan*, if you understand and realize the greatness of Śaivism, although you understand the greatness and supremacy of Śaivism, *yaḥ śāsanāntare āśvasto*, [and] are attached, you become attached, to other systems of Vedānta, or Rajneesh, or something else, *nottarītavyaṁ tena bheda mahārṇavāt*, he is never to come out from the ocean of differentiated perception. He will never come out from the ocean of differentiated perception. He will be drowned in that differentiated perception, the ocean of differentiated perception. There is no hope of his liberation in any way.

LJA TA04B (19:33)

श्रीकामिकायां प्रोक्तं च पाशप्रकरणे स्फुटम् ॥२५॥

śrīkāmikāyāṁ proktaṁ ca pāśaprakaraṇe sphuṭam //25//

In *pāśa prakaraṇa* also, the *prakaraṇa*[33] regarding these bondages (these *pāśā*), …*

Pāśā means …

SCHOLAR: Bondages?

SWAMIJI: Ropes by which you …

SCHOLAR: Nooses.

SWAMIJI: Nooses.

*… and in that *prakaraṇa* in the *Kāmikā Śāstra*, it is said:

33. Lit., treatise, section, explanation or discussion.

LJA TA04B (19:59)

वेदसाङ्ख्यपुराणज्ञाः पाञ्चरात्रपरायणाः ।
ये केचिदृषयो धीराः शास्त्रान्तरपरायणाः ॥२६॥
बौद्धार्हताद्याः सर्वे ते विद्यारागेण रञ्जिताः ।
मायापाशेन बद्धत्वाच्छिवदीक्षां न विन्दते ॥२७॥

vedasāṅkhyapurāṇajñāḥ pāñcarātraparāyaṇāḥ /
ye kecidṛṣayo dhīrāḥ śāstrāntaraparāyaṇāḥ //26//
bauddhārhatādyāḥ sarve te vidyārāgeṇa rañjitāḥ /
māyāpāśena baddhatvācchivadīkṣāṁ na vindate //27//

Those who are informed in Vedānta, who are informed in Sāṁkhya, in Purāṇa, in Pāñcarātra, and those *ṛṣis* (seers) who have become *dhīrāḥ* (resolute), *śāstrāntara parāyaṇāḥ*, by studying other systems of schools, other systems of thoughts, by studying other systems of thoughts they have become firm-minded,…*

JOHN: In their own system.

SWAMIJI: In their own system.

SCHOLAR: One-pointed in that.

SWAMIJI: That is [the meaning of] *dhīrāḥ*.

*… and those are Buddhists, Arhata (Jains), *sarve te*, all those philosophers, so-called philosophers, are *vidyā rāgeṇa rañjitāḥ*, they are attached by the *rāga* (attachment) of *vidyā*, limited information. They get limited information and they are attached to it. They say, they perceive that they know everything. *Māyā pāśena baddhatvā*, they are actually bound, they are actually encircled by the tug,…

DENISE: Noose.

SWAMIJI: … the noose, by the rope, of *māyā*, by the rope of the illusive energy of Lord Śiva. *Śiva dīkṣāṁ na vindate*, and there is no hope for them to get initiated in the system of Śaivism. They will never get that fortune. That fortune is away from them.

SCHOLAR: Until that *rāga* disappears.

SWAMIJI: Yes (laughs).

LJA TA04B (21:54)

रागशब्देन च प्रोक्तं रागतत्त्वं नियामकम् ।
मायीये तच्च तं तस्मिञ्छास्त्रे नियमयेदिति ॥२८॥

rāgaśabdena ca proktaṁ rāgatattvaṁ niyāmakam /
māyīye tacca taṁ tasmiñchāstre niyamayediti //28//

This is the power of that *rāga* in them. In those followers of other systems, this is the power of that *rāga* in them, that attachment that makes them established in that inferior wrong path. *Māyīye tacca taṁ tasmin śāstre niyamayediti*, so they get established, they get firmly established in that wrong system. And this is the power of that *rāga* which carries them from right to wrong. *Bas*.

LJA TA04B (22:45)

मोक्षोऽपि वैष्णवादेर्यः स्वसंकल्पेन भावितः ।
परप्रकृतिसायुज्यं यद्वाप्यानन्दरूपता ॥२९॥
विशुद्धचित्तमात्रं वा दीपवत्सन्ततिक्षयः ।
स सवेद्यापवेद्यात्मप्रलयाकलतामयः ॥३०॥

mokṣo'pi vaiṣṇavāderyaḥ svasaṁkalpena bhāvitaḥ /
paraprakṛtisāyujyaṁ yadvāpyānandarūpatā //29//
viśuddhacittamātraṁ vā dīpavatsantatikṣayaḥ /
sa savedyāpavedyātma-pralayākalatāmayaḥ //30//

The *mokṣa* (liberation) which is explained by other schools of thought, other schools of philosophy (that means, Vaiṣṇavites, etcetera), and that *mokṣa* they have concluded from their own imagination (*svasaṁkalpena bhāvitaḥ*). For instance, the Vaiṣṇavas accept that *para prakṛti sāyujya* is *mokṣa*. *Para prakṛti* means, that Being who possesses supreme *prakṛti*, that is Lord Nārāyaṇa.[34] And when you get oneness with him, that is liberation–*para prakṛti sāyujyaṁ* (not *sāmīpyam*).

SCHOLAR: Not *sāmyīpya*. *Sāyujyaṁ*.

SWAMIJI: *Sāyujyaṁ*. This is "union" we have explained in two ways. One is *sāmīpya*, one is *sāyujya*. *Sāmīpya* means, when you are existing near that Being–that is *sāmīpya mokṣa*. *Sāyujya mokṣa* is when you are one with that.

SCHOLAR: And *sālokyam* is? The third one?

SWAMIJI: *Sālokya* is very away from that, quite away.

SCHOLAR: But there are three stages in dualistic Śaivism.

SWAMIJI: Yes. *Sālokya* is from a distance, when you observe that state from a distance. That is *sālokya*. *Sāmīpya*, when you observe that state in front of you. *Sāyujya* is when you observe that state being one with Him. That is *sāyujya*, that is exact oneness.

SCHOLAR: This is *mahā vibhūti*, …

SWAMIJI: Yes, *mahā vibhūti*.[35]

SCHOLAR: … the highest glory of Nārāyaṇa.

SWAMIJI: And some Vedāntists accept that *ānanda rūpatā*[36] is *mokṣa*; when you are absolutely given to complete oneness of *ānanda* (bliss), that is *mokṣa*. Uninterrupted bliss is *mokṣa* from the Vedānta point of view. *Viśuddha citta mātraṁ vā* (verse 30), and another way of thought is *viśuddha citta mātraṁ vā*, when your mind is completely purified, that is liberation, that is the state of liberation.

SCHOLAR: That is Vijñānāvāda, a Buddhist's doctrine.

SWAMIJI: Yes, a Buddhist doctrine–some.

SCHOLAR: Pure consciousness?

SWAMIJI: Yes.

SCHOLAR: Pure of any contingent factors, *kleśa*, etcetera.

SWAMIJI: Yes. *Dīpavat santatikṣayaḥ*, another school of thought accepts that *dīpavat santatikṣayaḥ*: When, for instance, there is a candle, when the fuel in that is finished, you don't know how that flame disappears; by-and-by that flame also disappears along with the

---

34. An appellation of Lord Viṣṇu.

35. Lit., the great wealth or prosperity.

36. The formation (*rūpatā*) of bliss (*ānanda*).

disappearing of, the finishing of, this fuel in that. It may be oil, it may be that wax or something. In the same way, when all *vāsanās* (impressions), all *vikalpas* (thoughts) have disappeared, you can't understand how that limited being also disappears with it. That is the *mokṣa* [that] they have accepted.

SCHOLAR: Vaibhāṣika Buddhists.

SWAMIJI: Vaibhāṣika Buddhists. *Sa savedyāpavedyātma pralayākalatāmayaḥ*, from our point of view, this kind of *mokṣa* is *savedya pralayākala* or *apavedya pralayākala*. When they observe that that is *ānanda*, that *mokṣa* is filled with bliss, a blissful state, you may call it *savedya pralayākala*. When they call it *santatikṣaya* (*dīpavat santatikṣaya*) or *viśuddha cittamātram*, that would be *apavedya pralayākala*, it will go to *apavedya pralayākala*, not above that. So some *mokṣas* (liberations), from our point of view, are resting in *apavedya pralayākala* and some are resting in *savedya pralayākala*, not above. [The states of] *vijñānākala* or Śuddhavidyā or Īśvara and Sadāśiva, the question does not arise.[37]

SCHOLAR: Could you define for us exactly what is the state of *pralayākala* as opposed to *vijñānākala*?

SWAMIJI: *Pralayākala* is when all senses stop functioning. [Where] the mind stops functioning, the mind is not functioning, the senses are not functioning, nothing is functioning, and there is no awareness at the same time, that is *pralayākala*, that is *apavedya pralayākala*. *Savedya pralayākala* is when the same state [takes place], but you are aware that everything is finished–that is *savedya pralayākala*.

SCHOLAR: So there is some notion of a subject there, some *vedaka* (knower).

LJA TA04B (28:36)

SWAMIJI: For instance, take the state of sound sleep. When you are resting in sound sleep, sometime when you [awaken] after that, when your eyes open and you say, "But I don't know where I was,

---

37. According to Kashmir Shaivsm, there are seven states of consciousness (*pramātṛs*, perceivers). In ascending order, they are *sakala*, *pralayākala* (*apavedya* and *savedya*), *vijñānākala*, Śuddhavidyā, Īśvara, Sadāśiva, Śiva-Śakti.

I was absolutely away from everything", that is *apavedya pralayākala*. "I was peacefully resting, I don't know anything about it, only peaceful, I was peacefully situated in dreams", ...

SCHOLAR: *Sukhamāsvapasama.*

SWAMIJI: ... that is *savedya pralayākala*. This is the difference between *savedya pralayākala* and *apavedya pralayākala*.

JOHN: But you say in *savedya* there is some...

SWAMIJI: In *savedya*, there is some impression, an impression of...

JOHN: Subjectivity of awareness, of any, of...?

SWAMIJI: ... subjectivity of that experience, experiencing that state of *pralayākala*. When you experience that state of *pralayākala*, that is *savedya pralayākala*. When you don't experience that state of *pralayākala*, that is *apavedya pralayākala*. This is the difference.

SCHOLAR: It's experienced from a distance after the state. He says, "I experienced bliss" or ...

SWAMIJI: It is after, not in that.

SCHOLAR: "... I was one with Vasudeva."

SWAMIJI: Yes. If you were experiencing this state in the body of *pralayākala*,[38] then it was *vijñānākala*, then it would be *vijñānākala*, then it wouldn't be *pralayākala*.

SCHOLAR: If there was awareness there.

SWAMIJI: Awareness is not there, awareness is afterwards, after you come out from that.

JOHN: In *pralayākala*, in this *savedya* and *apavedya*.

SWAMIJI: Yes, in the state of *pralayākala*, awareness is outside *pralayākala*, awareness comes in memory. You remember that you were asleep, sound sleep, "[I was] peacefully situated in myself", but not [experiencing it] in the center of that being.

SCHOLAR: So it's not really possible to construct a metaphysical view from that state, just as the Buddhist says that, "*Nirvāṇa* is indescribable, I can't say anything about it. It is in relation to *saṁsāra*."

SWAMIJI: No, it is not, no, it is abs- ...

SCHOLAR: It's without knowledge.

SWAMIJI: Yes. Knowledge (i.e., awareness) must be there. If knowledge is not there, then it is *pralayākala*.

---

38. That is, while in the state of *pralayākala*.

JOHN: In *vijñānākala*, knowledge is there.

SWAMIJI: Yes. In *vijñānākala*, you …

JOHN: With or without *svātantrya*.[39] You said one time that in *vijñānākala* you can have *svātantrya* without …

SWAMIJI: [Without] *svātantrya* means, when it is not in your hands to hold it. You are in *vijñānākala*, but you have no strength to hold it. You come out of its own accord. That is *svātantrya rāhityam*[40] in *vijñānākala*.

JOHN: Without *svātantrya*.

SWAMIJI: And as soon as you come out, *vijñānākala* disappears, the state of *vijñānākala* disappears.

SCHOLAR: So, Śaṅkara's Absolute would fall into *pralayākala*, or would it fall into…?[41]

SWAMIJI: *Savedya pralayākala*.

SCHOLAR: *Savedya pralayākala*. So it's really low?

SWAMIJI: Yes. Because they perceive *ānanda rūpatā*, and *ānanda rūpatā* they explain: "*Ānanda rūpatā* cannot be explained." They give this example: when you take a piece of sweet on your tongue, you can't explain what sort of taste you feel. They give this example. But it can be explained in the Śaivite way.

SCHOLAR: So Śaivites, must they necessarily experience this state in their progress?

SWAMIJI: Yes, they must experience.

SCHOLAR: And own this *pralayākala bhāva* as well.

SWAMIJI: Yes, yes, in *ahaṁ bhāva*; in *ahaṁ bhāva*, not *idaṁ bhāva*: they experience it in a subjective way, not in an objective way.

SCHOLAR: But in *āṇavopāya*, *sādhaka*s can fall into this *pralayākala* state commonly.

SWAMIJI: Yes, first, first, first. At first this is the way, *pralayākala* is the way. From *sakala*, you have to pass *pralayākala*, and then in *vijñānākala*, then Śuddhavidyā, then Īśvara, and then Sadāśiva, and finally in Śiva.

---

39. Freedom of will.

40. Non-possession (*rāhityam*) of the freedom of will (*svātantrya*).

41. Śaṅkara was the formulator of Advaita Vedānta.

LJA TA04B (32:46)

तं प्राप्यापि चिरं कालं तद्भोगाभोगभुक्ततः ।
तत्तत्त्वप्रलयान्ते तु तदूर्ध्वां सृष्टिमागतः ॥३१॥
मन्त्रत्वमेति सम्बोधादनन्तेशेन कल्पितात् ।

taṁ prāpyāpi ciraṁ kālaṁ tadbhogābhogabhuktataḥ /
tattattvapralayānte tu tadūrdhvāṁ sṛṣṭimāgataḥ //31//
mantratvameti sambodhād-ananteśena kalpitāt /

Now, what comes the result? What is the result of this state of *savedya pralayākala* and *apavedya pralayākala* for those Vaiṣṇavites, etcetera, Buddhists, etcetera? *Taṁ prāpya api*, although they achieve that state of *savedya pralayākala* or *apavedya pralayākala*, *ciraṁ kālaṁ tat bhoga abhoga bhuktataḥ*, for a great span of time they enjoy the bliss of that state after leaving their body. *Tat tattva pralayānte tu*, when that *tattva*, when that state of the *pralayākala* state is destroyed at the time of destruction, *tad ūrdhvāṁ sṛṣṭim āgataḥ*, they naturally are carried towards higher states, not [lower] states. This is the only way of *pralayākala*. When you are established in *savedya pralayākala* (not *apavedya pralayākala*; in *apavedya pralayākala* there is no hope of rising), in *savedya pralayākala* there is hope of rising because in *pralayākala*.... You already know, in *sakala*, all the three *mala*s (impurities) are existing and functioning in fullness–in *sakala pramātā*. In *pralayākala pramātā*, only two *mala*s are functioning (*kārmamala* is finished).

SCHOLAR: There's no action.

SWAMIJI: No, *kārmamala* has kept only impressions. Only *māyīya-mala* and *āṇavamala* are functioning there.[42] In which state?

42. For a complete explanation of the three *mala*s, see: *Light on Tantra in Kashmir Shaivism, Tantrāloka, Vol. Two*, Appendix 3, p. 447. See also: *Kashmir Shaivism–The Secret Supreme*, Swami Lakshmanjoo, ed. John Hughes (Lakshmanjoo Academy, Los Angeles, 1985–2015), chapter 4.

SCHOLAR: In *pralayākala bhāva.*

SWAMIJI: In *pralayākala pramātā.*[43] And in *vijñānākala pramātā*, *kārmamala* is finished and *māyīyamala* is finished, along with the impressions. There are no impressions [of *kārmamala* and *māyīya-mala*] remaining in *vijñānākala pramātā*. In *pralayākala*, impressions are existing of all the three *mala*s, and in *sakala* also, impressions and the functioning of all of these three *mala*s exist, but not in *vijñānākala*. In *vijñānākala pramātā*, the traces of impressions of *kārmamala* and the traces of the impressions of *māyīyamala* have also disappeared – in *vijñānākala pramātā*.

SCHOLAR: So, how does *āṇavamala* function in that?

SWAMIJI: *Āṇavamala* is functioning [in *vijñānākala*], but in the state of *didhvaṁsiṣu bhāva*, it is towards destruction. It is functioning, just as Kṛṣṇa was singing songs, our Kṛṣṇa Brahmacāri, on my birthday, [the last] birthday. His singing songs was just towards its end. In the same way, in *vijñānākala pramātā*, *āṇavamala* is towards its end, it has got the tendency of ending tendency, in nothingness.

JOHN: But that functioning of *āṇavamala* is that consciousness is somewhat limited there. You said at one point that in *vijñānākala pramātṛ bhāva*, there could be *svātantrya* at some point, but not…

SWAMIJI: Yes, but not *vijñāna*, not *bodha* (consciousness). When *bodha* is there, then *svātantrya* is not there. When *svātantrya* is there, *bodha* is not there in *vijñānākala pramātā*.

SCHOLAR: So, it is not real *svātantrya*, it's not *para svātantrya*.

SWAMIJI: No, it is not real *svātantrya*, it is only half-way *svātantrya*. But the *āṇavamala* there is towards its destruction. It will be destroyed in the next step of being, that is, Śuddhavidyā.[44] So, it is why he says, *tat tattva pralayānte tu*, and *savedya pralayākala* is near *vijñānākala pramātā*, *apavedya pralayākala* is absolutely away from *vijñānākala pramātā*. *Savedya pralayākala* could be called "with nearness to *vijñānākala pramātā*". *Vijñānākala pramātā* and *savedya pralayākala* differ very little with each other.

---

43. The subjectivity (*pramātā*) of *pralayākala*.

44. In the ninth *āhnika* (verse 94), Abhinavagupta will explain how *āṇavamala* persists even up to Sadāśiva *pramātā*, and is completely destroyed in Śiva-Śakti *pramātā*.

SCHOLAR: And in relation to the state of deep sleep, where does *apavedya pralayākala* stand and *savedya pralayākala*?

SWAMIJI: Deep sleep, that is *suṣupti*, that is not *pralayākala*. In *pralayākala*, breath is not functioning. In sound sleep, breath is functioning. So, that is not *pralayākala*, that is *suṣupti*.

SCHOLAR: That is the major point of distinction between *pralayākala* and *suṣupti*.

SWAMIJI: *Pralayākala* is achieved by yogis. The state of *pralayākala* is achieved when you control the mind and breath-lessness comes, the breath stops, everything stops, the functioning of the senses stop, and you are in *samādhi*. And that *samādhi* is *pralayākala bhāva*.

SCHOLAR: But this *samādhi* is without *cit unmeṣa*,[45] there's no rise of *kuṇḍalinī*.

SWAMIJI: There is no rise of…no, that is not…the question does not arise there.

DENISE: Is it a stable state that remains–*pralayākala*?

SWAMIJI: It is stable for those unfortunate persons. But it must not remain, it must go (laughs), it must be removed, and you must step in a higher state.

DENISE: Quickly. How long? Does it last a long time?

SWAMIJI: It depends upon the capacity of the *sādhaka*. When the *sādhaka* is absolutely purified, towards his purification, then he will leave it aside in a short period and get entry in *vijñānākala pramātā*.

Tad bhogābhoga bhuktataḥ, this depends upon the capacity of the *sādhaka*. When, in his mind, impressions have disappeared, the *vāsanā*s of worldly enjoyments have disappeared, *tat tattva pralayānte tu*, when *pralayākala tattva* (that is, *māyā tattva*) is destroyed, then he gets entry in *vijñānākala pramātā*. That *savedya pralayākala pramātā* gets entry, automatic entry, in the *vijñānākala* state (*tat ūrdhvam sṛṣṭiṁ āgataḥ*), and *ananteśena kalpitāt sambhodhāt*, Anantabhaṭṭāraka infuses awareness in him afterwards.[46] When *māyā tattva* is destroyed, at the time of

45. The rise (*unmeṣa*) of consciousness (*cit*).

46. Lit., the infinite/eternal (*ananta*) highly venerated lord (*bhaṭṭāraka*). Anantabhaṭṭāraka (Aghoranātha) is Lord Śiva's "immediate assistant" (or demiurge), who governs creation from Sadāśiva to the element of earth. See *Tantrāloka* 5.171–173 (LJA archives).

destruction, then Anantabhaṭṭāraka infuses awareness in that *sādhaka*.

JOHN: What is this? Universal destruction or which destruction is this?

SWAMIJI: This is universal destruction up to *māyā*, not above. There is the *prakṛti*-destruction up to *prakṛti*. And there is *brahmāṇḍa*-destruction. There is *brahmāṇḍa* (*pṛthvyaṇḍa*), *pṛthvyaṇḍa* is destroyed (this is the first destruction), then *prakṛtyaṇḍa* is destroyed (the second destruction), *māyāṇḍa* is destroyed (the third destruction), *śaktyaṇḍa* is destroyed (fourth destruction). The destruction of *śaktyaṇḍa* is the final destruction of the universe. So, everything is finished and only Śiva remains there, shining everywhere (laughs).[47]

JOHN: From the point of view of Śaivism, between these *yuga*s (eras), which kind of destruction takes place?

SWAMIJI: *Yuga*s?

JOHN: Between this Kali Yuga…there is no destruction.

SWAMIJI: No, these *yuga*s are inferior destructions. These are very low destructions.

SCHOLAR: This is awareness.

JOHN: Up to the point of *māyā*, there would be no destruction at all.

SWAMIJI: No, in the *yuga*'s destruction (that is, the end of Kali Yuga, the end of Satya Yuga, the end of Tretā Yuga, the end of Dvāpara Yuga), these ends are not called "final destructions". These are only individual destructions.

---

47. *Brahmāṇḍa* (*pṛthvyaṇḍa*), *prakṛtyaṇḍa*, *māyāṇḍa*, and *śaktyaṇḍa* are synonymous with the *kalā*s (circles) of *nivṛtti kalā*, *pratiṣṭhā kalā*, *vidyā kalā*, and *śāntā kalā*, respectively. "These *kalā*s are enclosures for all the thirty-six elements, the thirty-six *tattva*s, from earth up to Śiva. The first and outermost enclosure is called *nivṛtti kalā*. In *nivṛtti kalā* you will find the first *tattva*, *pṛthivī tattva*, the element 'earth.' The next *kalā* or enclosure is *pratiṣṭhā kalā*. In *pratiṣṭhā kalā* you find the twenty-three *tattva*s from *jala tattva*, the element 'water,' up to and including *prakṛti tattva*. The next enclosure is known as *vidyā kalā*. *Vidyā kalā* contains the seven *tattva*s, from *puruṣa tattva* up to and including *māyā tattva*. The next enclosure is called *śāntā kalā*. *Śāntā kalā* contains the four *tattva*s from Śuddhavidyā *tattva* up to and including Śakti *tattva*, the thirty-fifth *tattva*. The fifth and last enclosure is known as *śāntātītā kalā*. Here, you will only find the existence of Śiva *tattva*." *Kashmir Shaivism–The Secret Supreme*, chapter 2, p. 12.

JOHN: So it has nothing to do with this at all then here.

SWAMIJI: No (affirmative). These four destructions are great destructions. First is the destruction of this *pṛthivī* (earth). You won't find this planet existing afterwards. This is the destruction of *pṛthivī*. And then the destruction of *prakṛti*; up to *prakṛti*, all the elements are finished, you can't perceive any element existing in this universe. That is the destruction of *prakṛti*.[48] And then above that, the destruction of Śakti; up to Śakti *tattva*, all is destroyed, you won't find any element except the Śiva-element existing.

JOHN: That's the fourth. What is the third?

SWAMIJI: *Pṛthivī* is the first, *prakṛti* is second, *māyā* is third, and *śakti* is the fourth.[49]

SCHOLAR: But not destruction in the sense of that Śiva is empty of those things in the way that a monastery is empty of monks when they go out of it.

SWAMIJI: No, Śiva has withdrawn everything, Śiva has withdrawn in His own consciousness. Śiva withdraws everything, because everything is there in its seed form.

Tat tattva pralayānte tu tat ūrdhvāṁ sṛṣṭimāgataḥ, naturally, automatically, he (the *sādhaka*) rises towards another state, that is, *vijñānākala*. *Mantratvam eti*, then *anantešena kalpitāt sambodhāt*, when Anantabhaṭṭāraka infuses awareness in him, in that *vijñānākala pramātā*, *mantratvam eti*, he gets entry in Śuddhavidyā *pramātā* also, *etat cāgre*, and so on, and onwards.

SCHOLAR: The state of subjective awareness–*mantratvam.*

SWAMIJI: Yes. But that awareness is infused by Anantabhaṭṭāraka, not Śiva Himself.

---

48. Here, Swamiji is referring to *prakṛtyaṇḍa*, the circle or egg of *prakṛti* that extends from the water element (*jala*) up to and including the element of *prakṛti*, and contains *brahmāṇḍa* (*nivṛtti kalā*). See Appendix 3, p. 387, for an explanation of *prakṛti*.

49. *Māyāṇḍa* extends from element of *puruṣa* to *māyā*, that is, the *kañcuka*s plus *māyā*. *Śaktyaṇḍa* contains the pure elements (*śuddha tattva*s) of Śuddhavidyā, Īśvara, Sadāśiva, and Śakti.

SCHOLAR: What is the meaning of that from the point of view of awareness by…?

SWAMIJI: Huh?

SCHOLAR: What does that mean from point of view of self-experience–"infused by Anantabhaṭṭāraka"?

SWAMIJI: Because, when he is established in *vijñānākala*, perceiving the *vijñānākala* state, at that time he gets infusion and automatically he gets entry in Śuddhavidyā *pramātā*.

SCHOLAR: But not into Śiva *bhāva*, so it's…

SWAMIJI: No (affirmative).

SCHOLAR: [He] experiences himself drawn into the state of Anantabhaṭṭāraka in Śuddhavidyā.

SWAMIJI: No. Anantabhaṭṭāraka is the infuser.

LJA TA04B (43:41)

एतच्चाग्रे तनिष्याम इत्यास्तां तावदत्र तत् ॥ ३२ ॥

etaccāgre taniṣyāma ityāstāṁ tāvadatra tat //32//

Let us drop this point here because it will be clarified in the 13th *āhnika*.

DENISE: Good.

SWAMIJI: (laughs) Why good?

DENISE: Well, I need more clarification.

SWAMIJI: Yes.

तेनाज्ञजनताक्लृप्तप्रवादैर्यो विडम्बितः ।
असद्गुरौ रूढचित्स मायापाशेन रञ्जितः ॥ ३३ ॥

tenājñajanatāklṛpta-pravādairyo viḍambitaḥ /
asadgurau rūḍhacitsa māyāpāśena rañjitaḥ //33//

So, the one who is misled by the discussions and theories of *ajñajanatā* (*ajñajanatā* means, all those masters of the Sāṁkhya System, the masters of the Vedānta theory – all those masters are called *ajñajanatā*[50]), …

SCHOLAR: Ignorant.

SWAMIJI: … and those who have put that *pravāda* (discussions) from their point of view, by that discussion, he who is befooled, he who is misled, in other words, he will be called *asadgurau rūḍhacit sa*, he has established his mind towards the wrong master, he is being sentenced towards the wrong master. *Māyāpāśena rañjitaḥ*, the conclusion is that he is *māyāpāśena rañjitaḥ*, he is colored by *māyāpāśa*; he is dyed, he is dyed by the *māyāpāśa*, by the bondage of *māyā*, by the bondage of illusion – he who has been directed towards the wrong master. Wrong masters are all wrong masters except Śaivites. All other masters are wrong masters from our point of view (laughter).[51]

LJA TA04B (45:55)

सोऽपि सत्तर्कयोगेन नीयते सद्गुरुं प्रति ।
सत्तर्कः शुद्धविद्यैव सा चेच्छा परमेशितुः ॥३४॥

so'pi sattarkayogena nīyate sadgurum̐ prati /
sattarkaḥ śuddhavidyaiva sā cecchā parameśituḥ //34//

But that also, that disciple also, who has been directed towards the wrong master by his misfortune, but *sattarka yogena*, when he puts *sattarka* in himself, …

SCHOLAR: *Sattarka*: true discrimination, true logic.

---

50. Ignorant (*ajña*) schools (*janatā*).

51. According to Kashmir Shaivism, other philosophies are not wholly "wrong" per se, but rather, incomplete. As Abhinavagupta says, "A master should find the difference of all the systems; the difference between what is lacking in Vedānta, what is not lacking in Buddhism, or what is lacking in Buddhism and what is not lacking in other systems. You must find out the difference afterwards and be complete in information, all-round information, and you'll become an all-round best master." *Tantrāloka* 13.343 (LJA archives).

SWAMIJI: ... true logic, *nīyate sadguruṁ prati sattarkaḥ śuddha*[*vidyaiva*]–true logic is not discussion, true discussion–he says, *sattarkaḥ śuddhavidyaiva*, true logic is just entry in Śuddhavidyā. When you get entry in Śuddhavidyā, there you find the discrimination between Śiva and ignorance.

SCHOLAR: You see from your point.

SWAMIJI: Yes.

JOHN: You really see.

SWAMIJI: *Sā ceccha parameśituḥ*, and that too is dependable to his will, the will of Lord Śiva. If he wills, you will be directed towards a *sadguru* (real master). You will be carried from a wrong master to a right master by His will.

LJA TA04B (47:12)

श्रीपूर्वशास्त्रे तेनोक्तं स यियासुः शिवेच्छया ।
भुक्तिमुक्तिप्रसिद्ध्यर्थं नीयते सद्गुरुं प्रति ॥ ३५ ॥

śrīpūrvaśāstre tenoktaṁ sa yiyāsuḥ śivecchayā /
bhuktimuktiprasiddhyarthaṁ nīyate sadguruṁ prati //35//
(not recited)

Śrīpūrva śāstre tenoktaṁ, it is why in the *Mālinīvijaya* [*Tantra*] it is also said, *sa yiyāsuḥ śivecchayā*, the desire comes in him who is directed towards the wrong master, by the will of Lord Śiva or by his blessed grace, this desire comes in him...the desire of what?

SCHOLAR: Let me go to this master.

SWAMIJI: To find out the real master. *Bhukti mukti prasiddhyarthaṁ*, for the fulfillment of *bhoga* and *mokṣa* he is carried to the right master. *Bhoga* means, the enjoyment of the universe. *Mokṣa* means, the establishment in one's own Self.

SCHOLAR: *Viśvamāyātvam, viśvatirṇattvam.*[52]

SWAMIJI: This also could be explained like that way. But *bhukti*

52. Immanence and transcendence, respectively.

mukti prasiddhi arthaṁ, as long as there is no *bhukti* (enjoyment), *mukti* (liberation) is not possible from our point of view. There must be *bhoga* in *mokṣa* and *mokṣa* in *bhoga*.

JOHN: So then Śaivism does not agree with the *sannyāsi* (renunciate) point of view of leaving …

SWAMIJI: No, *sannyāsi*, that question does not arise.[53] You can enjoy the universe and be one with Lord Śiva.

JOHN: Just for clarification, why does the Śaivite say that you have to have the fulfillment of desire in order to be established in *mokṣa*?

SWAMIJI: But desire, as long as there is no desire. For instance, Dr. Vasu is there, or Rangānandanātha is there. He has no desire to go to a real master. He is misled altogether because there is no will of God, there is no grace of God in him to find out the real master. He goes in this conclusion that, "All religions are one. One hundred and twelve centers we have opened and we will open more centers." But for what centers? They are no centers at all. The real center is the center of Universal consciousness. You must establish that. That is the real center of philosophy.

JOHN: So, why is *bhoga*, then, the fulfillment of desires, so important in Śaivism? I mean …

SWAMIJI: Huh?

JOHN: In so many systems, desire is to be excluded.

SWAMIJI: Not in Śaivism.

JOHN: No, not in Śaivism. So why is the fulfillment of desire tied up with *mokṣa* in Śaivism?

SWAMIJI: Because it is the expansion of Lord Śiva.

JOHN: Of your own nature.

SWAMIJI: Yes.

---

53. "In the Kula and Kālī *śāstras*, it is well-explained that those who are followers of Viṣṇu, Brahmā, all those gods, and who always massage their bodies with ashes, those *sadhus*, saints, they are not fit to get entry in the Trika system. You have to tell them, 'No, you have no authority to enter here.' They have to leave all these habits of putting *jaṭā* (growing long hair), or rubbing ashes [on their bodies], or wearing those dyed clothes, and putting those beads, all those are excluded from this system, they are kicked out." *Tantrāloka* 13.306 (LJA archives).

SCHOLAR: But the gross desire, "I want this, I want that, I am hungry, I want to eat, I feel sexually aroused, I want this woman", do you mean desire…?

SWAMIJI: That also is included.

SCHOLAR: But only with awareness, otherwise it is just…

SWAMIJI: Yes, when awareness is there, not otherwise.

SCHOLAR: But awareness here is something *heavy*, it is not just…

SWAMIJI: (laughs) It is heavy. It is not heavy, it is filled with the *mala*s (impurities). Because your desire for getting that girl was a desire with the *mala*s, so this desire was likely to be destroyed. When there would be a desire without *mala*s, then you wish for that girl and she would be yours at once, at that very moment, without any hindrance. That is the desire from the Lord. This [desire of yours] was the desire from the individual mind (laughs).

LJA TA04B (50:35)

शक्तिपातस्तु तत्रैष क्रमिकः सम्प्रवर्तते ।
स्थित्वा योऽसद्गुरौ शास्त्रान्तरे वा सत्पथं श्रितः ॥ ३६ ॥

śaktipātastu tatraiṣa kramikaḥ sampravartate /
sthitvā yo'sadgurau śāstrāntare vā satpathaṁ śritaḥ //36//

And this *śaktipāta* is *kramika śaktipāta*, it is the successive way of the grace of Lord Śiva. One is the direct way of the grace of Lord Śiva (that is direct grace, direct grace from Śiva to you), and there is successive grace from Śiva. Successive grace is, e.g., first you go to a Vaiṣṇavite master and you are initiated there, and afterwards you come to this conclusion that, "This path is exactly a wrong path, I am misled, I must find out some higher way". Then Lord Śiva directs you towards the right master. This is the grace of Lord Śiva functioning in a successive manner. [The direct] grace of Lord Śiva is, for instance, [take] me. I, from my very childhood, was directed towards Śaivism. This was direct grace. It was not successive grace. So there is successive grace and indirect grace also.

SCHOLAR: So, full successive grace would be that where [a person is] initiated in the Vaiṣṇava doctrine, and then in Śaiva Siddhanta, then in Vāma, then in Dakṣiṇa, then in Kula, then in Kaula, then in Mata, and then in Trika, *bas*.

SWAMIJI: ... then in Trika, that is the successive way of grace.

JOHN: In its fullest sense.

SCHOLAR: A long way from Śaiva Siddhānta.

SWAMIJI: Yes. *Śaktipātastu tatraiṣa kramikaḥ sampravartate*, so this is *kramikaḥ śaktipāta*: *sthitvā yo asadgurau*, the one who is established [with] the wrong master first, and *śāstrāntare*, or the wrong theory also, and then in the end, *satpatham śritaḥ*, is established [with] a real master and the real *śāstra* (scripture).

LJA TA04B (52:30)

गुरुशास्त्रगते सत्त्वेऽसत्त्वे चात्र विभेदकम् ।
शक्तिपातस्य वैचित्र्यं पुरस्तात्प्रविविच्यते ॥ ३७ ॥

guruśāstragate sattve'sattve cātra vibhedakam /
śaktipātasya vaicitryaṁ purastātpravivicyate //37//

Vibhedakam, distinction, the way of distinction, how to distinguish between a real master and a wrong master, how to distinguish between the real *śāstra* and the wrong *śāstra* (the wrong theory), the agency by which you distinguish this, this agency is *śaktipātasya vaicitryam*, the differentiated way of *śaktipāta*, the differentiated way of His grace. *Purastāt pravivicyate*, it will be described in the 13th *āhnika*, not here, because there is no time for this to be discussed (laughs).

DEVOTEES: (laughter)

SWAMIJI:

LJA TA04B (53:10)

उक्तं स्वच्छन्दशास्त्रे तत् वैष्णवाद्यान्प्रवादिनः ।
सर्वान्भ्रमयते माया सामोक्षे मोक्षलिप्सया ॥ ३८ ॥

uktaṁ svacchandaśāstre tat vaiṣṇavādyānpravādinaḥ |
sarvānbhramayate māyā sāmokṣe mokṣalipsayā ||38||

In the *Svacchanda Śāstra* also this is described, this is explained, that all these followers of other schools (that is, Vaiṣṇavites, etcetera), *sarvān bhramayate māyā*, *māyā* is putting them in the world of delusion always, *māyā* is sentencing them in the world of delusion, or kicking them in the world of delusion, because *sāmokṣe*, *amokṣe mokṣa lipsayā*, because they get a conception of *mokṣa* which is not *mokṣa*; exactly, that is not *mokṣa*, that is not liberation, but they perceive that this is liberation.

LJA TA04B (51:42)

Ataḥ paraṁ bhavetmāyā sarvajantuvimohinī (comm.), from here is the sphere of *māyā*, the kingdom of *māyā*, *sarva jantu vimohinī*, which puts into illusion each and every being. Each and every being is put into illusion by that energy of *māyā*, the illusive energy of *māyā*.

SCHOLAR: Swamiji, did you translate *mokṣa lipsayā* here?

SWAMIJI: Yes, *mokṣa lipsayā*, they consider *mokṣa* on the point which is not *mokṣa* exactly–*amokṣe*. *Sā* means, *māyā*. That *māyā* is *bhramayate*, misleads them because of conceiving, with this conception that *mokṣa amokṣe mokṣa lipsayā*. Now this reference: *ataḥ param bhavet māyā sarva jantu vimohinī*, from here is the kingdom of *māyā*, which puts illusion in each and every being.

LJA TA04B (52:44)

Nirvairaparipanthinyā (comm.), it is *nirvaira paripanthi*.[54] One is a misleader with some purpose, anybody misleading you with some purpose, [for example], that, "She will be mislead and she will come to me, she will come in my clutches afterwards. I will mislead her and she will come in my clutches afterwards." It is *paripanthi* (adversarial) with some object. [Another misleader is] *nirvaira paripanthinyā*, in

54. An amicable (*nirvaira*) adversary (*paripanthi*).

friendly terms: she just–this *māyā*, this energy of *māyā*–misleads you just for play, not for any purpose (laughs). So, this way of misleading you is very difficult to overcome. You could overcome that [first] way of misleading, when you are misled [by someone] with some purpose, [but] that is a very inferior [way of] misleading. You can overcome that misleading easily. But when misleading is done without purpose, it is great, you can't overcome it, you are misled for good. That is *nirvaira paripanthinyā*, without any purpose she (*māyā*) misleads everybody.

LJA TA04B (54:03)

Idam tattvamidam neti vivadantīha parāspadaṁ (comm.),[55] and the conclusion comes in their minds that, "This is the reality that I have understood: Śaivism is a very inferior way of understanding, Vedānta is the real way of understanding, Sāṁkhya is the real way of understanding." They come to this conclusion, but this is the after-effect of being misled by *māyā* without any purpose.

SCHOLAR: But there is one point that no philsophy in India has taken on Trika philosophically. No one has tried to approach that...

SWAMIJI: No (affirmative).

SCHOLAR: ... or to begin to try and refute its doctrines.

SWAMIJI: Yes (affirmative). *Yastu rūḍho'pi tatrodyat-parāmarśa*... the next *śloka*:

LJA TA04B (57:36)

यस्तु रूढोऽपि तत्रोद्यत्परामर्शविशारदः ।
स शुद्धविद्यामाहात्म्याच्छक्तिपातपवित्रितः ॥ ३९ ॥
आरोहत्येव सन्मार्गं प्रत्यूहपरिवर्जितः ।

yastu rūḍho'pi tatrodyat-parāmarśaviśāradaḥ /
sa śuddhavidyāmāhātmyāt-śaktipātapavitritaḥ //39//
ārohatyeva sanmārgaṁ pratyūhaparivarjitaḥ /

---

55. Swamiji says "*parāspadam*" in place of of the published "*vādinaḥ*".

Although he is established, that Vaiṣṇavite is established, in that wrong state of being, but by the grace of God, *sa parāmarśa viśāradaḥ*, when he puts his awareness in the real sense of understanding his being/reality, *sa śuddhavidyā māhātmyāt śaktipāta pavitritaḥ*, you must think, you must come to this understanding, that he is purified by the greatness of Śuddhavidyā.[56] By the greatness of Śuddhavidyā, he is purified, and is purified by *śaktipāta*, by the real grace of Lord Śiva. *Ārohatyeva sanmārgaṁ pratyūhapari-varjitaḥ*, without any interruption he is sentenced to the real path of Śaivism.

Bas. There is something else now to be [discussed].

LJA TA04B (58:48) end
LJA TA04C (00:00) start

Now he will explain the states of masters. There are so many various states of masters, and who is who, he will explain that–which master is [which]. There are so many masters. You must first realize masters in their real position and then get initiated by them. Without understanding masters, to get initiated is just being misled.

56. Lit., pure (*śuddha*) knowledge (*vidyā*). At the level of Śuddhavidyā *pramātṛ bhāva*, "you find the discrimination between Śiva and ignorance."

Gurusatattvakam — The Essence of Masters[57]

LJA TA04C (00:35)

स तावत्कस्यचित्तर्कः स्वत एव प्रवर्तते ॥४०॥
स च सांसिद्धिकः शास्त्रे प्रोक्तः स्वप्रत्ययात्मकः ।

sa tāvatkasyacittarkaḥ svata eva pravartate //40//
sa ca sāṁsiddhikaḥ śāstre proktaḥ svapratyayātmakaḥ /

First he had explained *vikalpa saṁskāra*, then *tarka* (the reality of *tarka*), now he explains the differentiated explanations of masters.

Sa tāvat kasya cit tarkaḥ, that *tarka* ...*

SCHOLAR: How will we translate "*tarka*"?

SWAMIJI: *Tarka*? That perception which differentiates.

SCHOLAR: Discrimination.

SWAMIJI: Discriminating logic. That discriminating logic which is absolutely one with Śuddhavidyā.

SCHOLAR: Transcendental knowledge.

SWAMIJI: Transcendental knowledge.

*... that *tarka* rises in some masters without being dependent to masters and the *śāstra*s. They don't read *śāstra*. They don't go to masters. Without depending upon these two, this rises automatically in them–this *tarka*, this transcendental discriminating logic.

SCHOLAR: Would "transcendental logic" be a good term for it? "Transcendental logic."

SWAMIJI: Yes, "transcendental logic" is good. Transcendental logic is where you find what is your nature and what is not your nature, to discriminate that. That rises in those masters without depending on

57. For an explanation of the lineage of masters in Trika Shaivism, see *Kashmir Shaivism–The Secret Supreme*, chapter 13, "The Birth of the Tantras", pp. 87–93. For a list of the various classes of masters as explained in the following verses of this chapter, see Appendix 2, p. 387.

masters and the *śāstras*. And that kind of master is called, is named, as a *sāṁsiddhika*[58] master, because *svapratyayātmaka*, this discriminating transcendental logic has risen in them automatically, *sva pratyayātmaka*, by their own force.

SCHOLAR: *Sāṁsiddhika* [means], *svabhāvata siddha.*

SWAMIJI: *Svabhāvata siddha …*

SCHOLAR: Spontaneously established.

SWAMIJI: … perfectly a *siddha.*

SCHOLAR: *Samyak siddha.*

SWAMIJI: *Samyak siddha*, not *svabhāvata siddha. Samyak siddha.*[59]

LJA TA04C (03:12)

किरणायां यदप्युक्तं गुरुतः शास्त्रतः स्वतः ॥४१॥
तत्रोत्तरोत्तरं मुख्यं पूर्वपूर्व उपायकः ।

kiraṇāyāṁ yadapyuktaṁ gurutaḥ śāstrataḥ svataḥ //41//
tatrottarottaraṁ mukhyaṁ pūrvapūrva upāyakaḥ /

Although in the *Kiraṇa Tantra* it is said that this state of transcendental logic rises by the grace of a master, by the grace of *śāstras*, and by your own grace, [that] these three graces are needed for attaining this kind of logic (and this kind of logic is not book logic, it is internal logic where you discriminate between the individual and the universal Being), although in the *Kiraṇa Śāstra* it is said this logic rises by these three (master, *śāstra*, and your own experience), *tatra uttara uttaraṁ mukhyaṁ pūrvapūrva upāyakaḥ*, in these three, *uttarottara* (the latter) is predominant, *uttarottara* is predominant and the previous is the means to get the other. For instance, a master becomes the means to achieve the reality of *śāstra*, and *śāstras* becomes the means to achieve the reality of your own experience. So, the most predominant is your own experience.

---

58. Lit., effected naturally, self-existent.

59. Completely (*samyak*) accomplished/perfected (*siddha*). *Svabhāvata siddha* means, inherently or innately perfected.

When you experience it, that is the final means. The final means is experience (the supreme), the medium is *śāstra*, and the inferior is a master.

SCHOLAR: So, *uttarottaram*, each successive one of these three is greater than the previous.

SWAMIJI: Greater than the previous.

SCHOLAR: And the previous is the means to it.

SWAMIJI: Yes. The guru is inferior and greater than the guru is *śāstra*. *Śāstra* is inferior and greater than *śāstra* is your own *anubhava* (experience). So, to whom this *anubhava* rises without being dependent to *śāstra* and the master, he is called a *sāṁsiddhika* master.

LJA TA04C (05:51)

यस्य स्वतोऽयं सत्तर्कः सर्वत्रैवाधिकारवान् ॥४२॥
अभिषिक्तः स्वसंवित्तिदेवीभिर्दीक्षितश्च सः ।

yasya svato'yaṁ sattarkaḥ sarvatraivādhikāravān //42//
abhiṣiktaḥ svasaṁvitti-devībhirdīkṣitaśca saḥ /

That master in whom the rise of this *sattarka* (transcendental logic) rises automatically without being dependent to a master or the *śāstras*, *sarvatraivādhikāravān*, he is capable of initiating the whole universe; *sarvatraivādhikāravān*, he becomes the master of the universe.

SCHOLAR: He has the capacity to initiate anyone.

SWAMIJI: Everyone, everyone–*sarvatraiva adhikāravān*, *sarvatraiva*. *Abhiṣiktaḥ svasaṁvitti devībhir dīkṣitaśca saḥ*, but it is said in the *śāstras* that without a master nothing can be achieved. How he achieves without a master and without *śāstras*? But for that [Abhinavagupta] says, "His own internal energies of Lord Śiva (*śakti cakra*) have initiated him."

SCHOLAR: The deities of his consciousness.

SWAMIJI: Yes. They become his masters–*sva saṁvitti devībhir*. *Abhiṣiktaḥ* and *dīkṣitaḥ ca*, he is initiated and he is *abhiṣikta*.

SCHOLAR: *Abhiṣikta*, consecrated.

SWAMIJI: Consecrated? What is "consecrated"? Sprinkle, when you sprinkle, when you…

DENISE: Make holy.
SWAMIJI: No, not whole.
SCHOLAR: Like the pouring on of water from the *kumbha* (pot).
SWAMIJI: Yes. *Abhiṣeka*. What we do in the *jag* (havan) ceremony – *abhiṣeka*, [when we] sprinkle that water [on the devotees]. Those *devī*s (goddesses) sprinkle water on him, that purifying water, and those *devī*s initiate him internally. So he is absolutely free from dependence on masters and *śāstra*s.

LJA TA04C (08:01)

स एव सर्वाचार्याणां मध्ये मुख्यः प्रकीर्तितः ॥४३॥

sa eva sarvācāryāṇāṁ madhye mukhyaḥ prakīrtitaḥ //43//

He is [said] to be the predominant master in all masters, in all the classes of masters – *mukhya pravartate*.

तत्सन्निधाने नान्येषु कल्पितेष्वधिकारिता

tatsannidhāne nānyeṣu kalpiteṣvadhikāritā /44a

Before him, in his presence, no other master has authority, no other master has the right to initiate others before him, in his presence. [Another master] must ask his disciples to be initiated by him if he is present there, if that kind of master is present there. He has no right to initiate [a disciple] before such a master. Have you understood it?
JOHN: Before this automatic …
SWAMIJI: Automatic master.
SCHOLAR: This *adhikāra* (authority) is only in initiation or also in the interpretation of *śāstra* or…?
SWAMIJI: Yes, *śāstra* and…
SCHOLAR: Everything.
SWAMIJI: Yes.
JOHN: He has more…?

SCHOLAR: Authority.

SWAMIJI: Most authority! The only authority!

JOHN: This automatic master.

SWAMIJI: Automatic master, yes (laughs).

SCHOLAR: And these other one's of *kalpiteṣu*.[60]

JOHN: Why would he have more authority? He may not have any knowledge of the *saṁpradāya*[61] at all.

SWAMIJI: Because that knowledge of *saṁpradāya* comes in him within, from within.

JOHN: What about these masters, lets say, like Rajneesh, who falls out of a tree and says he's enlightened?

SWAMIJI: Those things are not recognized here (laughs).

Yathā bhedenādisiddhāt...this reference [in the commentary]:

LJA TA04C (09:37)

यथा भेदेनादिसिद्धाच्छिवान्मुक्तशिवा ह्यधः

yathā bhedenādisiddhācchivānmuktaśivā hyadhaḥ //

Just as in this *bhedavāda* (I mean, the dualistic school, the school of dualistic thought) it is said, *anādi śiddhāt śivāt mukta śivā hyadhaḥ*, ...*

Mukta-śiva means, those Śiva's who have become liberated after being initiated by masters–those are called *mukta-śivas*. *Anādisiddha-śiva* is that Śiva who was never in ignorance, who had never fallen in ignorance, who is always in his own real nature–that is *anādisiddha-śiva*. And *mukta-śivā* is that Śiva who has become Śiva by getting initiation from masters.

*... in that dualistic school of thought, it is said that *anādisiddha-śiva* is more high, more supreme, than *mukta-śiva*. *Mukta-śiva* is very inferior (that Śiva who has become liberated), and that Śiva who is always there, always in his own nature (that is, *anādisiddha-śiva*), *anādisiddha-śiva* is [much] higher than *mukta-śiva*.

---

60. The *kalpita* master, who is completely dependent upon masters and scripture, will be discussed onwards.

61. *Saṁpradāya* is the knowledge which passes through a lineage of masters.

LJA TA04C (11:05)

तथा सांसिद्धिकज्ञानादाहृतज्ञानिनोऽधमाः ।

tathā sāṁsiddhikajñānād-āhṛtajñānino'dhamāḥ /75a[62]

In the same way, *āhṛtajñāni*, those masters who have achieved knowledge from others, from other agencies, [from] the other two agencies, …*

What are the two agencies?

SCHOLAR: Guru and *śāstra*.

SWAMIJI: Guru and *śāstra*.

*… and those masters are inferior, those masters are called [more] inferior masters than the *sāṁsiddhika* master, than the automatic master.

LJA TA04C (11:38)

तत्संनिधौ नाधिकारस्तेषां मुक्तशिवात्मवत् ॥

tatsaṁnidhau nādhikārasteṣāṁ mukta-śivātmavat //75b

Just as *mukta-śiva* has no right to do anything before an *anādisiddha-śiva*, in the same way, *āhṛtajñāni*, that person who has obtained knowledge from other agencies, the other two agencies, is called *adhama*, is called inferior than *sāṁsiddhika*, that automatic master.

किन्तु तूष्णीं स्थितिर्यद्वा कृत्यं तदनुवर्तनम् ॥

kintu tūṣṇīṁ sthitir-yadvā kṛtyaṁ tadanuvartanam /76a

62. In his commentary for this verse, Jayaratha quotes verses 75 and 76 from this *āhnika*.

If he does not want to be away from interfering, if he wants to interfere in his actions – in whose actions? – in the *sāṁsiddhika*'s actions (the automatic master's actions), then he should do one thing; if he wants to interfere in his [actions], then he should do one thing: *tūṣṇīṁ sthiti*, whatever he does, he must keep quiet before him. *Yadvā*, or, *kṛtyam tad anuvartanam*, whatever that automatic master has initiated, he must agree [with] that, he must have full agreement with that.[63] This is what he has to do. Otherwise, he has no right to indulge in his actions, in the actions of the automatic master.

LJA TA04C (13:07)

स समस्तं च शास्त्रार्थं सत्तर्कादेव मन्यते ॥४४॥

sa samastaṁ ca śāstrārthaṁ sattarkādeva manyate //44//

How can *saṁpradāya* come in his perception? That secret of *saṁpradāya*, how he knows the secret of *saṁpradāya* without reading *śāstras* or without depending on other masters? For that he says, *sa samastaṁ ca śāstrārtham*, he experiences all *śāstras*, all the *artha* (meaning) of the *śāstras*, by this transcendental state of discrimination, discriminating logic, because:

LJA TA04C (13:47)

शुद्धविद्या हि तन्नास्ति सत्यं यद्यन्न भासयेत् ।

śuddhavidyā hi tannāsti satyaṁ yadyanna bhāsayet /

63. In his translation of the complete verse onwards in this chapter, Swamiji gives this example: "If *anādisiddha-śiva* has ordered for rains, and it is raining, this *mukta-śiva* has no right to interfere in this action. What he has to do is only to keep quiet when it is raining."

Śuddhavidyā is so great! *Śuddhavidyā hi*, Śuddhavidyā is that, *tat nāsti yat satyaṁ yadyanna* [*bhāsayet*], it is true that everything is revealed by Śuddhavidyā, and that Śuddhavidyā has risen in him automatically.

SCHOLAR: Pure knowledge.

JOHN: This Śuddhavidyā is the Advaita Śaivist Śuddhavidyā.

SWAMIJI: Pure knowledge of God consciousness–universal.

JOHN: No, I mean, I'm saying that, say some master comes along who, like Rajneesh, who says he is automatically enlightened without a master, without *śāstra*, and then he begins to teach another doctrine, a different doctrine, he teaches God knows what…

SWAMIJI: But that is not recognized here.

JOHN: So then how do we differentiate these automatic masters from all those masters who pop up here and there and say that, "One day I was walking…"

SWAMIJI: But this existence of being an automatic [master] shines everywhere, everybody knows that. It is not [just] by telling you that I am an automatic master and you have to believe [me].

Śuddhavidyā hi tat nāsti satyaṁ yadyanna bhāsayet, Śuddhavidyā can reveal everything, nothing is secret there, nothing is unrevealed there.

LJA TA04C (15:13)

सर्वशास्त्रार्थवेत्तृत्वमकस्माच्चास्य जायते ॥४५॥

sarvaśāstrārthavettṛtvam-akasmāccāsya jāyate //45//

In the *Mālinīvijaya Tantra* it is said, the knowledge of all *śāstra*s comes in his experience all of a sudden–*sarva śāstrārtha vettṛtvam akasmāt cāsya jāyate*.

SCHOLAR: Inexplicably, *akasmāt*.

SWAMIJI: Unexpectedly, all of a sudden.

JOHN: So this automatic master, then, is very rare, super rare.

SWAMIJI: Very rare, very rare. The automatic master is one with Lord Śiva.

JOHN: I mean, even Abhinavagupta wasn't automatic.

SWAMIJI: Yes, he was automatic.

DEVOTEES: (laughter)
SCHOLAR: But he had so many masters?
SWAMIJI: He was automatic (laughs). I will tell you, you will come to this understanding that he was automatic in …
JOHN: A few minutes.
SWAMIJI: Yes.

LJA TA04C (16:04)

इति श्रीपूर्ववाक्ये तद् अकस्मादिति-शब्दतः ।

iti śrīpūvavākye tadakasmāditi-śabdataḥ /

It is in the *Mālinīvijaya* explained by this word "*akasmāt*", unexpectedly, without depending upon masters, without depending, going through *śāstra*s, without any other of these things, …*
SCHOLAR: An uncaused effect.
SWAMIJI: Yes.

LJA TA04C (16:25)

लोकाप्रसिद्धो यो हेतुः सोऽकस्मादिति कथ्यते ॥४६॥

lokāprasiddho yo hetuḥ so'kasmāditi kathyate //46//

*… (*akasmāt* means, unexpectedly), unexpected knowledge means, *loka aprasiddha hetuḥ*, that means which is *loka aprasiddha*, which is not found in the sphere of the world. In the sphere of the world, it is found [that] the cause of being inserted, being one with God consciousness, the cause of that is only a master, *śāstra*, and your own *anubhava* (experience).
SCHOLAR: It does not come from the field of causality in the ordinary way.
SWAMIJI: No (affirmative). *Loka aprasiddho he-*, but to whom this comes automatically, that is *akasmāt*, that is the meaning of *akasmāt* (unexpectedly, all of a sudden).

स चैष परमेशानशुद्धविद्याविजृम्भितम् ।

sa caiṣa parameśāna-śuddhavidyāvijṛmbhitam /

And that *akasmāt* rises only by the grace of Lord Śiva – that *akasmāt*, the process of *akasmāt*.

SCHOLAR: It is the expansion of the Śuddhavidyā, the pure knowledge of Śuddhavidyā.

SWAMIJI: Yes, Śuddhavidyā is *śaktipāta* (grace).

LJA TA04C (17:37)

अस्य भेदाश्च बहवो निर्भित्तिः सहभित्तिकः ॥४७॥
सर्वगोऽंशगतः सोऽपि मुख्यामुख्यांशनिष्ठितः ।
भित्तिः परोपजीवित्वं परा प्रज्ञाथ तत्कृतिः ॥४८॥

asya bhedāśca bahavo nirbhittiḥ sahabhittikaḥ //47//
sarvago'ṁśagataḥ so'pi mukhyāmukhyāṁśaniṣṭhitaḥ /
bhittiḥ paropajīvitvaṁ parā prajñātha tatkṛtiḥ //48//

There are differentiated classes of this also, of this automatic knowledge, automatic perception. *Nirbhitti* [*sāṁsiddhika*], one is *nirbhitti*, without being dependent to a master and the *śāstras*.[64]

SCHOLAR: No background.

SWAMIJI: [The other is] *sahabhittiki* [*sāṁsiddhika*]. *Sahabhittika* means, one is dependent, one [is found] to depend on masters and the *śāstras* partly.

SCHOLAR: There is some *bhitti* (some background) to his knowledge.

SWAMIJI: That is *bhitti*, dependent.

SCHOLAR: *Bhitti* means, background.

---

64. As explained above.

SWAMIJI: That is the background, that is a master and *śāstra*. *Sarvago aṁśagataḥ* (verse 48), and that *bhitti* is also needed in excess or by parts. For instance, you need something, there is some defect, some incompletion in your experience. If you are an automatic master, if you have become an automatic master, you need to ask about some points from other masters also for your satisfaction (that is *aṁśagata*). *Sarvaga* means, you need more information from other masters for this experience, otherwise you are not satisfied with it. *So'pi mukhya amukhya aṁśa niṣṭhita*, and that, too, is also in predominance and not in predominance; when you are dependent in predominance (sometimes you have to depend on *śāstra*s and masters in predominance), and sometimes it is not predominant (depending on *śāstra*s and masters is not predominant), and this also is according to the fall of *śakti*, *śaktipāta*, *anugraha* (grace). *Bhittiḥ paropajīvitvam*, in conclusion, when there is dependence of these two, that is *paropajīvitvam*: you find life from others, you calculate and get satisfaction from others (that is *paropajīvitvam*). *Parā prajñātha tatkṛtiḥ*, and this is *parā prajñā*, supreme *prajñā* (wisdom). Supreme *prajñā* is *nirbhitti* (without support). And *tat kṛti*, and his *śāstra*s; *tat kṛtiḥ*, whatever is explained by those [masters], those are *śāstra*s; whatever they speak, whatever comes from their lips, they become *śāstra*s.

SCHOLAR: Could you explain how it is that this class of master is spontaneously realized and yet at the same time you have here a class of *sahabhittika*, *sarvaga sahabhittika*.

SWAMIJI: *Saha-*, all-round, you need *sahabhittika* for each and every experience of yours.

SCHOLAR: So then how is he a *sāṁsiddhika*?

SWAMIJI: For instance, the rise of that perception comes automatically within you, but you are not satisfied. You want to confirm it from masters and *śastra*s – sometime. But sometime, if it rise *with* confirmation, that is absolutely the highest.

JOHN: So some person might think he was going crazy if he had this. Some master might have this autmoatic rise – he wouldn't be a master when he had this – if he didn't know masters and *śastra*s, he would just be an ordinary person before having this perception. Or was he already doing…? He couldn't be doing practice…

SWAMIJI: No, it does not rise by practice. This kind of…

JOHN: No, automatically.

SWAMIJI: Automatically.

JOHN: So this person may not know…

SWAMIJI: He may not know perfectly what it is.

SCHOLAR: How could that be enlightenment if he had some doubt about what it was?

SWAMIJI: Because it is *sahabhitti*, he wants confirmation from others. And that master tells him, confirms him, that this is the real way that he has experienced. So he is satisfied.

SCHOLAR: But how could he have doubt if he had experienced Śuddhavidyā?

SWAMIJI: Because it is *sahabhitti*, it is not that [first] kind of automatic master. That [first] kind of automatic master is very rare. [*Sahabhitti*] is still automatic because the rise of that God consciousness has come by his own way.

SCHOLAR: Spontaneously.

SWAMIJI: Spontaneously.

SCHOLAR: But if that's the rise of God consciousness, how could he have a doubt?

SWAMIJI: Because there is some defect, there is some…

SCHOLAR: Then he would be a *kalpita kalpaka*.

SWAMIJI: No, it is not *kalpita kalpaka* yet, because the rise has taken place automatically in him.

SCHOLAR: The rise of what if he has some doubts still?

DENISE: He doesn't know what to call it maybe?

SWAMIJI: Not doubts, not doubts. He wants to confirm if it is…

SCHOLAR: Yes. That I understand, that I understand. But how can we talk of doubt?

SWAMIJI:…that experience is right.

JOHN: He may think, if he had no idea what this was before from his limited intellectual point of view, he may be confused somewhat about what this is.

SWAMIJI: Yes. It is why he depends upon confirmation of other masters, others who have …

SCHOLAR: He is confused?

SWAMIJI: He's a bit confussed…not confused! Not satisfied perfectly. But the first who is perfectly satisfied, he has nothing to do with other masters. So there are sections in *sāṁsiddhika* guru also: *sahabhitti sāṁsiddhika* guru, *nirbhitti sāṁsiddhika* guru.

SCHOLAR: But this revelation of his then is not complete.

SWAMIJI: He is not as complete. He is not as complete as that *sāṁsiddhika* guru was.

SCHOLAR: So how is he different from *kalpita kalpaka*, if his revelation was not completely perfect, he needs to go to masters.

SWAMIJI: No, *kalpita kalpaka* is something else. It will be explained in the near future.

And whatever he speaks, that is *śāstra*; whatever he says, that is *śāstra*, that becomes *śāstra*.

LJA TA04C (24:16)

अदृष्टमण्डलोऽप्येवं यः कश्चिद्वेत्ति तत्त्वतः ।
स सिद्धिभाग्भवेन्नित्यं स योगी स च दीक्षितः ॥४९॥
एवं यो वेत्ति तत्त्वेन तस्य निर्वाणगामिनी ।
दीक्षा भवेदिति प्रोक्तं तच्छ्रीत्रिंशकशासने ॥५०॥

adṛṣṭamaṇḍalo'pyevaṁ yaḥ kaścidvetti tattvataḥ /
sa siddhibhāgbhavennityaṁ sa yogī sa ca dīkṣitaḥ //49//[65]
evaṁ yo vetti tattvena tasya nirvāṇagāminī /[66]
dīkṣā bhavediti proktaṁ tacchrītriṁśakaśāsane //50//

This is also explained in the *Triṁśika Śāstra*, the *Parātrīṁśikā Śāstra* (not the *Vivaraṇa*), the text of the *Parātrīṁśikā Śāstra*, that, *adṛṣṭa maṇḍa-lo'pi*, although he has not been blessed by perceiving the *maṇḍala*,...*

That guru draws that *maṇḍala*, the *kriyādīkṣā maṇḍala*, and by seeing the *maṇḍala* of those masters and *mantra*s (and all those are written on the ground), he has to see that (have *darśana* of that) and he gets initiation from within. That is *maṇḍala darśana*.

---

65. *Parātriśīkā Laghu Vṛtti*, verse 19.
66. Ibid., 24ab.

*... although he has not done that, he has not seen that, the one who has perceived *tattvataḥ*, in the real sense the reality of the nature of himself, *sa siddhibhāk bhavet nityam*, he is eternally the possessor of all powers, all yogic powers, he is called a yogi, and he is really initiated. *Evaṁ yo vetti tattvena*, by this way, he who experiences God consciousness in the real sense, for him, *nirvāṇa gāminī dīkṣā bhavet*, *dīkṣā*, he has achieved that *dīkṣā* (initiation) which will carry him right to the utmost state of liberation, final beatitude. It is said in the *Trīṁśikā Śāstra* also, the *Parātrīṁśikā Śāstra*.

LJA TA04C (26:23)

अकल्पितो गुरुर्ज्ञेयः सांसिद्धिक इति स्मृतः ।

akalpito gururjñeyaḥ sāṁsiddhika iti smṛtaḥ /51a

He has another name, there is another name for him, nominated for the *sāṁsiddhika* guru: *akalpita* guru. He is also called an *akalpita* guru; *akalpita*, because it is not...

SCHOLAR: Unconditioned. He is not determined by any other factor.

SWAMIJI: Yes, unconditioned, not [conditioned]. *Akalpita*, he is not manufactured by other agencies, he is not made by other masters.

JOHN: By masters or *śāstras*.

SWAMIJI: Yes.

LJA TA04C (26:55)

यस्तु तद्रूपभागात्मभावनातः परं विना ॥५१॥
शास्त्रवित्स गुरुः शास्त्रे प्रोक्तोऽकल्पितकल्पकः ।

yastu tadrūpabhāgātma-bhāvanātaḥ paraṁ vinā //51//
śāstravitsa guruḥ śāstre prokto'kalpitakalpakaḥ /

And the *akalpita* guru, although he is an *akalpita* guru, there is another class of these *akalpita* gurus, that is, *akalpita kalpaka*.[67] *Yastu tad rūpa bhāk*, although he is a *sāṁsiddhika* guru, he is residing in the level of a *sāṁsiddhika* master, *magar* (but) *ātma bhāvanātaḥ paraṁ vinā śāstravit*, he realizes *śāstra* by his own nature, by his own power, by his own power of understanding without asking masters. For instance, I am an *akalpita* guru; take for two minutes that I am an *akalpita* guru. I have not read *śāstra*s or anything, but I need to see to confirm, just to confirm, not from masters, [but] from *śāstra*s, if it is said like this that I have experienced (*ātma bhāvanātaḥ*). *Paraṁ vinā*, without a master, without depending [upon a] master, without reading under the guidance of masters, and he gets *śāstra vit*, he gets the confirmation of *śāstra*, that this is the reality.

SCHOLAR: *Ātma bhāvanātaḥ*.

SWAMIJI: [By] *ātma bhāvanātaḥ*.

SCHOLAR: Contemplation on his own nature?

SWAMIJI: Yes. And he is said [to be an] *akalpita kalpaka*. He is another master, another [kind of *sāṁsiddhika* master]. He is [more] inferior than that [*akalpita* master] – the *akalpita kalpaka*.

SCHOLAR: Because he goes to *śastra*.

SWAMIJI: He goes to *śastra* but without the support of masters.

SCHOLAR: Now in the case of the *sahabhittika sāṁsiddhika*, what is the difference? What is the difference there between this and the *sahabhittika sāṁsiddhika* guru?

SWAMIJI: *Sahabhittika* and *sāṁsiddhika* guru. The *sāṁsiddhika* guru is already explained – *sāṁsiddhika* guru.

SCHOLAR: But what is the difference between *akalpita kalpaka* and that class of *sāṁsiddhika* called…?

SWAMIJI: He takes the support of masters also, in getting information of *śastra*s.

SCHOLAR: So why is this man inferior to him?

SWAMIJI: Because he understands *śastra*s by his own self.

SCHOLAR: That is superior, isn't it?

SWAMIJI: That is superior, so this is *akalpita kalpaka*. *Akalpita kalpaka* is [more] supreme.

---

67. A non-manufactured (*akalpita*) guru who is manufactured (*kalpaka*).

JOHN: So he is more superior than this other one.

SWAMIJI: Which one?

JOHN: *Sahabhittika.*

SWAMIJI: *Sahabhittika.* Yes, *sahabhittika* is inferior. These are so many classes of masters explained in this *Tantrāloka.* He is confused (laughter). *Yastu tadrūpabhā-*...this is the next section, and in [the section of] *akalpita kalpaka* also, there will be the same line of inferiority and superiority.

SCHOLAR: So he is unconditioned by any other factor, but he also conditions himself, *kalpaka*, through *ātma bhāvana.* He develops his own awareness through...

SWAMIJI: This is the difference. But he has to depend on master's saying.

SCHOLAR: So pure *sāṁsiddhika* is spontaneously realized without any question even of *kalpanā.*

SWAMIJI: Realized. No *kalpanā.* No need of *śāstra*s rises there.

SCHOLAR: So, the *sāṁsiddhika* is superior to the *akalpita kalpaka.* This is the next level.

SWAMIJI: This is the next level. In this level also, there are other inferior states of *akalpita kalpaka* also, as there were inferior states of the *sāṁsiddhika* previously.

SCHOLAR: But it remains the case that any class of *sāṁsiddhika* is superior to any class of *akalpita kalpaka.*

SWAMIJI: Exactly.

SCHOLAR: So how then can *sahabhittika sāṁsiddhika* be said to be inferior to *akalpita kalpaka* guru, as you just said.

SWAMIJI: *Akalpita kalpaka*, there are many ways of *akalpita kalpaka*; there are many stages of *akalpita kalpaka.* This is the chief state. This chief state is superior than that *sahabhittika sāṁsiddhika* guru, the *sāṁsiddhika* guru who is *sahabhitti.*

JOHN: These are both *sāṁsiddhika* gurus, right? This *akalpita kalpaka.*

SWAMIJI: Yes, this is also *saṁsiddhika* guru, but not to that extent.

SCHOLAR: But he is not pure *sāṁsiddhika*, because pure *sāṁsiddhika*, or any class of *sāṁsiddhika*, is *akalpita guru geya sāṁsiddhiketi smṛta.*

SWAMIJI: Yes, that is an admitted fact.

SCHOLAR: And the next class, the lower class...

SWAMIJI: Next class of *sāṁsiddhika* guru is lower.

JOHN: Yes, but this *sahabhittika*, is he also *sāṁsiddhika*?

SCHOLAR: The *sahabhittika* is also *sāṁsiddhika*.

SWAMIJI: It is also *sāṁsiddhika*, but it is inferior.

SCHOLAR: But it is inferior within the class of *sāṁsiddhika* gurus.

SWAMIJI: It is inferior to this also, to this supreme class of *akalpita kalpaka* also.

SCHOLAR: So then this is also *sāṁsiddhika* guru.

SWAMIJI: *Akalpita kalpaka*. But there are *akalpita kalpaka*s defined variously, and those are inferior to that. Those masters are inferior to that *sahabhitti*.

SCHOLAR: So first we have a description of a pure *sāṁsiddhika*.

SWAMIJI: Pure *sāṁsiddhika*, then his sections, then his sections. For instance, Abhinavagupta was a *sāṁsiddhika* guru, but he read the *śāstra*s under the guidance of masters, [so] he became a *sahabhitti*. He became a *sahabhitti* maybe out of curiosity or out of dissatisfaction in his state. He became...this does not mean that he was not [a *sāṁsiddhika* guru].

SCHOLAR: He took initiations, didn't he?

SWAMIJI: Yes, he took. He was a *sāṁsiddhika*; at the same time he was also a *sāṁsiddhika*.

SCHOLAR: Because he was a *yoginībhūḥ*?

SWAMIJI: Yes, he was a *yoginībhūḥ*.[68]

JOHN: So then the reason that this [*akalpita kalpaka*] is superior, why you are saying this is superior, is because this person only turns to the *śāstra*s, not to masters.

SWAMIJI: *Śāstra*, not masters.

JOHN: And this one here, the *sahabhittika*?

SWAMIJI: The *sahabhitti* depends on a master.

JOHN: Yes, because masters are lower than *śāstra*s and these, that's why you're saying this is ...

SWAMIJI: Yes.

LJA TA04C (33:07)

68. Lit., an offspring of a *yoginī*, which will be discussed in verses 141 and 142 of this *āhnika*.

तस्यापि भेदा उत्कृष्टमध्यमन्दाद्युपायतः ॥५२॥

tasyāpi bhedā utkṛṣṭa-madhyamandādyupāyataḥ //52//

And this *akalpita kalpaka* also, this master who has become an *akalpita kalpaka*, there are many classes of *akalpita kalpaka* also, because *utkṛṣṭa madhya manda upāyataḥ* (*utkṛṣṭa* means, *tīvra*; *madhyā* means, medium; and *manda* means, inferior), ...*

SCHOLAR: *Tīvra* (intense), medium, and weak.

SWAMIJI: *... *upāyataḥ*, by the grace, the grace of God sometimes is in the *tīvra* way (sometimes intense), sometimes medium, and sometimes inferior. When it is *tīvra*, then he is *akalpita kalpaka*. When it is *manda* [grace], then he is an *akalpita kalpaka* also, but he depends upon *śāstra*s and masters because there is *mandatā* (dullness), and this kind of master is inferior [to the *tīvra* and *madhyā*] *akalpita kalpaka*.

SCHOLAR: But there has been no mention of masters here. It just says that he goes to *śāstra* (*śāstravit*)–*sa guru śāstre prokta akalpita kalpakaḥ*. So, that remains true of all the sub-classes–*tīvra*, *madhya*, and *manda*. So how does the guru come in here all of a sudden?

SWAMIJI: Guru, it is the section of all masters only here, the explanation of masters only here.

LJA TA04C (34:30)

भावनातोऽथ वा ध्यानाज्जपात्स्वप्नाद्व्रताद्धुतेः ।
प्राप्नोत्यकल्पितोदारमभिषेकं महामतिः ॥५३॥

bhāvanāto'tha vā dhyānāt-japātsvapnādvratāddhuteḥ /
prāpnotyakalpitodāram-abhiṣekaṁ mahāmatiḥ //53//

And this fortunate master achieves the highest *abhiṣeka*, the highest initiation, which is *akalpita* (unmanufactured), and which is the highest. He achieves that by *bhāvanā*, by *ātma bhāvanā*, by contemplation of his own.

JOHN: This is *utkṛṣṭa* (the highest)?

SWAMIJI: No, this he explains with the connection of this *akalpita kalpaka* guru. The *akalpita kalpaka* guru comes with *bhāvanā* also, in *dhyāna* (by *dhyāna*, by meditation), by recitation of *japa*, *svapnāt* (in dreams), *vratāt* (by performing some work), and *huteḥ*, by offering a sacrifice on the fire. And by these also, he can achieve this *akalpita uddhāra abhiṣeka*[69]–this supreme master. But these are inferior masters, these are inferior masters than that *sahabhitti sāṁsiddhika*. These masters are inferior.[70]

SCHOLAR: These classes of *akalpita kalpaka* who lift themselves up through these various ways: *bhāvanā*, *dhyāna*, *japā*, *svapnāt*, *vratā dhuteḥ*.

SWAMIJI: . . . various ways, are inferior than those *sahabhitti sāṁsiddhikas*.

SCHOLAR: Because he came automatically to that state.

SWAMIJI: He had to put effort, [so] they are inferior.

SCHOLAR: So, that is the situation.

SWAMIJI: That is the situation.

SCHOLAR: So he who conditions himself by *bhāvanā* is inferior to that *sahabhitti*.

SWAMIJI: *Sahabhitti*, yes, absolutely.

SCHOLAR: We have made that clear now.

SWAMIJI: But this first one is superior than *sahabhitti*.

JOHN: He doesn't clarify his nature by . . .

SWAMIJI: The first one.

SCHOLAR: But it says here, *bhāvanāto'tha vā dhyānāt*, they are all in the same category here.

SWAMIJI: Any way, by any means, he gets this *abhiṣeka* of *akalpita kalpaka bhāva*. But the one who is the first one, he is superior then *sahabhitti sāṁsiddhika*.

ALEXIS: Through *bhāvanā*, *ātmabhāvanā*.

SWAMIJI: *Ātmabhāvanā*, yes, *ātmabhāvana*.

SCHOLAR: But he does not say this here, does he?

SWAMIJI: But it is already clear, it's clear.

---

69. Initiation, which is *akalpita* (unmanufactured), and which is the highest.

70. That is, those *akalpita kalpakas* who are blessed with medium (*madhyā*) and inferior (*manda*) grace.

JOHN: In this 53rd *śloka*, he's not speaking about this person here, he is only speaking about these other three lower classes. Is there four classes?

SWAMIJI: There are so many classes here.

SCHOLAR: Those three classes, John, are contained within this one class.

JOHN: Yes, I know. Then how, if these *bhāvanās*, these conditions through *jāpa* and all these things, apply to this person here, then how is he superior to this *sahabhitti*?

SCHOLAR: Yes, exactly.

SWAMIJI: This is not superior. This is superior. And this is not superior.

JOHN: So this is different than this?

SWAMIJI: This is different…he has come down now. There are so many classes of *akalpita kalpaka*. The first class of *akalpita kalpaka* is superior, is supreme, yes.

JOHN: And that is left aside, we have left that.

SWAMIJI: And he says, *tasyāpi bhedā utkṛṣṭa madhya mandādyupāyataḥ. Tasyāpi bhedā*, they are also differentiated in so many sections, so many classes.

SCHOLAR: But that difference of *śaktipāta* also applies to *bhāvanā*, also to *dhyāna*, *japā*, *svapna*.

SWAMIJI: Yes, yes.

SCHOLAR: So in a way they don't affect the context.

SWAMIJI: What do you mean by that?

SCHOLAR: What I mean is that he is *akalpita kalpaka*, through *bhāvanā* predominantly…

SWAMIJI: As previously he has explained what is *sāṁsiddhika* guru. Then he has explained many sections of *sāṁsiddhika* gurus.

SCHOLAR: But still they are all *sāṁsiddhikas*, and they are a superior class.

SWAMIJI: There are *sāṁsiddhika*, yes, superior class. There are *sahabhitti*…*sahabhitti sāṁsiddhika* guru is inferior than *sāṁsiddhika* guru, the real *sāṁsiddhika* guru.

SCHOLAR: But he is still *sāṁsiddhika*.

SWAMIJI: He is called *sāṁsiddhika*.

SCHOLAR: So we are not moving to another class here. Just gradations within the one.

JOHN: And then *akalpita kalpaka*, is he also a *sāṁsiddhika* guru?

SWAMIJI: *Akalpita kalpaka* is not *sāṁsiddhika* guru.

JOHN: Then why is this one who is not a *sāṁsiddhika* guru superior to that *saha* …

SWAMIJI: *Akalpita kalpaka* guru has practiced this way of Self-realization. Whereas, the *sāṁsiddhika* guru has not practiced. It has come automatically.

SCHOLAR: How could he possibly be superior to *sahabhitti sāṁsiddhika*? Because he is still *sāṁsiddhika*.

SWAMIJI: But he is superior than *sāṁsiddhika* …

SCHOLAR: But you just said …

SWAMIJI: … the *sahabhitti sāṁsiddhika*. Not exact *sāṁsiddhika*. Exact *sāṁsiddhika* is above all – real *sāṁsiddhika*. *Sahabhittika sāṁsiddhika* is inferior than a real *sāṁsiddhika* guru.

JOHN: Then this *akalpita kalpaka* guru, this one here, is superior to this …

SWAMIJI: … *sahabhitti sāṁsiddhika*.

JOHN: … and then this *akalpita kalpaka* doesn't have to do practices.

SWAMIJI: But he does practice: *ātmabhāvanāta*.

JOHN: But only with *śāstra*, not in this way.

SWAMIJI: No, not *śāstra*. *Ātmabhāvanāta*, by his own contemplation of his own imagination; he has imagined that, "I will contemplate this way", without going to masters or without any other agency. He has contemplated and achieved. But this one, the *sāṁsiddhika* guru, has not contemplated at all!

JOHN: What about *sahabhitti*?

SCHOLAR: He only wants confirmation, nothing else.

SWAMIJI: Yes, confirmation.

SCHOLAR: So he is superior to this *akalpita kalpaka* …

SWAMIJI: No, not this [first] *akalpita kalpaka*.

SCHOLAR: … because he doesn't need to practice.

SWAMIJI: No, not this *akalpita*. Because there is dissatisfaction because he wants to confirm, as he wants to confirm from masters.

SCHOLAR: Why is this made a lower category?

SWAMIJI: Because a master is inferior, always a master is inferior than *śāstra*, and *śāstra* is inferior than *svataḥ* (one's own experience). But this *akalpita kalpaka* has got realization by *svataḥ*, so it is supreme than *sahabhitti*, not supreme than *sāṁsiddhika*. But he has to respect the master, he has to work for his master, he has to get things from the market for the master.

SCHOLAR: But then why didn't he put *sahabhitti* lower down *akalpita kalpaka* in this *prakaraṇa*...?

SWAMIJI: No...

SCHOLAR: He is moving through lower degrees.

SWAMIJI: No, this is the section of *sāṁsiddhika* masters. And this is the section *akalpita kalpaka* masters. And *akalpita kalpaka* master, the first *akalpita kalpaka* master is more than *sahabitti* master. And others are inferior than *sahabhitti* masters, other masters, these masters.

JOHN: So then what you are saying is that both these, this *sahabhitti* and this *akalpita kalpaka* master, both of these have some defect. This [*akalpita kalpaka*] resolved their defect through *śāstra* [and] this *sahabhitti* resolved his defect through going to a master,...

SWAMIJI: Yes, a master.

JOHN: ... so that's why he is lower. So they both had defects.

SWAMIJI: Yes, a master is lower, the master is always lower. You must take it for granted that the master is lower, *śāstra* is above that, and your own experience is above all. Wherever there is being dependent to a master, [it is] inferior, gone.

JOHN: So both these have some dependence.

SWAMIJI: But dependence on *śāstra*s!

JOHN: Right, that's why you're saying that because both...in other words, this one, this *sahabhitti*...

SWAMIJI: You can't go out of the circle, you see. The circle of this philosophy is limited. You can't cross that limitation. *Sahabhitti* is because he is dependent to masters. He does not get satisfaction from *śāstra*s.

SCHOLAR: But he is still *sāṁsiddhika*.

SWAMIJI: He is *sāṁsiddhika*, really he is *sāṁsiddhika*, above.

SCHOLAR: He is still *sāmsiddhika*. He only takes secondary dependence upon that.

SWAMIJI: Yes.

SCHOLAR: So in any sense he is surely superior to any class of *akalpita kalpaka*.

SWAMIJI: No, no, no, no, no (laughs). Not the first class of *akalpita kalpaka*.

SCHOLAR: Well then why isn't that class placed within *sāṁsiddhika*. Why has Abhinavagupta distinguished the two?

SWAMIJI: No, he places one section of *sāṁsiddhika* first. It does not mean all *sāṁsiddhika* masters are superior than the masters explained in the next class, the next section. It does not mean that.

JOHN: So this *akalpita kalpaka* master perfects his nature before. In other words, through *ātmabhāvanāt*, he perfects his nature before.

SWAMIJI: Without going to ...

JOHN: ... [without going] to *śāstra*s.

SWAMIJI: Yes.

JOHN: And this other, this *sahabhitti*, he perfects his nature after his perception. He has some perception, he is unclear...

SWAMIJI: No, *akalpita kalpaka*, he does not fulfill his knowledge by *śāstra*s. He understands the technique of *śāstra*s by his own self without going to a master.

SCHOLAR: *Tadrūpabhāgāpi.*

SWAMIJI: *Tadrūpābhāk.* It is not *api* there.

SCHOLAR: *Yaḥ punaḥ sāṁsiddhika rūpabhāgāpi svyamudite jñāne tāvatā pāripūrṇyasyābhāvāt*, etcetera.

SWAMIJI: But it is Jayaratha, it is not Abhinavagupta. It is *paripurṇa*.

SCHOLAR: But *tadrūpabhāk, sāṁsiddhika rūpābhāk.*

SWAMIJI: *Tadrūpabhāk* means, *sāṁsiddhika rūpābhāk. Ātma bhāvanātaḥ param vinā*; *ātma bhāvanātaḥ param vinā śāstravit bhavati.*

SCHOLAR: *Yas tu*, but he who is *sāṁsiddhika* but without another, simply through contemplation of his own nature understands *śāstras* ...

SWAMIJI: ... understands *śāstra*s, he is *akalpita kalpaka.*

SCHOLAR: He has called *akalpita kalpaka* in *śāstra*s.

SWAMIJI: Yes. And there are so many classes of *akalpita kalpaka*, which are inferior to those *sahabhitti sāṁsiddhika*s. Now he goes to a more inferior way of understanding.

JOHN: So then these practices here for this *akalpita kalpaka* isn't talking about this person here ...

SWAMIJI: No, no, no.

JOHN: This is other.

SWAMIJI: It is other of the same ...

SCHOLAR: *Tasyāpi*, of this very man ...

SWAMIJI: *Tāsyāpi, akalpita kalpaka*, not very man.

SCHOLAR: This very class.

SWAMIJI: Of this class of *akalpita kalpaka*. Because as *sāṁsiddhika* had also various classes ...

SCHOLAR: But they are all *akalipta kalpaka*, and it may take place thorough *bhāvanā*, it may take place through *jāpa*.

SWAMIJI: Yes, *akalpita kalpaka*.

SCHOLAR: But they are all *akalpita kalpaka*.

SWAMIJI: Yes, *akalpita kalpaka*.

SCHOLAR: And therefore because they are resorting to *ātmabhāvanā*, they are superior to…

SWAMIJI: Superior to *sahabhitti*, the next *sahabhitti*.

SCHOLAR: So this is, in fact, what you just said means that the whole class is superior to all *sahabhitti*.

SWAMIJI: Huh?

SCHOLAR: So the whole class of *akalpita kalpaka*s then, in accordance with what you just said, is superior to …

SWAMIJI: No, it is not superior than this.

JOHN: So which ones of these *akalpita*, only those that…?

SWAMIJI: You have to put *sāṁsiddhika* guru first, then next *akalpita kalpaka*.

JOHN: Which one of that?

SWAMIJI: First one!

JOHN: And so he's the one who just turns to *śāstra*s.

SWAMIJI: No, not *śāstra*s. *Akalpita kalpaka* …

JOHN: This one here.

SWAMIJI: Yes. *Ātmabhābanātaḥ paraṁ vinā śāstravitsa guruḥ śāstra prokto'kalpitakalpakaḥ*.

JOHN: Then how does he differ from other, *madhya* and *manda*?

SWAMIJI: They are inferior states of such masters also, of the same master, not only in that very master, in other masters of the same [class].

SCHOLAR: So their *ātmabhāvanāta* is *manda* or *madhyā*.

SWAMIJI: … *manda*, yes.

SCHOLAR: And their *japa* is *manda*, their *dhyāna* is *manda*, their *svapna* is *manda*, etcetera.

SWAMIJI: *Dhyāna* is *manda*, *svapna* is *manda*, yes.

SCHOLAR: But they are all *akalpita kalpaka*.

SWAMIJI: *Akalpita kalpaka*, yes. But the first *akalpita kalpaka* is supreme as the first *sāṁsiddhika* was supreme. The first *sāṁsiddhika* was supreme.

LJA TA04C (46:51)

श्रीमद्वाजसनीये श्रीवीरे श्रीब्रह्मयामले ।
श्रीसिद्धायामिदं धात्रा प्रोक्तमन्यत्र च स्फुटम् ॥५४॥

śrīmadvājasanīye śrīvīre śrībrahmayāmale /
śrīsiddhāyāmidaṁ dhātrā proktamanyatra ca sphuṭam //54//

It is already explained in the *Vājasanīya Tantra*, the *Śrī Vīra Tantra*, *Brahmayāmala Tantra*, and the *Siddha Tantra*, and other Tantras also.

तस्य स्वेच्छाप्रवृत्तत्वात्कारणानन्ततेष्यते ।

tasya svecchāpravṛttatvātkāraṇānantateṣyate /55a[71]

Tasya svecchā pravṛttatvāt, because…[how] has [Jayaratha] explained "*tasya*"? He has not explained "*tasya*".

SCHOLAR: *Tasya* [means], *akalpita kalpakasya*?

SWAMIJI: No. *Tasya svecchā pravṛttatvāt*, because Lord Śiva appears in his disciples by his own free will – *tasya svecchā pravṛttatvāt*. *Kārṇānantata iṣyate*, and the means are numberless, by numberless means he appears to those blessed souls.

LJA TA04C (47:54)

कदाचिद्भक्तियोगेन कर्मणा विद्ययापि वा ॥५५॥
ज्ञानधर्मोपदेशेन मन्त्रैर्वा दीक्षयापि वा ।

71. Swamiji recites "*icchate*" in place of the published "*iṣyate*", although he will recite "*iṣyate*" in his translation.

kadācidbhaktiyogena karmaṇā vidyayāpi vā //55//
jñānadharmopadeśena mantrairvā dīkṣayāpi vā /[72]
(not recited)

Kadācit bhakti yogena, sometimes by conducting *bhakti* yoga, he appears to them.

SCHOLAR: Through devotion, the path of devotion.

SWAMIJI: Yes. *Karmaṇā*, sometimes with some good actions; [sometimes by] *vidyā*, good knowledge; sometimes *jñāna-dharma-upadeśena*, by getting initiation of *jñāna* and *dharma*; …*

SCHOLAR: Which means?

SWAMIJI: *Jñāna* means, knowledge from masters, and *dharma* means, the best way of your conduct, conducting, how you conduct your actions in this universe.

SCHOLAR: Yes, that revelation might take place through some limited act.

SWAMIJI: *… *mantrairvā*, or with the recitation of *mantra*s; *dīkṣayā-pi vā*, by initiations.

LJA TA04C (48:39)

एवमाद्यैरनेकैश्च प्रकारैः परमेश्वरः ॥५६॥
संसारिणोऽनुगृह्णाति विश्वस्य जगतः पतिः ।

evamādyairanekaiśca prakāraiḥ parameśvaraḥ //56//
saṁsāriṇo'nugṛhṇāti viśvasya jagataḥ patiḥ /[73]
(not recited)

72. See *Wisdom in Kashmir Shaivism*, selected verses by Swami Lakshmanjoo (audio recordings, LJA archives 1988), verse 16.

73. Ibid., 17.

Evamādyairanekaiśca, by these numberless ways, this supreme master, Lord Śiva, uplifts/illuminates people because he is the protector of the whole universe (*viśvasya jagataḥ patiḥ*). So there are so many ways.

मातृमण्डलसम्बोधात्संस्काराात्तपसः प्रिये ॥५७॥
ध्यानाद्योगाज्जपाज्ज्ञानान्मन्त्राराधनातो व्रतात् ।
सम्प्राप्यं कुलसामान्यं ज्ञानं कौलिकसिद्धिदम् ॥५८॥

mātṛmaṇḍalasambodhāt-saṁskārāttapasaḥ priye //57//
dhyānādyogājjapājjñānān-mantrārādhanāto vratāt /
samprāpyaṁ kulasāmānyaṁ jñānaṁ kaulikasiddhidam //58//

By *mātṛ maṇḍala sambodha*. *Mātṛ maṇḍala sambodha* means–it should be explained in two ways–*mātṛ maṇḍala sambodha* is by putting awareness in your five senses; when you put awareness of God consciousness in the actions of your senses, that is *mātṛ maṇḍala sambodha*. Or automatic *mātṛ maṇḍala sambodha* is *yoginī melāpa*; *yoginī melāpa*, that is also *mātṛ maṇḍala sambodha*.

SCHOLAR: What do you mean by *yoginī melāpa* here? Do you mean *bāhyā* (external), *antara* (internal), what?

SWAMIJI: Huh?

SCHOLAR: What do you mean by *yoginī melāpa* here?

SWAMIJI: *Yoginī melāpa*, when you are absolutely absorbed in the awareness of God consciousness for sometime, and with no result, and you are weeping inside, you are imploring, craving, desiring to meet Him within, doing your meditation towards the Lord and nothing happens to you, and sometime when it gets ripened (your *tapa*s, your [penance], this kind of action is ripened), at once your eyes are closed and you feel yourself surrounded by divine ladies around you, and they illuminate you. That is *mātṛ maṇḍa-*…

SCHOLAR: This can be achieved through *mantra*.

SWAMIJI: By *mantra*, by imploring, by *bhakti* (by devotion).

SCHOLAR: And what is the difference between *haṭha krama*[74] here and *priya krama*[75], this *priya melāpa* and this *haṭha melāpa*?

SWAMIJI: This is *priya melāpa*. This is *priya melāpa*.

SCHOLAR: Just through your own contemplation,...

SWAMIJI: Contemplation and devotion, devotion, ...

SCHOLAR: ... and recitation of those *mantra*s given in [*āhnika*] thirty-one.

SWAMIJI: ... continuous devotion, yes.

SCHOLAR: Then what is *haṭha krama* here? What is the difference there in *yoginī melāpa*?

SWAMIJI: *Haṭha krama* is *śāmbhavopāya krama*.[76]

SCHOLAR: But in that *yoginī melāpa*, two *mantra*s are given, one for *priya melāpa* and one for *haṭha melāpa*.

SWAMIJI: *Haṭha melāpa* is more superior.

SCHOLAR: It says it involves *chidra-rakṣaṇa*; Abhinavagupta says that it involves *chidra-rakṣaṇa*.

SWAMIJI: *Cid-...?*

SCHOLAR: *Chidra-rakṣaṇa*.[77]

SWAMIJI: *Chidra-rakṣaṇa*, yes, where there is no leakage. For instance, *haṭha yoginī melāpa* is [when the divine ladies] make you lie down and have the sexual act with you. That is *haṭha yoginī melāpa*, like that. Or they throw that *praśāda*[78] which seems to you ...

SCHOLAR: *Jugupsyam*.

SWAMIJI: ... *jugupsyam*, absolutely filthy in your mouth. As soon as it is kept in your mouth, you get elevated.

SCHOLAR: *Mātṛ maṇḍala sambodha*.

SWAMIJI: That is *mātṛ maṇḍala sambodha* in *haṭha melāpa krama*, *haṭha yoginī*. And *yoginī melāpa* is inferior.

---

74. Lit., forceful process.

75. Lit., devotional/loving process.

76. Where "you have to jump in one instant and catch it." *Light on Tantra in Kashmir Shaivism, Tantrāloka, Vol. Two*, 3.108, p. 171.

77. Lit., leak (*chidra*) protection (*rakṣaṇa*).

78. Propitiatory offering or gift.

SCHOLAR: *Priya* …

SWAMIJI: *Priya melāpa*, [when] you get sweet things from the *yoginī* and get …

SCHOLAR: Not this *bhīmacaryākrama*.[79]

SWAMIJI: *Bhīmacaryā* is *haṭha melāpa*, but it is very effective.

JOHN: That one, *haṭha*.

SWAMIJI: *Haṭha melāpa* is very effective.

SCHOLAR: And the *sādhaka*, or the *sādhaka*'s master, can determine which will occur because there are different *mantra*s given for *haṭha melāpa* …

SWAMIJI: No, it is the *sādhaka*'s masters, only the *sādhaka*'s masters will inform him previously that, "You are reciting this *mantra*, *yoginī melāpa* may occur in this way, so you must not get confused there, you must accept whatever is given to you or whatever act is to be performed there."

JOHN: This is an internal state. Internal or external?

SWAMIJI: It is internal. In *samādhi* he does it.

SCHOLAR: This is not *cakra pūjā*.

JOHN: So these foul substances are given to him in *samādhi* by these [divine ladies]?

SWAMIJI: In *samādhi*, yes.

DENISE: This only happens to males?

SWAMIJI: Huh?

DENISE: This doesn't happen to females?

SWAMIJI: Females also with males.

DENISE: The same thing with males, not females.

SWAMIJI: With males, yes. That is *siddha yoginī*, it is *siddha yoginī melāpa*. It is not only *yoginī melāpa*. There are *siddha*s also.

SCHOLAR: But for males, only *yoginīs*, or it's also like in *cakra pūjā* you have *miśra cakra*?

SWAMIJI: That is *siddha melāpa*, automatic, this is automatic. That is to be [explained] in the 29th [*āhnika*].

SCHOLAR: Oh that, yes. You mean, *cakra-*, yes, that.

---

79. Where "you have to forcibly think of ugly things and see that God consciousness is also there pervading." Ibid., *Tantrāloka* 3.264, p. 416.

JOHN: So for ladies, men would appear, and for men, ladies appear.

SWAMIJI: Beautiful men, attractive men, not like John and me (laughs).

DEVOTEES: (laughter)

SWAMIJI: *Mātṛ maṇḍala sambodhāt saṁskārāt*…inspiring, elevating men. They are *siddhas*, you see.[80]

LJA TA04C (54:02)

mātṛmaṇḍalasambodhāt-saṁskārāttapasaḥ priye //57//
dhyānādyogājjapājjñānān-mantrārādhanāto vratāt /
samprāpyaṁ kulasāmānyaṁ jñānaṁ kaulikasiddhidam //58//
(verses repeated)

By the *mātṛ maṇḍala sambodha*, by the initiation got from *mātṛ maṇḍala* (*yoginī melāpa*), or awareness of your five senses, *saṁskārāt*, or by past impressions of your *karmas* (actions), *tapasaḥ*, or by penance, adopting penance, this can take place, *priye*, O dear Pārvatī. *Dhyānāt*, or by contemplation, *yogāt*, or by the practice of yoga, [or] *japāt*, by the recitation of *mantra*, [or] *jñānāt*, by getting knowledge from a master, [or] *mantra ārādhanāta*, by pleasing your Lord by the recitation of *mantras*, …*

SCHOLAR: How is that different from *japa*?

SWAMIJI: Huh?

SCHOLAR: Why does he mention that separately from *japa* here?

SWAMIJI: *Japa* is just to do the recitation of *mantra*. *Mantra ārādhanāta*, each *mantra* is recited, and at the same time, you implore the Lord, "Please bestow grace on me." That is *mantra ārādhanāta*.

SCHOLAR: This is given in these *Yāmala Tantras*.

SWAMIJI: Yes.

JOHN: So this *japa*, is this external repetition of *mantra* or internal?

SWAMIJI: No, it is internally, but it is recited, it is being recited.

*… *kulasāmānyamam jñānaṁ kaulika siddhidam, kula sāmānyam*, [one attains] that knowledge of *kula sāmāna*, knowledge which is [perceived to be] the same in each and every action of the world, and which

80. Accomplished yogis.

is the bestower of *kaulika siddhi*, which is the bestower of the power got from *kaulika bhāva*.[81]

SCHOLAR: The complete *cakreśvara*[82] state.

SWAMIJI:

LJA TA04C (56:01)

तत्त्वज्ञानात्मकं साध्यं यत्र यत्रैव दृश्यते ।
स एव हि गुरुस्तत्र हेतुजालं प्रकल्प्यताम् ॥५९॥

tattvajñānātmakaṁ sādhyaṁ yatra yatraiva dṛśyate /
sa eva hi gurustatra hetujālaṁ prakalpyatām //59//

But in conclusion, he wants to explain–Abhinavagupta–that *tattva jñāna* is the main point to be achieved.

SCHOLAR: Knowledge of reality.

81. "*Kaulika siddhi*, the *siddhi* (power) of totality, the totality of God consciousness, not unique God consciousness. One state is unique God consciousness and one state is the totality of God consciousness. When God consciousness digests everything, that is the totality of God consciousness. You can experience the state of God consciousness when you are doing your own business of daily life. That is in the totality of God consciousness. When you experience the state of God consciousness in your meditation room, that is another God consciousness, that is individual [viz., unique] God consciousness. He does not mention that individual God consciousness, he does not recognize that individual God consciousness, he recognizes the totality of God consciousness. He want's to find out the state of God consciousness in each and every action of life. That is the reality of God consciousness. If you find God consciousness only in a secluded corner of your meditation room, that is not real God consciousness. Is God consciousness absent in your daily life? It can't be! Your daily life cannot exist without God consciousness. So he says [that] that is *kaulika siddhi*." *Parātrīśikā Vivaraṇa,* with the commentary of Abhinavagupta, translation and commentary by Swami Lakshmanjoo (original audio recording, LJA archives, 1982–85), verse 1.

82. The lord of the wheel of energies.

SWAMIJI: Knowledge of reality. That is *sādhya*, that is to be achieved. *Yatra yatraiva dṛśyate*, wherever it is achieved, wherever it is perceived, that is the master, that you must confirm in your knowledge that it is the master. *Tatra hetu jālaṁ prakalpyatām*, other ways, other ways which have been explained (*mātṛ maṇḍala sambodha*, *saṁskāra*, *dhyāna*, *yoga*, *japa*, *jñāna*, *mantra ārādhanā*), all of these, maybe they are [used], maybe not, but the chief thing is guru *bhāva*.[83] Guru *bhāva* is *tattva jñāna*. *Tattva jñāna* is the essence of (inaudible)...

JOHN: The essence of what a guru is, what makes a guru.

SCHOLAR: The expansion of awareness.

SWAMIJI: Yes.

SCHOLAR: That is your guru if you are in this [class of] *akalpita kalpaka*.

SWAMIJI: Yes, that is...

SCHOLAR: That is your guru.

SWAMIJI: Yes.

JOHN: What?

SCHOLAR: *Avadhāna*, awareness.

SWAMIJI: Yes, *avadhāna*.

LJA TA04C (57:16)

तत्त्वज्ञानादृते नान्यल्लक्षणं ब्रह्मयामले ।

tattvajñānādṛte nānyallakṣaṇaṁ brahmayāmale /

In the *Brahmayāmala Tantra*, the definition of a master is only said, explained, that it is the awareness of your own knowledge [of *tattva jñāna*]–the definition of a master. Wherever awareness of [that occurs], the master has come, the master has appeared in you.

JOHN: So that is your master–your own awareness.

SWAMIJI: That is your master, yes, not these [masters] with physical bodies.

83. The state of the guru.

तत्रैव चोक्तं सेवायां कृतायामविकल्पतः ॥ ६० ॥
साधकस्य न चेत्सिद्धिः किं कार्यमिति चोदिते ।
आत्मीयमस्य सञ्ज्ञानक्रमेण स्वात्मदीक्षणम् ॥ ६१ ॥
सस्फुरत्वप्रसिद्ध्यर्थं ततः साध्यं प्रसिध्यति ।

tatraiva coktaṁ sevāyāṁ kṛtāyāmavikalpataḥ //60//
sādhakasya na cetsiddhiḥ kiṁ kāryamiti codite /
ātmīyamasya sañjñāna-krameṇa svātmadīkṣaṇam //61//
sasphuratvaprasiddhyarthaṁ tataḥ sādhyaṁ prasidhyati /
(not recited in full)

In that *Brahmayāmala Tantra*, Pārvatī had once put a question before Lord Śiva: "*Sevāyāṁ kṛtāyām*, although he has served his master, the disciple has served his master, *avikalpataḥ*, whole heartedly without putting any doubt in his [master's] state (*avikalpataḥ*, without doubt), *sādhakasya na cet siddhi*, if he does not achieve anything, what should be done afterwards, O Lord?" It was a question put by Pārvatī in the *Brahmayāmala* to Lord Śiva. And He explained this: He is initiated from within! He is not initiated from outer agencies. And *sasphuratva prasiddhyartham*, and that initiation illuminates him all-around. And *tataḥ sādhyam prasidhyati*, and whatever his [objective] is, that [objective] becomes fulfilled by that.

LJA TA04C (59:10)
LJA TA04D (00:00)

अनेन स्वात्मविज्ञानं सस्फुरत्वप्रसाधकम् ॥ ६२ ॥
उक्तं मुख्यतयाचार्यो भवेद्यदि न सस्फुरः ।

anena svātmavijñānaṁ sasphuratvaprasādhakam //62//
uktaṁ mukhya tayācāryo bhavedyadi na sasphuraḥ /

But this is only done, this way of initiating yourself by your own self, this way of initiation should take place when the initiator, a real initiator, is not in hand. Otherwise, if a real initiator is existing, you should get initiated by him, not try to initiate yourself by your own self.

LJA TA04D (00:37)

तत्रैव च पुनः श्रीमद्रक्ताराधनकर्मणि ॥६३॥
विधिं प्रोक्तं सदा कुर्वन्-मासेनाचार्य उच्यते ।
पक्षेण साधकोऽर्धार्धात्-पुत्रकः समयी तथा ॥६४॥

tatraiva ca punaḥ śrīmad-raktārādhanakarmaṇi //63//
vidhiṁ proktaṁ sadā kurvan-māsenācārya ucyate /
pakṣeṇa sādhako'rdhārdhāt-putrakaḥ samayī tathā //64//
(not recited in full)

In this *Brahmayāmala Tantra* also, this is also said in addition in the *Caṇḍikā Vidhāna* section, [where] there was the section of adoring Caṇḍikā (Durgā), in there it is said: *Vidhiṁ proktaṁ sadā kurvan*, anyone who follows the way which is given in that *Brahmayāmala Tantra*[84], *māsenācārya ucyate*, in one month he'll become a master by that…without depending on other masters, he will become himself a master in one month.

SCHOLAR: But not any *sādhaka*. Does that mean any *sādhaka*?

SWAMIJI: No, the way …

SCHOLAR: Or is it *akalpita kalpaka*?

SWAMIJI: No, that is over.

SCHOLAR: Why does he…? One month?

SWAMIJI: In one month, it will take him only one month to become a master.

---

84. That is, by *raktārādhana karmaṇi*, by offering propitiations (*rādhana*) to Raktā *devī* (Caṇḍikā *devī* or Durgā).

JOHN: But he has to have the capacity to follow that way.

SWAMIJI: Because there are four sections of initiations. The first initiation takes place for becoming disciplined (that is *sāmayika dīkṣā*), the second is a *putraka*,[85] the third is a *sādhaka* (aspirant), the fourth is a master (*ācārya*).[86] He becomes an *ācārya* within ...

JOHN: So this one who does this practice of the *Brahmayāmala Tantra* ...

SWAMIJI: In the *Caṇḍikā Vidhāna* [section of the] Tantra it is said.

JOHN: So this practice, then, is that practice, that last initiation.

SWAMIJI: It will carry him... yes, the last, yes.

SCHOLAR: But this is if he has no master.

SWAMIJI: No, there are so many, all the four initiations. *Vidhi* (injunction), this *vidhi*, [if] he will tread on this kind of action according to the sayings of the *Brahmayāmala Tantra*, he will become an *ācārya* (or a master) in one month. *Pakṣeṇa sādhaka*, he will become a *sādhaka* in fifteen days (a fortnight). *Ardhārdha putraka*, in seven days he will become a *putraka*.

DENISE: What is a *putraka*?

SWAMIJI: *Putraka* is a spiritual son, a spiritual son of a master.

DENISE: In how many days?

SWAMIJI: In seven days. And *samayī*, and he will become a disciplined *śiṣya* (disciple) in three days and a half, only three days and a half, without depending upon masters and all those humbug.

JOHN: Who is he a *putraka* of? His own consciousness?

SWAMIJI: *Putraka*, he becomes a *putraka*.

JOHN: Of who?

SWAMIJI: Of the master, Lord Śiva. The real master is Lord Śiva everywhere.

DEVOTEE: *Rakta-ārādhana-karmaṇi* means?

SWAMIJI: *Caṇḍikā vidhāna karmaṇi*.[87]

---

85. A spiritual son of a master.

86. The general order of initiation is *sāmayika*, *putraka*, *sādhaka* and *ācārya*, which is discipline, spiritual son, spiritual practice and teacher respectively. These four ways of *dīkṣa* (initiation) are explained in the 11th, 13th, 15th and 16th *āhnika*s of the *Tantrāloka*.

87. By performing the worship/recitation of Caṇḍikā.

LJA TA04D (03:21)

दीक्षयेज्जपयोगेन रक्तादेवी क्रमाद्यतः ।
गुरोरलाभे प्रोक्तस्य विधिमेतं समाचरेत् ॥ ६५ ॥

dīkṣayejjapayogena raktādevī kramādyataḥ /
guroralābhe proktasya vidhimetaṁ samācaret //65//
(not recited in full)

But who initiates that *sādhaka*, who initiates that *putraka*, who initiates that *sāmayī*, and who initiates that *ācārya*? He says this in [this] *śloka*.

Japayogena raktā devī, by this *japa* (the recitation), the recitation that he has done according to the sayings of the *Brahmayāmala Tantra*, by that recitation, *raktā devī* (Caṇḍikā) Herself comes and initiates him. *Guror alābhe proktasya vidhimetaṁ samācaret*, but this kind of action should take place only when the real master is not available in the market. If a real master is available, then he must do it.

JOHN: But then why if it only takes you one month to become a master through this following of the *Brahmayāmala Tantra*, why go to the market for a real master? Because one month is…

SWAMIJI: (laughs) Well said, yes (laughs)!

SCHOLAR: We have a manuscript of the *Brahmayāmala Tantra* now? *Acha* (okay).

SWAMIJI: But he says, *guror alābhe*, when those masters are not available, then it becomes fruitful, otherwise it won't become fruitful. If a master is available, [if a] master is watching you, you have not to ignore the master at the same time (laughs). You want to become master in one month?

SCHOLAR: But this is referring to the *sādhaka* who has great capacity, because how could I sit down with the *Brahmayāmala Tantra* up in my room and in one month become an *ācārya* (master)?

SWAMIJI: Yes, no, no. When there is capacity in the *sādhaka*.

JOHN: So there is also every tendency or every chance that this *sādhaka*, if he goes this way of the *Brahmayāmala*, he can get misled because he doesn't have real knowledge.

SWAMIJI: Yes, yes.

JOHN: He could read it wrong and do wrong things.
SWAMIJI: Because it is said:

LJA TA04D (05:29)

मते च पुस्तकाद्विद्याध्ययने दोष ईदृशः ।
उक्तो यस्तेन तद्दोषाभावेऽसौ न निषिद्धता ॥ ६६ ॥

mate ca pustakādvidyādhyayane doṣa īdṛśaḥ /
ukto yastena taddoṣābhāve'sau na niṣiddhatā //66//
(not recited in full)

In the *Mata Śāstra*, in the *Siddhāmata*,[88] it is written that from books, getting knowledge is very bad; *mate ca pustakāt vidyādhyayane*, by getting knowledge from books, it is said that it is not worthwhile, [that] you should not do that.

SCHOLAR: *Vidyādhyayane*, is that in the sense of *mantrādhyayane*?

SWAMIJI: *Mantra adhyayane*, *vidyā adhyayane*, just to achieve the knowledge of the *śāstra*s, just to achieve the knowledge of your nature through books ...

JOHN: Only, without a master.

SWAMIJI: ... without a master, is *doṣa* (defective). *Doṣa* is there, only there is a defect, in those who want to achieve this: it is those who are hypocrites, who don't want to serve their masters. Actually, they don't want to serve their masters, and they don't want to wait for so many years after following the master, just as [John noted].

SCHOLAR: One month course.

SWAMIJI: (laughs) But there is hypocrisy in them; in those disciples there is hypocrisy: they don't want to serve, the serving tendency is not there. But when the serving tendency is existing in *sādhaka*s, then they can achieve this, otherwise they will never achieve it.

SCHOLAR: Only if they can surrender.

88. The *Siddhayogeśvarīmāta* is the source of the *Mālinīvijaya Tantra*, which in turn is the foundational text for Abhinavagupta's *Tantrāloka*.

SWAMIJI: Yes.

JOHN: So, in other words, these hypocrites, they have more ego, this individual ego, pride, and …

SWAMIJI: Yes, they have, so they don't …

JOHN: … don't really understand the *śāstra*s.

SWAMIJI: *Bas*. The sixty-sixth [verse is completed].

SCHOLAR: I wonder if this is in there, the manuscript.

SWAMIJI: What?

SCHOLAR: I haven't yet read through this *Brahmayāmala* manuscript.

SWAMIJI: You must go through it.

SCHOLAR: It's huge. Maybe it will have this in, we'll see.

LJA TA04D (07:34)

SWAMIJI: Now he reads again the passage of the *Siddhāmata*, the *Siddhā Tantra*:[89]

मन्त्रद्रव्यादिगुप्तत्वे फलं किमिति चोदिते ।

mantradravyādiguptatve phalaṁ kimiti codite /

Because this is an extraordinary thing to get realization without depending upon a master. Generally we have to depend on a master in each and every case, but he says a *sāṁsiddhika* guru is without a master.

Mantra dravyādi guptatve phalaṁ kimiti codite, this question was put by Pārvatī before Lord Śiva: "Why *mantra* and *dravya* is kept secret?"

Dravya is three substances in the Kaula school. In the Kaula school, there are three substances to be used in worship, in internal worship (*ādiyāga*). The three substances you already know: *madhya*, *māṁsa*, and *maithuna*. *Madhya* means liquor, *māṁsa* is *mutton* (meat), and sex (*mithuna*). [These are] *dravya*. [These are] already kept a secret in this Kaula school. And *mantra* is also kept a secret. "Why this is kept a secret?" This was a question put by Pārvatī to Lord Śiva.

---

89. The *Siddhayogeśvarimāta*.

JOHN: Why these four things are kept secret – the three [*dravya*s] and *mantra*.

SWAMIJI: … *mantra*. The answer to that from Lord Śiva:

LJA TA04D (09:36)

पुस्तकाधीतविद्या ये दीक्षासमयवर्जिताः ॥ ६७ ॥
तामसाः परहिंसादि वश्यादि च चरन्त्यलम् ।
न च तत्त्वं विदुस्तेन दोषभाज इति स्फुटम् ॥ ६८ ॥

pustakādhītavidyā ye dīkṣāsamayavarjitāḥ //67//
tāmasāḥ parahiṁsādi vaśyādi ca carantyalam /
na ca tattvaṁ vidustena doṣabhāja iti sphuṭam //68//

Because those who get knowledge from books, not from masters, *pustaka adhīta vidyāye*, …*

SCHOLAR: *Vidyā mantra*? *Dhīta mantra ye ityartha*?

SWAMIJI: *Mantra*s and all *dravya*s. The ways of *dravya*s are defined in books and the ways of *mantra*s are also defined in books. Those who depend on those [books] without going to a master, because *dīkṣā samaya varjitā*, internally, in fact, they are away from the discipline of *dīkṣa*, they are away from maintaining the discipline of *dīkṣā*, the initiation of masters. When you are initiated by a master, you have to observe discipline then, all-around discipline. And they are without that discipline because they are not dependent to any masters. They just go on reading books and extracting the techniques from there and treading on that path by their own will.

*… *tāmasāḥ*, in fact, they are *tāmas*, they are given to the *tāmasic* state of mind.[90] And *parahiṁsādi vaśyādi ca carantyalam*, they want

90. Lit., darkness. "It comes out from *ajñānajaṁ*, from ignorance, it rises from ignorance. *Mohanaṁ sarvadehināṁ*, and it deludes everybody. It puts everybody in delusion, in the ocean of delusion. *Pramādālasyanidrābhi*, and that too binds you by *pramāda* (by forgetfulness), *ālasya* (by sluggishness), *nidrābhi* (and by sleeping,

to spoil the life of others.

JOHN: How to kill some person or make them sick or something.

SWAMIJI: How to kill some person, or madden some person, or divert some person from that person towards himself. Because they are *tāmasa*, *tāmasic*, and *parahiṁsādi vaśyādi ca*, they kill others, they want to kill others, by the aid of these *mantra*s, etcetera, and *vaśyādi*, and to *vaśa*. *Vaśa* means …

SCHOLAR: Subjugate.

SWAMIJI: … subjugate, subjugate ladies or gents towards their own self. *Na ca tattvaṁ vidus*, they do not know the exact position of *mantra*s, for which those *mantra*s are written in books. *Doṣabhāja iti sphuṭam*, they don't get the fruit of *mantra*s, so they become the victim of *doṣa*, the victim of giving bad impressions on books; afterwards they come to this conclusion that these books are nonsense because they don't get any fruit from those *mantra*s or *dravya*s.

SCHOLAR: But it says here that they do actually achieve *parahiṁsādi* with them, so they must have…

SWAMIJI: *Parahiṁsādi*, they try to kill others, and *vaśa*, or subjugate others, [but] *na ca tattvam viduḥ*, they do not know the exact position of *mantra*s, for which *mantra*s are produced, [why] *mantra*s are written. *Mantra*s are actually written for those occasions when it is very needful, but not to kill others, but not to [cause] destruction between a couple.

SCHOLAR: But those are described in the Vāma *Tantra*s (left-handed *Tantra*s).

SWAMIJI: Yes, in the *Svacchanda Tantra* it is …

SCHOLAR: So, when a man has *dīkṣāsāmaya* from a Vāmācāra master, then he does these things.

SWAMIJI: Then he will be successful in that. If he takes the aid of a master, then he will be successful. And the master will only give him aid if it is worthwhile to do, otherwise he won't agree with that suggestion to kill others.

LJA TA04D (13:51)

---

drowsiness)." *Bhagavad Gītā* 14.8 audio (LJA archive).

SCHOLAR: Under what circumstances would any of the *abhicāra*[91] processes be justifiable from a Śaivite point of view?

SWAMIJI: For instance, you marry a girl. She goes astray always and you are fed up with her, what to do with her, so you want to divert her attention towards your own self and keep her away from going to other persons. This is worthwhile.

SCHOLAR: Why is it worthwhile? If the woman is going astray, why…?

SWAMIJI: Why she should go astray to each and every [man]? She has become a prostitute like that.

SCHOLAR: But she is not worthy of the one person if she goes to others. Why should he try and artificially direct her attention?

SWAMIJI: Not the other person. I mean, that woman who is just like a prostitute. For that woman it is prescribed.

SCHOLAR: Who wants to divert the attention of a prostitute to themselves?

DENISE: If you love her.

JOHN: If she was your wife and you love her.

SWAMIJI: If you love her, then. And all these other things are also mentioned in that [*Tantra*]. It is just one point I…

SCHOLAR: It's still a problem to understand how, from a Śaiva point of view, people would use *mantric* power for such limited ends.

SWAMIJI: For instance, there is an enemy who destroys you and troubles you each and every moment in your life. And it is worthwhile, [if] he does not come to [his] senses in any case, then he must get his life ended. It is for your master to suggest. If he wants that, then that *māraṇa mantra*[92] is produced for him, so he will end his life. And there are so many other things also in this world happening. Because the *māraṇa mantra* is advisable, [but] not [physically] killing. By killing you will be caught by the government. By the *māraṇa mantra*, nobody will tell you anything. She or he is finished, that is all, nobody knows.

DEVOTEE: The perfect crime.

---

91. Employment of spells for a malevolent purpose.

92. *Mantra* of death (*māraṇa*).

SWAMIJI: Yes (laughs). No, that crime will take place only when it is advisable, not otherwise. It depends upon the suggestions of your masters, not your own free will.

SCHOLAR: But Abhinavagupta says in book thirty-seven that he should completely abandon *duratyaya*, these *kāmya siddhis*[93], these six limited practices.

SWAMIJI: Yes, that is [true]. In fact, this is the inferior way of the recitation of *mantras* and etcetera. But these people who want to find out the ways from books are generally like this, of this inferior class, they are not that superior class. *Na ca tattvaṁ viduḥ*, they don't know the reality of those *mantras* or *dravyas*. They just want to drink, they just want to have sex with girls, because it is said in the Tantras.

LJA TA04D (17:34)

पूर्वं पदयुगं वाच्यमन्योन्यं हेतुहेतुमत् ।

pūrvaṁ padayugaṁ vācyam-anyonyaṁ hetuhetumat /69a

He explains this verse of the *Siddha Tantra*, *pūrvaṁ padayugaṁ*, this 67th *śloka* which is from the *Siddha Tantra*, there are the last two words, the last two lines: *pustakādhītavidyā ye dīkṣāsamayavarjitāḥ*. This *pada yugam*, these two *padas* (quarters) of this *śloka* (*yugam* means, these two), *pustaka adhītavidyā*, *dīkṣā samayavarjitāḥ*, you must explain it in this way that it is *anyonyaṁ hetuhetumat*, it is cause and effect with each other. For instance, *pustaka adhīta vidyā ye*, those who extract knowledge of Śaivism, of this Tantric knowledge, from books, they are actually *dīkṣā samaya varjitā*, it is why they are *dīkṣā samaya varjitā*, they are carried away from the path of discipline and initiation of masters. Now again you have to explain in vice-versa way: those who are carried away from initiation and discipline of masters, they are actually *pustaka adhīta vidyā*, they come to study the knowledge of experience from books. Those who study knowledge

93. Unfathomable (*duratyaya*) powers (*siddhis*) performed through the desire (*kāmya*) of some object or personal advantage.

from books are actually carried away from the path of masters and initiation. And those who are carried away from the path and initiation of masters, they go to learn the technique of Śaivism from books. You should explain it this way.

SCHOLAR: *Anyonyaṁ hetuhetumat, ...*

SWAMIJI: That is *anyonyaṁ hetuhetumat.*

SCHOLAR: ... reciprocal causality.

SWAMIJI: *Yataḥ pustakādhītavidyā ataḥ dīkṣāsamaya varjitā, yataḥ dīkṣāsamaya varjitā, ato pustakādhītavidyā*–this way. Now he explains *kalpita* guru, an absolutely *kalpita* guru, not *akalpita kalpaka*, not *kalpitākalpita.*

SCHOLAR: *Kalpita, śuddhā kalpita.*

SWAMIJI: No, one was the *sāṁsiddhika*. The *sāṁsiddhika* was also nominated as an *akalpita* guru. The *sāṁsiddhika* and the *akalpita*, this is the first class of masters. The second class of masters was *akalpita kalpaka.*[94] Now the third class is *kalpita.*

LJA TA04D (20:41)

यस्तु शास्त्रं विना नैति शुद्धविद्याख्यसंविदम् ॥६९॥
गुरोः स शास्त्रमन्विच्छुस्तदुक्तं क्रममाचरेत् ।

yastu śāstraṁ vinā naiti śuddhavidyākhyasaṁvidam //69//
guroḥ sa śāstramanvicchus-taduktaṁ kramamācaret /

That master who cannot achieve the state of Śuddhavidyā, the pure knowledge of God consciousness, that person who cannot achieve the pure knowledge of God consciousness without depending on masters or *śāstras*, *guroḥ sa śāstram anvicchuḥ*, he must desire to get knowledge of *śāstras* through masters, *tad uktaṁ kramamācaret*, and must obey the commands of masters.

SCHOLAR: *Kramam* is "practice", this course of practice?

---

94. Here, Swamiji corrects himself. That is, the second class of masters are *akalpita kalpaka*, not *kalpita kalpaka.*

SWAMIJI: The way, the practice, yes.

SCHOLAR: Which his master gives him.

SWAMIJI: Yes. He must tread accordingly as he is told by masters. And if his masters do not tell him easily, then:

LJA TA04D (21:46)

येन केनाप्युपायेन गुरुमाराध्य भक्तितः ॥७०॥

yena kenāpyupāyena gurumārādhya bhaktitaḥ //70//[95]

You must please [the master], you must…

SCHOLAR: Court him.

SWAMIJI: Court him? What is "court"?

SCHOLAR: C-o-u-r-t, court. Like a young man courts his lover, to win favor.

SWAMIJI: Yes, yes, you must court your master by any means, according to the needs of the master. Because there are so many masters who are wealthy masters, they don't need money from you; some masters are wealthy, the wealthiest masters, they don't need money and they don't need that kind of help. And some masters are paupers, without money, they need money. And some masters do not want either of these, not money or…[but] they want service, they want to be served: punching and pinching [i.e., massage] and all of that sort of thing, or cooking for them, making so many dishes for the master. And there are some masters who do not like that also. So you have to see the [desire] of your master. According to the [desire] of the master, you must act. And there are some masters who like to learn a language, another language, e.g., the French language, the Canadian language, or the English language. So you must teach him that language if he likes to do so.

SCHOLAR: This is knowledge, giving knowledge.

SWAMIJI: That is *pratividyā*. Because these means are many, so you have to court the master according to the needs of your master.

---

95. See also *Wisdom in Kashmir Shaivism*, verses 19–20 (LJA archive).

LJA TA04D (23:43)

तद्दीक्षाक्रमयोगेन शास्त्रार्थं वेत्त्यसौ ततः ।
अभिषेकं समासाद्य यो भवेत्स तु कल्पितः ॥७१॥
सन्नप्यशेषपाशौघविनिवर्तनकोविदः ।

taddīkṣākramayogena śāstrārthaṁ vettyasau tataḥ
abhiṣekaṁ samāsādya yo bhavetsa tu kalpitaḥ //71//
sannapyaśeṣapāśaugha-vinivartanakovidaḥ /[96]
(not recited)

Taddīkṣākramayogena śāstrārthaṁ vetti, vetti asau, then *asau*, this disciple, gets the knowledge of the background of *śāstras*, gets the knowledge of *śāstras* by being initiated by that master accordingly. *Tataḥ abhiṣekam samāsādya*, then he gets complete *abhiṣeka* (initiation) of teacher (*ācārya*) *abhiṣeka*, not only *sāmayīka dīkṣā*. He gets *sāmayīka dīkṣa*, he gets *putraka dīkṣā*, he gets *sādhaka dīkṣā*, and he gets *ācārya dīkṣā*. These four ways of initiations he gets from that master.[97]

SCHOLAR: *Ācārya abhiṣeka* and *sādhaka abhiṣeka*.

SWAMIJI: *Ācārya abhiṣeka*, *sādhaka abhiṣeka*, *putraka abhiṣeka*, and *sāmayīka abhiṣeka*.[98]

SCHOLAR: There are *abhiṣeka* for *putraka* and *sāmayīka* or only for *sādhaka* and *ācārya*?

SWAMIJI: No, *abhiṣeka* is for all the four. *Yo bhavet*, and that person who becomes an *ācārya*, who becomes a master then, he has got a master's training from him, *sa tu kalpita san api*, although he is a *kalpita* guru because he is made by other masters, but even then, *aśeṣapāśaughavinivartana kovidaḥ*, he can remove all bondages of disciples. He is *pravīna*, he is clever, in removing away the bondages

96. Ibid.

97. See fn. 91, p. 102.

98. The four ways of *abhiṣeka* (consecration) are explained in the 23rd *āhnika* of the *Tantrāloka*.

of the mind or everything, all-around bondages of his disciples.

Have you understood it?

It is why he says in the commentary: *Kaściddhi śuśrūṣayā*, some masters are pleased, get pleased, by serving, by service. *Kaściddanena*, some masters do not want service, they want this cash, they want service in dollars–*kaściddanena*. *Kaścicca prātividyādinā*, some masters even do not want even dollars, they want to learn some other language from you.

SCHOLAR: They want some knowledge in return.

SWAMIJI: Some knowledge in return. That is *prātividyā*. It is why he has put, *yena kenāpyupāyena*, by any means, according to the needs of your masters. Because:

LJA TA04D (26:24)

यस्मान्महेश्वरः साक्षात्कृत्वा मानुषविग्रहम् ।
कृपया गुरुरूपेण मग्नाः प्रोद्धरति प्रजाः ॥

yasmānmaheśvaraḥ sākṣāt-kṛtvā mānuṣavigraham /
kṛpayā gururūpeṇa magnāḥ proddharati prajāḥ //

It is a reference in [Jayaratha's] commentary.

Lord Śiva has descended from his upper level of universal consciousness in the body of masters. So Lord Śiva is residing there; in the body of masters, you must feel Lord Śiva is there. And *kṛpayā guru rūpeṇa*, he takes the formation of the master, he becomes the master (Lord Śiva becomes the master) and elevates mankind in this universe.

Yo yathākrama yogena... now he explains *kalpita akalpita*; although he is a *kalpita* guru, he becomes partly *akalpita* also.

LJA TA04D (27:28)

यो यथाक्रमयोगेन कस्मिंश्चिच्छास्त्रवस्तुनि ॥७२॥
आकस्मिकं व्रजेद्बोधं कल्पिताकल्पितो हि सः ।

yo yathākramayogena kasmiṁścicchāstravastuni //72//
ākasmikaṁ vrajedbodhaṁ kalpitākalpito hi saḥ /

So in the *kalpita bhāga* (class) also, they differ with each other. One is a *kalpita*, an absolute *kalpita* guru, the other is *kalpita akalpita*. And *kalpita akalpita* is that master who *yathā krama yogena*, although he is a *kalpita* and he treads on the *kalpita* way because he depends upon the teaching of his masters, he has nothing to do, he does not cross the boundary of his [master's] teachings, but *kasmiṁścit śāstra vastuni ākasmikaṁ vrajet bodhaṁ*, sometime, with some grace of Lord Śiva, he gets the knowledge of the *śāstra*s. I mean, not *śāstra*s, not words, [but] the points, the important points, some important point he gets understood by himself–by the grace of Lord Śiva. This kind of master is said to be *kalpita akalpita*. Because:

LJA TA04D (28:42)

तस्य योऽकल्पितो भागः स तु श्रेष्ठतमः स्मृतः ॥७३॥

tasya yo'kalpito bhāgaḥ sa tu śreṣṭhatamaḥ smṛtaḥ //73//

That kind of knowledge that comes to him all of a sudden, ...*

Because, [for example], I am reading this as I am taught by my master. I am reading again and again but there is some point where I have a doubt, and the doubt is not cleared by my master because I am not capable of receiving that answer. I receive that answer from the mouth of my master but it is not digested in me properly. And sometime I go and go and go and read on, read on, and then automatically all of a sudden I perceive that point and it is exposed to me–all of a sudden. That is *akalpita bhāga* for him.

*... *tasya yo'kalpita bhāgaḥ*, and that *akalpita* way of understanding is said to be the supreme way of understanding. *Sa tu śreṣṭhatamaḥ*, that is the most supreme way of understanding, because:

LJA TA04D (29:55)

उत्कर्षः शुद्धविद्यांशतारतम्यकृतो यतः ।

utkarṣaḥ śuddhavidyāṁśa-tāratamyakṛto yataḥ /74a

This is the *utkarṣaḥ*, this is the rise of Śuddhavidyā in a successive way. This is not the rise of Śuddhavidyā in an *akrama* (non-successive) way. It is *tāratamya kṛta*.[99] The *akrama* way of rise is in the *sāṁsiddhika* guru.

SCHOLAR: Non-successive rise is in *sāṁsiddhika – akrama*.

SWAMIJI: Yes, non-successive. [Here] it is a successive rise. Successive rise: he has been initiated, he has been taught in books by masters, and after, all of a sudden some important point comes in his understanding – all of a sudden. That is *akalpita bhāga*.

LJA TA04D (30:44)

यथा भेदेनादिसिद्धाच्छिवान्मुक्तशिवा ह्यधः ॥७४॥

तथा सांसिद्धिकज्ञानादाहृतज्ञानिनोऽधमाः ।

yathā bhedenādisiddhācchivānmukta-śivā hyadhaḥ //74//
tathā sāṁsiddhikajñānād-āhṛtajñānino'dhamāḥ /

Just as *bhede* (*bhede* means, in the dualistic schools of thought), in the dualistic schools of thought, in *dvaita śāstra*s, it is said that, *anādi siddhāt śivāt mukta śivā hyadhaḥ, …**

SCHOLAR: There's a misprint. It should be "*bhede*", and then a gap – right? – and *avagraha*, and then "*nādi siddha śivāt …*"

SWAMIJI: Yes.

SCHOLAR: They have written "*bhedena adhi siddhāt*".

---

99. Gradations (*tāratamya*) of acquisition (*kṛta*).

SWAMIJI: "*Bhedena*", yes.[100] This is the importance in this person (laughs) because he is informed in the Sanskrit language.

*...*yathā bhede*, *yathā*, just as *bhede*, in the dualistic way of schools, the dualistic *śāstra*s, it is said, *anādi-siddhāt śivāt mukta śivā hyadhaḥ*, *mukta-śiva*s are [much more] inferior than *anādisiddha-śiva*s. *Anādisiddha-śiva* is supreme. *Anādisiddha-śiva* is that Śiva who has never come in the field of ignorance, who has never been ignorant. That is *anādisiddha-śiva*–eternal, eternally filled with his realization of God consciousness, forever! That is *anādisiddha-śiva*. He has never been ignorant. That Śiva is called *anādisiddha-śiva*. *Mukta-śiva* is that Śiva who has become Śiva by going to masters, by being initiated, and by treading on the path of yoga, etcetera, and *kuṇḍalinī* rise, and all this, and he becomes *mukta-śiva*, he is liberated afterwards in the end. But in the dualistic schools of thought, it is said, *anādisiddha-śiva* is more supreme, more superior, that *mukta-śiva*, but not in our system! In our system it is said [that] *mukta-śiva* is as supreme as *anādisiddha-śiva*. There is no difference between *anādisiddha-śiva* and *mukta-śiva* in our school of thinking. But in the dualistic way of schools, it is said that they are inferior. Who are inferior?

SCHOLAR: *Mukta-śiva*s, enlightened beings.

SWAMIJI: *Mukta-śiva*s are [more] inferior than *anādisiddha*s, [but] not from our point of view. Just as this is admitted in the *dvaita* school, *tathā*, in the same way, *sāṁsiddhika jñānādāhṛta jñānino adhamāḥ*, in our school of Śaivism, the *sāṁsiddhika* guru is [more] supreme than the *āhṛtajñāni*. The *sāṁsiddhika jñāni* is that person whose perception of God consciousness has risen without depending on others, the other two, for instance, masters and *śāstra*s. That is the *sāṁsiddhika jñāni* (he has already explained that *sāṁsiddhika* guru). And *āhṛtajñāni* is that person who has got realization by initiation, [from] others.

SCHOLAR: He has acquired knowledge.

SWAMIJI: Acquired knowledge. *Āhṛtajñāni* has acquired from masters, acquired from *śāstra*s–that is *āhṛtajñāni*. Those are *adhamā*, those are [more] inferior than that *sāṁsiddhika* from our point of view, from the Śaiva point of view, [just] as from their point of view, from the dualistic point of view, *mukta-śiva*s are inferior, supposed to be

100. It should read "*bhede'nādi siddhāt*" instead of "*bhede nādi siddhāt*".

[more] inferior, than *anādi-siddha-śiva*s.

SCHOLAR: Swamiji, may I ask a point on the side? What, from the point of view of Śaiva Siddhānta (*bhedeśvaravāda*), is the status of *mukta-śiva*?

SWAMIJI: Huh?

SCHOLAR: What is it in the dualistic Śaivite doctrine to realize Śiva? What does that mean if it is not to become identical?

SWAMIJI: He has become identical, ...

SCHOLAR: But he is still *adha* (inferior).

SWAMIJI: ... but because as there a was time when he was ignorant, there was a time previously when he was ignorant, when he was totally unaware of his God consciousness, so this is the defect in him. They believe, but we do not believe that!

SCHOLAR: They claim that ...

SWAMIJI: Śaivism does not believe that.

SCHOLAR: Non-dualistic Śaivism.

SWAMIJI: Non-dualistic Śaivism does not believe that he is inferior. Once he has realized God, he is as good as the *sāṁsiddhika* – the *anādisiddha-śiva*. There is no difference, there is no minor difference between *anādisiddha-śiva* and *mukta-śiva* from our point of view. From their point of view, they realize that he is inferior because he had, some time before, he had ignorance, he had this torture.

DENISE: But the impressions of that ignorance are gone after he realizes?

SWAMIJI: They have gone.

DENISE: Then there's no difference, is there?

SWAMIJI: From our point of view. They think that there is some bad impression, previous bad impression, in him.

JOHN: They don't believe that there is ever any absolute oneness with That.

SCHOLAR: Complete freedom of consciousness.

JOHN: You never attain that Absolute. You attain the oneness of being with Him.

SWAMIJI: That can't be because they conclude in the end that he becomes one with God consciousness when he leaves the body, as we do.

SCHOLAR: *Dehapātat śivaṁvrajet.*

SWAMIJI: *Dehapātat śivaṁvrajet.*[101] But they believe that as long as there was a time previously when he was ignorant, when he was a *jīva* (individual), when he was given to worldly senses, he was enjoying just like beasts previously, in the previous part of his life, so he is inferior to that *anādisiddha-śiva*.

SCHOLAR: So they have no notion of complete *jīvanmukti*.[102]

SWAMIJI: No (affirmative).

SCHOLAR: Because *nara* (the individual) and Īśvara (Lord Śiva) are…

SWAMIJI: Separate.

SCHOLAR: … separate in that doctrine.

SWAMIJI: Because *nareśvaravādi*, because they think that, just like in Sāṁkhya also, the same is the case.

SCHOLAR: *Seśvara* Sāṁkhya.[103]

JOHN: There's a difference between *prakṛti* and this.

SWAMIJI: No, between *puruṣa* and *jīva* there is a difference, some difference remains.

SCHOLAR: In the *seśvara* Sāṁkhya.

SWAMIJI: Yes, *seśvara* Sāṁkhya. So:

LJA TA04D (38:03)

तत्सन्निधौ नाधिकारस्तेषं मुक्तशिवात्मवत् ॥७५॥

tatsannidhau nādhikāras-teṣāṁ mukta-śivātmavat //75//

And they believe, those dualistic schools of thinkers believe, that *mukta-śiva* has no right to act before the *anādisiddha-śiva*. Whatever the *anādisiddha-śiva* [does, for example], the *anādisiddha-śiva* has

101. "*Dehapātāt śivaṁ*, and although they are initiated, but they don't get the realization of God consciousness in their lifetime. At the end, when they leave this physical frame, they realize God consciousness. There are some individuals like that, some disciples, because there is something lacking in their minds." *Tantrāloka* 13.203 (LJA archive).

102. Embodied liberation.

103. Sāṁkhya with the doctrine of God.

produced rains, he cannot interfere in this, the *mukta-śiva* cannot interfere, he cannot stop the rain.

SCHOLAR: He still has traces of impressions in his mind, because this is a lower stage of realization.

SWAMIJI: Yes. And in the same way, in our system also, before the *sāṁsiddhika jñāni*, before the *sāṁsiddhika* guru, the *āhṛtajñāni* has no right to initiate others before him, in his presence.

LJA TA04D (38:59)

किं तु तूष्णींस्थितिर्यद्वा कृत्यं तदनुवर्तनम् ।

kiṁ tu tūṣṇīṁsthitiryadvā kṛtyaṁ tadanuvartanam /
(not recited)

Kiṁ tu tūṣṇīṁsthitir, this is the only conclusion or substance [the *mukta-śiva*] should know: *tūṣṇīṁ sthitir*, he must keep quiet. If the *anādisiddha-śiva* has ordered for rains, and it is raining, this *mukta-śiva* has no right to interfere in this action of the *anādisiddha-śiva*. What he has to do is only to keep quiet when it is raining. [This example] is just to make you understand. *Kiṁ tu tūṣṇīṁ sthitir. Yadvā kṛtyaṁ tadanuvartana*, if he does not remain like that, if he does not want to remain quiet, *kṛtyaṁ tat anuvartanam*, then he must say that, "This was my desire also, this rainfall was my desire also." That is *kṛtyam tad anuvartanam.*

SCHOLAR: Either he be quiet or he move with him (laughs).

SWAMIJI: Yes (laughs). Either he should remain quiet or he should move with him. In the same way, before the *sāṁsiddhika jñāni*, the *āhṛtajñāni* must remain quiet or move with the *sāṁsiddhika jñāni*.

LJA TA04D (40:32)

यस्त्वकल्पितरूपोऽपि संवादद्दढताकृते ॥७६॥
अन्यतो लब्धसंस्कारः स साक्षाद्भैरवो गुरुः ।

yastvakalpitarūpo'pi saṁvādadṛḍhatākṛte //76//
anyato labdhasaṁskāraḥ sa sākṣādbhairavo guruḥ /

Now he explains the way in which he was treading – the author, Abhinavagupta.

Yastu akalpita rūpo'pi, Abhinavagupta says, that master who is already an *akalpita*, whose rise of God consciousness has come all of sudden without depending on masters or *śāstras*, but *saṁvāda dṛḍhatā kṛte*, just to make it more firm, *anyato labdha saṁskāra*, he is initiated by other masters also at the same time.

SCHOLAR: *Saṁvādadṛḍhatākṛte*, make it firmer through confirmation.

SWAMIJI: Confirmation, yes. *Anyato labdha saṁskāra* (*anyato* means, *śāstrataḥ gurutaśca*), he gets initiated by masters, other masters also, and *śāstras* also. He reads *śāstras*. *Sa sākṣāt bhairavo guruḥ*, there is no difference, he is already an *akalpita*; *sa sākṣāt bhairavo*, he becomes absolute Bhairava. So this was the position of Abhinavagupta.

SCHOLAR: He says that through going to many masters as he did, it is possible to attain complete fullness of understanding, complete fullness of awareness in all departments of Śaivism.

SWAMIJI: Yes. But at the same time he said:

धन्यस्तु ज्ञानवान एको ज्ञानार्थी लभते गुरुम्

dhanyastu jñānavāna eko jñānārthī labhate gurum /[104]

That fortunate person, fortunate disciple, attains a complete master, only one, who [removes] all his doubts.[105]

SCHOLAR: Abhinavagupta didn't have such a master who cleared everything.

---

104. Swamiji quotes *Tantrāloka* 13.342 which reads: *dhanyastu pūrṇavijñānaṁ jñānārthī labhate gurum.*

105. "That person who is most fortunate, he reaches at the feet of a *siddha* yogi who is complete with all-around knowledge." Ibid.

SWAMIJI: No. Abhinavagupta had so many masters, numberless masters. He said, "I am just like a bee. The disciple must remain just like a bee and he must suck the nectar from numberless masters and make himself filled with knowledge all-around." This was his way of thinking – of Abhinavagupta.

Yastu akalpita rūpo'pi, that person who is already an *akalpita*, but *saṁvādadṛdhatākṛte*, just to make his experience of that God consciousness confirmed, absolutely confirmed, and is initiated, gets initiation from masters and *śāstra*s, he becomes Bhairava completely. Because... another *śloka*:

LJA TA04D (43:28)

यतः शास्त्रक्रमात्तज्ज्ञगुरुप्रज्ञानुशीलनात् ॥७७॥
आत्मप्रत्ययितं ज्ञानं पूर्णत्वाद्भैरवायते ।

yataḥ śāstrakramāttajjña-guruprajñānuśīlanāt //77//
ātmapratyayitaṁ jñānaṁ pūrṇatvādbhairavāyate /

Because *śāstra kramāt*, by the successive way of *śāstra*s, understanding *śāstra*s, and *tad jña guru-prajñānu-śīlanāt*, and by going on or practicing the ways of perfect masters (*tad jña guru prajñā anuśīlanāt*, practicing the knowledge of fully-informed masters), and *ātma pratyayitam*, and at the same time, *ātma pratyayitam*, getting confirmation by your own experience...

SCHOLAR: *Ātmabhāvanāta*.

SWAMIJI: ... (*ātmabhāvanāta*), and that knowledge, because of its fullness, carries you to the real state of Bhairava.

SCHOLAR: That knowledge becomes the state of Bhairava – *bhairavāyate*.

SWAMIJI: *Bhairavāyate, bhairava vat ācarati*.

SCHOLAR: *Caitanyamātma*.[106]

---

106. "Supreme consciousness is the reality of everything." *Shiva Sutras – The Supreme Awakening*, Swami Lakshmanjoo, ed. John Hughes (Lakshmanjoo

SWAMIJI: Yes.

LJA TA04D (44:35)

तेन श्रीकिरणोक्तं यद्गुरुतः शास्त्रतः स्वतः ॥७८॥
त्रिप्रत्ययमिदं ज्ञानमिति यच्च निशाटने ।

tena śrīkiraṇoktaṁ yad-gurutaḥ śāstrataḥ svataḥ //78//
tripratyayamidaṁ jñānam-iti yacca niśāṭane /

Now he has left the classes of these masters. He has explained the *sāṁsiddhika jñānī* (that is, the *akalpita* guru), and *akalpita kalpaka*, and *kalpita*, and *kalpita akalpita*. These four sections of masters he has already explained. Now he puts the importance on these triple knowledge, threefold knowledge, that is, knowledge from the master, knowledge from *śāstra*, and knowledge from your own experience. He quotes the *Kiraṇa Śāstra* here for that.

SCHOLAR: This is a *bheda śāstra* (dualistic scripture).

SWAMIJI: *Bheda śāstra. Tena śrīkiraṇoktaṁ yat*, it is already said, related, explained, in the *Kiraṇa Tantra*, [that] *gurutaḥ śāstrataḥ svataḥ*, by your master, by *śāstra*s, and by your own experience, *tripratyayamidaṁ jñānam*, this knowledge of God consciousness is threefold, *tripratyayam*, has threefold understandings – *tripratyayam.*

SCHOLAR: Three means of knowledge.

SWAMIJI: Three means of knowledge. And it is also said in the *Niśāṭana Tantra* (the *Niśācāra Tantra*).

LJA TA04D (46:06)

तत्सङ्घातविपर्यासविग्रहैर्भासते तथा ॥७९॥

tatsaṅghātaviparyāsa-vigrahairbhāsate tathā //79//

Academy, Los Angeles, 2002), chapter 1, verse 1.

And that knowledge is revealed to a person by *saṅghāta* and *viparyāsa*.[107] *Saṁghaṭṭa* means, you need all the three, sometimes you need the aid of all the three: you need the aid of a master, you need the aid of *śāstra*s, and you need the aid of your own experience. Sometimes you need only two: the aid of a master and aid of your own experience. Sometimes you need only one: only the need of experience. But the need of experience is not excluded in any class!

SCHOLAR: It is the principal one.

SWAMIJI: Huh?

SCHOLAR: It is the first one.

SWAMIJI: It is the first one.

SCHOLAR: Like *śāmbhava*.

SWAMIJI: Yes, *śāmbhava*. Sometimes you need only your experience (that is *svataḥ jñāna*). Sometimes you need only two: *svataḥ* and *śāstra*. Sometimes you need all the three: *svataḥ* (your own experience), *śāstra*s, and a master also (the guidance of masters also).

LJA TA04D (47:25)

करणस्य विचित्रत्वाद्विचित्रामेव तां छिदम् ।
कर्तुं वासीं च टङ्कं च क्रकचं चापि गृह्णते ॥८०॥
तावच्च छेदनं ह्येकं तथैवाद्याभिसन्धितः ।

karaṇasya vicitratvād-vicitrāmeva tāṁ chidam /
kartuṁ vāsīṁ ca ṭaṅkaṁ ca krakacaṁ cāpi gṛhṇate //80//
tāvacca chedanaṁ hyekaṁ tathaivādyābhisandhitaḥ /
(not recited)

Karaṇasya vicitratvāt...why these three, then? Why not only one? Why not, if one can lead to you to the real goal, why to depend on the other two? He says, *karaṇasya vicitratvāt*, for instance, the means are various. For instance, you need to cut the trunk of the tree, you have

107. Lit., to combine (*saṅghāta*) or to separate (*viparyāsa*).

to cut the trunk of the tree at the root, [so] you need a hatchet, first you need a hatchet, [and] where a hatchet does not reach, you need a saw, [and] where a saw does not reach, you need some other tools. *Karaṇasya vicitratvāt*, and that *karaṇa* is *vicitra*, so the means are various, but *chedanam ekaṁ*, the cutting, the meant, is only one. What is the meant?

SCHOLAR: Cutting.

SWAMIJI: Cutting the trunk of the tree is only one, one act, and for that one act, to fulfill that one act, you have to use so many means. *Vicitrāmeva tāṁ chidam kartuṁ*, sometimes you need an axe, sometimes you need a saw, [sometimes you need] a *vāsī* (an adze). There are so many means needed there, *tāvat chedanaṁ hyekam*, but the cutting, the act of cutting, is only one. *Tathaivādyābhisandhitaḥ*, in the same way, for realizing God consciousness, you need all the three; sometimes you need your own experience, sometimes you need to ask your master about your own experience, sometimes you need to confirm your experience and the sayings of your master in books also, and then it is confirmed very well. Because whatever you have experienced, the same thing is told to you by your master, but still if you are not satisfied, and when you see the same thing in books also, then your knowledge is confirmed totally and you believe that, "Absolutely I am correct. My knowledge is absolutely correct."

SCHOLAR: Because the order is *gurutaḥ-śāśtrataḥ-svataḥ*, why is it not the case that you would seek confirmation of your own experience in *śāstra*, and then from *śāstra* in your master, if that is the order? It is not *śāśtrataḥ-gurutaḥ-svataḥ*, it is *gurutaḥ-śāstrataḥ-svataḥ*.

SWAMIJI: Because the case is always inferior. In each and every individual, the case is inferior.

SCHOLAR: Case?

SWAMIJI: The case of ignorance. The case of removing ignorance is an inferior way, so he has to go to a master first, and then the master will guide him and select a *śāstra* for him, which *śāstra* he should read, and then by that *śāstra* he will come to his own experience. And when once he has got confirmation, and when he has got experience, then he will rise again with the same level [of confirmation]–he will see if that experience is quoted in the *śāstra*s, and he will see if that experience is said by his masters also, then it is confirmed. It is vice versa: he has to travel first from a master, to the *śāstra*s, and [then] to

[his] own experience, and then travel again from [his] own experience, to the *śāstras*, and the master. This is the way of our thinking.

SCHOLAR: So a master is one who has realized the complete unity of those three.

SWAMIJI: Yes, yes, he must be an absolute master. He must not be just a hypocrite master. You have to find out first a master, if he is a real master.

SCHOLAR: Not just go to any master who says he is a master and looks like a master and has disciples, …

SWAMIJI: No, no.

SCHOLAR: … and do *prāṇaṁ* (obeisance) because you do *prāṇaṁ* to such people.

SWAMIJI: Or has so much gathering also of people and you will be impressed. No, that is not…that won't do.

SCHOLAR: Has a big reputation, has long hair and a beard, and quotes the *Upaniṣads*.

SWAMIJI: No, that won't do. Not that *tripuṇḍra*.[108] You must find out the reality in the master.

JOHN: He may have so many disciples [or] he may have no disciples.

SWAMIJI: He may not have one disciple. He may be living as a householder. But if he is a real master, he will guide you.

LJA TA04D (52:13)

इत्थमेव मितौ वाच्यं करणस्य स्वकं वपुः ॥८१॥

itthameva mitau vācyaṁ karaṇasya svakaṁ vapuḥ //81//

So, in this way, this is the way where *mitau*, for your understanding (*mitau; miti prāptyartham–naimittiki saptamī*[109]),…

SCHOLAR: In order to attain knowledge.

SWAMIJI: … to attain the knowledge of God consciousness, for attaining the knowledge of God consciousness, this is the way for

108. A triple sectarial mark consisting of 3 lines or marks on the forehead.

109. Seventh case, or locative, in Sanskrit grammar.

attaining the knowledge of God consciousness: *karaṇasya svakam vapuḥ*, should be adopted, the *svarūpa* (the formation) of *karaṇa*, the formation of…

SCHOLAR: Instrument.

SWAMIJI: … instrument, the formation of the means, is to be explained – the formation of the means. How many are these means here?

DENISE: Three?

SWAMIJI: Yes. And it is for *mitau*, for achieving the real knowledge of God consciousness – for achieving the real knowledge of God consciousness.

LJA TA04D (53:33)

न स्वतन्त्रं स्वतो मानं कुर्यादधिगमं हठात् ।

na svatantraṁ svato mānaṁ kuryādadhigamaṁ haṭhāt /

This *māna* (this *śāstra* or this master) is not *svatantra* (independent), it is dependent on your own experience. When your experience, your inner experience, believes that your master has told you the exact thing, then you should believe in the words of your master. When your *śāstra*s have told you according to your experience, then you should believe those *śāstra*s.

DENISE: If it is not according to your experience, you don't believe.

SWAMIJI: Huh?

DENISE: If it is not according to your experience…?

SWAMIJI: You should not believe [them], you should not believe [them] in any case, because *svatantram svato mānam*, this *māna* (*māna* means, *śāstra* and guru), *śāstra* and the guru are not independent, that independently they will thrust [knowledge] in your experience. This [knowledge] must be digested in your experience. If it is not digested in your experience, there is still the need of a master, there is still the need of *śāstra*, some other *śāstra*. If not that [master, then] some other master; if not that [*śāstra*, then] some other *śāstra*.

LJA TA04D (54:43) end

LJA TA04E (00:00) start

प्रमात्राश्वासपर्यन्तो यतोऽधिगम उच्यते ॥८२॥

pramātrāśvāsaparyanto yato'dhigama ucyate //82//
(not recited)

True knowledge, true knowledge of your God consciousness is said to be *pramātra āśvāsaparyanto*, when you are satisfied, when you are satisfied with your master (inaudible). In our way of thinking, although the individual is ignorant, he is absolutely ignorant, he does not know what to do, he does not know how to act, he does not know the way of practice, he does not know anything, so he is depending upon masters, but in the background of his consciousness, in the background of his consciousness he is one with Lord Śiva! So, that Lord Śiva must accept the sayings of the master. That Lord Śiva, in the background of his consciousness, must accept the sayings of *śāstra*s. If that does not get digested in his consciousness, in his sub-consciousness, [then] *śāstra*s have no value and that master has no value. You have to find out another master and you have to find out another *śāstra* which will suit your experience.

SCHOLAR: Reflect awareness.

SWAMIJI: Yes. So *pramātra āśvāsa paryantaḥ*, [as long as] the *pramātā* (the individual) is not satisfied with the answer or with the way of initiation from masters, that *adhigama* (acquisition) won't take place, that knowledge of God consciousness will never take place.

LJA TA04E (01:38)

आश्वासश्च विचित्रोऽसौ शक्तिपातवशात्तथा ।

āśvāsaśca vicitro'sau śaktipātavaśāttathā /

Āśvāsaśca vicitro'sau, and that *āśvāsa*, that satisfaction, that mode of getting digested in …

SCHOLAR: Conviction.

SWAMIJI: … the conviction, is also variously moving; the way of convictions move variously because of *śaktipāta*.

SCHOLAR: The degree of grace.

SWAMIJI: Because when you experience, for instance, you experience, you go in *samādhi*–for instance, for the time being, you go in *samādhi*–and experience various sounds, various music, and you ask your master [about them]. If the master is not to the point, he will tell you, "You are on the wrong path because these are only obstacles in the way that you experience this music and all that–divine music, and divine taste, divine touch, divine *rasa* (taste)." So it means your master is not complete. When you have got a complete master, he will tell you, "Yes, this is on the path. You are right, this experience comes on the path. Go on, go on, and you will find some more experiences." He is the real master. So, *āśvāśca vicitro'sau śaktipātavaśat*, according to the grace of Lord Śiva, this satisfaction moves in the field of individual consciousness, in the field of the consciousness of the disciple. So, when he has not experienced *cidānanda*[110], the master will tell him, "No, you are on the wrong path, you must experience *cidānanda*, you must not experience the taste. The divine taste is all humbug." So how can you believe in the word [of that master]? You are experiencing that taste, you are experiencing that *rasa* of *amṛta* (nectar), that juice which you taste in your *samādhi*. So, he must be a real master who guides you, and he will come to this conclusion that you are on the first path, you have reached the first step of yoga, and the next step is to be achieved in the future, and the third is to achieved after that. That thing your master must know. If he just destroys your experience by saying that, "You are on the wrong path", what will you think? You will think, "This experience was false. How do I experience this then?"

JOHN: That's what happens, though. People have these experiences, they go to some master or some person, …

SWAMIJI: They say, "No, you are wrong."

JOHN: … and they ask, and he says, "No, you are wrong", and then they get confused, and they stop their practice, or do some other…

SWAMIJI: Yes. So:

110. The bliss (*ānanda*) of God consciousness (*cit*).

LJA TA04E (05:10)

प्रमितेऽपि प्रमाणानामवकाशोऽस्त्यतः स्फुटः ॥८३॥

pramite'pi pramāṇānām-avakāśo'styataḥ sphuṭaḥ //83//

Although you have realized, there is yet more to be realized. Although you have once realized something, you have to realize more. You have to realize more again and again, again and again, until you become complete like Lord Śiva.

SCHOLAR: Like you look at some object and you recognize it, but also you can see its detail and go on and on and on.

SWAMIJI: Yes, yes. Because when you see specks (eye-glasses), I see, at the first moment, I see it has got a black color and white color, that is all. And afterwards I come to this conclusion when I go on seeing it again and again and again, I see some more things appearing in this very object. Details come afterwards.

SCHOLAR: So this is why there is a degree of conviction mentioned here in accordance with the intensity of grace.

SWAMIJI: *Pramite api pramāṇānām avakāśostyataḥ sphuṭaḥ*, so there is more room again and again, if you have already experienced the reality of Lord Śiva, there is yet to be experienced more and more.

SCHOLAR: So he is attacking the Buddhist's epistemology here.

SWAMIJI: Yes. Now he gives you a reference of sex:

LJA TA04E (06:32)

दृष्ट्वा दृष्ट्वा समाश्लिष्य चिरं सञ्चर्व्य चेतसा ।
प्रियां यैः परितुष्येत किं ब्रूमः किल तान्प्रति ॥८४॥

dṛṣṭvā dṛṣṭvā samāśliṣya ciraṁ sañcarvya cetasā /
priyāṁ yaiḥ parituṣyeta kiṁ brūmaḥ kila tānprati //84//

Dṛṣṭvā dṛṣṭvā, first you look at the body of a lady, well-dressed, good-looking, good-featured, *dṛṣṭvā dṛṣṭvā*, then you [feel the] need

[for] embracing her. If you had already experienced the reality of that lady, where was the need of embracing her? So there is yet to be understood something more. Although you have understood something, but there is more to be understood in the next moment. You first see that lady and then you embrace that lady, then *ciraṁ sañcarvya cetasā*, then you kiss her, then you embrace her, then you get more firm contact with her. Why? If you have embraced her and got satisfaction, why to get more contact?

DENISE: Because you want more satisfaction.

SWAMIJI: Huh?

DENISE: Because you want more satisfaction.

SWAMIJI: So you [have] more satisfaction. *Priyāṁ yaiḥ paritușyeta*, those people who do this kind of action with their beloveds, *kiṁ brūmaḥ kila tānprati*, what is the answer for those persons, those persons who get satisfaction after every moment, after every further moment, more satisfaction, not only by seeing, not only by embracing, not only by kissing, not only by the sexual act, but something more? He wants to undress her, he wants to sleep with her for the whole night, and so on. He gets some satisfaction afterwards in the end. So there is [the fact that], although you have experienced something in God consciousness of God consciousness, there is yet to be experienced something more. Something more is to be experienced. This is the way of Abhinavagupta to make you confirm by these references.

LJA TA04E (09:03)

इत्थं च मानसम्प्लुत्यामपि नाधिगते गतिः ।
न व्यर्थता नानवस्था नान्योन्याश्रयतापि च ॥८५॥

itthaṁ ca mānasamplutyām-api nādhigate gatiḥ /
na vyarthatā nānavasthā nānyonyāśrayatāpi ca //85//

This way, *māna samplutyām api*, if you are flooded with repeated initiations and repeated knowledge of *śāstras*–you have to get flooded with repeated knowledge of *śāstras* and repeated modes of initiation from masters–*nādhigate gatiḥ*, this is not *adhigate gatiḥ* (useless).

SCHOLAR: He is not trying to understand what is already been understood.

SWAMIJI: No. You are understanding something more! At first you have understood something, something very important, and when repeatedly you get initiated again and again from your master, you experience something more. And in the end, something more, something more, something more is understood by-and-by. In each and every step you understand something more. If you go and realize the ways of the *śāstra*s, first you understand something, and afterwards if you again try to get more knowledge from *śāstra*s, you experience something more. And something more comes in each initiation, in each way of thinking of *śāstra*s. So it is not *adhigate*, it is not useless. Once you have realized, there is yet to be realized something more. Once you have realized, you have no right to say that, "I have realized, I am fully realized, I don't need any master now, I don't need reading scripts of *śāstra*s or anything else. I am full!" You can't say that. There is yet to be understood something more. Because take the example of that lady, of that person who finds something more by embracing her, by keeping her in his contact always. So, *na vyarthatā*, it is not *vyarthatā*, there is no *vyartha doṣa*. It is not *vyartha*. *Vyartha* means, useless.

SCHOLAR: From a Buddhists point of view, it is *vyartha*, because once the object is grasped, it's grasped, *bas*.

SWAMIJI: It is grasped, yes.

SCHOLAR: So he is saying it is not like that.

SWAMIJI: *Na anavasthā*, it is not *anavasthā*. *Anavasthā* means, ...

SCHOLAR: Infinite regress.

SWAMIJI: ... infinite regress, yes. There is not infinite regress. By an infinite way of getting more and more knowledge, you get more. *Na anyonyāśrayatā*, and there is *na anyonyāśraya doṣa*. These are three kinds of defects (*doṣa*s) in logic. One is *vyarthatā*. *Vyarthatā* means, e.g., I will ask you, "Are you going to Srinagar? You should take my lawn mower and have it repaired." You have understood, huh? Then [if] I will again tell you the same thing, it is *vyartha*, it is useless. If I again [tell] you the same thing, and again after half an hour I will tell you the same thing, "Please take this lawn mower and have it repaired in Srinagar", this is *vyartha*. But here it is not the case. Such is not the case here in realizing God consciousness. In realizing God consciousness, you realize more and more from teachers, from masters, and from *śāstras*. And *na anavasthā*, it is [not] *anavasthā*. *Anavasthā* is another defect in knowledge, in logic.

SCHOLAR: In epistemology.

SWAMIJI: And there is *anyonyāśraya*, mutual dependence.

JOHN: What was the second one?

SWAMIJI: That is *anavasthā*.

JOHN: *Anavasthā* means?

SWAMIJI: *Anavasthā* means, e.g., to know this book there must be some other book to understand this book. When you come to this conclusion that this book will make you understood this [other] book, for understanding this book you need another…

JOHN: Infinite regress.

SWAMIJI: … for that you need another [book, and] for that you need another [book]. This is *anavasthā*. So this is incorrect logic.

SCHOLAR: So the Buddhist says that this knowledge is not established because it always needs more.

SWAMIJI: Yes.

SCHOLAR: So that is his objection.

SWAMIJI: Yes.

JOHN: And the third one is what?

SWAMIJI: *Vyarthatā*, useless. First one is *arthatā*. *Anavasthā* is *anyonyāśraya*. *Anyonyāśraya* is, e.g., there is an egg. It is produced by?

SCHOLAR: Chicken.

SWAMIJI: Chicken. Chicken is produced by?

DENISE: Egg.

SWAMIJI: Egg is produced by?

DENISE: Chicken.

SWAMIJI: Chicken is produced by?

DENISE: Egg.

SWAMIJI: So it is *anavasthā*. It goes in a line without its end. So this kind of logic is *anavasthā*, it is incorrect.

ALEXIS: That's *anavasthā*, yes.

SWAMIJI: Yes, that is *anavasthā*.

JOHN: That's infinite regress.

SWAMIJI: Because there is no end to this.

ALEXIS: But the *anyonyāśrayatā* …

SWAMIJI: Huh?

SCHOLAR: The third *doṣa* is *anyonyāśrayatā*.

SWAMIJI: *Anyonyāśraya. Anyonyāśraya*, depending on each other. That is also incorrect, yes. *Bas*, now this is another subject. Now *yogāṅga anupayogitvam* will be explained on Saturday. *Yogāṅga anupayogitvam, yogāṅga*s are not needed, the limbs of Yoga are not needed in Śaivism. These three subjects are over, huh?

JOHN: *Vikalpa saṁskāra*?

SWAMIJI: *Vikalpa saṁskāra*, yes, this was the first.

JOHN: And *tarka*, second.

SWAMIJI: *Tarka*. And the definition of masters.

LJA TA04E (15:50)

Yogāṅga Anupayogitvam – Limbs of Yoga in Śaivism

Now, *yogāṅga anupayogitvam*, the limbs of Yoga bear no fruit in this system of ours. From Patañjali's point of view, there are eight limbs of Yoga. From our point of view, we have recognized only six limbs. In eight limbs, they include *yama* and *niyama*s also; *yama*, *niyam*, *āsana* (third), *prāṇāyām* (fourth), *pratyāhāra* (fifth), *dhāraṇā* (sixth), *dhyāna* (seventh), and *samādhi* (eighth). But here we start with *prāṇāyāma*. *Prāṇāyāma*, *dhyāna*, *pratyāhāra*, *dhāraṇā*, and *tarka*, and *samādhi*.

SCHOLAR: Is *dhyāna* before *pratyāhāra* or after *dhāraṇā*?

SWAMIJI: After *prāṇāyām* is *dhyāna*, and after *dhyāna* is *dhāraṇā*. Then–*prāṇāyāmastatha dhyānam pratyāhāra*–then is *pratyāhāra*, then is *dhāraṇā* after *pratyāhāra*, and then *tarka*, and then *samādhi*.

LJA TA04E (17:37)

एवं योगाङ्गमियति तर्क एव न चापरम् ।
अन्तरन्तः परामर्शपाटवातिशयाय सः ॥८६॥

evaṁ yogāṅgamiyati tarka eva na cāparam /
antarantaḥ parāmarśa-pāṭavātiśayāya saḥ //86//

So in this body of the *yogāṅga*s, the six limbs of Yoga, only *tarka*, the fifth limb, is recognized. *Iyati*, in these six classes, *yogāṅgam tarka eva*, only *tarka* is *yogāṅga*, the chief and predominant, the only *aṅga*, the only limb of Yoga–*tarka* (discrimination, discriminating transcendental logic). *Na cāparam*, other limbs are not recognized here, because that *tarka* is *antarantaḥ parāmarśa pāṭavātiśayāya saḥ*; *saḥ*, that *tarka*, is meant for revealing the innermost center of *parāmarśa*, the innermost center of *ahaṁ parāmarśa*.

SCHOLAR: Self-awareness.

SWAMIJI: *Ahaṁ parāmarśa* is revealed by *tarka*, by maintaining *tarka*.

LJA TA04E (19:03)

अहिंसा सत्यमस्तेयब्रह्मचर्यापरिग्रहाः ।
इति पञ्च यमाः साक्षात्संवित्तौ नोपयोगिनः ॥८७॥
तपः प्रभृतयो ये च नियमा यत्तथासनम् ।
प्राणायामाश्च ये सर्वमेतद्बाह्यविजृम्भितम् ॥८८॥

ahiṁsā satyamasteya-brahmacaryāparigrahāḥ /
iti pañca yamāḥ sākṣāt-saṁvittau nopayoginaḥ //87//
tapaḥ prabhṛtayo ye ca niyamā yattathāsanam /
prāṇāyāmāśca ye sarvam-etadbāhyavijṛmbhitam //88//

Ahiṁsā means, not to hurt anybody in action (deed) and thought. These are the five *yamas* (moral restraints) and the five *niyamas* (positive observances) as are recognized in the system of Patañjali. [The five *yamas* are]: *ahiṁsā*, *satya*, *asteya*, *brahmacarya*, and *aparigraha*. *Ahiṁsā* is not to hurt anybody in deed (action) or thought. *Satya*, you should use only truth in your speech, you should never tell lies – that is *satya*. *Asteya* is, you should not snatch anything from others – *asteya*. *Brahmacarya*, you should maintain *brahmacarya*.[111] And *aparigraha*, you should not collect so many things – that is *aparigraha*. These are the five *yamas*. And there are five *niyamas* also: *śauca*, *santoṣa*, *tapas*, *svādhyāya*, and *īśvara praṇidhāna*. *Śauca* means, purity in body and mind, to keep your mind and body pure, absolutely pure – that is *śauca*. *Santoṣa* is just to be contented [with] what you have. *Tapas* is penance. *Svādhyāya*, be absorbed in reading and understanding spiritual books. *Śauca*, *santoṣa*, *tapas*, *svādhyāya*, and *īśvara praṇidhāna*. *Īśvara praṇidhāna* means, attachment for the Lord. These are the five *niyamas*. These are also not added in these limbs of Yoga [in the Śaiva system].

---

111. Continence, chastity.

SCHOLAR: *Saṁvittau nopayoginaḥ.*

SWAMIJI: *Saṁvittau nopayoginaḥ sākṣāt.*

SCHOLAR: They obviously have no ...

SWAMIJI: They have, they help you, but indirectly, not directly. There is no direct help from these limbs.

SCHOLAR: In the matter of awareness–*saṁvittau.* As far as awareness is concerned–*saṁvit apekṣayā.*

SWAMIJI: *Saṁvittau*, yes, awareness, yes. And these *tapas*, etcetera, these *niyamas* including *āsana* also (*āsana* is not also included in the limbs of Yoga in our system), the five *niyamas* and the five *yamas*, and *āsana* is also excluded. *Prāṇāyāmāśca ye*, and *prāṇāyām*, etcetera, which are admitted in our limbs, in our yogic limbs ...*

Prāṇāyāmā, because it is plural, so you should take it for granted that it is *prāṇāyāma*, it is *dhyāna*, it is *pratyāhāra*, it is *dhāraṇā*, and it is *samādhi*... not *samādhi, dhāraṇā.*

*... *te sarvam etat bāhya vijṛmbhitam*, [these are] all the external way of maintaining the strength of yoga. [According to Śaivism], you can't maintain the strength of yoga by these limbs. Only there is one predominant limb of Yoga, that is, *tarka* (discrimination, discrimination between the individual and the Universal, the discriminating logic in your own self).

LJA TA04E (23:28)

श्रीमद्वीरावलौ चोक्तं बोधमात्रे शिवात्मके ।
चित्तप्रलयबन्धेन प्रलीने शशिभास्करे ॥८९॥

śrīmadvīrāvalau coktaṁ bodhamātre śivātmake /
cittapralayabandhena pralīne śaśibhāskare //89//
(not recited)

Śrīmadvīrāvalau coktaṁ, in the *Vīrāvala Tantra* also it is said–it is the next [verse]–*bodhamātre śivātmake*, when Śiva, which is only *bodha* (absolute awareness of God consciousness), and there, when *citta pralaya bandhena*, when you adopt the *citta pralaya* way of contemplation, ...*

Citta pralaya, not *citta saṁbodha*, not *citta viśrānti*. *Citta viśrānti* and *citta saṁbodha* are discarded. Only *citta pralaya*. I think you know *citta pralaya*.

*... *citta pralaya bandhena pralīna śaśibhāskare*, when *śaśibhāskare*, the moon and sun are gone ("the moon and the sun are gone" means, *prāṇa* and *apāna*, breathing in and out, has stopped), *citta pralaya bandhena* ...*

SCHOLAR: Can you explain *citta pralaya bandhena* again? Can you explain that again for everyone?

SWAMIJI: But it is already explained in the end of [the discussion of] *śāmbhavopāya* when explaining the three ways of *visarga*.[112] One is *parā visarga* ('*ā*'), one is *parāparā visarga* ('*aḥ*'), and the other is *aparā visarga* ('*ha*'). In *parā visarga*, he has explained *citta pralaya*. In *parāparā visarga*, he has explained *citta saṁbodha*. In *aparā visarga*, he has explained *citta viśrānti*. *Citta viśrānti* is concerned with *āṇavopāya*, *citta saṁbodha* is in concerned with *śāktopāya*, and *citta pralaya* is concerned with *śāmbhavopāya*. *Citta pralaya* is the only direct way to get entry in God consciousness without any hindrance.

SCHOLAR: Complete melting away of limited awareness.

SWAMIJI: Yes.

*... *citta pralaya bandhena*, and there what you feel, first comes the stoppage of breath, breathing in and out is finished, there is no breathing, breathing does not exist. And then what happens?

LJA TA04E (25:42)

प्राप्ते च द्वादशे भागे जीवादित्ये स्वबोधके ।
मोक्षः स एव कथितः प्राणायामो निरर्थकः ॥९०॥

prāpte ca dvādaśe bhāge jīvāditye svabodhake /
mokṣaḥ sa eva kathitaḥ prāṇāyāmo nirarthakaḥ //90//
(not recited)

---

112. See *Light on Tantra in Kashmir Shaivism, Tantrāloka, Vol. Two*, pp. 211–220.

Prāpte ca dvādaśe bhāge, you get entry in *brahmarandhra*. *Dvādaśa bhāge* means, the place of *dvādaśānta* (inner *dvādaśānta*, not the outer *dvādaśānta*).

There are two *dvādaśānta*s: one is the outer *dvādaśānta* and one is the inner *dvādaśānta* (on the skull, on the *brahmarandhra*).[113] That is when this breath gets entry in *suṣumnā* and then it rushes straight up to *dvādaśānta* by maintaining the *citta pralaya* way of contemplation.

Jīvāditye svabodhake, when *jīva* (the individual) becomes shining, *jīva āditye*, just like the sun, so the state of *jīva* does not exist, *jīva* melts in universal Being. And it is just *svabodhake*, your own God consciousness, your own *bodha*, your own awareness. *Mokṣa sa eva kathitaḥ*, that is real *mokṣa*, that is real liberation. *Prāṇāyāmo nirarthakaḥ*, these *prāṇāyāma*s, etcetera, all these limbs are *nirarthaka*, useless, they have no value.

LJA TA04E (27:07)

प्राणायामो न कर्तव्यः शरीरं येन पीड्यते ।
रहस्यं वेत्ति यो यत्र स मुक्तः स च मोचकः ॥९१॥

prāṇāyāmo na kartavyaḥ śarīram yena pīḍyate /
rahasyaṁ vetti yo yatra sa muktaḥ sa ca mocakaḥ //91//
(not recited)

Prāṇāyāmo na kartavyaḥ, you should never adopt *prāṇāyāma*. The *prāṇāyāma* way is absolutely wrong. *Śarīram yena pīḍyate*, you

113. *Dvādaśānta* means, the end (*anta*) of twelve (*dvādaśa*) finger spaces. *Dvādaśānta* refers to the various centers in the body where the aspirant maintains awareness, i.e., heart, throat-pit, between the eyebrows, etcetera. Here, in this verse, the inner *dvādaśānta* is in *brahmarandhra*, and the outer *dvādaśānta* is twelve finger spaces directly above the head. For a detailed explanation of *dvādaśānta*, see *Vijñāna Bhairava–The Manual for Self-Realization* (with original audio), Swami Lakshmanjoo, ed. John Hughes (Lakshmanjoo Academy, Los Angeles, 2007), verse 29.

only get fatigue in the body by doing *prāṇāyāma*, you are exhausted. *Rahasyaṁ vetti yo yatra*, this secret position of God consciousness, wherever is found this secret state of God consciousness, *sa muktaḥ*, he becomes liberated, *sa ca mocakaḥ*, and he liberates others (*mocaka*, liberates others). *Yaḥ*, anybody, *yatra*, in that state, in which state that secret is realized, *sa muktaḥ*, he is liberated, *sa ca mocakaḥ*, he liberates others.

LJA TA04E (28:11)

शशिभास्करसंयोगाज्जीवस्तन्मात्रतां व्रजेत् ।
अत्र ब्रह्मादयो लीना मुक्तये मोक्षकाङ्क्षिणः ॥

śaśibhāskarasaṁyogāj-jīvastanmātratāṁ vrajet /
atra brahmādayo līnā muktaye mokṣakāṅkṣiṇaḥ //[114]

When *śaśibhāskara*, this breath, the in-going breath and the out-coming breath, has stopped (*śaśibhāskare saṁyogāt*), *jīvaḥ tan mātratām vrajet*, the *jīva* becomes universal, the individual gets entry in its universal state. *Atra brahmādayo līnā*, here, all these great beings (Brahmā, Viṣṇu, and Rūdra) are craving for that state. *Muktaye mokṣakāṅkṣinaḥ*, and those who wish to get liberation (*mumukṣuḥ*), they also are craving for this stage.

It is the negation of *prāṇāyāma*. Now, he negates *pratyāhāra* also, and then *dhāraṇā*, etcetera.

SCHOLAR: So the order is, in fact, *prāṇāyāma-pratyāhāra-dhāraṇā-dhyāna-samādhi*.

SWAMIJI: *Pāṭha kramāt artha kramo balīyāt*. The *pāṭha krama*[115] in the *Mālinīvijaya Tantra* is not this. The *pāṭha krama* in the *Mālinīvijaya Tantra* is:

114. Jayaratha references his own reference of a verse given in his commentary for *Tantrāloka* 29.275cd-276ab.

115. The successive (*krama*) listing (*pāṭha*) of the yogic limbs.

LJA TA04E (29:39)

प्राणायामस्तथा ध्यानं प्रत्याहारोऽथ धारणा ।
तर्कश्चैव समाधिश्च षडङ्गो योग उच्यते ॥

prāṇāyāmastathā dhyānaṁ pratyāhāro'tha dhāraṇā /
tarkaścaiva samādhiśca ṣaḍaṅgo yoga ucyate //[116]
(Abhinavagupta's *Tantrasāra*, chapter 4)

Where is that?
SCHOLAR: He doesn't seem to quote it here in the commentary.
SWAMIJI: It must be (gap in recording).

LJA TA04E (29:57)

Now he defines *pratyāhāra*:

प्रत्याहारश्च नामायमर्थेभ्योऽक्षधियां हि यः ।
अनिबद्धस्य बन्धस्य तदन्तः किल कीलनम् ॥९२॥

pratyāhāraśca nāmāyam-arthebhyo'kṣadhiyāṁ hi yaḥ /
anibaddhasya bandhasya tadantaḥ kila kīlanam //92//

Pratyāhāra, what is *pratyāhāra*? What is the meaning of *pratyāhāra* in the real sense? The meaning of *pratyāhāra* is, *arthebhyo akṣadhiyām hi yaḥ, anibaddhasya bandhasya tadantaḥ kila kīlanam, arthebhyaḥ*, from objects, from the objective world, you have to withdraw the senses, your senses, and your intellect; to withdraw your senses and intellect

116. The reading of the succession of the yogic limbs as described in the *Mālinīvijaya Tantra* is thus: *prāṇāyāma-dhyāna-pratyāhāra-dhāraṇā-tarka-samādhi*. This verse was quoted by Jayaratha in his commentary for verse 16 of this chapter.

from objective senses, this is withdrawing. Withdrawing is called *pratyāhāra*. But withdrawing from what? Withdrawing and binding it at one point. Binding what? Sentencing your mind and senses on one point. That is *pratyāhāra*. Withdrawing inside and keeping [your awareness] within, within your own point. *Anibaddhasya bandhasya*, but what is the use of putting that [awareness] in your own self? Is not God consciousness available in the outside world also? God consciousness is available everywhere, because it is said:

LJA TA04E (31:34)

संसारोऽस्ति न तत्त्वतस्तनुभृतां बन्धस्य वार्तैव का ।

saṁsāro'sti na tattvatastanubhṛtāṁ bandhasya vārtaiva kā /[117]

There is no *saṁsāra* (there is no wheel of repeated births and deaths), it is only the glory of Lord Śiva. When you are born, it is the glory of Lord Śiva. When you die, it is the glory of Lord Śiva. When you live, it is the glory of Lord Śiva. Everywhere there is the glory of Lord Śiva. And to find out the glory [of Lord Śiva] only [by] withdrawing all these things, that is not the real position of the glory of Lord Śiva. So *pratyāhāra* is useless. Wherefrom you have to withdraw and to which place you have to get establishment? That means, the reality of God consciousness is available only at one point, at one particular point. That is not true. That is the meaning of *anibaddhasya bandhasya*.

SCHOLAR: The literal meaning is that he fixes/nails within his own awareness, bondage, which was never tied in the first place.

SWAMIJI: It was never tied. It was already liberated everywhere. And what is *dhāraṇā*?

---

117. Jayaratha quotes verse 2 of Abhinavagupta's *Anuttarāṣṭaka* (*Eight Verses on the Supreme Reality–Anuttara*). For the full translation of this hymn, see *Light on Tantra in Kashmir Shaivism, Tantrāloka, Vol. Two*, Appendix 5, p. 449.

LJA TA04E (32:50)

चित्तस्य विषये क्वापि बन्धनं धारणात्मकम् ।
तत्सदृग्ज्ञानसंतानो ध्यानमस्तमिता परम् ॥९३॥

cittasya viṣaye kvāpi bandhanaṁ dhāraṇātmakam /93a

Dhāraṇā means, to establish your mind at one point. For instance, I gaze on Stephanie's face, *bas*, nowhere else. That is *dhāraṇā*. Just to establish and fix your mind…

JOHN: *Ekagraha*[118], kind of.

SWAMIJI: Yes.

…to one point, that is *dhāraṇā*.

तत्सदृग्ज्ञानसन्तानो ध्यानमस्तमिता परम् ॥९३॥

tatsadṛgjñānasantāno dhyānamastamitā param //93//

Tat sadṛg jñāna santāna, and to maintain such awareness on one point is *dhyāna*; to maintain awareness of that *dhāraṇā* on one point. For instance, I put my gaze on these specks, only specks, and then–or [on] Denise–I put my gaze and mind and my senses on that point, and afterwards…this is *dhāraṇā*. And what is *dhyāna*? *Dhyāna* is, *tat sadṛgjñāna santāna*, to produce, just like as you have been explained in *vikalpa saṁskāra*, to produce the same, the similar thought again and again on that very point.

JOHN: Refreshing of awareness on that.

SWAMIJI: Yes. Refreshing that similar thought, similar consciousness, on that very point, is *dhyāna*, because it is *param astamitā*, when you are absolutely withdrawn from all other things, only your consciousness is attached to that one point.

---

118. The fourth among the five yogic states.

JOHN: So there is a continuity here, then, between *dhāraṇā* and *dhyāna*.

SWAMIJI: Yes. *Dhāraṇā* is only one-pointedness. *Dhyāna* is just to maintain that one-pointedness by adjusting similar thoughts of that one point again and again in continuity. And it is *param astamitā*; *param astamitā* means, absolutely *astamitā*, when you are unaware of other [points and are aware of]…

JOHN: Only that point.

SWAMIJI: … only that point. Now it is *samādhi*:

LJA TA04E (35:32)

यदा तु ज्ञेयतादात्म्यमेव संविदि जायते ।
ग्राह्यग्रहणताद्वैतशून्यतेयं समाहितिः ॥९४॥

yadā tu jñeyatādātmyam-eva saṁvidi jāyate /
grāhyagrahaṇatādvaita-śūnyateyaṁ samāhitiḥ //94//

When your awareness becomes one with that objective point by maintaining *dhāraṇā* and *dhyāna* on that (*jñeya tādātmyam eva saṁvidi jāyate*, in your consciousness, only that point remains shining in your awareness), and *grāhya grahaṇatā dvaita śūnyata*, it is *dvaita śūnyata*[119], *grāhya* and *grahaṇa* do not remain.

SCHOLAR: The object and the means of knowledge.

SWAMIJI: The object and the means. The object means, that point on which you are fixing *dhāraṇā* and *dhyāna*. The means are the way by which you are maintaining that [awareness]. And *grahaṇa* and *grāhya* vanish altogether and there is only that consciousness of that point.

SCHOLAR: But that point is…it's consciousness of that point?

SWAMIJI: No, that point does not…no. It is *svarūpa śūnyam eva samādhi*, *svarūpa śūnyam eva*.

SCHOLAR: As though having no own being, no content.

---

119. Lit., the void (*śūnyata*) of duality (*dvaita*).

SWAMIJI: The perception that, "I am meditating on it, I am putting *dhāraṇā* and *dhyāna* on it", that perception vanishes.

SCHOLAR: Is this *apavedya pralayākala*?

SWAMIJI: This is *samādhi*. This is *apavedya pralayākala*. This can be *savedya pralayākala* also.

SCHOLAR: If it is *ānanda* (bliss), then it will be *savedya pralayākala*.

SWAMIJI: *Savedya pralayākala*.

SCHOLAR: But it is not higher than that.

SWAMIJI: It is never higher than that.

SCHOLAR: So there's *nopayogitaḥ*, …

SWAMIJI: No (affirmative).

SCHOLAR: … no use here of that.

SWAMIJI: This is *samāhitiḥ*. *Samāhitiḥ* means, *samādhi*.

LJA TA04E (37:28)

तदेषा धारणाध्यानसमाधित्रितयी पराम् ।
संविदं प्रति नो कञ्चिदुपयोगं समश्नुते ॥९५॥

tadeṣā dhāraṇādhyāna-samādhitritayī parām /
saṁvidaṁ prati no kañcid-upayogaṁ samaśnute //95//

So this way, thus, these triple states of *dhāraṇā*, *dhyāna*, and *samādhi*, this triple state, *saṁvidaṁ prati no kañcid upayogaṁ samaśnute*, they are not fruitful, they don't help in attaining the state of *saṁvit*, the state of God consciousness.

योगाङ्गता यमादेस्तु समाध्यन्तस्य वर्ण्यते ।
स्वपूर्वपूर्वोपायत्वादन्त्यतर्कोपयोगतः ॥९६॥

yogāṅgatā yamādestu samādhyantasya varṇyate /
svapūrvapūrvopāyatvād-antyatarkopayogataḥ //96//

But why these six limbs of Yoga are defined in our Śaivism, then? If there was no use of these limbs, why have they have been explained in our system? Only *tarka* ought to have been explained–only *tarka*. Why these six limbs? He says to that, for that the answer is, *yogāṅgatā yamādestu samādhyantasya varṇyate*, this *yogāṅgatā*, this being the limbs of Yoga, *yamadestu samādhyantasya*, beginning from *yama*, ending in *samādhi*, all these limbs of yogas are explained only *sva pūrva pūrva upāyātvāt*, because they become the means of their previous limbs. For the *yama*s, the *yama*s are the means to get entry in the *niyama*s; the *niyama*s becomes the means to get entry in *āsana*; *āsana* becomes the means to get entry in *pratyāhāra*, and so on–*svapūrva pūrva upāyatvāt. Antya tarka upayogataḥ*, and in the end, all these limbs are meant to get entry in *tarka*. *Tarka* is the final state and the supreme state of yoga.

LJA TA04E (40:10)

अन्तः संविदि रूढं हि तद्द्वारा प्राणदेहयोः ।
बुद्धौ वार्प्यं तदभ्यासान्नैष न्यायस्तु संविदि ॥९७॥

antaḥ saṁvidi rūḍhaṁ hi taddvārā prāṇadehayoḥ /
buddhau vārpyaṁ tadabhyāsān-naiṣa nyāyastu saṁvidi //97//

In your internal consciousness, what is already existing in your internal consciousness, these limbs are already existing in your internal consciousness, and *tad dvārā prāṇa dehayoḥ buddhau vārpyaṁ*, and what are already existing in your inner consciousness, and to find out that inner consciousness by those means, is it worthwhile? For instance, you are established in your inner consciousness–take for one minute that you are [practicing] a limb of Yoga to get entry in your inner consciousness–but this limb is already existing in that inner consciousness. Without that, it won't exist. That is what he says: *antaḥ saṁvidi rūḍham hi*, these [limbs] are established already in [your] inner consciousness, and to find out [your] inner consciousness by these means, is it worth[while]?

SCHOLAR: Possible.

SWAMIJI: It is not possible. On the contrary, [your] inner consciousness will make you realize these limbs. These limbs won't carry you to inner consciousness because they are existing, they are living in that inner consciousness. The inner consciousness is the life of all these limbs. And *tad dvārā*, by those means, *prāṇa dehayoḥ*, in *prāṇa* (breath), in *deha* (body), in *buddhi* (intellect), you are thrusting that inner consciousness. For instance, in *prāṇa*, by which means in *prāṇa*? By *prāṇāyāma*. In *deha*, by which means in *deha*? By *āsana*, by posture–*āsana*. And in *buddhi*, by which means? In *dhyāna*. By intellect, in *dhyāna*; in *deha*, in *āsana*; and in *prāṇa*, in *prāṇāyāma*. By *prāṇa* you maintain *prāṇāyāma* and get realization of God consciousness, and in *deha* you adopt *āsana*s and get entry in that God consciousness, and in *buddhi* (that is the intellect) you maintain, adopt this *dhyāna* and *dhāraṇā* and get entry in that God consciousness, but that God consciousness is the life of all these limbs! How can God consciousness be realized by these? So it is an incorrect process.

SCHOLAR: They are not the means of entry into God consciousness.

SWAMIJI: No (affirmative). They are already existing in God consciousness. *Naiṣa nyāyastu saṁvidi*, in God consciousness, it is not worthwhile to get the realization of God consciousness by the help of these means which are already existing in God consciousness. So it is an incorrect theory of getting entry in God consciousness. You will get entry in God consciousness by maintaining only *tarka*, the transcendental way of logic.

LJA TA04E (43:57)

अथ वास्मद्दृशिप्राणधीदेहादेरपि स्फुटम् ।
सर्वात्मकत्वात्तत्रस्थोऽप्यभ्यासोऽन्यव्यपोहनम् ॥९८॥

atha vāsmaddṛśi prāṇa-dhīdehāderapi sphuṭam /
sarvātmakatvāttatrastho'pyabhyāso'nyavyapohanam //98//

Or this is also possible from our point of view, not from other points [of view], I mean, from the points [of view] of other systems: In our system it is possible that we can realize God consciousness by maintaining, by adopting, and by treading on these yogic limbs. In our system only it is possible in some respect, because *asmaddṛśi*, in our system (*asmaddṛśi* means, in our way of thinking, in the Śaivite way), *prāṇa dhī dehāderapi sphuṭam*, *prāṇa* is already filled with God consciousness, the intellect (*dhī*) is also filled with God consciousness, and the body (*deha*) is also filled with God consciousness. Why not adopt the ways which are existing in *prāṇa*, the intellect, and the body also? By that also we'll get entry in God consciousness because they are not other than God consciousness. *Prāṇa* is also one with God consciousness, the intellect is also one with God consciousness, and the body is also one with God consciousness. As *prāṇa* is also one with God consciousness, so we can adopt *prāṇāyāma* and get entry in God consciousness. Because we don't believe *prāṇa* to be away from God consciousness as other schools of thought believe that *prāṇāyāma* is the means, the meant is God consciousness. We don't believe that. We mean, *prāṇa* is also God consciousness, and the means and the meant are one here in our system. So, we can adopt these means also in one way. In one way, it is also admitted, we can admit that. By *prāṇāyāma* we will get entry, by *dhī* (intellect, that is, *dhyāna* and *dhāraṇā*), and in *deha* (by *āsana*s also we can get entry in God consciousness), because they all reside in the field of God consciousness from our point of thinking, because *sarvātmakatvāt*, because *sarvam sarvātmakam*, everything rests in everything. *Tatrastho'pi abhyāsa anyavyapohanam*, so *abhyāsa* (discipline) could be admitted there also, [the observance of] which is *anavyapohanam*, which is negating the other opposite ways. For instance, *ahiṁsā*, not to hurt any living being by mind, body, and action. Hurting any being by mind, body, and by action would be rejected by maintaining not-hurting. That is *anyavyapohanam*, this [violence] is rejected.

SCHOLAR: Isn't it therefore limited?

SWAMIJI: *Hiṁsā* (violence) is rejected. *Hiṁsā* is rejected, but it can't be [said to be] limited because *hiṁsā* could be rejected, *ahiṁsā* could be owned, and *satya* (truthfullness) could be owned and *asatya* (false, lies, telling lies) could be rejected, [only] in our way of thinking.

SCHOLAR: Or vice versa?

SWAMIJI: Not vice versa.

SCHOLAR: Why not?

SWAMIJI: Because it is *abhyāsa*, it is *abhyāsa*s...you mean, [in terms of] *sarvātmakatvāt*? No...

SCHOLAR: From the point of view of awareness, what shadow does theft cast on awareness?

SWAMIJI: Shadow?

SCHOLAR: How can it limit awareness?

SWAMIJI: No, he says it is just [to] make you understood that *yama*, *niyama*, *āsana*, *prāṇāyāma*, all these limbs could be also adopted in our system – in our system. They are not fruitful, they don't give any help to us, but from the Śaiva point of view, they can help also.

SCHOLAR: From a higher point, from the *śāktopāya* point of view.

SWAMIJI: From a higher point also, they can help, but only in our system, not in other systems. In other systems, they don't help at all, they are only false. The procedure of those *yama*s and *niyama*s, all these limbs, is incorrect.[120] In our point [of view], it is correct, it can be correct, because, e.g., when I have maintained *ahiṁsā*, nobody has the right to tell me, "Why don't you do *hiṁsā*? Why don't you do *hiṁsā*?" I have adopted *ahiṁsā*, that is all, finished.

SCHOLAR: *Svātantrya.*

SWAMIJI: *Svātantryavāda.*[121]

LJA TA04E (49:32)

देह उत्प्लुतिसम्पात धर्मोज्जिगमिषारसात् ।
उत्प्लाव्यते तद्विपक्षपाताशङ्काव्यपोहनात् ॥९९॥

deha utplutisampāta-dharmojjigamiṣārasāt /
utplāvyate tadvipakṣa-pātāśaṅkāvyapohanāt //99//

He has said – the commentator:

120. Because of their mistaken belief in the duality of the means and the meant. This is another example of why *tarka* is given supreme importance in Kashmir Shaivism.

121. The Doctrine (*vāda*) of Freedom (*svātantrya*), which is another name for Kashmir Shaivism. See *Light on Tantra in Kashmir Shaivism, Tantrāloka, Vol. One*, Appendix 7, p. 387.

तत्र प्राणादावविस्थितोऽपि यमादीनामभ्यासः, अन्येषां भेदनिष्ठानामयमादिरूपाणां हिंसादीनामपोहनम्, एवं हि यथात्मनि हिंसा न कार्या

tatra prāṇā[yāma]dāvavasthito'pi yamādīnānāmabhyāsaḥ; anyeṣāṁ bhedaniṣṭhānāmayamādirūpāṇāṁ hiṁsādīnām apohanam, evaṁ hi yathātmani hiṁsā na kāryā[122]

If you like to keep yourself filled with happiness, in the same way, you must like others also to remain happy. Why not that? So that can also be maintained, because when you don't want to hurt your body, you must not want to hurt any other body. That could be maintained in our way of thinking. And when you don't want to tell lies, you should not ask…when everybody wants not to tell lies, you should also not tell lies. It is *apohana*; *apohana*, you are rejecting telling lies. But why telling lies is rejected? Why telling the truth is owned? It is *svātantrya*, it is the *svātantrya* of these *yama*s, and the *yama*s are adopted in this way in our system, and they will carry you to God consciousness in the end.

SCHOLAR: Could it be from a Śaivite point of view that these *ahiṁsā*, etcetera, are less *bhedaniṣṭhā*, they are less grounded in duality because if I say, "I shouldn't hurt you", then that is eliminating the distinction?

SWAMIJI: They are actually, they are actually less, they are actually grounded on that lower system, but at the same time, that lower system is also residing in that God consciousness.

SCHOLAR: Yes. So, from the higher point of view, *hiṁsā* and *ahiṁsā* are completely irrelevant.

SWAMIJI: Yes, from the higher point of view.

SCHOLAR: Because the tyranny of awareness doesn't care for such things.

SWAMIJI: Yes.

---

122. Part of Jayaratha's commentary for verse 4.98.

DENISE: But from our point of view, from the *sādhaka*'s (aspirant's) point of view, in *āṇavopāya* it's important to tell truth and…

SWAMIJI: It is important, yes.

DENISE: … do honest acts, isn't it?

SWAMIJI: Not from the *śākta* point of view. From the *āṇava* point of view it is important. *Deha utpluti sampāta dharma ujjigamiṣārasāt* (verse 99), *deha utplāvyate*, when you want to jump up, what is the purpose of jumping up? The purpose of jumping up is rejecting falling down, you reject falling down (*utpluti sampāta dharma ujjigamiṣārasāt*); *utpluti sampāta dharma udgantum icchā*, *utpluti*, when you jump higher up, by jumping higher up you ignore falling down, you reject falling down at the same time. But it is not in your mind that you are rejecting falling down, but it is automatically understood that you reject falling down. You see (Swamiji gives a practical demonstration), *bas*. When it goes up, you are rejecting falling down. Falling down is this. You reject that while going up. *Deha utplāvyate*, your body is *utplāvyate*, is being carried up, by the *rasa*, by the taste, of *utpluti sampāta dharma ujjigamiṣā*, by *utpluti*, by getting up, by getting on the higher level. And, at same time, side-by-side, simultaneously, *tadvipakṣa pāta āśaṅkāvyapohanāt*, falling down is also rejected at the same time. There is no other means for that [opposite act]. You adopt only one means, you have to adopt only one means to go up, and the other adoption of falling down is [simultaneously] rejected. In the same way, when you observe silence, talking too much is rejected. When you observe seclusion, going in a crowd is rejected. When you adopt, when you focus your mind towards, God consciousness, focusing your mind towards differentiated perception is rejected. It is why these yogic limbs are also fruitful in our system; by *dhāraṇā*, by *dhyāna*, *samādhi*, and *yama*, *niyama*, all these are fruitful in our system.

LJA TA04E (54:56)

गुरुवाक्यपरामर्शसदृशे स्वविमर्शने ।
प्रबुद्धे, तद्विपक्षाणां व्युदासः पाठचिन्तने ॥ १०० ॥

guruvākyaparāmarśa-sadṛśe svavimarśane /
prabuddhe, tadvipakṣāṇāṁ vyudāsaḥ pāṭhacintane //100//

But he joins this logic now to the main point: *Guru vākya parāmarśa sadṛśe svavimarśane*; *svavimarśa*, your own *vimarśa* of God consciousness (awareness of God consciousness is *svavimarśane*), *guru vākya parāmarśa sadṛśe*, it is *guru vākya parāmarśa sadṛśe*, it is just like the *parāmarśa* of what is told to you by your master, the point which has been explained to you by your master, and when you think over that, it is *svavimarśa*, it is your *ahaṁ parāmarśa*. When *ahaṁ parāmarśa* has risen (*prabuddhe*)–put a comma there–*guru vākya parāmarśa sadṛśe svavimarśane prabuddhe sati*, when that [*ahaṁ parāmarśa*] has risen in you, *tad vipakṣāṇāṁ pāṭhacintane vyudāsaḥ*, then going through books and reading this knowledge and taking help of dictionaries and all those things disappear (*pāṭhacintane*: *pāṭha* and *cintana*). *Pāṭha* and *cintana*…

SCHOLAR: *Tad vipakṣāṇāṁ vyudāsaḥ*.

SWAMIJI: Yes. *Vimarśa* (*svavimarśa*), *pāṭha*, and *cintana*. First is *pāṭha* (reading this book knowledge), then *cintana* (*cintana* is just contemplating on what you have read in books), then the rise of your own *vimarśa* (the rise of your I-consciousness), that is *svavimarśa*, that is the end.

SCHOLAR: So, is Abhinavagupta saying that once that has been achieved, then in *pāṭha-cintana*, other positions are completely automatically rejected?

SWAMIJI: No, that *pāṭha-cintana* automatically goes away, automatically they are vanished (*vyudāsa*).

SCHOLAR: He says, *vyudāsa tadvipakṣāṇāṁ pāṭha cintane*…

SWAMIJI: Yes.

SCHOLAR: *Pāṭhacintanāmaye viṣaye*, in reading and contemplating…

SWAMIJI: In reading and contemplating.

SCHOLAR: …then those other positions is the *vyudāsa* (rejection) of those *vipakṣa*s (opposites).

SWAMIJI: *Vyudāsa*, they vanish.

SCHOLAR: They vanish automatically in that truth.

SWAMIJI: Automatically, yes, when *svavimarśa* has risen.

SCHOLAR: So it is not *pāṭha* and *cintana* that are rejected, it's *tadvipakṣa* (the opposite) that is rejected.

SWAMIJI: No.

pāṭha-cintanādau viṣaye punaḥ punarabhyasatiśāyāt, gururvākya parāmarśa-anuguṇe svaparāmarśe[123], *uditasya svaparāmarśasya vipakṣabhūtānāṁ mauḍhyādīnām*[*api*]*vyudāsaḥ* / (commentary)

All those fields of ignorances are vanished.

LJA TA04E (57:52)

नह्यस्य गुरुणा शक्यं स्वं ज्ञानं शब्द एव वा ।
धियि रोपयितुं तेन स्वप्रबोधक्रमो ध्रुवम् ॥१०१॥

nahyasya guruṇā śakyaṁ svaṁ jñānaṁ śabda eva vā /
dhiyi ropayituṁ tena svaprabodhakramo dhruvam //101//

But this *svavimarśane*, your own *vimarśa*, must rise, no matter if already your master has made you [understand] the reality of your God consciousness. But unless your God consciousness has risen in you, the preaching of your master won't have any effect. Understand? The preaching of the master is necessary for the time being, but [as long as] your rise of God consciousness does not take place automatically in you, the guru will be of no help to you. The master will help you only to induce that strength in you, and you have to rise by your own self, you have to do that practice by your own strength. That is what he says in [this] *śloka*: *nahyasya guruṇā śakyam*, the guru has not this power, the guru has not this strength, the master has not this strength, that he will induce, he will inject, his knowledge and his word in you, in your consciousness. *Tena svaprabodhakramo dhruvam*, so, your own consciousness must get development, your own consciousness must get developed in you.

SCHOLAR: *Dhruvam*?

SWAMIJI: *Dhruvam* (absolutely) it is *niścayam* (ascertained). *Svaprabodha krama*[124] is *dhruvam*, it is established, it is confirmed.

---

123. Swamiji says "*svavimarśe*" in place of the published "*svaparāmarśe*", which are essentially synonymous terms.

124. The course (*krama*) of self (*sva*) awakening (*prabodha*).

LJA TA04E (1:00:23) end
LJA TA04F (00:00) start

अत एव स्वप्नकाले श्रुते तत्रापि वस्तुनि ।

ata eva svapnakāle śrute tatrāpi vastuni /

It is why in *svapna kāla*, in the time of the dreaming state also, *śrute tatrāpi vastuni*, whatever you have heard or experienced in wakefulness ...

तादात्म्यभावनायोगो न फलाय न भण्यते ॥१०२॥

tādātmyabhāvanāyogo na phalāya na bhaṇyate //102//

... *tādātmya bhāvanā yoga* takes place in the dreaming [state] also. It is the strength of your maintaining the strength of your God consciousness.[125]

SCHOLAR: *Tādātmya bhāvanā yogaḥ*?

SWAMIJI: *Tādātmya bhāvanāyoga phalāya na na bhaṇyate*? *Bhaṇyate eva*, it gives fruit, it bears fruit.

JOHN: What is *tādātmya*?

SWAMIJI: *Tādātmya bhāvanā yoga*? *Tādātmya bhāvanā yoga* is, for instance, this is Alexi, he has seen that girl with whom he was in love. She has gone to America or a foreign [place] or somewhere else, but

125. "If that awareness does not remain, does not persist in the dreaming state, it means, in wakefulness there were some gaps. In wakefulness, if there are no gaps in awareness, awareness is in continuity, [then] in the dreaming state also, you will be there, [and] in the dreamless state also, you will be enjoying God consciousness, the state of God consciousness. This is what yogis have felt." *Bhagavad Gītā* audio (LJA archive, 1978). "If you, in your dreaming state, only dream that you are doing *abhyāsa* (meditation), there is liberation, there is no rebirth, you won't be born again. This is the certificate of your being liberated." *Vijñāna Bhairava–The Manual for Self-Realization*, verse 55.

still that girl is in his mind. When he dreams of her in his dreaming state, he can get the real enjoyment of that with her in the dreaming state also – *tādātmya bhāvanā yoga*. This is the strength of your own consciousness.

SCHOLAR: So this *tādātmya bhāvanā yoga* means, the process of becoming one with.

SWAMIJI: Yes.

SCHOLAR: Identification.

SWAMIJI: *Ata eva svapna kāle*, although it is believed by people that [the dreaming state] is false, but in that false world also, you get *tādātmya yoga*, and that bears fruit, actual fruit. So, it is your own strength of awareness that will carry you to God consciousness, not the strength of your master, the master's preaching. The master's preaching has the strength only to some extent, to some point, but after that point, you have to travel yourself.

LJA TA04F (02:20)

सङ्केतानादरे शब्दनिष्ठमामर्शनं पठिः ।
तदादरे तदार्थस्तु चिन्तेति परिचर्च्यताम् ॥ १०३ ॥

saṅketānādare śabda-niṣṭhamāmarśanaṁ paṭhiḥ /
tadādare tadarthastu cinteti paricarcyatām //103//

Saṅketa anādare.[126] What is *saṅketa*? *Saṅketa* is "God consciousness". This word "God consciousness" is *saṅketa* (is a sign) for that state.

SCHOLAR: The word is.

SWAMIJI: The word "God consciousness" …

SCHOLAR: God consciousness.

SWAMIJI: "God consciousness", this word is *saṅketa*, this is *saṅketa* (a signboard) for that state. Which state?

SCHOLAR: God consciousness.

---

126. Disrespect (*anādara*) for the *saṅketa* (the signboard).

SWAMIJI: That actual God consciousness. When this word has come in your consciousness–*saṅketa*, God consciousness–you must not have any respect on this *saṅketa*. Find out the reality of that, find out the reality of that, what is behind that, what is behind that "God consciousness". *Saṅketa anādare*, when you do not respect the *saṅketa*, *śabda niṣṭham*, and your mind is focused on words only, that is *paṭhiḥ*.[127]

SCHOLAR: When you *do* respect *saṅketa*.

SWAMIJI: No, I will tell you. Give me...for instance, I write here "God consciousness". "God consciousness", this is a signboard for something else. "God consciousness" is written in books, [that] "God consciousness must be owned." When you read this line, "God consciousness must be owned", but the line is *saṅketa* (this is the sign) for diverting you towards the actual state of God consciousness. When you don't respect that sign, when you don't respect the point that it is directing to...it is directing you to that point. These are not only words, "God consciousness", "The state of God consciousness." When you read "The state of God consciousness" and just write, "The state of God consciousness" ("s-t-a-t-e, state of God consciousness"), that is *saṅketa anādare*[128], and *śabda niṣṭham āmarśanaṁ*, you focus your mind and body and intellect on these words only. You don't try to carry your mind towards its [signification], towards what is representing this word. Have you understood?

SCHOLAR: Yes.

SWAMIJI: That is *saṅketa anādare*. *Śabda niṣṭham*, when your *āmarśana* (awareness) is *śabda niṣṭha*, only focused on these sounds, words, that is *paṭhiḥ*, that is reading and writing, that is called reading and writing. Actual reading and writing is that. When you read books, it means, you don't have any *saṅketa* of it, you don't know what it really means.

SCHOLAR: So just in the act of recitation.

SWAMIJI: Recitation of these words, that is "*paṭhiḥ*". That is *paṭhiḥ* means, that is *pāṭha*.[129] *Tadādare*, when a time will come when you will have respect, you will create respect for that *saṅketa* also, ...*

---

127. Being a student.

128. Disrespecting the signboard.

129. Reciting, reading, studying.

Which *saṅketa*?

DENISE: Those written words of "God consciousness".

SWAMIJI: Not the words.

DENISE: Of the place, of the state, that it points to.

SWAMIJI: Of the place, yes, state – *tadādare.*

*... and *tadarthastu*, when you get entry, when you force your mind to enter in the meaning of that "God consciousness", the word "God consciousness", *cinteti paricarcyatām*, that is *cinta*, that is *cintana*, that is called *cintana. Pāṭha* is, *bas*, only reading and writing. *Cintana* is just to find out the background of those words.

LJA TA04F (06:51)

तदद्वयायां संवित्तावभ्यासोऽनुपयोगवान् ।
केवलं द्वैतमालिन्यशङ्कानिर्मूलनाय सः ॥ १०४ ॥

tadadvayāyāṁ saṁvittāv-abhyāso'nupayogavān /
kevalaṁ dvaitamālinya-śaṅkānirmūlanāya saḥ //104//

So, in the same way, *advayāyāṁ saṁvittau*, for maintaining the undifferentiated and monistic state of God consciousness (*advyāyāṁ saṁvittāu*, it is *naimittike saptamī – saṁvitti prāptyartham*[130]), *advāyaṁ saṁvittāu abhyāso'nupayogavān*, this *abhyāsa* (practice), this *yamādīnāṁ*[131] *abhyāsa*, is *anupayogavān*, it is not helping you in any way. It helps you only in one point, that is, *dvaita mālinya śaṅkānirmūlanāya saḥ*, it purifies the impurity in your mind. Only impurity is washed off in your mind, but you can't be carried to that state of God consciousness by adopting these *yamādis*, the yogic limbs.

SCHOLAR: Only *tarka* has *sākṣādupāyatvam.*

SWAMIJI: *Tarka* has *sākṣādupāyatvam.*[132]

---

130. The locative case, which indicates obtaining (*prāpti*) to the highest aim (*artha*), God consciousness (*saṁvitti*).

131. The *yamas*, etcetera.

132. The means of direct revelation.

LJA TA04F (08:10)

द्वैतशङ्काश्च तर्केण तर्क्यन्त इति वर्णितम् ।
तत्तर्कसाधनायास्तु यमादेरप्युपायता ॥ १०५ ॥

dvaitaśaṅkāśca tarkeṇa tarkyanta iti varṇitam /
tattarkasādhanāyāstu yamāderapyupāyatā //105//

And these doubts of differentiated perceptions in this world are removed away by *tarka*, by that supreme transcendental way of logic. *Iti varṇitam*, this is already explained by us. *Tat tarka sādhanāyāstu*, just to build up the body of *tarka*, you can adopt other means of these yogic limbs. The other means, they will give you some help.

SCHOLAR: Like a ladder,

SWAMIJI: Like a ladder, yes.

SCHOLAR: But from the point of view of *tarka*, from *tarka*'s point of view, …

SWAMIJI: … it is direct. From *tarka*'s point of view …

SCHOLAR: … these others are meaningless – *anupayogavān.*

SWAMIJI: … these are meaningless, these are meaningless.

LJA TA04F (09:13)

उक्तं श्रीपूर्वशास्त्रे च न द्वैतं नापि चाद्वयम् ।
लिङ्गपूजादिकं सर्वमित्युपक्रम्य शम्भुना ॥ १०६ ॥
विहितं सर्वमेवात्र प्रतिषिद्धमथापि वा ।
प्राणायामादिकैरङ्गैर्योगाः स्युः कृत्त्रिमा यतः ॥ १०७ ॥
तत्तेनाकृतकस्यास्य कलां नार्हन्ति षोडशीम् ।

uktaṁ śrīpūrvaśāstre ca na dvaitaṁ nāpi cādvayam /
liṅgapūjādikaṁ sarvam-ityupakramya śambhunā //106//
vihitaṁ sarvamevātra pratiṣiddhamathāpi vā /
prāṇāyāmādikairaṅgair-yogāḥ syuḥ kṛttrimā yataḥ //107//
tattenākṛtakasyāsya kalāṁ nārghanti ṣoḍaśīm /

It is already described in the *Mālinīvijaya Tantra*: there is no meaning for maintaining a dualistic way of thinking, *nāpi cādvayam*, there is no meaning for maintaining a monistic way of thinking – a monistic way of thinking has no meaning.

SCHOLAR: If it excludes *dvaitam* (duality).

SWAMIJI: Yes. *Liṅga pūjādikaṁ sarvam*, the worshiping of *liṅga pūjā* is also condemned – *liṅga pūjā*.

SCHOLAR: *Adikam* means, all outer worship. Is that right?

SWAMIJI: All outer worships. *Ityupakramya*, and so on. It is said by Lord Śiva: *vihitaṁ sarvam eva atra* (verse 107), you can do all of these, you can do all of these if you are aware of God consciousness. If you are aware, if you do all these outer worships also with awareness of God consciousness, then it is all right. If the awareness of God consciousness is not there and you do worship, you do other things, you go to mosques, churches, temples, [then] it is useless. *Vihitaṁ sarvam-evātra*, it is not prohibited, you can do it [or] you cannot do it. You may do it, you may not do it, but maintain awareness of God consciousness. Because *prāṇāyāma adikair aṅgair yogāḥ syuḥ kṛttrimā*, the yoga [that is] produced by these limbs of yoga, the yogic limbs, [is] artificial. Artificial yoga is produced by these limbs of Yoga. The real yoga is produced only by *tarka*. *Tat tenākṛta kasyāsya kalāṁ nārghanti ṣoḍaśīm*, so, this is the un-artificial state of God consciousness, and in view of that state, *kalāṁ nārghanti ṣoḍaśīm*, these [limbs] are not worth [even] one-sixteenth part of God consciousness.

SCHOLAR: Of *tarka*.

SWAMIJI: So they are useless. Of *tarka*.[133]

---

133. That is, the other yogic limbs are not worth even one-sixteenth part of *tarka*.

LJA TA04F (11:44)

किं त्वेतदत्र देवेशि नियमेन विधीयते ॥ १०८ ॥
तत्त्वे चेतः स्थिरं कार्यं तच्च यस्य यथास्त्विति ।

kiṁ tvetadatra deveśi niyamena vidhīyate //108//
tattve cetaḥ sthiraṁ kāryaṁ tacca yasya yathāstviti /

Only there is one binding for *sādhaka*s, one binding for *sādhaka*s is only, O Pārvatī, that *tattve cetaḥ sthiraṁ*, you have to focus your mind on God consciousness. If your mind is focused on God consciousness by inferior ways of thinking, do that. That is the reality. If your mind is focused on God consciousness by telling lies, [then] tell lies, but focus your mind on God consciousness. If the mind is focused on God consciousness by doing adultery, that adultery must be done. But focusing the mind on God consciousness is the main point to be achieved. You must focus [on] God consciousness at any cost. Don't think of any other *niyama*s or not-*niyama*s.[134] *Tattve cetaḥ sthiraṁ kāryaṁ tat ca yasya yathāstviti*, that focusing on God consciousness should be adopted by anyone with any means, good or bad. If focusing of God consciousness does not take place by worshipping Lord Śiva day and night, that worshipping of Lord Śiva is a sin! You [must] leave it aside. If your mind is focused on God consciousness by sinning, by doing butchering, [then] do that. That is the real way of doing. This is [Abhinavagupta's] thought (laughs). Focusing of God consciousness must be done.[135]

---

134. Positive observances or their opposites.

135. "[When] you come to the point of Śaivism afterwards, then at that moment, right and wrong has nothing to do [with it]. But till then, we have to follow all the rules and regulations of the *śāstra*s–till then." *Kashmir Shaivism and the Transformation of Life*–Abhinavagupta's *Bodhapañcadaśikā*, Webinar 4, Verse 9, commentary, p. 71.

SCHOLAR: So the question is where that man's awareness is.

SWAMIJI: Yes.

SCHOLAR: It's not a question of even a choice.

SWAMIJI: Yes (affirmative).

SCHOLAR: If he is not touched, if his awareness is there, if he see that those things are just things, they are.

SWAMIJI: They are, but focusing of God consciousness must be done.

SCHOLAR: Yes, that's what I mean.

SWAMIJI: Yes.

JOHN: In other words, he must find in these things, or whatever acts he's doing, that must always sentence his mind to God consciousness in these acts.

SWAMIJI: ... God consciousness. If that is not done, nothing is done. If that is done, everything is done. If that is done and nothing is done in this world, [or] from a worldly point of view he is a butcher, he is a first-class rogue, he is a thief, but he is maintaining God consciousness, [then] he has done everything. *Bas*? This much we will do.

LJA TA04F (14:48)

Kalpitārcānādaraḥ – Artificial Worship

Kalpitārcānādaraḥ, artificial worships is condemned now. This is another subject now. Because these are artificial! If you worship Lord Śiva from morning to evening, remain in seclusion for the sake of maintaining His consciousness every second, and with no result, that is a sin, you must leave it aside. If you can maintain God consciousness in the cinema hall, you must remain in the cinema hall. That is the reality.

DEVOTEE: This is *śāktopāya*.

SWAMIJI: (Kashmiri) I am reading it to myself (laughs).

SCHOLAR: So there's a point of difference here: the Trika System is saying everything is possible and everything is forbidden, it depends on where your awareness is.

SWAMIJI: Yes.

SCHOLAR: Whereas the Kula system says that this *liṅga pūjā*, this *bhasma* (ashes), this *jaṭa*[136], all of these …

SWAMIJI: That is Kula system.

SCHOLAR: … it rejects those and so does the Māta [system]. Whereas Trika says, "We neither reject nor accept, only the mind must be made firm in reality."

SWAMIJI: Yes, it will be discriminated now in *niṣedha vidhi tulyatām*.[137]

JOHN: Why do those other systems reject these? So strongly reject, why do they feel…? This Kula system and the Māta, why do they reject?

SWAMIJI: By all these *caryas*, all these attributes, outer attributes of Śaivism, in some systems they are rejected, in some systems they are owned, they are respected, and here [in Trika] they are respected and rejected also, you can have them or you cannot have them. *Iha sarvātmake kasmāt tat vidhi pratiṣedhane*,[138] there is no *vidhi* (injunction), there is no *pratiṣedha* (prohibition), in our system.

---

136. Coconut hair.

137. The discussion of the equal position (*tulyatā*) of prohibitions (*niṣedha*) and injunctions (*vidhi*).

138. This is verse 257a of this text, p. 363.

SCHOLAR: But in the Kula system, because it is emphasizing *śākta* path …

SWAMIJI: *Kulādiṣu niṣedhasau*, because *dehe viśvātmā vidhe*,[139] *viśvātmā vidhe*, for maintaining awareness in your own body. *Iha sarvātmake kasmāt tat vidhi pratiṣedhane*, this is the *sarvātmaka* system[140] (this Kaula system or the Trika System), there is no *vidhi* (injunction) and there is no *niṣedha* (prohibition).

JOHN: Everything in everything.

LJA TA04F (17:32)

SWAMIJI:

एवं द्वैतपरामर्शनाशाय परमेश्वरः ॥१०९॥
क्वचित्स्वभावममलमामृशन्ननिशं स्थितः ।

evaṁ dvaitaparāmarśa-nāśāya parameśvaraḥ //109//
kvacitsvabhāvamamalam-āmṛśannaniśaṁ sthitaḥ /

So, Lord Śiva, just to remove the differentiated *parāmarśa*, the differentiated perception of the universe, for removing that differentiated perception in the universe, he shines in some fortunate soul and reveals in him his pure Self.

SCHOLAR: *Aniśaṁ*?

SWAMIJI: *Aniśaṁ*, in continuity, he realizes his nature, his real nature. And it is functioned by Lord Śiva himself just to remove *dvaita parāmarśa*, just to remove the differentiated perceptions of the universe.

139. Ibid., verse 256.

140. The system expounding the doctrine that everything is everything (*sarvātmaka*).

LJA TA04F (18:47)

यः स्वभावपरामर्शो इन्द्रियार्थाद्युपायतः ॥ ११० ॥
विनैव तन्मुखोऽन्यो वा स्वातन्त्र्यात्तद्विकल्पनम् ।

yaḥ svabhāvaparāmarśa indriyārthādhyupāyataḥ //110//
vinaiva tanmukho'nyo vā svātantryāttadvikalpanam /

This realization of one's Self takes place in two ways. One way is *indriya artha upāya vinaiva*, without taking hold of the means of the organs (*śabda*, *sparśa*, *rūpa*, *rasa*, and *gandha*). That is the way of *śāmbhavopāya*. They don't take the support of *śabda*, *sparśa*, *rūpa*, *rasa*, and *gandha*. And in *śāktopāya* and *āṇavopāya*, he reveals his nature by the support of these organic sections–*śabda*, *sparśa*, *rūpa*, *rasa*, and *gandha*. Concentrate on sound, touch, and so on, and they get entry in God consciousness. But some fortunate souls get entry without taking the support of this organic field. [They] just take hold of that nature and they are inside.

LJA TA04F (20:21)

तच्च स्वच्छस्वतन्त्रात्मरत्ननिर्भासिनि स्फुटम् ॥ १११ ॥
भावौघे भेदसन्धातृ स्वात्मनो नैशमुच्यते ।
तदेव तु समस्तार्थनिर्भरात्मैकगोचरम् ॥ ११२ ॥
शुद्धविद्यात्मकं सर्वमेवेदमहमित्यलम् ।

tacca svacchasvatantrātma-ratnanirbhāsini sphuṭam //111//
bhāvaughe bhedasandhātṛ svātmano naiśamucyate /
tadeva tu samastārtha-nirbharātmaikagocaram //112//
śuddhavidyātmakaṁ sarvam-evedamahamityalam /

And that twofold experience of God consciousness takes place in the purified, absolutely independent, and shining just like a jewel, the Self. This is the qualification of the Self: The Self which is absolutely purified (*nirmala*, pure), and absolutely independent, and shining just like a jewel. And in that consciousness, when this whole collection of the objective world, which is not away from the differentiated perception from your own nature, is called "the means concerned with *māyā*." This is the means of *māyā*, the means of illusion. So, *śāktopāya* is the means of illusion and *āṇavopāya* is also the means of illusion (*naiṣam* means, concerned with *māyā*). *Tadeva tu samastārtha nirbharātmaika gocaram*, and another means where you find, where the *sādhaka* finds, that the totality of the universe is centered in one nature of God consciousness, and when that Self is revealed in that way, this is Śuddhavidyā *parāmarśa*; and where you find this-ness (*idam*) absolutely united with I-ness (*ahaṁ*), and I-ness absolutely united with this-ness (*sarvam eva idam ahaṁ ityalam*).

LJA TA04F (22:55)

इदं विकल्पनं शुद्धविद्यारूपं स्फुटात्मकम् ॥ ११३॥
प्रतिहन्तीह मायीयं विकल्पं भेदभावकम् ।

idaṁ vikalpanaṁ śuddhavidyārūpaṁ sphuṭātmakam //113//
pratihantīha māyīyaṁ vikalpaṁ bhedabhāvakam /

This *vikalpa*, this mode of experience, or this mode of the means concerned with Śuddhavidyā, is absolutely vividly removed away (*pratihanti*, removes away or sets aside) the *vikalpa* concerned with differentiated perception (*māyī vikalpa*). So, *māyī vikalpa*[141] does not remain, does not exist there, at the time [when] Śuddhavidyā *parāmarśa* has taken place.

141. Mayic thought.

शुद्धविद्यापरामर्शो यः स एव त्वनेकधा ॥ ११४ ॥
स्नानशुद्ध्यर्चनाहोमध्यानजप्यादियोगतः ।

śuddhavidyāparāmarśo yaḥ sa eva tvanekadhā //114//
snānaśuddhyarcanāhoma-dhyānajapyādiyogataḥ /
(not recited)

And this Śuddhavidyā *parāmarśa*, this experience of Śuddhavidyā *parāmarśa*, is not onefold, is not only onefold; *sa eva tvanekadhā*, it is differentiatedly experienced by *sādhakas*, i.e., by taking a bath (*snāna*), by purifying one's own nature (*śuddhi*), by worshipping Lord Śiva (*arcane*), by offering oblations in a fire (*homa*), by meditation (*dhyāna*), and by the recitation of *mantra* (*japa*). But these things concerned with bath, purification, worship, oblations, meditation, and recitation, [are] divine, [they are] not an ordinary thing. That he will explain in the following *ślokas*.

LJA TA04F (24:40)

विश्वमेतत्स्वसंवित्तिरसनिर्भरितं रसात् ॥ ११५ ॥
आविश्य शुद्धो निखिलं तर्पयेदध्वमण्डलम् ।

viśvametatsvasaṁvitti-rasanirbharitaṁ rasāt //115//
āviśya śuddho nikhilaṁ tarpayed-adhva-maṇḍalam /

When one observes by the force of the taste of Śuddhavidyā, not by the force of your effort (effort does not work there, your effort does not work there),...*

In *Spanda* also, it is said, "Whatever this state tells me, I will do that. I won't do according to my efforts, I [won't] act according to my choice, I will do whatever is ordered from above."[142] So it is *rasāt* (*rasāt* means, *antar mukhatā rasāt*),[143] by the taste of your own Self.

*... when the *sādhaka* gets entry in the universe–in which universe?–which is already filled by the *rasa*, by the nectar, of one's own consciousness, *svasaṁvitti rasa nirbharitam viśvam*, when he finds this whole universe is filled with [his] own nectar of [his] own consciousness, Self-consciousness, when he gets entry in that (*āviśya*), he becomes purified; when he becomes purified, *nikhilam adhva maṇḍalam tarpayet*, then he purifies this whole universe in one glance without any effort.

SCHOLAR: *Tarpayet.*

SWAMIJI: *Svātmasāt kuryāt.*

SCHOLAR: He offers that into his own nature.

SWAMIJI: Yes. Offers that in his own nature or purifies this whole universe by that *rasa*.

SCHOLAR: This is *śuddhi prakaraṇam* or *tarpaṇa prakaraṇam*?[144]

SWAMIJI: *Tarpaṇa prakaraṇam*: each and every being in the objective world is satisfied by his existence in this universe. It is why in the *Śiva Sūtra* it is called *lokānanda samādhi sukham*[145]: when he gets entry in *samādhi*, that is, from another point of view, it means his remaining in *samādhi* is a boon for this whole universe (*lokānanda*; *samādhi asya samādhi sukham lokānanda bhavati*).

---

142. See *The Mystery of Vibrationless-Vibration in Kashmir Shaivism*, Vasugupta's *Spanda Kārikā* and Kṣemarāja's *Spanda Saṇdoha*, Revealed by Swami Lakshmanjoo, ed. John Hughes (Lakshmanjoo Academy, 2016), chapter 1, verse 23. See also commentary for verse 151, fn. 284, p. 261.

143. See commentary for verse 150 of this text.

144. The explanation (*prakaraṇa*) of purification (*śuddhi*) or satisfaction (*tarpaṇa*).

145. Verse 1.18.

LJA TA04F (27:49)

उल्लासिबोधहुतभुग्दग्धविश्वेन्धनोदिते ॥ ११६ ॥
सितभस्मनि देहस्य मज्जनं स्नानमुच्यते ।

ullāsibodhahutabhug-dagdhaviśvendhanodite //116//
sitabhasmani dehasya majjanaṁ snānamucyate /

In this 115th *śloka*, he has explained the general way of Śuddhavidyā *parāmarśa*, the general way of experiencing Śuddhavidyā. Now he explains one-by-one [what] he has already nominated, pointed out. He has pointed out first Śuddhavidyā *parāmarśa* in taking a bath. In taking bath (*snāna*) is the first chapter, thing.

Ullāsi bodha huta bhuk dagdha viśvendhanodite sita-bhasmani dehasya majjanaṁ snānam ucyate, he defines what is a real bath, taking a bath. *Yadi muktirjalasnānānmatsyānāṁ sā na kiṁ bhavet* (comm.), if by taking a bath in water, ordinary water, you would get liberated, [then] why these fish in the water are not liberated? They are always in water. *Yadi muktir jala snānāt matsyānāṁ sā na kiṁ bhavet.*

SCHOLAR: It is [from the] *Kularṇava* [*Tantra*].

SWAMIJI: Yes (laughs). So, this bath is something else, something special. And that bath is *ullāsi bodha hutabhuk*, when the fire of consciousness is brightened, or is inflamed, *ullāsi bodha hutabhuk*, and when by that inflamed fire of consciousness this whole differentiated perception of the universe is burnt totally, is burnt to ashes, the differentiated perception of the universe is burnt totally to ashes, then what remains afterwards? By burning these differentiated perceptions, there remains *sita bhasmani*, absolutely white ashes, and those white ashes are the state of *para pramātṛ bhāva*, and when in those white ashes of *para pramātṛ bhāva*, …

SCHOLAR: The supreme subject.

SWAMIJI: … you dive your body of wakefulness, you dive your body of the dreaming state, and you dive your body of the dreamless state, all these three bodies dive in that *bhasma*, in those ashes of *para pramātṛ bhāva*, this is, in the real sense, a bath, taking a bath – *majjanaṁ snānam ucyate*. And this bath is not an ordinary bath, this is a bath according to the way of Śuddhavidyā.

SCHOLAR: *Śāktopāya.*
SWAMIJI: *Śāktopāya.* Yes, next:

LJA TA04F (31:12)

इत्थं च विहितस्नानस्तर्पितानन्तदेवतः ॥ ११७॥
ततोऽपि देहारम्भीणि तत्त्वानि परिशोधयेत् ।

ittham ca vihitasnānas-tarpitānantadevataḥ //117//
tato'pi dehārambhīṇi tattvāni pariśodhayet /

When he has once taken a bath in such a way (*ittham ca*, this way, when he has *vihita snāna*, taken this divine bath), *tarpitānanta devataḥ*, when all your organic class, the class of organs…

SCHOLAR: *Devatā karaṇeśvarī.*

SWAMIJI: …*karaṇeśvaryaḥ*, all the classes of organs are fulfilled in their own way (*tarpitānanta devataḥ*)–fulfilled in which way?–not by seeing, the eyes are not satisfied by seeing, [but when] the eyes are satisfied by seeing the beauty of your own God consciousness, and similarly, *śabda*, *sparśa*, *rūpa*, *rasa*, and *gandha*, all these five senses get the experience of God consciousness (that is, in the real sense, to satisfy them), …*

Because once you want to embrace your beloved [and have embraced him], you are not fulfilled, your desire is not fulfilled, because you want to embrace him again after a while. And that time, too/also, your desire is not fulfilled because you want to embrace again, and you want to again, again, again, again, again–there is no end. But once when you embrace in such a way, this embrace of your God consciousness with all these five senses, there is no further desire remaining for your lifetime–never! *Ittham ca vihita snānaḥ tarpitānanta devataḥ*, all these *karaṇeśvaryas*, all these divine organs, get the fulfillment of their desire. "The fulfillment of their desire", it would be the appropriate [translation].

*… *tato'pi dehārambhīṇi tattvāni parośodhayet*, and then there is something more to be done–after the fulfillment of the desires of your five senses in [their] divine way, there is something more to

be done – that is, *dehārambhīṇi tattvāni parośodhayet*, the thirty-six elements are to be purified afterwards. Those thirty-six elements, which have given the rise to the body, those also must be purified with the experience of God consciousness. When they are purified with the experience of God consciousness, you leave the body at once, you shake it [off].

SCHOLAR: This is *unmīlanā* here?

SWAMIJI: It is just leaving the limited physical frame. Because [as long as] you don't leave this limited frame, you are entangled in limitation. Although there may be God consciousness everywhere in all your five senses, but still their limitation is there – you want to take food, you want to drink water, you want to have touch with your beloved, you want everything afterwards (laughs). So that must not remain. If you have become one with God consciousness, that [desire] must not remain. So you have to purify these thirty-six elements.

SCHOLAR: With effort or spontaneously?

SWAMIJI: No, not with effort, with consciousness.

SCHOLAR: Is this *unmīlanā*?

SWAMIJI: *Unmīlanā*, yes.[146]

SCHOLAR: So he says, *anantadevataḥ*, the infinite deities.

SWAMIJI: *Ananta* means, these, the *ananta devataḥ* residing in your body. Those *devata*s which are existing already in your body, they are being…

SCHOLAR: Those *pīta śakti*s, etcetera.

SWAMIJI: Yes. There are not only the five senses. They have got offshoots also, many offshoots of the senses.

---

146. "For instance, this is a calf, you look at it, you look at it and see that *unmīlanā* state. [You] won't touch [the calf], it is only looking (*ālocana*). First you have to experience this state in the *alocana* world, then in act, then you can touch it, then you can kiss it, then you can embrace it, then you can do whatever you like in *unmīlanā samādhi*. It is to be realized first in one's own consciousness, and when it is realized, then you have to realize that *unmīlanā* state experience in actions also." *Interview on Kashmir Shaivism*, Swami Lakshmanjoo (original audio recordings, LJA archives, Los Angeles 1980).

LJA TA04F (35:42)

शिवात्मकेष्वप्येतेषु बुद्धिर्या व्यतिरेकिणी ॥११८॥
सैवाशुद्धिः, पराख्याता शुद्धिस्तद्धीविमर्दनम् ।

śivātmakeṣvapyeteṣu buddhiryā vyatirekiṇī //118//
saivāśuddhiḥ, parākhyātā śuddhistaddhīvimardanam /

After "*saivāśuddhi*" you must put a comma.

Śivātmakeṣu api eteṣu, in these thirty-six elements, although these thirty-six elements are one with Lord Śiva, they are not separate from Lord Śiva, but as long as your intellectual perception is experiencing these elements in your body separately, …*

For instance, "This is my hand", "These are my nails", "This is my tongue", "This is my nose", "This my face", "I am beautiful", "I am ugly", "I am black", "I am fair", that is *vyatirekiṇī buddhi*. *Vyatirekiṇī buddhi* means, that intellect which makes you perceive differentiatedness in your body. When you perceive that, "I am the universal body, I am not this body; I am not this limited body, I am the universal body", then you are undifferentiated, your body is undifferentiated. So all these [differentiated] thirty-six elements have been diluted in the cosmic thirty-six elements. Your body is not existing there then.

*… *saiva aśuddhiḥ*, that is impurity. As long as this differentiated perception lives there, that is impurity. *Parākhyātā śuddhiḥ tad dhīvimardanam*, when that intellect of that differentiated perception is removed, that is, in the real sense, absolute purification.

Why do you smile?

DENISE: Because when children are very small, they are taught, "This is your finger", "This is your fingernail." Now repeat, what is this? "This is your finger." "This is my finger." All the different parts of the body we're taught to believe that…

SWAMIJI: But there also, you come to this conclusion in the end that, "This whole [body] is my body, only one." You first talk [about it] separately, then you talk [about its] oneness – "This whole [body] is my body." But leave that perception also aside and think that this whole universe is your body. Then you have come to the real conclusion.

SCHOLAR: Swamiji, this is discussing *snānam* (this bathing), and he says that it's immersion in the state of *para pramātṛ bhāva*, ...

SWAMIJI: Yes.

SCHOLAR: ... in Śiva *bhāva*, ...

SWAMIJI: Yes.

SCHOLAR: ... and in that state, all the deities of the senses receive complete ecstatic fulfillment, ...

SWAMIJI: Yes.

SCHOLAR: ... and in book three, it is described how in Śiva *bhāva*, *ṛ-ṝ-ḷ-ḹ* and *a-i-o-au*, the eight *mātṛ*s pervading each other, the *cakra* of the sixty four, ...

SWAMIJI: *Aṣṭāṣṭaka cakra.*[147]

SCHOLAR: ... the eight senses pervading each other, ...

SWAMIJI: Yes.

SCHOLAR: ... *aṣṭāṣṭaka cakra*. Is that referred to here?

SWAMIJI: No, that is from the *śāmbhavopāya* point of view there in the third *āhnika*.

SCHOLAR: But he is entering Śiva *bhāva*.

SWAMIJI: This is Śiva *bhāva*, yes. This Śiva *bhāva* also comes in *śāktopāya*.

SCHOLAR: So if he enters in Śiva *bhāva*, that state is experienced or not?

SWAMIJI: Yes, that state is experienced in the end.

LJA TA04F (39:16)

एवं स्वदेहं बोधैकपात्रं गलितभेदकम् ॥११९॥
पश्यन्संवित्तिमात्रत्वे स्वतन्त्रे तिष्ठति प्रभुः ।

147. *Aṣṭāṣṭaka cakra* refers to the sixty-fourfold *cakra* where the eight principal *devis* are Brahmāṇī, Śāmbhavī, etcetera. See *Dehasthadevatācakrastotram* of Abhinavagupta, translation and commentary by Swami Lakshmanjoo (original audio recording, LJA archives, Los Angeles, 1980). See also *Light on Tantra in Kashmir Shaivism, Tantrāloka, Vol. Two*, 3.109, p. 173, and Appendix 12, p. 462.

evaṁ svadehaṁ bodhaika-pātraṁ galitabhedakam //119//
paśyansaṁvittimātratve svatantre tiṣṭhati prabhuḥ /

In this way, when he experiences in this way of taking a bath, then he experiences his own body just as one with one's own consciousness (*bodhaikapātram*).

"*Bodhaika-pātraṁ*" is not quite to the point. "*Bodhaika-mātram*" would be to the point. "*Bodhaika-mātram*" is "only *bodha*". His body becomes one with *bodha* (consciousness)."

SCHOLAR: There is no *pātra* (a pot, vessel).

SWAMIJI: That is no *pātra*. When there is "*pātra*", when [you are a] pot, you are not worthy of God consciousness.

SCHOLAR: Receptacle.

SWAMIJI: It means, God consciousness won't exist in you. So there are two: "You are one with God consciousness", that is divine, that is real. "You are not worthy of having God consciousness, you are not worthy of possessing God consciousness", it means, there is a possessor and a possessed. "You are one with God consciousness", there is no possessor, there is no possessed. So, instead of "*pātram*", you should put "*mātram*".

Evaṁ svadehaṁ bodhaika mātram, when your body becomes one with God consciousness, *galita bhedakam*, and this differentiatedness is removed (the differentiatedness that, "This is the body of Denise", "This is the body of John", "This is the body of Swamiji", "This is the body of Kamala", etcetera), this differentiated perception is removed totally, then there remains only one body, and that body is the universal body.

SCHOLAR: So all of this *snāna*, etcetera, is all just *saṁvit cakrodaya*.

SWAMIJI: Yes (laughs), it is *saṁvit cakrodaya*.[148]

SCHOLAR: There is nothing separate from that.

SWAMIJI: *Paśyan*, when he experiences that, *saṁvitti mātratve svatantre tiṣṭhati*, then he is established in absolute independent consciousness, God consciousness, and he becomes *prabhu* (*prabhu* means, *samartha*, capable), he is capable of being established in absolute independent God consciousness.

148. Lit., the rise (*udaya*) of the wheels (*cakra*) of consciousness (*saṁvit*). In this fourth *āhnika*, *saṁvit cakrodaya* refers to the rise of the wheel of the twelve Kālīs.

SCHOLAR: *Tiṣṭhati prabhuḥ: prabhavanaśīla.*
SWAMIJI: *Prabhavanaśīla, samartha.*

LJA TA04F (41:57)

यत्किञ्चिन्मानसाह्लादि यत्र क्वापीन्द्रियस्थितौ ॥१२०॥
योज्यते ब्रह्मसद्धाम्नि पूजोपकरणं हि तत् ।

yatkiñcinmānasāhlādi yatra kvāpīndriyasthitau //120//
yojyate brahmasaddhāmni pūjopakaraṇaṁ hi tat /

This *sāmagrī* (offering) of *pūjā* (worship) is to be sought first. I mean, the things by which you will adore/worship to Lord Śiva, that is, flowers, *chandana* (sandalwood), scent, essence, all these things you have to collect first before you adore Him. And that collection is to be done from where? Not from the garden, not from flowers, [but from] *yat kiñcit mānasāhlādi*, whatever is digested in your brain, whatever is digested peacefully in your brain, happily, joyfully in your brain. For instance, you (Denise) are digested in the brain of John. John thinks that you are very beautiful. *Yat kiñcit mānasāhlādi*, whatever gives [enjoyment to] your mind, whatever thing, whatever object, [gives enjoyment to] your mind, ...

SCHOLAR: Gives joy to.

SWAMIJI: ... gives joy to your mind, absolute joy, complete joy, it does not matter whatever organ, in which organic field that joy appears, it may appear in sex, it may appear in *rūpa* (form), *śabda* (sound), *sparśa* (touch), any organ (*yatra kvāpi indriya sthitau*), *yojyate brahmā saddhāmni pūjopa karaṇaṁ hi tat*, that, in reality, is the collection of those things for the adoration of Lord Śiva. You must collect those things to adore Lord Śiva.

SCHOLAR: "*Yojyate brahmā saddhāmni*", that means?

SWAMIJI: *Yojyate. Yojyate: tarkeṇa saṁpadyate*, by logic it is proved that this is to be collected. For instance, you get joy by embracing a girl, a beautiful girl – you get joy [from] that. That is the *pūjopakaraṇam*, that is the *sāmagrī* for the adoration of Lord Śiva. You have not to embrace her for *your* joy. You have to embrace her just to offer that joy to your Lord Śiva who is residing in your heart. That is *pūjopakaraṇam.*

SCHOLAR: So that *brahmā saddhāma*?

SWAMIJI: *Brahmā saddhāmni*, the real place of Brahman, the real place of Brahman. This is *pūjā upakaraṇam* for that reality of Brahman.

SCHOLAR: So "Brahmā" here is the Universal state of Consciousness?

SWAMIJI: Universal state of God consciousness.

SCHOLAR: This *sa-kāra*?

SWAMIJI: Why *sa-kāra*?

SCHOLAR: Universal field as well.

SWAMIJI: Not only *sa-kāra*. That will also do, but "Brahmā" is there, it is not that *bījākṣara* here.[149]

SCHOLAR: No, no, I did not mean that should be inserted here, but in the sense of understanding what state was referred to here, this *amṛta* state.

SWAMIJI: "Brahmā" means, the supreme state of Lord Śiva, not *sa-kāra*.

SCHOLAR: So it is not Sadāśiva *bhāva*[150] indicated here.

SWAMIJI: No, [it is] Śiva *bhāva. Brahmā saddhāmni pūjopakaraṇam hi tat*, that is *pūjā-upakaraṇam*, that is the collection for *pūjā*, that is the collection of all those things to be adored to Lord Śiva. You have to adore Lord Śiva, e.g., just see that divine flower from the garden and offer that beauty of that flower to Lord Śiva who is residing in your heart. This is *pūjā*. Or a beautiful boy you are embracing, and that joy, carry that joy to Lord Śiva, who is all-consciousness, and offer that joy to Him. Don't taste that joy yourself (laughs). It is for Him.

But why this is called "real worship"? To explain that, he explains the next *śloka*:

---

149. By *bījākṣara* (the first syllable of a *mantra*), Swamiji is referring to the letter *sa* (*sa-kāra*), which is also called *tritiya brahmā*, the third Brahmā (viz., *śa*, *ṣa*, and *sa*).

150. In Mātṛkā *cakra* (the wheel of the alphabet) as related to the thirty-six *tattvas* (elements), the letter '*sa*' refers to the *tattva* of Sadāśiva. See *Light on Tantra in Kashmir Shaivism, Tantrāloka Vol. Two*, chapter, 3, Appendix 14, p. 464.

LJA TA04F (47:11)

पूजा नाम विभिन्नस्य भावौघस्यापि सङ्गतिः ॥१२१॥
स्वतन्त्रविमलानन्तभैरवीयचिदात्मना ।

pūjā nāma vibhinnasya bhāvaughasyāpi saṅgatiḥ //121//
svatantravimalānanta-bhairavīyacidātmanā /

In fact, worshipping is that, in the real sense, when *vibhinnasya bhāvaughasyāpi*, this differentiated world of objectivity is being united with that pure, infinite, independent, and all-consciousness of Bhairava. When this differentiated objective perception is united in that, that is in the real sense *pūjā*, that is the real *pūjā*. That *pūjā* like in those temples, it is not *pūjā*; or the *pūjā* of bowing down before the image of Christ in a Church is not *pūjā*; or bowing to Hazrat Mohammad in a mosque is not *pūjā*. Real *pūjā* is that *pūjā* when you unite this objective world in that God consciousness. When this objective world is digested in that God consciousness, the state of God consciousness, that, in fact, is the real *pūjā*. So, whatever you do in daily life, you have to offer that, you have to carry that to God consciousness, the state of God consciousness where Brahman[151] is seated. That is, in the real sense, *pūjā*.[152]

This will be explained now onwards that your own God consciousness is multiplied in each and every objective world, and that will be explained in the next lesson. And that is *saṁvit cakrodaya*, the twelve Kālīs.

When this differentiated world of objectivity is united with the consciousness of Bhairava, that is, in fact, worship. But these two things are absolutely different from each other: whereas Bhairava is *svatantra* (absolutely independent), Bhairava is *vimala* (absolutely pure), *ananta* (unlimited), and filled with consciousness (*cidātmanā*); whereas this objective world is not *svatantra*, it is dependent

151. "In Kashmir Shaivism, Brahmā (the creator) refers to the state of Śakti, and Brahman refers to the state Lord Śiva." *Tantrāloka* 10.168 commentary (LJA archive).
152. This process of internal worship is beautifully explained by Abhinavagupta in his hymn, *Dehastadevatacakra*. See footnote 157 for reference.

to *pramātṛ* (the subject), and it is not *vimala*, it is impure, and it is not *ananta*, it is *sānta*, it is limited, and it is unconscious. So how can this unconscious and all this limited universe of objectivity be united with that independent pure Being of consciousness, Bhairava? How can two things of different aspects be united, Bhairava with the objective world? For this he explains this next *śloka*, 122nd.

LJA TA04F (50:45)

तथाहि संविदेवेयमन्तर्बाह्योभयात्मना ॥ १२२ ॥
स्वातन्त्र्याद्वर्तमानैव परामर्शस्वरूपिणी ।

tathāhi saṁvideveyam-antarbāhyobhayātmanā //122//
svātantryādvartamānaiva parāmarśasvarūpiṇī / [153]

The answer to this objection is that, in fact, this state of Consciousness has taken two forms: internally and externally. Internally She is one with Bhairava, and externally She is absolutely filled in the universal objective world. And it is His free will that *vartamānaiva*, She is always one in objectivity and in the subjective world also. So there is no question of... the question of differentiation does not arise.

SCHOLAR: *Svātantryāt.*

SWAMIJI: Because of Her *svātantrya* (independence).

SCHOLAR: *Parāmarśa svarūpiṇī.*

SWAMIJI: And *parāmarśa svarūpiṇyeva bhavati.* And that *parāmarśa* (experience) of Consciousness he differentiates now in the following *ślokas*:

LJA TA04F (52:05)

स च द्वादशधा तत्र सर्वमन्तर्भवेद्यतः ॥ १२३ ॥
सूर्य एव हि सोमात्मा स च विश्वमयः स्थितः ।
कलाद्वादशकात्मैव तत्संवित्परमार्थतः ॥ १२४ ॥

153. See also *Interview on Kashmir Shaivism* 2, audio 351 (32:16).

sa ca dvādaśadhā tatra sarvamantarbhavedyataḥ //123//
sūrya eva hi somātmā sa ca viśvamayaḥ sthitaḥ /
kalādvādaśakātmaiva tatsaṁvitparamārthataḥ //124//

That *parāmarśa* [of Consciousness] is actually twelvefold only. It is not sixteenfold, it is not eightfold, it is not fourfold, it is twelvefold. In fact, the real state of this *parāmarśa* is twelvefold because *tatra sarvam antar bhavet yataḥ*, in that twelvefold Being, all other three are digested. The sixteenfold state is digested in the twelvefold state, and the eightfold state is also digested in the twelvefold state, and the fourfold state is also digested in the twelvefold state. Because *sūrya eva hi somātmā*, the objective world is sixteenfold, the cognitive world is twelvefold, the subjective world is eightfold, and beyond the subjective world, that is, supreme consciousness, pure consciousness, the state of *pramiti bhāva*, is fourfold. And these four states of consciousness are digested in one state, that is, the twelvefold cognitive state. Because *sūrya eva hi somātmā* (verse 124), in fact, the cognitive state is concerned with the sun, the objective state is concerned with the moon, and the subjective state is concerned with [fire, viz.], *śuddha* (pure) *pramātṛ bhāva*, and the last one is concerned with pure *pramiti bhāva*.

There is a difference between *pramātṛ bhāva* and *pramiti bhāva*. *Pramātṛ bhāva* is that state of consciousness where objective perception is attached. When that state of *pramātṛ bhāva* is attached with objective perception, that is the pure state of *pramātṛ bhāva*. When it moves to the state where there is no objective perception, [where] there is no touch of objective perception, [where] it is beyond objective perception, that is *pramiti bhāva*.

JOHN: Pure subjectivity.

SWAMIJI: Pure subjectivity …

JOHN: Without an object.

SWAMIJI: … without an object, just like *śāstrajña*, the one who knows, he is well-informed in, *śāstra*. Without taking *śāstra*s in his hands, he is supposed to recognize everything without the help of *śāstra*s. That is [like] the state of *pramiti bhāva*. Now he says how all these other three states are digested in the cognitive state (*pramāṇa bhāva*).

Sūrya eva hi somātmā, *sūrya* (sun) is the state of cognition, and the moon is the state of the objective world, and *agni* (fire) is the state of the subjective world, and beyond *agni* it is *pramiti bhāva*. *Sūrya eva hi somātmā*, because as *sūrya* (the sun) has become *soma* (the moon), *sūrya* has taken the state of the objective world (because the objective world cannot exist when it is not perceived in cognition; when there is cognition, then the objective world exists), ...*

SCHOLAR: *Prāgyevartho'prakāśasyat*.[154]

SWAMIJI: Yes.

*... and that cognition also remains then when *pramātṛ bhāva* is also in that (so, the state of *pramātṛ bhāva* is diluted in cognition and the state of objective world (*prameya bhāva*) is also diluted in the cognitive state), so there are only twelvefold states of consciousness (*dvādaśakātma*), and he will give rise to the twelve Kālīs from this.

JOHN: All these are included in the cognitive state except *pramiti* or also *pramiti bhāva*?

SWAMIJI: *Pramiti* also. *Kalādvādaśakātmaiva tat saṁvit paramārthataḥ*, *tat*, so, thus, *saṁvit*, this consciousness, is *paramārthataḥ*, in fact, *kalā dvādaśakātmaiva*, twelvefold, only twelvefold; it will be accepted only twelvefold, not sixteenfold as in the objective world, not eightfold in the subjective world, not fourfold in *pramiti bhāva*, the state of *pramiti bhāva*.

SCHOLAR: So, from the point of view of *saṁvit krama*[155], only *anākhya cakra* is here.

SWAMIJI: Oh, this is all *anākhya cakra*! *Anākhya cakra* is pervading in each and every movement of this state. It is only *anākhya cakra* because the state of *turya* is governing in all these four states.[156]

---

154. "There is no such existence before perception." See *Tantrāloka* 10.94 discussion (LJA archive).

155. The course (*krama*) of consciousness (*saṁvit*).

156. Lit., the wheel (*cakra*) of the unknowable (*anākhya*). Swamiji will explain that *anākhya* is the "Absolute void which is known in the state of the unknown. It is unknown and, at the same time, it is known. That is the absolute void." "*Anākhya* is the state of *pramiti bhāva*." "*Anākhya* is more than *turya*." "The state of *turya* (lit., 'the fourth') is said to be the penetration of all energies simultaneously, not in succession. All of the energies are residing there but are not in manifestation. They are all together without distinction. *Turya* is called *savyāpārā* because all of the energies get their power to function in that state. At the same time, this

SCHOLAR: *Tailavalasya.*
SWAMIJI: *Tailavat*, yes.[157]

LJA TA04F (58:06)
LJA TA04G (00:00)

सा च मातरि, विज्ञाने माने करणगोचरे ।
मेये चतुर्विधं भाति रूपमाश्रित्य सर्वदा ॥१२५॥

sā ca mātari, vijñāne māne karaṇagocare /
meye caturvidhaṁ bhāti rūpamāśritya sarvadā //125//

Sā, that consciousness, that energy of consciousness, *mātari*, in *pramātṛ bhāva* (after "*mātari*" you have to put a comma), *vijñāne māne*, and in the *vijñāna* (knowledge) which is *pramāṇa bhāva* (*māne* means, *vijñāne eva māne*), *karaṇa gocare*, and the object of the organic field (in the object of the organic field, that is, *prameya, prameya bhāva*), so that consciousness in *pramātṛ bhāva*, in *pramāṇa bhāva*, and in *prameya bhāva*, *caturvid rūpām āśritya sarvadā bhāti*, fourfold formations, fourfold faces of Her own nature, getting hold of these fourfold natures of Her nature, *sarvadā bhāti*, She shines always. In *pramātṛ bhāva*, She takes fourfold stages, in *vijñāna* also (that is, *pramāṇa*) fourfold stages, and in *karaṇa gocare* [viz., *prameya bhāva*] also taking hold of fourfold stages. That is, *sṛṣṭi*, *sthiti*, *saṁhṛtī*, and *anākhya*. [In the field of *pramātṛ bhāva*], *sṛṣṭi* means, the creation of *pramātṛ bhāva*; *sthiti* means, the establishment in *pramātṛ bhāva*; *saṁhritī* means, the destruction of *pramātṛ bhāva*; *anākhya* means, the gap of *pramātṛ bhāva*. Between *pramātṛ bhāva* and *pramāṇa bhāva* there is a gap, in that gap, that is *anākhya*. *Sṛṣṭi*, *sthiti*, *saṁhṛtī*, and

state is known as *anāmaya* because it remains un-agitated by all of these energies." *Kashmir Shaivism–The Secret Supreme* 11.72–84

157. *Triṣu caturthaḥ tailavadāsecyam.* "The fourth state (*turya*) must be expanded like oil so that it pervades the other three: waking, dreaming, and deep sleep." *Shiva Sutras–The Supreme Awakening*, 3.20, p. 180.

anākṣa. *Anākṣa* means, that gap, *śūnya* (void).[158] In the same way, *vijñāne māne*, in *vijñāna* (that is, *pramāṇa bhāva*, the cognitive sphere of Her consciousness), in the cognitive sphere also, She creates *sṛṣṭi*, *sthiti*, *saṁhṛtī*, and *anākṣa* (creation, establishment, destruction, and *anākṣa* means, the gap, the gap between *pramāṇa* and *prameya*). And *karaṇa gocare meye*, in *karaṇa gocare*, the object of the organic field, which is *meye* (*prameya bhāva*, the objective world), in that also, She takes hold of fourfold states, that is, creation, establishment (*sthiti*), *saṁhāra* means, destruction, and *anākhya* means, the gap. In this way, She takes the formation of twelve Kālīs.[159]

JEREMY: So that gap in *prameya*, then, is the gap between what? *Prameya* and…?

SWAMIJI: In *pramātā* (the subject) there is a gap, which will be found in-between *pramātṛ bhāva* and *pramāṇa bhāva*. And after *pramāṇa bhāva* there is a gap after destruction, which will be found between *pramāṇa bhāva* and *prameya bhāva*. And in *prameya bhāva* there is also a gap, that is, *anākhya*, which will be found in[-between] *prameya bhāva* and *pramātṛ bhāva*. Because it is a round circle. So there are twelve Kālīs. Now the 126th [*śloka*].

नन्वेवंरूपत्वेनावभासमानाया अस्या
वैशिष्ट्यमवश्याश्रयणीयम्

nanvevaṁrūpatvenāvabhāsamānāyā asyā
vaiśiṣṭyamavaśyāśrayaṇīyam (commentary)

When it is such that She takes twelvefold stages to manifest Her nature (Her nature is manifested in twelvefold stages), in this way, *vaiśiṣṭyam avaśyam āśrayaṇīyam*, there must be some difference between these twelve states of Consciousness. I want to [clarify] this differentiation where in which differentiation She is existing. What is

158. That is, the void of pure consciousness.

159. See Appendix 4, p. 390, on the twelve Kālīs.

the difference between the state of *pramātṛ bhāva* and *pramāṇa bhāva*, and *pramāṇa bhāva* and *prameya bhāva*, and *prameya bhāva* and *pramātṛ bhāva*? Where is that difference?

LJA TA04G (05:30)

शुद्धसंविन्मयी प्राच्ये ज्ञाने शब्दनरूपिणी ।
करणे ग्रहणाकारा यतः श्रीयोगसञ्चरे ॥१२६॥

śuddhasaṁvinmayī prācye jñāne śabdanarūpiṇī /
karaṇe grahaṇākārā yataḥ śrīyogasañcare //126//

It is indicated in the *Yogasañcara Tantra*[160]: *śuddha saṁvit mayī prācye jñāne*, in the first consciousness (*pramātṛ*), She is filled with pure *saṁvit*, pure consciousness. In *karaṇe* (*pramāṇa*), She is just *śabdana rūpiṇī*, She is just *śabdana* (*śabdana* means, filled with knowledge). She is partly known, partly not known. Because one's own nature is not known, it is [just] there (that is pure consciousness, that is in *pramātṛ bhāva*). In *jñāna*, [She] is *śabda*; *śabda* means, it is known, it is known there, She finds the state of consciousness there, She realizes that state of consciousness. But in the first [consciousness], it is not a realization, it is just there.

JOHN: Why do they use the word *śabda*? Isn't that to do with sound?

SWAMIJI: *Śabda* means, *parāmarśa*. *Śabda* is *parāmarśa*.

JAGDISH: *Pramāṇa* (cognition).

SWAMIJI: It is *pramāṇa*, yes. In the first *jñāna* (that is, *pramātṛ bhāva*), it is just Her nature.

JAGDISH: Pure nature.

SWAMIJI: Yes, pure nature. In *śabdana rūpiṇī*, *karaṇe* (cognition) is *grahaṇākārā*.[161] It is *grahaṇākārā* because She knows Her nature there in the state of *pramāṇa bhāva*.

JEREMY: She recognizes Her nature.

---

160. A Kula text.

161. The act of grasping.

SWAMIJI: Yes…not "recognizes". She "knows". "Recognizes" is in the field of Recognition (Pratyabhijñā). It is not the question of Pratyabhijñā here. It is said in the *Yogasañcare*. And this *Yoga Tantra*, he gives the reference of the *Yoga*[*sañcara*] *Tantra* in the next *śloka*:

LJA TA04G (07:52)

ये चक्षुर्मण्डले श्वेते प्रत्यक्षे परमेश्वरि ।
षोडशारं द्वादशारं तत्रस्थं चक्रमुत्तमम् ॥१२७॥

ye cakṣurmaṇḍale śvete pratyakṣe parameśvari /
ṣoḍaśāraṁ dvādaśāraṁ tatrasthaṁ cakramuttamam //127//

Ye cakṣur maṇḍale śvete pratyakṣe parameśvari, O Pārvatī ("Parameśvari" is *āmantraṇam*, it is *āmantraṇa pada*[162]), …

JAGDISH: Yes.

SWAMIJI: … take the reference of one's eyes (eye-*golakas*).[163] *Śvete maṇḍale, cakṣur śvete maṇḍale ye.*

JAGDISH: *Dve* (two).

SWAMIJI: *Ye dve sthita*. Those *śvete maṇḍala*, *śveta maṇḍala* means, white pockets. First you will come with the white [circles] in this [eye]. Those are absolutely white, and *pratyakṣe*, it is *pratyakṣa* (evident) in each eye, [and also] in each organ, but in the eye it is vividly seen. In the ear also, the same thing is existing. In the nose also. In *śabda*, *sparśa*, *rūpa*, *rasa*, and *gandha*, in all these five senses, these *maṇḍalas* are existing, but to make it quite clear, he gives the reference of one's eyes.

JAGDISH: So, *maṇḍala* here he refers to these round shapes …

SWAMIJI: Round, round shapes.

JAGDISH: … of this white part [of the eye].

SWAMIJI: Because there are two [circles], so it is in *maṇḍale*, *dve-maṇḍale* (two circles).

162. The vocative case.

163. Lit., the eye balls.

JAGDISH: *Dve-maṇḍale.*

SWAMIJI: *Soḍaśāraṁ dvādaśāraṁ tatrasthaṁ cakram uttamam*, there you will find the wheel of *ṣoḍaśāraṁ* (sixteen spokes) and the wheel of twelve spokes.

JAGDISH: In these?

SWAMIJI: In these *maṇḍalas*. This is a sixteen-spoke *maṇḍala* here, and inside this it is a twelve-spoke *maṇḍala.* and inside that, in the center of that eye where there is the pupil, that is *aṣṭa maṇḍala*, an eightfold *maṇḍala*. So, the first round one is …

DEVOTEES: Sixteen.

SWAMIJI: … sixteen … he will [clarify] it because there is another *maṇḍala* also. *Ye cakṣur maṇḍale śvete pratyakṣe* (*pratyakṣe* means, [it is evident] in each and every organ), Parameśvarī, O Pārvatī, *ṣoḍaśāraṁ dvādaśāraṁ* … it does not mean that there are sixteenfold spokes and twelve spokes only. There are eightfold spokes, there are fourfold spokes also. So there are four *maṇḍalas* in each organ. That is, *sṛṣṭi*, *sthiti*, *saṁhṛitī*, and *anākṣa*. *Sṛṣṭi*, *sthiti*, *saṁhṛitī*, and *anākṣa*, [they] will be connected with [the four *maṇḍalas*]. The outside organ is sixteenfold, inside that is twelvefold, inside that is eightfold, and inside that it is fourfold. Now he [clarifies] it in the next *śloka*:

LJA TA04G (11:48)

प्रतिवारणवद्रक्ते तद्बहिर्ये तदुच्यते ।
द्वितीयं मध्यगे ये ते कृष्णश्वेते च मण्डले ॥१२८॥

prativāraṇavadrakte tadbahirye taducyate /
dvitīyaṁ madhyage ye te kṛṣṇaśvete ca maṇḍale //128//
(not recited in full)

Prativāraṇavat rakte ye maṇḍale, *prativāraṇavat*, when there is *prativāraṇavat*, when you close your eyelids, you will find there is some redness in whiteness in another twofold *maṇḍalas* – there is reddish-whiteness. First it is absolutely white. Inside that is reddish-whiteness in another two *maṇḍalas* (*prativāraṇavat rakte tadbahir*, *tadbahir* means, after that, after that white *maṇḍala* there is a reddish-white [*maṇḍala*], *tad ucyate dvitīyam*, that is the second *maṇḍala*). *Madhyage ye te kṛṣṇaśvete ca maṇḍale*, and in that center, after that center, there is *kṛṣṇa śvete*, a black and white [*maṇḍala*]. First is white, then is reddish-white, then is black and white (that is *kṛṣṇa śvete ca maṇḍale*).

LJA TA04G (13:11)

तदन्तर्ये स्थिते शुद्धे भिन्नाञ्जनसमप्रभे ।
चतुर्दले तु ते ज्ञेयेऽग्नीषोमात्मके प्रिये ॥१२९॥

tadantarye sthite śuddhe bhinnāñjanasamaprabhe /
caturdale tu te jñeye'gnīṣomātmake priye //129//

And inside that [is the *maṇḍala*], which is just *bhinnāñjana*, just like…you know *suramā*? *Añjana* means, *suramā* (collyrium), when you put that black dust on your eyes with some stick. That is *bhinnāñjana samaprabhe*, inside that, in the pupil, there is *bhinnāñjana sama*, it is just like *bhinnāñjana*, just like the mixture of that [black] dust, that color. *Caturdale tu te jñeye*, those are the fourfold *maṇḍala*s.

So there are sixteenfold *maṇḍala*s (that will go in *prameya bhāva*), twelvefold *maṇḍala*s (that will go in *pramāṇa bhāva*), eightfold *maṇḍala*s (that will go in *pramātṛ bhāva*), and fourfold *maṇḍala*s (that will go in *pramiti bhāva*).[164]

Agnīṣomātmake priye, and those are *agnīṣomātmake*, you will find there *pramātā* (*agnī*) and *prameya* (*soma*); *pramātā-prameya bhāva*, one is subjective, one is objective. Subjectivity and objectivity is existing in every *maṇḍala*, each *maṇḍala*–subjectivity and objectivity. Subjectivity is when it is there, objectivity is when it is found, when it is realized. That is *agnīṣomātmake*, *priye* (O Beloved).

---

164. As Swamiji will say onwards, *pramiti bhāva* is *anākhya*.

मिथुनत्वे स्थिते ये च चक्रे द्वे परमेश्वरि ।

mithunatve sthite ye ca cakre dve parameśvari /130a[165]

So they are in *mithuna bhāva*, there is *agni* and *soma* (*pramātā* and *prameya*). Inside there is the consumption of *pramāṇa bhāva* and *pramiti bhāva*–inside both. The predominant *cakra*s are only two existing, that is, *pramātṛ bhāva* and *prameya bhāva*.

GEORGE: That "*mithuna*" means, there's two.

SWAMIJI: *Mithuna* means, two.

LJA TA04G (15:43)

सम्मीलनोन्मीलनं तेऽन्योन्यं विदधातके ॥ १३० ॥

sammīlanonmīlanaṁ te'nyonyaṁ vidadhātake //130//

And they do *sammīlana* (closing) and *unmīlanā* (opening). Sometimes *pramātṛ bhāva* is on the top, sometimes *prameya bhāva* is on the top. When *prameya bhāva* is on the top, then you go astray. When *pramātṛ bhāva* is [on the top], then you go introverted, you become introverted. [This occurs] in each and every organ. When there is *pramātṛ bhāva* [in predominance], you are elevated, you are elevated in God consciousness. When there is *prameya bhāva* [in predominance], you are outside, in the outside world. So, *pramātṛ bhāva* and *prameya bhāva* is always there, they are functioning in each and every moment.

JOHN: What about in the *jagadānanda*, the state?[166] What is functioning there?

SWAMIJI: No, *jagadānanda* is a state of *samādhi*.[167]

---

165. See also *Interview on Kashmir Shaivism*, audio 351 (33:28) (LJA archives).

166. Lit., the state of rejoicing the world.

167. "*Unmīlanā* (extroverted *samādhi*) and *nimīlanā* (introverted *samādhi*) in one body is *jagadānanda*." *Tantrāloka* 13.186 (LJA archive).

JOHN: But it is also an extroverted state, it's an extroverted state of *samādhi*, I mean, you are outside in the world.

SWAMIJI: No, [*jagadānanda*] is not [only] extroverted. It is introverted in extroverted, extroverted in introverted. It is not [referring to] that [here].

JOHN: So this is question of *prameya* …

SWAMIJI: This is a question of manifestation, it is [the way of] manifestation in each and every way of life.

JOHN: No, I know. I am saying, in here, *prameya* means that you're astray …

SWAMIJI: *Jagadānanda* is only in *samādhi*.

JOHN: If *prameya* is in predominance, you are astray; if *pramātṛ* is in predominance, you become introverted in this, and this is in all states of life. What about in *jagadānanda*? Is also *prameya* predominant there?

SWAMIJI: No. *Prameya* is diluted in *pramātṛ bhāva*, *pramātṛ bhava* is diluted in *prameya bhāva*, there in *jagadānanda*. It is not the question [here].

GEORGE: So those senses take a different function there.

SWAMIJI: Yes. [Here] it is a question of the Kālīs, the twelve Kālīs, which have [created] this manifestation of the whole universe, inside and outside.

Now go to the 131st *śloka*. Now, how is it like? How the combination of both of these function simultaneously? They function simultaneously. Simultaneously does not mean, at once. Simultaneously means, one first, then the second, then the first, then second, then the first, then the second. This is the way of Kālīs. To be alert…because there are two states: one is introverted, one is extroverted. But it is not the question of *jagadānanda*. *Jagadānanda* is the state of *samādhi* [where] in introverted nature you will find extroverted nature, in extroverted nature you will find introverted nature–there [in *jagadānanda*].

LJA TA04G (18:52)

यथा योनिश्च लिङ्गं च संयोगात्स्रवतोऽमृतम् ।
तथामृताग्निसंयोगाद्-द्रवतस्ते न संशयः ॥१३१॥

yathā yoniśca liṅgaṁ ca saṁyogātsravato'mṛtam /
tathāmṛtāgnisaṁyogād-dravataste na saṁśayaḥ //131//

There is no doubt about it, just as ...*

[Abhinavagupta] gives a reference. He always gives odd references, which are not liked by saints. He is tough!

*...*yathā yoniśca liṅgaṁ ca*, take two organs (*yoni* means, the organ of a woman, and *liṅga* means, the organ of a man), *saṁyogāt*, when they unite, when they are united with each other, *sravato amṛtam*, they create nectar, that blissful state (that is sexual pleasure; in sexual pleasure they create that blissful state), *tathāmṛtāgni saṁyogāt dravataste na saṁśayaḥ*, in the same way, ...*

This is not to be done. This is just an example. He has put this example because he puts such examples, odd examples (laughs).

DENISE: To make it quite clear.

SWAMIJI: To make it clear.

*... *tathāmṛtāgni saṁyogāt dravataste na saṁśayaḥ*, in the same way, *amṛtāgnisaṁyogāt*, when *amṛta* and *agni* are united with each other...

JOHN: *Amṛta* and *agni* means, *prameya* and *pramātṛ*?

SWAMIJI: Yes.

JAGDISH: *Soma-agni*.

SWAMIJI: *Soma* and *agni*. *Soma* is *amṛta*.

JOHN: *Prameya* and *pramātṛ*.

SWAMIJI: *Pramātṛ* is fire.

JOHN: Fire, *agni*.

SWAMIJI: Yes.

JOHN: *Soma* is *prameya*?

SWAMIJI: *Pramātṛ* is *agni* (fire). That will go to the male class. He is just fire, without any blissful state. Blissful state comes out from *soma*. That is a woman.

JOHN: *Soma* means, *soma rasa* here? How will we translate *soma*?

SWAMIJI: *Soma* means, the moon, not *soma rasa*.

JOHN: So it takes reflection of fire, like that.

SWAMIJI: No, when they are united, [when] fire and *soma* are united, *amṛta* is created. *Amṛta* is created, that is what he says here.

JAGDISH: Actually, these are two terms to indicate male and female.

SWAMIJI: Yes.

JAGDISH: *Soma* and *agni.*

SWAMIJI: *Soma* and *agni*, yes. But why he gave this reference, this odd reference? [Jayaratha] said it is not...

लिङ्गशब्देन विद्वांसः सृष्टिसंहारकारणम् ।
लयादागमनाच्चाहुर्भावानां पदमव्ययम् ॥

liṅgaśabdena vidvāṁsaḥ sṛṣṭisaṁhārakāraṇam /
layādāgamanāccāhur-bhāvānāṁ padamavyayam //[168]

JAGDISH: *Padam paramam.*

SWAMIJI: "*Paramam padam*" is the real reading. "*Padam avyayam*" is there.

JAGDISH: Yes, Sir.

SWAMIJI: In place of "*padam avyayam*", you should put "*paramam padam*" – "*bhāvānāṁ paramam padam.*"

In "*liṅga*", you will find '*la*' and '*ga*', the [letter] '*la*' and the [letter] '*ga*'. So that [person] who realizes the reality of *liṅga* must understand that *liṅga* does not mean this male organ. It means, actually, *laya* and *āgaman* (*laya* means, absorption; *āgaman* means, manifestation), when there is absorption, when there is manifestation. You go in the introverted state, that is *laya.* You go in the extroverted state, that is *āgaman.* That is *liṅga*, that is the state of *liṅga.* And *liṅga* does not exist only in men, it exists in the organ of a woman also – *liṅga.*

168. This verse from an unknown source in quoted in Jayaratha's commentary.

LJA TA04G (22:55)

तच्चक्रपीडनाद्रात्रौ ज्योतिर्भात्यर्कसोमगम् ।
तां दृष्ट्वा परमां ज्योत्स्नां कालज्ञानं प्रवर्तते ॥ १३२ ॥

taccakrapīḍanādrātrau jyotirbhātyarkasomagam /
tāṁ dṛṣṭvā paramāṁ jyotsnāṁ kālajñānaṁ pravartate //132// [169]

Tat cakra pīḍanāt, when these *cakra*s, these four *cakra*s, are *pīḍanāt*, squeezed with each other, united with each other, diluted with each other, …*

These *cakra*s, four *cakra*s: One is that of *prameya* (that is with sixteen spokes), another *cakra* is *pramāṇa* with twelve spokes, the third is of *pramātṛ bhāva* with eight spokes, and the fourth is *pramiti bhāva* with four spokes.

*… and these fourfold *cakra*s (wheels), when they are united with each other, absorbed, diluted in each other (that is *pīḍana*), *rātrau jyotir bhātyarka somagam* (*rātrau* means, *rātrau satyāmapi*, *māyāmapi*, *māyā daśāyāṁ api*–that is *rātrau*), *rātrau*, in the space of *rātri* (*rātri* means, illusion[170]; in the space of *rātri*, that is, the illusive surface of the world or all these extroverted activities of the world), in those activities of the world, also *arka somagam jyotirbhāti*, that *prakāśa* (light) is existing there. *Tāṁ dṛṣṭvā*, one who realizes that *prakāśa* in each and every objective field, *paramāṁ jyotsnāṁ*, he realizes *paramāṁ jyotsnāṁ*, the supreme state of *soma* (the moon), *kāla jñānaṁ pravartate*, and he realizes the nature of *kāla* (time), that is, the nature of time is timeless.

Actually, *kāla* (time) has nothing to do with time, *kāla* is just the variation of activities. When there are a variety of activities, there is time. When there is nothing to do, there is no time. Because, e.g., you have to cook, you have to clean the pots, put water in that, put sugar in that, put *ghee* in that, then fry it, then put some water in that, then boil it, put salt in it. It will take time. When there is nothing to be done,

169. See also *Interview on Kashmir Shaivism* 2, audio 531 (45:05).
170. *Rātri* literally means, night.

there is no time. Although you are existing in the cycle of time, but there is no time. When you are only doing one thing only, where is the time? You are above time. That is *kāla jñāna*.[171]

That *paramā jyotsnā*, when you realize the state of the supreme moon, supreme consciousness, that supreme consciousness will rise only at the crash, at the dilution, mixture of all these *cakras*. That is the actual state of the twelve Kālīs. You have to find *sṛṣṭi*, *sthiti*, *saṁhrīti*, and *anākṣa* in *prameya* first, then after you find *sṛṣṭi*, *sthiti*, *saṁhrīti*, and *anākṣa* [in *prameya bhāva*], then you have to step in *pramāṇa bhāva*. There you have to find out another four states–*sṛṣṭi*, *sthiti*, *saṁhrīti* and *anākṣa*. *Sṛṣṭi* means, white; *sthiti* means, reddish-white; *saṁhrīti* means, black-white; and *anākhya* means, that…

JAGDISH: Pupil, fourfold pupil.

SWAMIJI: … pupil, [which is] black. [This is observed] in the organic field. Inside also it is *pramātṛ bhāva*, *pramāṇa bhāva*, *prameya bhāva*, and *pramiti bhāva*.

JAGDISH: So that light appears from *arka* and *soma*, is that right?

SWAMIJI: The contact of, the absolute contact of, *arka* and *soma*; the absolute contact of man and woman; the absolute contact of *prameya* (object) and *pramātṛ* (subject).

JOHN: So that's *amṛta*.

SWAMIJI: No, *amṛta* is created.

GEORGE: Is created.

JAGDISH: That is light.

JOHN: Out of that contact.

SWAMIJI: Yes, con- …

JOHN: And that's *pramiti bhāva*?

SWAMIJI: No, that is above *pramiti bhāva*.

GEORGE: So in the reference that he gave, man and woman …

SWAMIJI: That was only an example!

GEORGE: No, that was an analogy. Yes, but what I am saying, in each of the senses, when some experience comes, it also gives that pleasure.

SWAMIJI: Yes, in the ear, in… *bas*, just to make it clear, he has taken the example of the eyes only here.

JOHN: So this happens in all organs.

171. Knowledge of time.

SWAMIJI: Yes.

JOHN: And the reason he takes the example of man and woman is because that is also found in that state. That's why he also clarifies the sexual thing in this. Is this creation, preservation, destruction, and *anākhya* is the void state?

SWAMIJI: Yes.

JOHN: Those three plus the void.

SWAMIJI: Yes.

JOHN: Why do they call it *anākhya*? That means, not spoken?

SWAMIJI: *Anākhya* means …

JOHN: Unspeakable or…?

SWAMIJI: Yes, it is an absolute void. You may call it just "an absolute void".

GEORGE: Unknowable.

SWAMIJI: Absolute void which is known in the state of the unknown. It is unknown, and at the same time, it is known. That is the absolute void. Now [Jayaratha] says:

ननु यदि एवं, तत् विश्वस्यावभास एव न स्यात्

nanu yadi evaṁ, tat viśvasyāvabhāsa eva na syāt (commentary)

When this contact will take place, when this contact of all these four *cakra*s will take place, then this whole world should not exist. Where is the space for the world to exist?

LJA TA04G (29:52)

सहस्रारं भवेच्चक्रं ताभ्यामुपरि संस्थितम् ।

sahasrāraṁ bhaveccakraṁ tābhyāmupari saṁsthitam /133a

Then you have to find out in, you have to step again ahead, you have to step ahead again and see that it is not only fourfold *cakra*s (*ṣoḍaśāra cakra*, *dvādaśāra cakra*, *aṣṭāra cakra*, and *caturāra cakra*), it is not only these fourfold *cakra*s, it is *sahasrāra cakra*, you will get entry in *sahasrāra cakra*, then you will find activity in full, the activity of God consciousness in full–*sahasrāra cakra.*

JAGDISH: Thousand.

SWAMIJI: A thousand spokes. It is not actually a thousand spokes, it is *asaṁkhyāra* (numberless) *cakra*! In the long run, it will touch that *cakra* which has got *asaṁkhyāra cakra*. *Asaṁkhyāra cakra*, it has no number, it has numberless *cakra*s. When numberless *cakra*s are found, is realized, in this state of life, in this daily routine of life, numberless *cakra*s, then you are God yourself. You have nothing to do.

GEORGE: So then that process of the senses takes a different role. Instead of that individual *amṛta* being produced, there's *amṛta*s all-around. Is that what you...?

SWAMIJI: Yes, *amṛta* is all-around, yes.

GEORGE: Fulfilling every sense organ, no matter what experience.

SWAMIJI: The whole universe also. He becomes one with the universe. That is *sahasrāra cakra*.

LJA TA04G (31:36)

Sahasrāraṁ bhaveccakraṁ tābhyāmupari saṁsthitam, *tābhyām upari* (*tābhyām upari* means, *somāgnicakrābhyām upari*), *soma* and *agni*, beyond *soma* and *agni*, beyond these two *cakra*s. Because first there are fourfold *cakra*s, and when these fourfold *cakra*s are diluted, they become twofold *cakra*s, because he takes *pramātṛ cakra* and *prameya cakra*, and in those two *cakra*s, the other two *cakras* are diluted.

JOHN: Other two *cakra*s means, *pramāṇa* and *pramiti cakra*?

SWAMIJI: ...*pramiti cakra*, yes. *Pramiti cakra* will be attached to *pramātṛ bhāva* and *pramāṇa cakra* will be attached to *prameya bhāva*. And *sahasrāra cakra* will exist afterwards.

JEREMY: What? When those two are united?

SWAMIJI: When those two are united, then *sahasrāra cakra* will [arise].

LJA TA04G (32:55)

ततश्चक्रात्समुद्भूतं ब्रह्माण्डं तदुदाहृतम् ॥ १३३ ॥

tataścakrātsamudbhūtaṁ brahmāṇḍaṁ tadudāhṛtam //133//[172]

Then the creation of this whole universe takes place by those *cakras*. In the same way, when you have conducted the contact with two *cakras* (*soma cakra* and *agni cakra*) physically, …*

What is physical contact?

JOHN: Sexual intercourse.

SWAMIJI: Sex, yes.

*… you get creation, e.g., you get Viresha. Viresha is created, [then] another, Shanna is created[173], everything is created. In the same way, when this *sahasrāra cakra* takes place, *brahmāṇḍa* is created (the whole one hundred and eighteen worlds are created). This is through that super-sexual [contact between *soma cakra* and *agni cakra*].

JOHN: Everything is sexual.

SWAMIJI: Yes, everything is sexual. *Tataścakrātsamudbhūtaṁ brahmāṇḍaṁ tadudāhṛta*, that is nominated as *brahmāṇḍa*. *Brahmāṇḍa* means, the whole universe. The whole universe has come out by this contact.

JOHN: Is that why, if you are in *śāktopāya* awareness, that this sexual practice will carry you to God consciousness at once?

SWAMIJI: Yes, yes, at once!

LJA TA04G (34:16)

तत्रस्थां मुञ्चते धारां सोमो ह्यग्निप्रदीपितः ।
सृजतीत्थं जगत्सर्वमात्मन्यात्मन्यनन्तकम् ॥ १३४ ॥

tatrasthāṁ muñcate dhārāṁ somo hyagnipradīpitaḥ /
sṛjatītthaṁ jagatsarvam-ātmanyātmanyanantakam //134//[174]

---

172. See also *Interview on Kashmir Shaivism* 2, audio 531 (51:45).

173. The son and daughter of John and Denise Hughes.

174. See also *Interview on Kashmir Shaivism* 2, audio 531 (46:55 and 57:53).

This is the best *śloka* that I have found in his book.

Tatrasthāṁ muñcate dhārāṁ somo hyagnipradīpikaḥ[175], *somo* (*somo* means, *soma, soma cakra*), *agni pradīpitaḥ*, *soma cakra* (not an unaware *soma*[176]), ...*

JAGDISH: *Pradīpitaḥ.*

SWAMIJI: *...*pradīpitaḥ*, when you induce fire in *soma*, *soma* will induce *amṛta* (nectar) in fire. Do you understand? Don't go only to sex (laughter) and lose the ...

DEVOTEES: (laughter)

JOHN: But everything is sex, I'm not going only to sex. But "inducing fire" in this means that *pramātṛ* (subjectivity) induces fire in *prameya* (objectivity).

SWAMIJI: Yes, this is Śaivism. *Tatrasthāṁ muñcate dhārāṁ somo hyagnipradīpikaḥ, agni pradīpitaḥ soma, dhārāṁ muñcate* (*jñāna dhāraṁ muñcate*; *jñāna dhārā* means, the flow of knowledge; *muñcate* [means], flows), ...

JAGDISH: Releases.

SWAMIJI: ... [this contact] releases the flow of knowledge, and that releases the flow of *amṛta*. That sex, it releases the flow of knowledge that, "I am this whole universe, one hundred and eighteen worlds and above it." *Sṛjatītthaṁ jagat sarvam ātmany-ātmany-anantakam*, in the same way, *ātmani ātmani* (*ātmani ātmani* means, *pratyātmani*), in each and every individual, *soma* and *agni*, you will find that it is created, it is created by the contact.

JOHN: Every perception, everything, everything, everything.

SWAMIJI: Yes. It is universal creation. Now he will connect it with individual creation in the next *śloka*–it is individual creation. Universal creation is from Lord Śiva. This is the functioning of Lord Śiva himself here. Now, the individual state also, in individuality also, you find the same process.

---

175. Swamiji recites "*dīpikaḥ*" in place of the published "*dīpitaḥ*".

176. That is, objectivity devoid of subjectivity.

LJA TA04G (36:50)

sṛjatītthaṁ jagatsarvam-ātmanyātmanyanantakam //134//
(repeated)

Itthaṁ, in this very way, this wheel of *soma* creates an uncommon world also in each individual. That [was] a common world.

SCHOLAR: *Sādhāraṇā*.

SWAMIJI: The *sādhāraṇā* world is the common world, which is created by Lord Śiva. The *asādhāraṇā* world is an uncommon world.

SCHOLAR: Individual.

SWAMIJI: It is created by individuals (man and woman). That world which is created by these two is called an "uncommon world".

SCHOLAR: So, in these preceding verses, the *adhikāra* (topic) of *caryākrama* is not so present.[177] It really starts here.

SWAMIJI: The *adhikāra* of *caryākrama* is…

SCHOLAR: … there, too.

SWAMIJI: Yes, it is touching [the topic].

SCHOLAR: But here, the emphasis is on the universal process in realization, and this [topic] is outside that…

SWAMIJI: But that [was] the *caryākrama* of Lord Śiva. When the *caryākrama* of Lord Śiva does not take place, the *caryākrama* of the individual will not exist. *Caryākrama* is functioned by Lord Śiva himself first, and then it shines in the individual formation also.

LJA TA04G (37:53)

षोडशद्वादशाराभ्यामष्टारेष्वथ सर्वशः ।
एवं क्रमेण सर्वत्र चक्रेष्वमृतमुत्तमम् ॥ १३५॥
सोमः स्त्रवति यावच्च पञ्चानां चक्रपद्धतिः ।

177. *Caryākrama* is a technical term in Kashmir Shaivism referring to sexual union, more specifically, the sexual union between a yogi and a yoginī. See also *Light on Tantra in Kashmir Shaivism, Tantrāloka, Vol. Two*, fn. 289, p. 159.

ṣoḍaśadvādaśārābhyām-aṣṭāreṣvatha sarvaśaḥ /
evaṁ krameṇa sarvatra cakreṣvamṛtamuttamam //135//
somaḥ sravati yāvacca pañcānāṁ cakrapaddhatiḥ /

This individual creation he explains in these one *śloka* and a half. *Ṣoḍaśa dvādaśārābhyām*, by the sixteenfold and twelvefold wheels, when you get entry in *aṣṭāreṣu* (*aṣṭāreṣu* means, the eightfold and also the fourfold wheels), when you get entry in the eightfold wheel and fourfold wheel (that is, when you get entry in *pramātṛ bhāva* and *para pramātṛ bhāva*[178]; the eightfold wheel is *pramātṛ bhāva* and the fourfold wheel is *para pramātṛ bhāva*), ...*

SCHOLAR: Eightfold is that *khecarī*.

SWAMIJI: Yes.

SCHOLAR: And this is *vyomavameśvari*, this [*para pramātṛ bhāva*].

SWAMIJI: Yes.[179]

*... *ṣoḍaśa dvādaśārābhyām*, and this is to be functioned by these two wheels: by *ṣoḍaśa* (sixteenfold), by the objective way of functioning, and the cognitive way of functioning (*dvādaśa*, twelvefold).

SCHOLAR: This "*atha*" here is in sense of, "then"? *Ānantaryārthe*?[180]

SWAMIJI: *Ānantaryārthe*. *Atha* is "after this".

SCHOLAR: In succession. So first in *ṣoḍaśāra*, then *dvādaśāra*.

SWAMIJI: *Dvādaśārābhyām, aṣṭāreṣu*. "*Aṣṭāreṣu*", it is *saptamī* (locative case). *Aṣṭāreṣu* means, in *aṣṭāra cakra*. It is understood in the fourfold *cakra* also.

SCHOLAR: That is the meaning of the plural here. *Bahuvacanam* is for that.

---

178. That is, *pramiti bhāva*.

179. "*Vāmeśvarī* is the chief energy of all these four energies (*khecarī*, *gocarī*, *dikcarī*, and *bhūcarī*). *Khecarī* is that of the vacuum [of voidness], *gocarī* is that of the organs, *dikcarī* is that of your own personal world, *bhūcarī* is the universal world. *Vāmeśvarī* is the chief energy who handles all these fourfold worlds. And these are internal *cakras*, internal energies." *The Mystery of Vibrationless-Vibration in Kashmir Shaivism, Vasugupta's Spanda Kārikā and Kṣemarāja's Spanda Sandoha*, Revealed by Swami Lakshmanjoo, ed. John Hughes (Lakshmanjoo Academy, Los Angeles, 2016), 393.

180. Immediate sequence or succession.

SWAMIJI: Yes. *Aṣṭāreṣu atha sarvaśaḥ*, all-around, *evaṁ krameṇa sarvatra cakreṣu*, in all these *cakra*s, this *soma*, *uttamam amṛtam sravati*, discharges that supreme nectar of bliss.

SCHOLAR: So he is not just referring to…

SWAMIJI: …*caryākrama* direct yet.

SCHOLAR: But he is saying here, *asādhāraṇāmapi jagat sṛjati*.

SWAMIJI: Yes, it is *asādhāraṇā* (uncommon).

SCHOLAR: So here it is…

SWAMIJI: It is *asādhāraṇā*. It is not *sādhāraṇā jagat* (the common world).

SCHOLAR: But it is still *rahasya* (a mystery), this is not just an ordinary experience of *paśu* (the individual).

SWAMIJI: Because [Abhinavagupta] cannot explain it in clear words. It is a secret.

SCHOLAR: But do these verses refer simply to *paśu bhāva*, how one experiences the emergence of objects in experience?

SWAMIJI: *Paśu bhāva* does not remain here when…*paśu bhāva* does not remain in this function, although it is in [the field of] *paśu*. *Cakreṣu uttamam amṛtam sravati*, the *soma* discharges the supreme nectar of *rasa*, *yāvacca pañcānāṁ cakra paddhati*, until these fivefold wheels get manifested (the fivefold wheels means, *śabda*, *sparśa*, *rūpa*, *rasa*, and *gandha*, the fivefold senses).

SCHOLAR: And *karmendriya*s and *jñānendriya*s?[181]

SWAMIJI: *Jñānendriya*s only. First the *jñānendriya*s, and then he will connect it with *karmendriya*s also.

JOHN: So, whose *soma* is this, then? This nectar, if it is not *paśu*'s, you said it is not the coming into objectivity of…

SWAMIJI: …*paśu bhāva*. It is not *paśu bhāva*…

SCHOLAR: It is *agni-dīpita*[182].

SWAMIJI: Yes. It is already in the state of *paśu bhāva*, but you are above *paśu bhāva* there, when you function this way of the sexual process.

SCHOLAR: So, why does he have the order [as] *ṣoḍaśa-dvādaśa-aṣṭāra*, when there is "*evaṁ krameṇa*"…?

---

181. Organs of action (*karmendriya*s) and knowledge (*jñānendriya*s).

182. Lit., the excited or inflamed (*dīpita*) fire (*agni*), i.e., when subjective consciousness (fire) is united with objective consciousness (moon).

SWAMIJI: No, *ṣoḍaśa-dvādaśārābhyām*, [the sixteenfold and the twelvefold *cakra*s are] the means to get entry in *aṣṭāra* (eightfold) *cakra* and the fourfold wheels. You can't get entry in the fourfold wheels and the eightfold wheels without any means. [You can get entry] by the means of *ṣoḍaśāra cakra* and *dvādaśāra cakra*. *Ṣoḍaśara cakra* means, objectivity; *dvādaśara cakra* is [cognition]. *Ṣoḍaśara cakra* is connected with the woman, *dvādaśara cakra* is connected with the man. Because the man has transformed his consciousness in the cognitive world there, he has become the embodiment of the cognitive world, and the woman has become the embodiment of the objective world.

SCHOLAR: But she has awareness there, so from the point of view of awareness she is ...

SWAMIJI: Awareness, you have to maintain awareness. Without maintaining awareness, you will get entry in *paśu bhāva*.

SCHOLAR: So from her point of view, the *siddha* (the yogi) is *prameya*.

SWAMIJI: Huh?

SCHOLAR: It is says here that she is resting in *ṣoḍaśāra* by emphasis, in the objective, and he is resting in *pramāṇa* by emphasis. That's *saṅgatāvastha* (the state of union).

SWAMIJI: *Pramāṇa bhāva*, because his *pramātṛ bhāva* (subjective state) is not excited at that moment. What is excited there?

SCHOLAR: *Pramāṇa*.

SWAMIJI: In *pramāṇa*, the all-organic field [is excited], and those organs also with connection to cognition, the cognitive organs only. The cognitive organs are only functioning there, and they get excited.

[Gap in recording]

LJA TA04G (43:24)

Along with the sixteenfold and the twelvefold wheels in all the wheels of eightfold and fourfold, this *soma* discharges out the supreme nectar until the state of the fivefold wheels is created, which is the creation of the five senses.

JOHN: So how do you move from twelvefold and sixteenfold, which is man and woman, to eight and fourfold?

SWAMIJI: You get entry in that by functioning that process.

JOHN: By the process which we have already spoken about here.

SWAMIJI: Yes, that is *pīḍana* (squeezing).

SCHOLAR: This is *avaroha krama.*

SWAMIJI: Yes, it is *avaroha krama.*[183]

SCHOLAR: So, Jayaratha hasn't understood this because he takes it as *krama* from first *ṣoḍaśāra* (sixteen), then *dvādaśa* (twelve), then *aṣṭāra* (eight), then *caturāra* (four). That's incorrect.

SWAMIJI: *Aṣṭāra* and *caturāra* is the entry [point]. You get entry in *aṣṭāra* and *caturāra.*

SCHOLAR: And this *ṣoḍaśa-dvādaśa* is *pīṭhakā*, that is the means of entry.

SWAMIJI: Yes, that is the means. Because ["*ṣoḍaśa-dvādaśārābhyām*"] is [in the] instrumental case, and "*aṣṭāreṣu*" is [in the] *saptamī* (locative) case.

SCHOLAR: [Jayaratha] hasn't understood this. He says, "*ṣoḍaśadvādaśārābhyāṁ saha*".

SWAMIJI: No, it is not.

DEVOTEE: No, *dvitiyādhivacana.*

JOHN: So, this *pīḍana* is the means – this squeezing.

SWAMIJI: Squeezing.

JOHN: Which you haven't explained quite what…

SWAMIJI: No, to get the essence out of it,…

SCHOLAR: Through awareness.

SWAMIJI: … both parties are squeezed [together] to get the creation.

JOHN: And its the process…as an outcome of that squeeze is this *soma*, this *rasa*, is it?

SWAMIJI: Yes.

JOHN: Is that the same as seminal fluid? Is that…?

SWAMIJI: Yes, yes, yes. But it is *kuṇḍa-gola*, it is not *śukra* (semen)-*śoṇita* (blood) there.[184]

JOHN: That's ordinary.

SWAMIJI: It is not ordinary.

JOHN: It's super-ordinary.

SWAMIJI: Yes. Now he explains how to withdraw this also.

---

183. A descending (*avaroha*) process (*krama*).

184. "*Kuṇḍa-golaka* is both feminine energy and masculine energy, universal semen and blood." *Tantrāloka* 3.139 (LJA archive).

JOHN: "Withdraw" means?
SWAMIJI: To rise in your God consciousness also.
JOHN: Through this act.
SWAMIJI: Yes, through this act.
JOHN: *Pīḍana.*
SWAMIJI:

LJA TA04G (45:27)

तत्पुनः पिबति प्रीत्या हंसो हंस इति स्फुरन् ॥ १३६ ॥
सकृद्यस्य तु संश्रुत्या पुण्यपापैर्न लिप्यते ।

tatpunaḥ pibati prītyā haṁso haṁsa iti sphuran //136//
sakṛdyasya tu saṁśrutyā puṇyapāpairna lipyate /

That universe of *pramātṛ* and *prameya*, that universe of *pramātṛ* and *prameya bhāva*, is dissolved or is gobbled …

SCHOLAR: *Alaṁgrāsa*, it is dissolved, absorbed.

SWAMIJI: … dissolved by the way of *svātantrya* (*prītyā* means, by the way of *svātantrya*), when you preserve the *svātantrya śakti* there. That is:

LJA TA04G (46:09)

शिवशक्त्यात्मकं रूपं भवयेच्च परस्परम् ।
न कुर्यात् मानवीं बुद्धिं रागमोहादिसंयुताम् ॥

śivaśaktyātmakaṁ rūpaṁ bhavayecca parasparam /
na kuryāt mānavīṁ buddhiṁ rāgamohādisaṁyutām //[185]

---

185. From *Tantrāloka* 1.1, commentary, *KSTS* vol. 23, p. 14. "You must not think that you are mating with your wife or you are mating with your husband. You should not think like that. You should think that, 'My husband is Śiva and I am Pārvatī and we are mating like that.' It is divine mating." *Stava Cintāmaṇi of Bhaṭṭa*

You must not be attached to bodies there. If you are attached to bodies, each other's body, then everything is ruined, all the process…

SCHOLAR: There is no *yāga*, then.

SWAMIJI: There is no *yāga* (sacrifice), yes.

SCHOLAR: [Abhinavagupta] said, *tathātvena samastāni bhāvajātāni paśyataḥ.*[186]

SWAMIJI: Yes. *Haṁso haṁsa iti sphuran*, you have to take the state of *haṁsa* (*haṁsa* means, *para pramātṛ bhāva*) – how? – *haṁsa iti sphuran*, when you, by flashing (*sphuran*, by flashing or throbbing), throbbing *ahaṁ* (I-ness) in *idam* (this-ness). *Haṁsa* means, "*ahaṁ-saḥ*": "This object, which is functioning with me, is inseparable [from] me, is absolutely one with me." And it is done by both parties.

SCHOLAR: Yes.

SWAMIJI: By both parties. The woman believes, understands, that, "I am one with that Śiva", and the man believes that, "I am one with Śakti." There is no difference between the two. That is *haṁsa iti sphuran*.

SCHOLAR: But not *vikalpa krameṇa* (by the process of thoughts).

SWAMIJI: No, it is *nirvikalpa krama* (by the process of thoughtlessness). *Sakṛdyasya tu saṁśrityā*, when, only for once, you get entry, you get the *sākṣātkāra* (realization) of this state, *puṇyapāpairnalipyate*, you are not touched by *puṇya* and *pāpa*, vice and …

SCHOLAR: Virtue.

SWAMIJI: Virtue and vice. All virtues and all vices end there.

SCHOLAR: He has destroyed even the ash of impressions.

SWAMIJI: Yes. This is not connected with this [current topic]. This is above that. He has only touched it just to give you …

JOHN: This is above this.

SWAMIJI: Above our subject. This is not our subject.

SCHOLAR: He is explaining what is the fruit of that in the *nirañjana* state.

SWAMIJI: *Nirañjana* state.[187]

Nārāyaṇa, translation and commentary by Swami Lakshmanjoo ed. John Hughes (Lakshmanjoo Academy, Los Angeles, 2018), verse 87, p. 107.

186. First line from *Tantrāloka* 29.5, which describes the nature of the Kula sacrifice.

187. Lit., spotless, pure, supreme. "There are three states in this sexual act. The

JOHN: In this act, if there was [the awareness of] bodies, then there would be *vikalpa saṁskāra.*

SWAMIJI: No, bodies are not to be experienced.

SCHOLAR: It is completely impression-less.

SWAMIJI: Body, beauty, *rasa* (taste), all this ends there.

JOHN: At this point.

SWAMIJI: At this point.

SCHOLAR: But before that, then you have that *carvaṇā* (tasting) and…

SWAMIJI: Before that it is there.

JOHN: Body is there and sensation is there. For a man, it is mainly sensation. As you said, he is *pramāṇa.*

SWAMIJI: Yes.

JOHN: So then he moves in the cognitive field of sensation and feeling and…

SWAMIJI: Yes. And that *pramāṇa* also is diluted in *prameya bhāva*, and *prameya bhāva* is diluted in *pramāṇa bhāva.* Both are united with each other, in awareness.

SCHOLAR: So, from the point of awareness, this *ṣoḍaśa* (sixteen-fold) and *dvādaśa* (twelvefold) doesn't really apply to the *siddha* and the *yoginī* because they are both in *pramāṇa*, they are both in the field of cognitivity.

SWAMIJI: Yes. It can't be without *pramāṇa.* When *pramāṇa bhāva* is not there, this process won't act.

SCHOLAR: So he is writing here from the point of view of *vīra* rather than…

SWAMIJI: *Vīra* and *yoginī.*

SCHOLAR: But from the *yoginī*'s point of view, he is resting in *ṣoḍaśa* [viz., *prameya bhāva*].

---

first state is *kāma tattva*, the reality of *kāma*; the second is the reality of *viṣa tattva*; and the third is *nirañjana tattva.* First is excitement, and that will go to *kāma tattva.* Then there is the climax, and that will go to *viṣa tattva.* And the third act is *samāveśa* (absorption). *Samāveśa* means, *bas*, the state of appeasement, when you are absolutely free from any thought." *Tantrāloka* 3.170 (LJA archive). "*Kāma tattva* is in desire, in will, in the energy of will; *viṣa tattva* is in the energy of knowledge; and *niraṇjana tattva* is in the energy of action (*kriyā*)." Swami Lakshmanjoo, trans., *Kuṇḍalinī-Vijñāna-Rahasyam* (LJA archive).

SWAMIJI: Yes.

JOHN: From her point of view.

SCHOLAR: From her point of view. From his point of view he is resting in *pramāṇa*.

SWAMIJI: No. From his point of view, she is resting in *dvādaśāra cakra* [viz., *pramāṇa*], and from her point of view, he is resting in *ṣoḍaśāra cakra* [viz., *prameya*]. Do you understand?

SCHOLAR: Yes. That is why I was clearing that.

SWAMIJI: From his point of view, she is resting in *dvādaśāra cakra*.

SCHOLAR: She is resting in *dvādaśāra cakra*?

SWAMIJI: She is resting in *dvādaśāra cakra*.

JOHN: So she is in *pramāṇa*?

SCHOLAR: From his point of view?

SWAMIJI: She has united herself in *pramāṇa bhāva* and he has united himself in *prameya bhāva*. *Prameya* and *pramāṇa* are one.

SCHOLAR: He only experience *pramāṇa* there.

SWAMIJI: Yes…huh?

SCHOLAR: *Kevalaśaktayastvaham*.

SWAMIJI: Yes.

SCHOLAR: *Nāhamasmi nacānyo'sti kevalā śaktayastvaham iti …*[188]

SWAMIJI: Yes.

JOHN: So the secret of this whole thing, which you haven't quite told us yet, is this *pīḍana*, which you will explain. So that's the secret, the squeezing …

SWAMIJI: Squeezing, squeezing.

JOHN: … is the secret of how to squeeze, is the secret of this whole …

SWAMIJI: By excitement.

JOHN: By excitement. Excitement is squeezing. The more excitement, the more you're squeezed.

SWAMIJI: Yes (laughs).

SCHOLAR: Whereas when there is no excitement, then these two *cakra*s are away from each other, there is *prameya* and *pramāṇa*.

SWAMIJI: Yes.

JOHN: So one other clarification. Now I'm trying to be clear. He understands her as the twelvefold *cakra* …

---

188. The scholar is reciting the first line of *Tantrāloka* 29.64.

SWAMIJI: Yes, because it is a union with each other.

JOHN: So, in other words, he is functioning in *pramāṇa* ...

SWAMIJI: He is she and she becomes he. Now this is a *prasaṅga*[189], this was not our subject. Now he connects his explanation with his own subject.

LJA TA04G (51:13)

पञ्चारे सविकारोऽथ भूत्वा सोमस्रुतामृतात् ॥ १३७ ॥
धावति त्रिरसाराणि गुह्यचक्राण्यसौ विभुः ।

pañcāre savikāro'tha bhūtvā somasrutāmṛtāt //137//
dhāvati trirasārāṇi guhyacakrāṇyasau vibhuḥ /

This Lord, *para pramātṛ* (*vibhuḥ* means, this Lord, *para pramātṛ*), when *pañcāre savikāro'tha bhūtvā*, when in the body (*pañcāre* means, in *pañcāra cakra*; *pañcāra cakra* is the body, the body containing the five elements: earth, water, *agni* (fire), *vāyu* (air), and *ākāśa* (ether)–that is *pañcāra cakra*, that is in the body), when in the body, by the flow of nectar from *soma*, *soma* creates the flow of nectar in that body, and *savikaro'tha*, he gets excited and she also gets excited, ...*

JOHN: So this nectar comes from *soma*. The *soma* causes ...

SWAMIJI: No, not only *soma*, because *soma* is one with *sūrya* there.

JOHN: So we are talking about *soma* here in the objective sense.

SWAMIJI: Yes, objective sense. But objectivity has taken the position of cognitivity, and cognition has taken the position of objectivity. So *soma* can be connected with both man and woman.

*... *soma srutā amṛtāt savikāro'tha bhūtvā*, they get excited, this *para pramātṛ*, the state of *para pramātṛ bhāva*, gets excitement, ...*

JOHN: What kind of excitement? This is not ordinary. This is not cognitive excitement.

SWAMIJI: This is cognitive excitement in that higher scale, not in *paśu bhāva*.[190]

---

189. Incidental discussion.

190. Lit., the beastial state, i.e., individuality.

SCHOLAR: So he is explaining here, *yāvacca pañcānāṁ cakrapad-dhatiḥ* (verse 135), then he has that *prasaṅga*, and then he goes [to the topic of] *pañcāra savikāro'tha.*

SWAMIJI: Yes, in this *pañcāra cakra*, in the body [composed of five elements].

SCHOLAR: So this is *avaroha* (descending), this is *unmīlanā krama*[191] he is explaining in that previous verse (135), *ṣoḍaśa-dvādaśā*, etcetera.

SWAMIJI: Yes.

*... *dhāvati trirasārāṇi guhyacakrāṇyasau vibhuḥ*, and he is sentenced to these three *rasa*s, threefold fluids, *trirasa arāṇi guhya cakrāṇi*, which are connected with *guhya cakra*, the *cakra* which is absolutely secret, hidden.

JOHN: These threefold fluids.

SWAMIJI: Fluids. The watery element of blood, and the element of semen, and the element of blood direct.

JOHN: So two kinds of blood and one semen.

SWAMIJI: The watery element of blood first takes place, and then semen and blood are united. That is *trirasārāṇi*. That is *vāma*, *mad-hyamā*, and *dakṣā*.[192] So then the Lord, *para pramātra*, runs towards the wheel of the private parts of body where the threefold fluids are functioning.

JOHN: When this excitement occurs.

SWAMIJI: Yes.

LJA TA04G (54:30) end
LJA TA04H (00:00) start

The three fluids.

JOHN: Why this *para pramātṛ bhāva* runs after this ...

SWAMIJI: ... these three fluids of *rasa*s. He says:

191. Extroverted process.

192. *Vāma* (left), *madhyamā* (center), and *dakṣa* (right).

यतो जातं जगल्लीनं यत्र च स्वकलीलया ॥ १३८॥

yato jātaṁ jagallīnaṁ yatra ca svakalīlayā //138//

By the *svātantrya* (freedom) of the Lord from where everything is created, and in that, everything is absorbed.

SCHOLAR: *Yasyonmeṣanimeṣābhyāṁ jagat* ...[193]

SWAMIJI: No, it is not that. *Yato jāta*, *ratistatra*; *ye pītā*, *te ca marditaḥ*: from where you have come out in this manifestation of the world (that is the organ, that sexual organ), *ratistatra*, you are directed towards that when you get entry in youth, your attention is diverted towards that same point. From which point you have come out in this manifestation, you go after that very point in youth.

SCHOLAR: But from the universal point of view, in awareness here, he experiences the whole objective field created and destroyed in *mukhya cakra*.[194]

SWAMIJI: The whole objective field is created by *para pramātṛ bhāva*, and that *para pramātṛ bhāva* takes place in the objective world, and the objective world takes place in *para pramātṛ bhāva*. *Yato jātam jagat līnam yatra ca*, *yato jātam jagat*, wherefrom this whole universe has been created, and *yatra ca jagat līnam*, and in which this whole universe merges, ...*

JOHN: So this has a twofold sense.

SWAMIJI: * . . this is the way of the *svātantrya śakti* of Lord Śiva.

JOHN: This has a twofold sense in the sexual act, why *para pramātṛ bhāva* moves to this point, and also in the universal sense, why Lord Śiva moves back to his own nature.

SWAMIJI: Yes, own Self, own nature.

SCHOLAR: So this is here we have already passed *viṣa tattva* here.

SWAMIJI: Yes.

---

193. The first *śloka* of the *Spanda Kārikās*.

194. Lit., the principal wheel, also known as *saṁvit cakra* (the wheel of Consciousness). Swamiji will later explain that *mukhya cakra* is "the point of God consciousness inside."

SCHOLAR: This is not explaining …

SWAMIJI: He does not explain it quite vividly because it is a secret!

SCHOLAR: Yes, I know, I know. One hundred times I've read this.

JOHN: What is this secret *cakra*, this super-hidden *cakra*, that's these three fluids? That is that threefold *cakra*?

SWAMIJI: Yes, three fluids, yes, that is *guhya cakra*.

LJA TA04H (02:21)

तत्रानन्दश्च सर्वस्य ब्रह्मचारी च तत्परः ।
तत्र सिद्धिश्च मुक्तिश्च समं सम्प्राप्यते द्वयम् ॥ १३९ ॥

tatrānandaśca sarvasya brahmacārī ca tatparaḥ /
tatra siddhiśca muktiśca samaṁ samprāpyate dvayam //139//

Because everybody gets bliss there at that point. Not only worldly people get bliss, but even *brahmacāri ca tatparaḥ*, a *brahmacāri* who is residing in the state of Lord Śiva, he also is bent upon finding out the secret of that organ.

SCHOLAR: *Ānandacāri*.

SWAMIJI: *Ānandacāri* (*brahmā* means, *ānanda*). *Tatra siddhiśca muktiśca*, there you attain the worldly powers, the great worldly powers, and there you attain the power of getting liberated from this universe.

SCHOLAR: That's why in these Vāma Tantras, there are so many practices for gaining powers.

SWAMIJI: *Samaṁ samprāpyate dvayam*, and this is obtained equally; the *siddhi* (power) and *mokṣa* (liberation) is attained equally there. But *siddhi* is attained by those who are functioning this process, and *mukti* is attained by those who are functioning the process of introverted consciousness (that is *brahmacāri*).

JOHN: What is the difference between these two?

SWAMIJI: Huh?

JOHN: The introverted process is still a sexual act …

SWAMIJI: It is a sexual act.

JOHN: … but he's carried to his own nature through that act. But for the other person, what happens to him? The one who wants powers, what happens to him?

SWAMIJI: The rise of *prāṇa kuṇḍalinī* takes place in him. And the rise of *parā kuṇḍalinī*[195] takes place in that other person, the *brahmacāri*.[196]

JOHN: So that one who wants powers, his *prāṇa kuṇḍalinī* rises only to one *cakra* or other. It doesn't rises to *sahasrāra cakra*, huh?

SWAMIJI: All *cakra*s up to this, yes. *Sahasrāra cakra* is…

SCHOLAR: To *rūpātīta* (i.e., *turya*), but not to *sarvātīta*.

SWAMIJI: No (affirmative), *rūpātīta*.

SCHOLAR: He goes into that *turya*, but not into *turyātīta*.[197]

SWAMIJI: Yes.

JOHN: So he gets all powers through that rising to that…?

SWAMIJI: Yes.

---

195. *Parā kuṇḍalinī* is functioned by Lord Śiva and takes place in a universal body, not in an individual body; *cit kuṇḍalinī* is functioned in consciousness, and *prāṇa kuṇḍalinī* is functioned in breath. See *Light on Tantra in Kashmir Shaivism, Tantrāloka, Vol. Two*, Appendix 7, p. 455.

196. "*Brahmacāri vrata* (celibacy) is not the type of being a bachelor always. *Brahmacāri*, from the Śaiva point of view, is that you should see, you should observe in your mind, that death, life, success, failure, pain, pleasure, sadness, sorrow, happiness, joy, rise, fall, all these are the expansion of His glory. *Brahmacāri vrata* is to perceive that everywhere Brahman is moving, [that everything] is the movement of God consciousness, death is the movement of God consciousness, life is the movement of God consciousness. So there is no fear, because the soul is always living, the soul will never die. The body is already dead." *Bhagavad Gītā* audio 1978, 6.15 (LJA archives). "*Brahmacāri* is the one who experiences this *kuṇḍalinī*. He is *brahmacāri*." *Kashmir Shaivism, The Secret Supreme*, Swami Lakshmanjoo (original audio recording, LJA archives, Los Angeles, 1972).

197. "The difference between *turya* and *turyātīta* is, in *turya*, you find in *samādhi* that this whole universe is existing there in the seed form, germ. The strength, the energy, of universal existence is existing there, but here he has [yet] to come out [into activity]. In *turyātīta*, he comes out in action and feels universal consciousness. This is the difference between *turya* and *turyātīta*." See *Tantrāloka* One, Appendix 14, *Turya* and *Turyātīta*.

LJA TA04H (04:29)

अत ऊर्ध्वं पुनर्याति यावद्ब्रह्मात्मकं पदम् ।
अग्नीषोमौ समौ तत्र सृज्येते चात्मनात्मनि ॥ १४० ॥

ata ūrdhvaṁ punaryāti yāvadbrahmātmakaṁ padam /
agnīṣomau samau tatra sṛjyete cātmanātmani //140//

Now he explains why *guhya cakrāṇi*, [as] the *guhya cakra* was only one, why he has put it in the plural form. Are *guhya cakras* many or only one – that sexual organ? Because everybody knows the *guhya cakra* is only the sexual organ.

JOHN: This hidden *cakra*.

SWAMIJI: The hidden *cakra*. But he says, *ata ūrdhvam*, by functioning in this sexual organ (*guhya cakra*, only one *guhya cakra*), *punaryāti yāvat brahmātmakaṁ padam*, he travels to the extent of the supreme state of Brahman. From this *janmādhāra*[198] (*guhya cakra*), some blessed souls – not everybody – some blessed souls are being carried to the state of Brahman where *agnīṣomau samau tatra sṛjyete*, when *agni* and *soma* are created in an equal state, equilibrium. That is, *ahaṁ* becomes *idam*, *idam* becomes *aham*. *Aham* and *idam* (this-ness and I-ness) are united in one state. So, it means that he is carried to the state of Śuddhavidyā; he is carried to the state of Śuddhavidyā by this functioning in the *janmādhāra cakra*. So, up to Śuddhavidyā, these are all *guhya cakras* where *agni* and *soma* are created in oneness.

JOHN: Up to…?

SWAMIJI: Śuddhavidyā and onwards – Śuddhavidyā, Īśvara, and Sadāśiva. So, the Śuddhavidyā *bhāva* (*mantra bhāva*), and the *mantreśvara bhāva* (Īśvara), and *mantra maheśvara bhāva* (Sadāśiva) are achieved. And the state of *mantra bhāva* and the state of *mantreśvara bhāva* and *mantra maheśvara bhāva* are also *guhya cakras*. So it is why he has put it in the plural form – "*guhya cakraṇī*".

198. Lit., the basis (*ādhara*) of creation/life (*janma*).

JOHN: So up to Śuddhavidyā *tattva*, there is only one secret *cakra*.

SWAMIJI: Yes.

JOHN: And then after that, these all *mantra*, *mantreśvara*, and…

SWAMIJI: These are also *guhya cakra*s internally, introverted.

SCHOLAR: So this process he is describing of this *pañcāra vikāra*[199], etcetera,…

SWAMIJI: Yes.

SCHOLAR: …which is *unmīlanā* (external), and now again he is moving into *ata ūrdhvam punaryāti*, he is going into *nimīlanā* (internal) again.

SWAMIJI: *Nimīlanā* again–again, yes.

SCHOLAR: And this in the *nirañjana* state after the completion of that process?

SWAMIJI: After the completion of the *nirañjana* state, he moves into…

SCHOLAR: So this is not actually the rise of *cit kuṇḍalinī* (*kuṇḍalinī unmeṣa*) at that point.

SWAMIJI: No.

SCHOLAR: It is not the rise of *viṣa tattva* here.

SWAMIJI: The rise of *viṣa tattva* he has already taken place.

SCHOLAR: So this is the state of *uccāra* (rise) after that act.

SWAMIJI: Yes, after that act.

SCHOLAR: This is the real *uccāra* of that rising in awareness.

SWAMIJI: Now he goes down again, he comes down again, in this next *śloka*. It is why [Jayaratha] says in [this] context:

LJA TA04H (07:49)

यदा पुनः सोमात्मनः प्रमेयस्योद्रेकस्तदा विश्वोल्लासः

yadā punaḥ somātmanaḥ prameyasyodrekastadā viśvollāsaḥ
(commentary)

199. Transformation (*vikāra*) into the body composed of five elements (*pañcāra*).

When *prameya udreka*[200] takes place, then *viśva ullāsa*[201] comes in function.

SCHOLAR: *Udita* state.

SWAMIJI: Yes.

तत्रस्थस्तापितः सोमो द्वेधा जङ्घे व्यवस्थितः ।

tatrasthastāpitaḥ somo dvedhā jaṅghe vyavasthitaḥ |141a

Tatrasthaḥ, when already situated in that state, so that when one resides in that state of the sameness of I-ness and this-ness, *soma tāpitaḥ, tatrasthaḥ soma bhuya tāpitaḥ, tatrasthaḥ soma tāpitaḥ*, when *soma* is *tāpitaḥ*, inflamed, or put into excitement again, *dvedhā jaṅghe vyavasthitaḥ*, he takes the seat in universal objects also.

SCHOLAR: *Dvedhā*, yes.

SWAMIJI: *Dvedhā jaṅghe vyavasthitaḥ*, he takes the seat in the universal state also and he is born.

SCHOLAR: *Jaṅghe*? *Carācare.*

SWAMIJI: *Carācare*, yes.[202] *Jaṅgha* does not mean only *jaṅgha* (movable). [It means], *sthāvara* (immovable) and *jaṅghama* (movable).

SCHOLAR: But "*jaṅghe*" is *dvivāchanam* (plural) here.

SWAMIJI: Yes. *Jaṅghe* means, *carācaraste jagati.*

JOHN: So after the state of Śuddhavidyā, where this-ness and I-ness is equal …

SWAMIJI: No …

JOHN: He has left that [topic].

SWAMIJI: … he has left that, he has left that aside. He has taken his own subject now. This was not his subject.

SCHOLAR: Which one?

SWAMIJI:

---

200. Excess (*udreka*) of objectivity (*prameya*).

201. The manifestation (*ullāsa*) of the universe (*viśva*).

202. Moveable and immoveable (animate and inanimate) objects of the universe.

LJA TA04H (09:33)

ata ūrdhvaṁ punaryāti yāvadbrahmātmakaṁ padam /
agnīṣomau samau tatra sṛjyete cātmanātmani //140//
(repeated)

SCHOLAR: This is not in the context of *caryākrama.*
SWAMIJI: This was not connected with this, our subject. And…

tatpunaḥ pibati prītyā haṁso haṁsaḥ iti sphuran //136//
(repeated)

…this is not connected with our subject. In connection with [our subject] it was just by *prasaṅga* (extension). Our subject is just sex here.

SCHOLAR: In this context here.

SWAMIJI: Yes. Because it is creation, we are dealing with creation, we are not dealing with residing in your own nature.

SCHOLAR: *Vāma vāmanata.*

SWAMIJI: Yes.

JOHN: So in this state, then, "there" (*tatra*), what is that "there"? In this act?

SWAMIJI: Yes, in this act, when *soma* is again put into excitement, he takes place in *sthāvara jaṅgama*, he takes place in *sthāvara jaṅgama*, in the universal states [of the moving and unmoving]. So he is created, he gets conceived.

JOHN: Is this in a physical sense that he gets conceived, or is this in the real sense that he becomes his own nature, maybe? How is it?

SWAMIJI: No, it is physical.

JOHN: This talking about giving birth…

SWAMIJI: Yes.

SCHOLAR: So we are back to *unmīlanā* again here.

SWAMIJI: Yes.

SCHOLAR: *Soma-udreka*[203] is again in *unmīlanā.*

---

203. The discussion about the abundance or excess (*udreka*) of objectivity (*soma*).

SWAMIJI: Yes, because it was not our subject, that *nimīlanā*.[204]

SCHOLAR: But *nimīlanā* is a pre-condition of that *unmīlanā*.

SWAMIJI: Yes, a pre-condition, because he touches that *nimīlanā* because that is our object, that is the real object of all this *caryākrama* (divine sexual act). The real object of *caryākrama* is to attain that one consciousness with God, so he is touching that [topic] side-by-side.

JOHN: So what is this birth here, then? That is what I am confused about.

SWAMIJI: Birth?

JOHN: In this 141a.

SWAMIJI: Your birth is also the same.

JOHN: He is talking about ordinary birth, when I was born, that kind of birth.

SWAMIJI: No.

JOHN: No, no, not that.

SWAMIJI: It is *yoginībhūḥ*. It is *yoginībhūḥ*. It is *yoginībhūḥ*.

JOHN: This is giving rise to *yoginībhūḥ*.[205]

SWAMIJI: Yes.

LJA TA04H (11:41)

JOHN: So this is giving rise to *yoginībhūḥ* by again exciting *soma*.

SWAMIJI: Yes. How is *soma* excited? That he explains in the next *śloka*.

SCHOLAR: But this "*tatra*" (there) is this *brahmātmake pade*.[206]

SWAMIJI: *Sāmyātmani pade*[207], because *sāmyātāmani pada* must come, it is touched, because he has touched it.

SCHOLAR: *Ataḥ ūrdhvam punaryā–punaḥ*.[208]

JOHN: So this state of equality of I-ness and this-ness, this comes for the participants.

SWAMIJI: Yes.

---

204. Lit., closing, that is, the absorption back into one's own real nature as it was discussed in verse 136 and 140.

205. *Yoginībhūḥ* is the divine offspring of a yoginī and a yogi.

206. The stage (*pada*) of Brahman.

207. The stage of union (*samyātma*).

208. From verse 140.

JOHN: And through that state comes the rising of *yoginībhūḥ*, …
SWAMIJI: Yes.
JOHN: … which is this. Is that right?
SWAMIJI: Yes. [As long as] you are not connected with that supreme God consciousness, *yoginībhūḥ* won't take place. *Yoginībhūḥ* takes place only by maintaining the full awareness of God consciousness there.
JOHN: At that moment.
SCHOLAR: Although we have gone through this passage many times, I am still not entirely clear where the *adhikāra* (rules) of what ends and begins.
SWAMIJI: This will be clarified to you in an individual way when you come to me privately in one room, you and me. How can we expose this? You can't expose everything.
SCHOLAR: It should not be in published translation in detail.
SWAMIJI: Yes. There also, in the translation also, you must not expose it fully.
SCHOLAR: Only with …
SWAMIJI: With hints.
SCHOLAR: … hints here and there.
SWAMIJI: Yes.

LJA TA04H (13:11)

नातिरहस्यमेकत्र ख्याप्यं न च सर्वथा गोप्यम् ॥२२५॥

nātirahasyamekatra khyāpyaṁ na ca sarvathā gopyam |[209]

This must not be kept a secret, this must not be exposed, too, even.
SCHOLAR: But it should be revealed here a little bit and hidden there a little bit.
SWAMIJI: Yes (laughs).

209. This verse appears in the fourth *āhnika* of Abhinavagupta's *Tantrasāra* and is quoted by Jayaratha in his commentary on *Tantrāloka* 5.130. Swamiji elaborates on this in his commentary of *Tantrāloka* 6.43.

LJA TA04H (13:25)

अधस्तं पातयेदग्निरमृतं स्रवति क्षणात् ॥ १४१ ॥
गुल्फजान्वादिषु व्यक्तं कुटिलार्कप्रदीपिता ।
सा शक्तिस्तापिता भूयः पञ्चारादिक्रमं सृजेत् ॥ १४२ ॥

adhastaṁ pātayedagnir-amṛtaṁ sravati kṣaṇāt //141//
gulphajānvādiṣu vyaktaṁ kuṭilārkapradīpitā /
sā śaktistāpitā bhūyaḥ pañcārādikramaṁ sṛjet //142//

Now he says how to function this.

When *soma* is placed in the state of *idam bhāva* (*adha* means, *idam bhāva*), *soma* is placed in the state of *idam bhava* (this-ness), *adhastaṁ pātayet agni*, then the fire (that is, *pramātṛ*), …*

The commentator has not translated it correctly. He has translated it that, *soma amṛtam sravati*. He has translated it as *soma amṛtam sravati*.[210]

SCHOLAR: *Sravati iti arthāt agni tāpitaḥ somaḥ.*

SWAMIJI: How he could guess this? Here, Abhinavagupta has in clear words said that *agni amṛtam sravati* (*agni* is the subjective case).[211]

*… *agni amṛtam sravati*, *pramātṛ* (the man) discharges *amṛta* when this *soma* is placed in the state of *idam bhāva*.

SCHOLAR: So, *adha pāta* is *carama dhātu prasara*.[212]

SWAMIJI: Yes, *carama dhātu prasara*.

JOHN: So *soma* here is?

SWAMIJI: *Soma* is the woman, lady, yes. *Adhastam pātayet agnir amṛtaṁ sravati kṣaṇāt*, in one second, this *amṛta* is discharged. Which *amṛta*? The qualification of *amṛta* he says: that *amṛta* which absolutely appears, which is absolutely vivid, vividly found (*vyaktam*, vividly

210. Jayaratha comments that the nectar (*amṛta*) flows (*sravati*) from *soma* (objectivity).

211. Abhinavagupta says that the nectar flows from *agni* (subjectivity).

212. Descending (*pāta*) into the lower region (*adhasta*), which is the stratum (*dhatu*) where the flow (*prasara*) terminates (*carama*).

found) in *gulphajānvādiṣu*, in all the limbs of the body. The *amṛta* is found, not only in the producer of *amṛta*, not only in that organ which produces *amṛta*, but the *amṛta* is found in all the limbs of the body, in all *anu-cakra*s: in the arms also, in the face also, in the mouth also, in the body also, in the legs, knees, ankles, everywhere! *Jāyayā saṁpariśakto nabāhyaṁ vetti nāntaraṁ*[213], when you are absolutely embraced with your beloved, *nabāhyaṁ vetti nāntaraṁ*, you don't recognize what is going on outside, what is going on inside–you don't recognize it at all. You are only diverted towards each other. This is the way how this sexual act functions. The sexual act functions in oneness. You forget all other things. While eating (eating also is a sexual act in one sense), but while eating you are aware of other things also, while observing form you are aware of other things also, while hearing sounds you are aware of other things also, but when you are actually embraced with each other, you forget everything.

JOHN: So is this distinction being made here, where you brought to our attention in the third *āhnika*, this idea that in memory, excitement only comes in the sexual organ, but in the real act, excitement is in…?

SWAMIJI: *Anu-cakra*s also, in all the limbs.

JOHN: … in all the limbs, in the real sexual act.

SWAMIJI: Yes.

SCHOLAR: So the point is though that his awareness is not *liṅgaparā*.[214]

SWAMIJI: No (affirmative).

SCHOLAR: Actually he experiences impression-less sex.

SWAMIJI: That impression of *ānanda*, that supreme *ānanda* (bliss). [When] *adhastam pātayet*[215], then *agni*, *kṣaṇāt amṛtaṁ sravati*, [discharges *amṛta* in one second]. What kind of *amṛtaṁ*? Which is actually existing, vividly found, in *gulphajānvādiṣu*, in all the limbs of the body. When *amṛta* is created, then it is said, outwardly also, you must rest; if you want to make your wife conceive, you must rest, you

213. This verse from an unknown source does not appear in the commentary. Swamiji also references this verse in his translation of *Tantrāloka* 3.170.

214. The scholar perhaps means to say *liṅgaparāmarśa*: an inference drawn from an invariable sign or characteristic.

215. Directed towards the lower region.

must not leave each other at once.

JOHN: Leave the act.

SWAMIJI: You must not leave the act soon. *Arka pradīpitā sā kuṭila śaktiḥ*, that energy (that is, the woman), which is *arka pradīpitā*, excited, put into excitement by the *arka*[216], ...*

Arka is the man there, because *arka* has been transformed in the cognitive world there, he has become only one with that [female] sexual organ, that is why he nominates *pramātṛ* as *arka*, because he has descended in *pramāṇa bhāva*.

SCHOLAR: This is the same process for the *yoginī* there.

SWAMIJI: Yes.

*... *arka pradīpitā*, *sā kuṭila śakti*, that *śakti* which is *kuṭila*, which is curved, and *arka pradīpitā*, when you [make] her more excited, pour more into excitement after that, after the discharge also, *pañcārādikramam sṛjet*, then there takes place of conceiving.

JOHN: Of the *yoginībhūḥ*.

SWAMIJI: That is *yoginībhūḥ*. The man or the woman who appears from that womb is *yoginībhūḥ*, is divine.

JOHN: *Kuṭila* means, curved?

SWAMIJI: Curved, yes.

SCHOLAR: So this is not that *prāṇa kuṇḍalinī* that Jayaratha takes it to be.

SWAMIJI: *Prāṇa kuṇḍalinī* is also there because *prāṇa kuṇḍalinī* takes place there in this act. In this act of the sexual way, the *prāṇa kuṇḍalinī* must rise.

SCHOLAR: Successively?

SWAMIJI: Yes.

SCHOLAR: This is not *cit kuṇḍalinī* rise.

SWAMIJI: No, *prāṇa kuṇḍalinī*.

SCHOLAR: But in the actual *viṣa tattva*, that is *cit kuṇḍalinī*.

SWAMIJI: That is *cit kuṇḍalinī*.

SCHOLAR: Whereas here...

SWAMIJI: This is *prāṇa kuṇḍalinī*.

---

216. Lit., the sun, viz., *pramāṇa* (cognition).

SCHOLAR: But if the *vīra* (man[217]) has experienced the rise of *cit kuṇḍalinī*…

SWAMIJI: Then he will go to that supreme state of God consciousness.

SCHOLAR: Then why here…? Are we going right back to the act now, to the whole act?

SWAMIJI: Because it is creation, it is the act, it is the act that we are…

SCHOLAR: Of the *yoginībhūḥ*.

SWAMIJI: *Yoginībhūḥ*.

JOHN: So this act was done for creating *yoginībhūḥ*, was it?

SWAMIJI: Yes.

JOHN: For that very reason.

SCHOLAR: For Self-realization.

SWAMIJI: *Bas*, the act of the sexual way is over. Now he will connect it with the other senses also, the next time.

JOHN: Now this act, in speaking about *yoginībhūḥ*, was this act done for Self-realization and *yoginībhūḥ* comes as extra, or was this act done for *yoginībhūḥ* primarily?

SWAMIJI: *Yoginībhūḥ*. It is creation, sir, because it is [the discussion of] the rise of the twelve Kālīs.

SCHOLAR: In this *krama catuṣṭayam*.[218]

SWAMIJI: Yes. *Bas*, that is all for today's lesson.

SCHOLAR: But I still don't understand this *prāṇa kuṇḍalinī* function here, why he introduces *prāṇa kuṇḍalinī*.

SWAMIJI: I will tell you privately. What are you writing, sir?

MARK D: I'm scribbling down what you are saying.

SWAMIJI: (laughs)

LJA TA04H (21:15)

[Questions]

… but that *kuṇḍalinī* is not understood. It is misunderstood.

SCHOLAR: It's also mispronounced

DEVOTEES: (laughter).

---

217. Lit., hero.

218. The fourfold process of *sṛṣṭi*, *sthiti*, *saṁhṛti*, and *anākhya*.

SWAMIJI: It was a tough subject today.

SCHOLAR: Yeah it is! The toughest piece in the whole of *Tantrāloka*.

SWAMIJI: Now this is more tough, the next [subject], on Saturday.

SCHOLAR: And Abhinavagupta never really explains this *krama catuṣṭayam*, the way that functions. He deals with twelve Kālīs in that *Kramakeli* a bit, ...

SWAMIJI: Yes.

SCHOLAR: ... the *Kramastotra*, but not on that process of holding awareness in the senses fully.

SWAMIJI: But it has come from mouth-to-mouth. It must come from mouth to mouth. It must travel there. It must not travel in books.

LJA TA04H (22:04)

So this explanation of that sexual course (that is, *mukhya cakra*), it is already explained. The purpose of these twelve Kālīs, you know what is the purpose of the twelve Kālīs: in *prameya* (in the objective world), in the cognitive world (*pramāṇa*), and in the subjective world (*pramātṛ*), you have to find *sṛṣṭi*, *sthiti*, *saṁhāra*, and *anākhya*, in each – creation, protection, destruction, and withdrawal.[219]

JOHN: Is *anākhya* the same as *turya*?

SWAMIJI: It is more than *turya*. And the purpose of twelve Kālīs is to find that state in each and every state. In *sṛṣṭi* also, you have to find *anākhya*. These twelve Kālīs are the explanation of *anākhya cakra* only. It is not the explanation of objectivity or cognitivity or subjectivity. You have to find that real transcendental state of nothingness in each and every act. It is why it is called *anākhya cakra*. It is *anākhya cakra*.

SCHOLAR: So *anākhya* is *saṁhāra-saṁhāra* in some sense, it is *saṁhāra bhakṣiṇī*.[220]

SWAMIJI: Not *saṁhāra bhakṣiṇī*. When it is destroyed, when this whole differentiated perception is destroyed, then there remains

---

219. The twelvefold states of consciousness, or Kālīs, "are the main connecting rod between individuality and universality. You will be sentenced to universality through *pramāṇa cakra* (the wheel of cognition)." *Interview on Kashmir Shaivism* (LJA archive).

220. To the extent of the devouring (*bhakṣa*) of destruction (*saṁhāra*).

impressions, impressions that this whole universe is destroyed, impressions to understand that this whole universe is destroyed. But that impression, too, is not existing there in *anākhya cakra*. That is *anākhya cakra* in the real sense.

JOHN: What is *anākhya cakra* in *sṛṣṭi* and *sthiti* and…? You said you have to find this *anākhya cakra* in all these…

SWAMIJI: But he will explain that now in the explanation of the twelve Kālīs.

SCHOLAR: *Saṁvit cakrodaya*, the spontaneous rise [of the wheel of consciousness].

SWAMIJI: Huh?

SCHOLAR: *Saṁvit cakrodaya.*

SWAMIJI: *Saṁvit cakrodaya.*

LJA TA04H (24:22)

एवं श्रोत्रेऽपि विज्ञेयं यावत्पादान्तगोचरम् ।

evaṁ śrotre'pi vijñeyaṁ yāvatpādāntagocaram /143a

The same process is to be held in the other organs of perceptions (or the other organs of the senses, the cognitive organs), *yāvat* (until) *pādānta gocaram*, these organs of actions also have the same process.

SCHOLAR: "*Pāda*" is *upalakṣaṇam.*

SWAMIJI: "*Pāda*" is *upalakṣaṇam* (designation) for the other *karmendriyas*. *Pāda* does not mean only "foot", [it means the] hand also. When you hold something in hand, some soft thing, you should not discard…for the time being, you have to discard those things which are not creating your [*vīrya*], that energy. For instance, bad things, bad smells, discard [them] for the time being. Afterwards, when your consciousness is established firmly, then you can play with those also, bad things also. When you see some soft thing, that soft thing will carry you and give strength to that *vīrya* inside. Soft words, soft touch, soft words, [good] smell, they all carry you to that *mukhya cakra*. These *cakras* are called *anu-cakras*. *Anu-cakras* are meant to strengthen the *mukhya cakra*. *Mukhya cakra* is the sex, internal sex.

LJA TA04H (26:23)

पादाङ्गुष्ठात्समारभ्य यावद्ब्रह्माण्डदर्शनम् ॥ १४३ ॥

pādāṅguṣṭhātsamārabhya yāvadbrahmāṇḍadarśanam //143//

Pādāṅguṣṭhāt samārabhya, just as it is found that *mukhya cakra* is being strengthened, is filled with energy by these organs of cognition and organs of action, in the same way, *pādāṅguṣṭhāt samārabhya yāvat brahmāṇḍa darśanam*, from the toe of the foot (*pādāṅguṣṭha*, from the toe of the foot) to *brahmāṇḍa darśanam* (*brahmāṇḍa darśanam* is up to the state of *brahmarandhra*, the skull, the top surface of the skull in the body), in the body also you have to find out that state of *mukhya cakra*.

Why this is explained? Why so [much] importance to *mukhya cakra* is explained here? For that he [clarifies] in this *śloka*, 144th:

LJA TA04H (27:30)

इत्यजानन्नैव योगी जानन्विश्वप्रभुर्भवेत् ।
ज्वलन्निवासौ ब्रह्माद्यैर्दृश्यते परमेश्वरः ॥ १४४ ॥

ityajānannaiva yogī jānanviśvaprabhurbhavet /
jvalannivāsau brahmādyair-dṛśyate parameśvaraḥ //144//

Ityajānan, that person, that yogi, who does not know the way of carrying each and every organ of senses and organ of action to the point of *mukhya cakra*, he is not supposed to be nominated as a yogi. He is not a yogi. He is not in any case a yogi from our point of view. *Jānan viśva prabhur bhavet*, but the one who knows how to carry these *anu-cakras* to that *mukhya cakra*, ...*

It is not just to take a flower of roses with fragrance, [to] just smell it. It is not only that. This sensation of smell must be sentenced to that point of God consciousness inside (that is *mukhya cakra*). You have to do that.

*... and the person who does that, *viśva prabhur bhavet*, he becomes the master of the universe–*viśva prabhur bhavet. Jvalan-ivāsau brahmādyair*

dṛśyate parameśvaraḥ, the effulgent and shining Lord (*jvalanniva parameśvaraḥ*, *parameśvaraḥ* who is *jvalanniva*; *jvalanniva* means, shining and effulgent), …*

SCHOLAR: Why does he says "*iva*"[221]?

SWAMIJI: Because the word is "*jvalana*". *Jvalana* is, he who is set on fire, who is [enflamed]. It is not firing, you are not firing the Lord.

SCHOLAR: *Vikasita karaṇa cakra.*

SWAMIJI: *Vikasita karaṇa cakrāḥ.*[222] *Jvalanniva*, it is why he has put "*iva*".

*…*jvalanniva parameśvaraḥ*, that *parameśvaraḥ*, who is effulgent and shining just like fire, is perceived by *brahmādyair* (*brahmādyair* means, from Brahmā to any individual); by each and every individual, it is seen there at that point.

LJA TA04H (29:51)

अत्र तात्पर्यतः प्रोक्तमक्षे क्रमचतुष्टयम् ।
एकैकत्र यतस्तेन द्वादशात्मकतोदिता ॥ १४५ ॥

atra tātparyataḥ proktamakṣe kramacatuṣṭayam /
ekaikatra yatastena dvādaśātmakatoditā //145//

Atra, here, the purpose or the aim of this subject (*atra tātparyataḥ proktam*, the purpose or the aim of this subject) is that in each and every organ (*ekaikatra akṣe*; *ekaikatra akṣe* means, in each and every organ), *krama catuṣṭayam*, the fourfold successions are found (the fourfold successions, that is, *sṛṣṭi*, *sthiti*, *saṁhṛti*, and *anākhya*). For instance, this is *sṛṣṭi* (creation).[223] When this is known as "This is the case of specks", this is *sthiti* (preservation). Before that is *sṛṣṭi*, when you don't know that it is the case of specks – that is *sṛṣṭi*.

SCHOLAR: *Didṛkṣāyām.*

---

221. Lit., like, in the same manner.

222. The cause (*karaṇa*) of the expansion (*vikasita*) of the wheels (*cakra*).

223. Swamiji uses the example of perceiving an eye-glass case.

SWAMIJI: *Didṛkṣāyām.*[224] At the state of *didṛkṣā*, when you see only some black shade there, that is *sṛṣṭi*. When you see that, "This is the case of specks", that is *sthiti*.[225] When you are satisfied, "I have known it, I know what it is", that is *saṁhṛti* (destruction) because there is no curiosity to see it again and again.

JOHN: So it means, in the destructive act, you move away from it, your perception moves away from it or you…?

SWAMIJI: You are satisfied, you have no curiosity, curiosity is finished.

SCHOLAR: So then you can go to more *sṛṣṭi* or you can realize *anākhya* at that point?

SWAMIJI: No, *anākhya* is found when that *saṁhṛti* is over and the *sṛṣṭi* of another object has not begun yet–there is *anākhya*, that is *anākhya* of this.

SCHOLAR: When that object is withdrawn into consciousness, either it's *vāsanā* (impression) is completely destroyed…

SWAMIJI: [When] the impression is destroyed, that is *pramiti bhāva*–that is, in fact, *pramiti bhava. Anākhya* is the state of *pramiti bhāva*.[226]

SCHOLAR: *Para pramātṛ bhāva.*

SWAMIJI: *Para pramātṛ bhāva*. And these fourfold sections are found in each and every organ, maybe the organs of cognition or the organs of actions. So, in each and every state of the organs, *dvādaśātmakata-uditā*, the twelvefold states of consciousness [i.e., the Kālīs] are found, get rise.

JOHN: So, in walking, between two steps, is that *anākhya* in that sense in terms of…?

SWAMIJI: *Anākhya* is found there also. *Anākhya* is found in each and every action of the universe. And you have to find out *anākṣa*, not

224. The desire or tendency of seeing something. "Just about to see. You have not seen yet, but you want to see; you will, you are going to see it the next moment." *The Mystery of Vibrationless-Vibration in Kashmir Shaivism, Vasugupta's Spanda Kārikā and Kṣemarāja's Spanda Sandoha*, Revealed by Swami Lakshmanjoo, ed. John Hughes (Lakshmanjoo Academy, Los Angeles, 2016), 256.

225. Preservation, protection, or establishment.

226. Pure subjectivity without the touch of objectivity.

only in the state of *anākṣa*, you have to find *anākṣa* in the state of creation, in the state of protection, in the state of destruction also.

JOHN: Is that *unmīlanā samādhi*? To find *anākhya* in these states…

SWAMIJI: *Anākhya* is *unmīlanā*, all-around *unmīlanā* here in the explanation of the twelvefold Kālīs.

SCHOLAR: When that *saṁvit cakra* has risen, then it is *unmīlanā*.

SWAMIJI: Yes.

SCHOLAR: But in the process of practice, from *śāktopāya*, it is *asphuṭam* (not vivid) *unmīlanā* …

SWAMIJI: Yes.

SCHOLAR: … leading to *nimīlanā*.

SWAMIJI: Yes.[227]

LJA TA04H (33:12)

न व्याख्यातं तु निर्भज्य यतोऽतिरहस्यकम् ।

na vyākhyātaṁ tu nirbhajya yato'tirahasyakam /146a

This subject of the twelvefold ways is not explained clearly here, I am not going to [clarify] it clearly. I have not [clarified] this subject in the real sense, *yato ati rahasyakam*, as it is the most secret subject. So you will get hints by your own awareness. If you maintain awareness in hearing my words, you will get hints of that real explanation of this.

SCHOLAR: *Śiva niśamaya*.[228]

SWAMIJI: Yes.

LJA TA04H (33:51)

मेयेऽपि देवी तिष्ठन्ती मासराश्यादिरूपिणी ॥ १४६ ॥

meye'pi devī tiṣṭhantī māsarāśyādirūpiṇī //146//

227. "This is the essence of these twelve Kālīs: this going up and coming in *nimīlanā*, and then coming down in *unmīlanā*." *Interview on Kashmir Shaivism* (LJA archive).

228. When you are perceiving (*niśamaya*) Śiva.

In the objective world also, you find twelvefold ways everywhere. *Meye api*, in the objective world also, *devī*, this energy of consciousness, is found, the twelvefold energy of consciousness is found. For instance, take [the fact that the] months are twelve [in number]. *Rāśī* means...you call that *rāśī*, "zodiacs", or what?

JOHN: Signs of the zodiac.

SWAMIJI: The signs of the zodiacs, those are also twelve. Suns are also twelve.[229] So, twelvefold ways are found everywhere because in the original state of their source, there is the twelvefold energy. So the twelvefold energy is the real energy which is found in the introverted state and the external state also. Next.

SCHOLAR: And twelve vowels.

SWAMIJI: Twelve vowels also, there are twelve vowels, without the *napuṁsaka yoni*s.[230]

JOHN: So this twelvefold energy is a special energy. In other words, its not...

SWAMIJI: The twelvefold energy is the energy of *anākhya.*

JOHN: It's the predominant energy in this universe.

SWAMIJI: Yes, the predominant energy in the universe. The only...

SCHOLAR: But not by excluding any other.

SWAMIJI: If you exclude, then it is not *anākhya.*

JOHN: Excluding what?

SWAMIJI: Exclude that which are not *anākhya*. For instance, the state of creation, the state of protection, the state of destruction, you exclude it. When you exclude it, you are not entering in *anākhya cakra*. You have to get entry from the very beginning to the end. You have to get entry in *anākhya cakra* from the very beginning and to the end. Where there is a clear entry, the clear entrance is in *anākhya cakra*. *Asphuṭa* (non-vivid) entrance is in creation, *sphuṭa* (vivid) entrance is in protection, *sphuṭatara* (more vivid) entrance is in destruction, and *sphuṭatama* (most vivid) entry is in *anākhya*. But the Śaivite yogi has to see that the *asphuṭa*, *sphuṭa*, *sphuṭatara*, and *sphuṭatama*, these four states are held in one level. In the *asphuṭa* state, you must find and see and perceive

---

229. A different sun is said to shine in each of the twelve months of the year.

230. That is, without the *śāntha bīja*s 'ṛ', 'ṝ', 'ḷ', and 'ḹ', which are also nominated as *napuṁsaka* (eunuchs).

that in the *asphuṭa* state is the *sphuṭatama* state of *anākhya*. That is the purpose of the twelve Kālīs. The purpose of the twelve Kālīs is to see that the beginning is the end. There is no starting point. You have not to start. You have to begin from the end, to the end.

JOHN: So there is nothing excluded in the twelve Kālīs.

SWAMIJI: No (affirmative).

SCHOLAR: *Kaulārṇava.*[231]

JOHN: Whereas in *āṇavopāya*, some things are excluded.

SWAMIJI: *Āṇavopāya* is not excluded, *śāktopāya* is not excluded, *śāmbhavopāya*, too, is not excluded.

JOHN: Is this more predominant than the threefold energies of Trika?

SWAMIJI: Huh?

JOHN: These twelvefold energies, which he is saying are in vowels and so many things, the zodiac, is this a more predominant energy than the threefold…?

SWAMIJI: No. Threefold, when you say "threefold", then it is [more] predominant than threefold. When you say "Trika", [then] threefold means, not three; threefold means, one. From one point of view, you see something, from another point of view, you see some other thing, and from another point of view, you see some other thing. Where you see all these three things abruptly in one body, that is Trika. That is the purpose of the Trika System.

SCHOLAR: So Trika and this twelvefold are exactly the same, really.

SWAMIJI: Yes. That is the real Trika.

JOHN: So Trika, then, has been expanded in twelvefold ways.

SWAMIJI: Yes.

SCHOLAR: Trika is twelvefold, it is already expanded.

SWAMIJI: The explanation of the twelvefold energies is the explanation of the kingdom of Trika. This is the kingdom of Trika, the Trika *śāstra*.

LJA TA04H (38:33)

अत एषा स्थिता संविदन्तर्बाह्योभयात्मना ।
स्वयं निर्भास्य तत्रान्यद्भासयन्तीव भासते ॥ १४७॥

231. The foaming sea (*arṇava*) of Kaula.

ata eṣā sthitā saṁvid-antarbāhyobhayātmanā /
svayaṁ nirbhāsya tatrānyad-bhāsayantīva bhāsate //147//

Ata, thus, *eṣā saṁvit*, this supreme Consciousness, *sthitā*, is existing, *antar bāhya ubhayātmanā*, internally and externally also; *antar bāhya ubhayātmanā*, internally and externally, that internal state and external state, are created by this Being, by this transcendental Consciousness of *svātantrya*; *antar bāhya ubhayātmanā svayaṁ nirbhāsya*, is created by Her own *svātantrya*. And in that Self (*tatra*, in that *svātmanī*, in that Self) She shines, She exists Herself realizing Her own nature; not only realizing Her own nature in Her own Self, [but] *anyat bhāsayantī*, She realizes Her own nature not in Her own nature only – what is Her own nature? The state of *anākhya* – She realizes *anākhya cakra* in creating other sections of Herself (the other three sections: *sṛṣṭi*, *sthiti*, and *saṁhṛti* also), the three so-called excluded aspects of *anākhya*, so-called excluded. Those who are actually ignorant of the real point of *anākhya*, they realize that *sṛṣṭi* is excluded, *sthiti* is excluded, *saṁhāra* is excluded, only *anākhya* is there.

JOHN: Vedānta. The Vedāntic point of view.

SWAMIJI: Predominant. There is no predominance of *anākhya* and not the predominance of the other three.

SCHOLAR: *Kramākramātīta*.[232]

LJA TA04H (40:42)

SWAMIJI: Now he'll explain in succession the way of the twelve Kālīs.

232. Lit., beyond succession and non-succession.

1. Sṛṣṭikālī – *sṛṣṭi* (creation) in *prameya* (objectivity).

ततश्च प्रागियं शुद्धा तथाभासनसोत्सुका ।
सृष्टिं कलयते देवी तन्नाम्नागम उच्यते ॥ १४८ ॥

tataśca prāgiyaṁ śuddhā tathābhāsanasotsukā /
sṛṣṭiṁ kalayate devī tannāmnāgama ucyate //148//

So, *iyam*, this supreme energy of Consciousness, *prāk* (*prāk* means, in Her previous state), in Her previous state, …*

For instance, this [eye-glass case] is an object. The real state of [this] object is–do you know what is the real state of [this] object?–the real state of [this] object is, "This is the case of specks." Knowing that, "This is the case of specks", this is the real state of this object. But he says, *prāk*, before that; before that, what happened? Before this feeling that, "This is the case of specks", before that something [else] happened previous to this thought, previous to this sensation. That is the meaning of "*prāk*".[233]

233. "It is *prathmābhāsa*, the first impulse. When we hear, taste, see, etcetera, all the five *rasas*, whatever it may be, when we first go to it, when we want some *śabda* (sound), then we are attracted to that first. Then in the first *kṣaṇa* (instant), there is some *ābhāsa* (appearance) which is *nirvikalpa*, indeterminate, it is without *vikalpas* (thoughts). And this *nirvikalpa-ābhāsa* is called *prathamika ālocana* (*alocana* means, to see; *prathamālocana*, the first impulse to perceive). In this *daśā* (state), *pramātā* (the subject) does not have *savikalpa jñāna* (differentiated knowledge). It is *nirvikalpa*, there is no thought. 'I see this', 'I eat this', he has not this *jñāna* (knowledge). It is only a sprout, he does not see differentiated thought. But *nirvikalpita saṁvit rūpitā* he feels." *Shri Kramanaya Pradīpikā–Shining Light on the Twelve Kālīs*, Swami Lakshmanjoo (Hindi), 1958. English translation by Pranath Kaul, 2003, verse 1 (LJA archive).

*…there, this supreme consciousness is *śuddha*, absolutely pure, pure from differentiatedness–*śuddha. Tathābhāsana-sotsukā*, but She is too much curious to create this other state. Which other state?

DENISE: Of what it is.

SWAMIJI: "This is the case of specks." "This is the case of specks", to create this perception that, "This is the case of the specks", She is fond of creating this next state. That is the meaning of "*tathābhāsana sotsukā*".

SCHOLAR: *Sisṛkṣu.*

SWAMIJI: *Sisṛkṣu.*[234] *Sṛṣṭiṁ kalayate*, and She creates the state of that [pure] consciousness first, [that] previous [state]. *Tat nāmna āgama ucyate*, in the Tantras, that state of consciousness is called Sṛṣṭikālī. This is Sṛṣṭikālī. And there you find the state of *anākhya* shining.

SCHOLAR: *Mantrodaya.*[235]

SWAMIJI: Yes. We are not going to explain this [commentary] here. We will go with the *śloka*s (verses) only. Next:

LJA TA04H (43:30)

2. Raktakālī – *sthiti* (establishment) in *prameya* (objectivity).

तथा भासितवस्त्वंशरञ्जनां सा बहिर्मुखी ।
स्ववृत्तिचक्रेण समं ततोऽपि कलयन्त्यलम् ॥ १४९ ॥
स्थितिरेषैव भावस्य.................... ।

tathā bhāsitavastvaṁśa-rañjanāṁ sā bahirmukhī /
svavṛtticakreṇa samaṁ tato'pi kalayantyalam //149//
sthitireṣaiva bhāvasya.................... /

234. Lit., wishing to let flow or emit.

235. "The rise of *mantra* means, meditation upon the center." *Tantrāloka* 6.125 (LJA archives).

Now there is the next state. Some ancient masters have explained that the next state of this *anākhya* is called Sthitikālī, but Abhinavagupta does not recognize that. He says:

अतः परं श्रीरक्तकाल्या भगवत्याः स्थितिः संभाव्यते

ataḥ paraṁ śrīraktakālyā bhagavatyāḥ sthitiḥ saṁbhāvyate (commentary)

I feel from my observing way of awareness that from that point there is not Sthitikālī, next to Sṛṣṭikālī is not Sthitikālī, next to Sṛṣṭikālī must be Raktakālī, not Sthitikālī; *ataḥ paraṁ raktakālyā bhagavatyāḥ sthitiḥ saṁbhāvyate*, *saṁbhāvyate*, it is from my experience, I experienced that Raktakālī is the next state of this *anākhya*.

And [Abhinavagupta] explains that Raktakālī here in these one and half *śloka*s.

Tathā bhāsita vastvaṁśa rañjanāṁ, then, when this is perceived that, "This is the case of specks", ...*

This is the next state of conscious energy. God consciousness is nowhere found here. He will nominate it as "conscious energy" because it is "Kālī", feminine gender.

*... *tathā bhāsita vastvaṁśa rañjanāṁ*, when you are absolutely attached with this perception that, "This is the case of specks", *sā bahirmukhī*, She is extroverted, She becomes extroverted. Her previous introverted state is over, Her previous introverted state is over, and She holds now this extroverted state.

SCHOLAR: The previous state [of Sṛṣṭikālī] was introverted-cum-extroverted (*nimeṣonmeṣa*).

SWAMIJI: Yes, *nimeṣonmeṣa madhye*.[236] *Svavṛtti cakreṇa samaṁ tato'pi kalayanti*, She *kalayanti*, observes, that energy observes this state, *svavṛtti cakreṇa samaṁ*, along with Her field of sensations (*svavṛtti cakreṇa samaṁ tato'pi kalayanti*), and [when] She observes that, *sthireṣaiva bhāvasya*, this is Raktakāli. This is the state of

236. *Madhye* (in the center) of *nimeṣa* (introverted) and *unmeṣa* (extroverted).

Raktakāli when you are absolutely mixed with that state. And in that state also, you have to observe the state of *anākhya*. *Anākhya bhāva* is to be observed at the very center of agitation, the agitation of action. In agitated action also, you have to find out the *anākhya* state, the un-agitated state of Being. This is Raktakāli.

LJA TA04H (46:56)

You see, here [Jayaratha] has [stated]:

tadvivṛtau śrīsṛṣṭikālyādistutiśloka-vyākhyānānantaraṁ
śrīraktakālyā bhagavatyāḥ ataḥ paraṁ sthitiḥ saṁbhāvyate

I find these words of Abhinavagupta as shoots, it shoots and gets pricked in my heart–his words, Abhinavagupta's words.[237] *Śrīsṛṣṭi*...these are [Abhinavagupta's] words. You see, *śrīsṛṣṭi-kālyādi-stuti-śloka-vyākhyānān-antaraṁ śrīraktakālyā bhagavatyāḥ ataḥ paraṁ sthitiḥ saṁbhāvyate*, these are the divine words which have come out from the lips of Abhinavagupta.

SCHOLAR: What is the difference of the real sense between "Raktakālī" and "Sthitikālī"? Is there actually a real distinction since the senses are *bhāva sthiti*[238]? Is it just a difference in name?

SWAMIJI: No, because Raktakālī is due, Sthitikālī is not due. Sthitikālī means, the strengthening of the previous state.

SCHOLAR: Of *sṛṣṭi*.

SWAMIJI: Sṛṣṭi. But that is not there.

SCHOLAR: There's just *rañjanā* (delight).

SWAMIJI: It is *rañjanā*! *Rañjanā* will be next.

SCHOLAR: Yes.

SWAMIJI: *Sthiti* will give you the sense of strengthening the previous state (Sṛṣṭikālī), but that is not in our *anubhava krama*, that is not in the world of experience, this is not experienced by yogis. The yogis

237. The commentator (Jayaratha) indicates that Abhinavagupta's words were like arrows piercing his heart.

238. Fixed or rooted.

have experienced from the previous state there is Raktakālī, there is *rañjanā*, when you are given to it in an external way.

SCHOLAR: But why then does Abhinavagupta say, "*sthitiraiṣaiva bhāvasya, sthitiḥ bhāvasya*"?

SWAMIJI: *Bhāvasya sthitiḥ*, not Sthitikālī.

SCHOLAR: *Atra sthiti*, it is establishment of the thing, he's saying.

SWAMIJI: Not *praktanasya bhāvasya. Bhāvasya*, [that] which was to be observed, it's *sthiti* is there. This is not the *sthiti* of *sṛṣṭi*. This is not the *sṛṣṭi* of *sthiti*, this is the *sthiti* of *bhāva*.

LJA TA04H (49:22)

Now from Raktakālī, he will start the next state of consciousness:

3. Sthitināśakālī – *saṁhāra* (destruction) in *prameya* (objectivity).

...................तामन्तर्मुखतारसात् ।
सञ्जिहीर्षुः स्थितेर्नाशं कलयन्ती निरुच्यते ॥ १५० ॥

...................tāmantarmukhatārasāt /
sañjihīrṣuḥ sthiternāśaṁ kalayantī nirucyate //150//

There is no Sthitikālī at all. He has not accepted Sthitikālī at all. Sthitināśakālī he has accepted. Although the Tantras have accepted, nominated, this state as Sthitikālī (some Tantras, not all). And the third state of God consciousness, the third state of conscious energy, is Sthitināśakālī, because *tām antar mukhatārasāt*, *tāṁ pramāṇa rūpāṁ sthitiṁ* (comm.), when you are externally given to this perception that, "This is the case of specks", when you know that and observe that and perceive, "There is no doubt about it that I realize that this is the case of specks", *tām antar mukhatā rasāt sañjihīrṣuḥ*, when She withdraws the curiosity of observing this, when that energy withdraws the curiosity of observing this that, "This is the specks, this is the case of specks", when this curiosity is over, that is *antar mukhatārasāt sañjihīrṣuḥ*.

SCHOLAR: Eager to destroy through the flavor of Her internal…

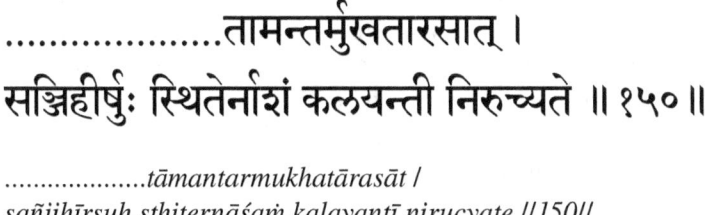

SWAMIJI: No, that curiosity is over. "What is this? What is this?" This is *sṛṣṭi* (creation). "Oh, this is specks; Oh, this is specks", [then] there is no curiosity to see the specks again [because] "*jñāto'yam mayārthaḥ.*"[239] That is *antar-mukhatā-rasāt sañjihīrṣuḥ*, when the *rasa* (taste of perception) will be sentenced to *antar mukha bhāva* (the internal state), not *bahir mukha bhāva* (the external state).

ALEXIS: Yes. So it is internal impulse, *saṁjihīrṣu*, the impulse to withdraw that objective...

SWAMIJI: Withdrawal, this is the state of withdrawal.

ALEXIS: ... in the flavor of internal nature.

SWAMIJI: Yes, internal state.

DEVOTEE: *Saṁhartum.*

SWAMIJI: *Saṁhartum-icchu* (comm).[240]

LJA TA04H (51:31)

Sthiternāśam kalayantī, so She observes the *nāśa* of that *sthiti*, the destruction of this *sthiti*. So it is Sthitināśakālī. Sthitināśakālī is the third state of Kālī. Sthitināśakālī, that destroys the state of *sthiti*, that, 'This is the specks, and this is ...", when that curiosity is over.

These states are found predominantly in the sexual course–in predominance.[241] In other senses also, they are found, [but] not in predominance. But you have to find out how it is like that. For instance, you take food, you take good tasteful paneer (*tzaman*, cheese) and taste it, and you have to find out all these states. First, when nothing was there in your brain that this is *tzaman* [viz., Sṛṣṭikālī], then *tzaman*, and then the tasting of the *tzaman* (that is the *sthiti* of Raktakālī), [and] when the taste is over, that is Sthitināśakālī. *Carvaṇān antaram*[242], Sthitināśakālī, there is no curiosity to eat the *tzaman* anymore.

JOHN: How do these fit into the sexual act in terms of *viṣa tattva* and...?

SWAMIJI: ... *kāma tattva* and *nirañjana tattva*. *Nirañjana tattva* will carry you to that state when there is no curiosity.

---

239. "I have understood this."

240. The desire (*icchu*) to draw together or collect.

241. "Predominance" in the sense of being vivid.

242. Tasting (*carvaṇa*) internally (*antaram*).

Tām antar mukhatārasāt sañjihīrṣuḥ, when She withdraws that state by touching the flavor of *antarmukha bhāva*, the flavor of introverted-ness, *sthiternāśam kalayantī*, then She observes Her state of *sthitināśa*. So this is Sthitināśakālī, this is the state of Sthitināśakālī. It is *nirucyate*, it is well-explained in the Tantras.[243]

Now, in *prameya* (objectivity), he has explained the *sṛṣṭi* in *prameya*, *sthiti* in *prameya*, *saṁhāra* as *prameya*. In creation in the objective world, you have to find out *anākhya cakra*, and in the protection of the objective world, you have to find out *anākhya cakra*, and in destroying the objective world, you have to find out *anākhya cakra*. Now, this *saṁhāra* (destruction) of *prameya* is over, is explained. Then *anākhya* of *prameya* is now described here – *anākhya* of *prameya*:

LJA TA04H (54:43)

4. Yamakālī – *anākhya* (the gap[244]) of *prameya* (objectivity).

ततोऽपि संहाररसे पूर्णे विघ्नकरीं स्वयम् ।
शङ्कां यमात्मिकां भागे सूते संहरतेऽपि च ॥ १५१ ॥

243. "She merges both the objective and subjective worlds in Herself and She is called Sthitināśakālī. When these *karaṇeśvarī devī*s are *tṛpta* (full, satiated), then they are united with *cit*-Bhairava and they feel satisfied and contented. And when these *yoginī*s are satisfied, they become introverted. Here, this *samvit devī* has merged this *mita-pramātā* (the limited experient) in Her own *svarūpa* (nature). And that *pramāṇa-prameya-adi-kṣobha-śūnya*, which is without these two, [*pramāṇa* and *prameya*], which is above these, or which is *prāṇa-apāna-adi-kṣobha-śūnya*, where there is neither *prāṇa* nor *apāna*, that is *atyanta śānta nirvikalpa-rūpa sthiti*, that is *śānta sthiti*, where there is *nirvikalpa*, where there are no thoughts. That is Sthitināśakālī. That is the actual Śivarātri where everything melts away." *Shri Kramanaya Pradīpikā*, Verse 3 (LJA archive).

244. The *parasaṁvitti rūpa*, the supreme formation of consciousness.

tato'pi saṁhārarase pūrṇe vighnakarīṁ svayam /
śaṅkāṁ yamātmikāṁ bhāge sūte saṁharate'pi ca //151//
(not recited)

Tato'pi saṁhārarase pūrṇe, when this *saṁhāra rasa*, the flavor of *saṁhāra*, the flavor of withdrawal of all these threefold acts is over (*saṁhāra rase pūrṇe*), *vighnakarīṁ svyam*, now this state of *anākhya* becomes twofold there, it takes the position of twofold states.[245] The onefold state of *anākhya* is for those fully elevated yogis. This is the first state of *anākhya*. And those yogis who are not fully elevated, they fall.[246] You must have read in the *Spanda Nirṇaya*, the *Spanda* [*Kārikā*]:

LJA TA04H (55:43)

तदा तस्मिन्महाव्योम्नि प्रलीनशशिभास्करे ।
सौषुप्तपदवन्मूढः प्रबुद्धः स्यादनावृतः ॥२५॥

245. "So *anākhya dāśa* is in two forms. One is *bahir-mukha svarūpa-acchadana-rūpā*, it is tending towards the objective world. And the next is *antar-mukha svarūpa-unmīlanā-rūpa*, internal. The *parameśvarī bhagavati* [i.e., Yamakālī] is always playing with these two *rasas* of *mahā-grāsa* and *mahā-vilāsa* (*grāsa* means, digestion, and *vilāsa* means, expansion or creation). *Yama* means, that which controls, so it digests and it throws out. This takes place in the *anākhya* of *sṛṣṭi*, so it is the highest level in *prameya bhāva* (objectivity)." *Shri Kramanaya Pradīpikā*, Verse 4 (LJA archive).

246. "If we go to this previous state of *parapramātṛ-rūpā* of Sthitināśakālī, where *prāṇa* and *apāna*, these two horses of *prameya* and *pramāṇa* were fixed in one place in that *sandhi sthāna* of *bahir-dvadaśānta* or *antar-dvadaśānta*. There the yogi has to be most aware in his *svātmānusaṁdhāna*. *Ānusaṁdhāna* means, in awareness, he has to be most aware because even the slightest trace of going astray will push him to the state of sound sleep, and there he will be *kiṁkarttavya-mūḍha*, wondering what to do next. He will lose everything, and he will be in *śaṅkā-samudra*, he will be in the sea of *śaṅkās* (suspicions and doubts). Then afterwards he will come out of that state, and instead of going inward he will go outward, he will be thrown out." Ibid.

tadā tasminmahāvyomni pralīnaśaśibhāskare /
sauṣuptapadavanmūḍhaḥ prabuddhaḥ syādanāvṛtaḥ //[247]
(not recited in full)

Mūḍhaḥ becomes *sauṣupta padvat* (deep sleep)–he falls. This is the gap where there is the [possible] apprehension of falling down also in *anākhya*, this first *anākhya*.

SCHOLAR: But *śaśi* and *bhāskara* are already dissolved there.

SWAMIJI: *Śaśi-bhāskara* is dissolved.[248]

SCHOLAR: So he is already entering into *anākhya*, but he falls at this point.

SWAMIJI: He falls because he cannot maintain that strong and full awareness. He cannot maintain that strong and full awareness. He has no capacity to hold it.[249]

SCHOLAR: But *apāna* (exhale) and *prāṇa* (inhale) have melted away?

SWAMIJI: Yes.

SCHOLAR: But he can't proceed further than that.

SWAMIJI: *Prāṇa-apāna*, there is no question of the rise of *prāṇa-apāna* there. But only that state of consciousness will vanish in one second if he does not hold it properly. *Pūrṇe vighnakarīṁ svayam śaṅkāṁ* (verse 151), then doubt rises. The doubt of what? "Is it *anākhya*?

---

247. *Spanda Kārikā*, 1.25. See also *Wisdom in Kashmir Shaivism*, verse 46 (LJA archives).

248. The moon and the sun, respectively.

249. "Because this point of God consciousness is so refined that it requires full attention. If you are [unaware] just for half a second, one hundredth part of a second, if you don't maintain attentiveness, you will fall down." *Spanda Kārikā* and *Spanda Sandoha*, 1.25. "And it is said in the *Śiva Sutras*, '*Udyamo Bhairavaḥ*', you have to be *udyamo* Bhairava, here you have to maintain great effort just to remain awake at this stage. There is no *prāṇa-apāna*, and you have to be very aware there. When the function of *prāṇa-apāna* is one, then you can go to sleep. So Yamakālī is connected with '*udyamo bhairavaḥ*'. It is very interesting. He says: When you go for this *udyamo bhairava*, then this *udyama* does not leave him, he is after it because he want's to go to *anākhya dāśa*." *Shri Kramanaya Pradīpikā* (LJA archive).

It is the real *anākhya* or not?" This doubt shines only in that yogi who has not maintained it properly. The one yogi who has maintained this *anākhya* properly, there is no question of the rise of doubt in him. So, *śaṅkāṁ yamātmikām*, this is *yamātmikā śaṅkāṁ*.[250] So, what happens afterwards? When he goes in this *anākhya* state, the inefficient yogi, when he enters in this next state of *anākhya*, he, after coming out from this kind of *samādhi*, he goes to the master again [and says], "O master, I am not completely satisfied with this *samādhi*, please instruct me something more." Because the reality he has not touched. The one who has maintained that full awareness, he has touched the reality and there is no need for him to go to the master. So this is the *anākhya* of *prameya*. *Bas*. Next lesson we will do another eight states of Kālīs. Four states of the Kālīs [concerned with objectivity] are over. Sṛṣṭikālī is first.

SCHOLAR: You didn't complete the verse. Actually, you commented it but you didn't actually translate the verse.

SWAMIJI: *Yamātmikāṁ śaṅkām*, this *śaṅkā*, this doubt-ness, *bhāge sūte saṁharate'pi ca*, on one side, from one point of view, it creates that doubt [for the inefficient yogi], and from another point of view, it destroys that doubt [for the efficient yogi].[251]

SCHOLAR: But that presupposes the existence of the doubt that is to be destroyed. So does it arise in the form of an impression for that *prabuddha*[252]?

---

250. The destruction of doubt.

251. "Doubt is *mala* (impurity) and doubt is also *glāni*, going away from God consciousness, doubt is being shrunken [viz., duality]. *Saṁsārakārāgārāntaḥ sthūla*, and doubt is that thing which makes you tied like an animal to a stake in the imprisonment of the universe. *Tatha ahi śaṅkā mālinyaṁ*, *mala* means, the dirt arising from *śaṅkā*s and *glāni* (*glāni* means, when some bad or disgusting thing is put in front of you, you feel an aversion, or a sickly feeling towards it). *Saṅkoca* means, the impression that, 'If I do such-and-such action, I will be *saṅkoca* (shrunken).' These are all *mala*s, the dross of doubts. *Saṁsārakārāgārāntaḥ*, these are *saṁsāra-rūpi*, and this *sthūla-sthūṇa-aghaṭāyate*, these are always there in gross form – these *śaṅkā*s, *malinya* (dross), *glāni* (aversion), *saṅkoca* (shrunkenness), and they exist up to Sadāśiva-*dāśa*." *Shri Kramanaya Pradīpikā*, Verse 4 (LJA archive)

252. The awakened one, i.e., the efficient yogi.

SWAMIJI: The form of impression: "Is it really *anākhya* or not?"

JOHN: But for both people it arises?

SWAMIJI: Not for both people.

SCHOLAR: So why does he say, "*bhāge sūte, bhage saṁhārite'pi*"? *Kiṁ saṁhārite*?

SWAMIJI: *Bhage saṁhārite, śaṅkāṁ* (doubt) [is destroyed].

SCHOLAR: So *śaṅkā* has already arisen.

SWAMIJI: *Śaṅkā* is there because you don't know... *tadā tasmin yāmavasthāṁ samāvalambya*... you refer to that *Spanda* of Vasugupta:

LJA TA04H (59:47)

यामवस्थां समालम्ब्य यदयं मम वक्ष्यति ।
तदवश्यं करिष्येऽहमिति सङ्कल्प्य तिष्ठति ॥

yāmavasthāṁ samālambya yadayaṁ mama vakṣyati /
tadavaśyaṁ kariṣye'hamiti saṁkalpya tiṣṭhati //1.23//[253]
(not recited in full)

"I won't [use] my brain there. *Yadayam mama vakṣyati*, whatever that *dhātā*, the *parameśvaraḥ* (Lord), will instruct me [to do], I will do that." Because this is the way, this is the state of the yogi which is called, the journey of *bhramavega*.[254] It is not a journey of... this is not

---

253. *Spanda Kārikā*, 1.23. See also *Wisdom in Kashmir Shaivism*, verse 4 (LJA archives), and *Self-Realization in Kashmir Shaivism–The Oral Teachings* of Swami Lakshmanjoo, ed. John Hughes (State University of New York Press, Albany, 1995), "Talks on Practice", fn. 21, p. 51.

254. "*Bhramavega* means, the unknowing force. Here you have to put your force of devotion without knowing what is to happen next. You cannot use your *mantra* because when your breath is gone, your mind is also gone as the mind has become transformed into the formation of consciousness (*cit*). Here, breathing takes the form of force (*vega*). It is this *vega* which pierces and penetrates *mūlādhāra cakra* so that you pass through it." *Kashmir Shaivism–The Secret Supreme*, "*Seven States of Turya*", p. 113.

traveling with your consciousness. This is traveling with *bhrama-vega*. You have to thrust, you have to thrust without understanding. You thrust, go on, go on inside, get entry, get entry! Don't [use] your brain! As soon as you [use] your brain, how to thrust and enter, finished![255]

LJA TA04H (1:00:46) end
LJA TA04I (00:00) start

255. The *Spanda Kārikā* verses 1.22 and 1.23 are speaking of the moments when one is overjoyed, or filled with wrath, or overcome with fear, and at these moments one's organs remain at a standstill position and consequently *sāmānya spanda* (viz., *anākhya*) is vividly perceived. "When this wrath, etcetera, has been transformed in that supreme God consciousness, at that moment also there is another problem, there is another problem there. When your breath has stopped, it has rushed in *suṣumnā nāḍī*, and from *mūlādhāra* it has risen to the state of *sahaśrārdha cakra*. At that moment also, if you are not fully attentive in that God consciousness, you are kicked down on the path of *suṣupti*, you will become just asleep. If you don't have the character and strength of maintaining that, there you will just fall on the ground unconscious and doctors will be attending you when you will wake up [and they will wonder], 'What has happened to this man?'" *Spanda Kārikā* 1.25. "And it is said in the *Śiva Sutras*: '*Udyamo Bhairavaḥ*', you have to be *udyamo*-Bhairava, here you have to maintain great effort just to remain awake at this stage. There is no *prāṇa-apāna* and you have to be very aware there. When the function of *prāṇa-apāna* is one, then you can also fall asleep. So Yamakālī is connected with *udyamo*-Bhairava. It is very interesting. He says, "When you adopt this *udyamo*-Bhairava, then this *udyama* (strenuous exertion) does not leave you, because you want to go to *anākhya dāśa*. And that *anākhya dāśa* is beyond description. It is why in the *Veda*s it is said: '*utiṣṭhata jāgrata prāpyabharān nibodhataḥ*, O soul, be attentive, be awake, hear this message of Lord Śiva: *kṣurasyadhārā*, this is treading on the path on the edge of sword; *durgam-patha*, this is a very difficult path to tread; just for a one second mistake you will be kicked down, because it is so precious. So you must maintain it, you must devotedly have it.'" *Shri Kramanaya Pradīpikā*, Verse 4 (LJA archive).

5. Saṁhārakālī – *sṛṣṭi* (creation) in *pramāṇa* (cognition)

संहृत्य शङ्कां शङ्क्यार्थवर्जं वा भावमण्डले ।
संहृतिं कलयत्येव स्वात्मवह्नौ विलापनात् ॥ १५२ ॥

saṁhṛtya śaṅkāṁ śaṅkyārtha-varjaṁ vā bhāvamaṇḍale /
saṁhṛtiṁ kalayatyeva svātmavahnau vilāpanāt //152//

So this starts the function in the organic [i.e., cognitive] field. Previously it was in the objective field; *sṛṣṭi*, *sthiti*, *saṁhāra*, and *anākhya* [were] in the objective field. Now it is *sṛṣṭi*, *sthiti*, *saṁhāra*, and *anākhya* in the cognitive field.

Saṁhṛti śaṅkām, when all doubts are removed, or *śaṅkyārtha varjaṁ*, or the basis of doubts [is removed], ...*

SCHOLAR: That arose in Yamakālī.

SWAMIJI: Yes, that rose in Yamakālī, in previous the Kālī, the fourth Kālī.

*... *bhāvamaṇḍale saṁhṛtiṁ kalayatyeva svātmavahnau vilāpanāt*, then that *parā saṁvitti*, that supreme consciousness, directs the *maṇḍala* (the classes) of all the objective field and destroys them in the fire of Her own nature, and so functions the state of *saṁhāra* (destruction).

SCHOLAR: *Śaṅkyārtha varjaṁ*?

SWAMIJI: *Śaṅkyārtha varjaṁ*, when *śaṅkyārtha*, all these objects, which had created doubt, are also removed. And this is nominated as Saṁhārakālī. Saṁhārakālī is the *sṛṣṭi* of *pramāṇa*.[256]

---

256. "Saṁhārakālī is *bhāva-saṁhāra rūpī kālī*, whatever the object we see, it destroys it. This is the Kālī who destroys objective differentiatedness. Previously we said that Yamakālī digests and again throws it out. Now here, Saṁhārakālī destroys all differentiated objectiveness. Because the duality, all these *śaṅkās* (doubts), e.g., 'This is to be taken', 'This is not mine', 'This is bad', 'This is good', all these thoughts which arose in that *prameya maṇḍalaṁ sarva-bhāva*, they are all digested. So this is for that yogi who remained awake by virtue of that great effort (*udyamo*

But how this *saṁhāra* takes place, he explains that in the next verse:

LJA TA04I (02:01)

विलापनात्मिकां तां च भावसंहृतिमात्मनि ।
आमृशत्येव येनैषा मया ग्रस्तमिति स्फुरेत् ॥ १५३ ॥

vilāpanātmikāṁ tāṁ ca bhāvasaṁhṛtimātmani /
āmṛśatyeva yenaiṣā mayā grastamiti sphuret //153//

This supreme consciousness (that *saṁvitti* or Kālī), when in Her own nature this *bhāva saṁhṛti*, the destruction of the objective world has taken place (that is *vilāpanātmikām bhāva saṁhṛtim*), and then She observes and perceives that, "I have totally/completely destroyed the universe of the objective world. I have absolutely destroyed or finished this objective world."

SCHOLAR: *Grastam*, devoured, taken in.

SWAMIJI: Yes, taken in, swallowed.[257] This is the nature of this first Kālī, Saṁhārakālī, which has taken place in the *sṛṣṭi* (creation) of *pramāṇa*, in the *sṛṣṭi* of the cognitive field. Now he explains the *sthiti* of the cognitive field, how *sthiti* takes place in the cognitive field.[258]

---

bhairava). He has approached the next state which is Saṁhārakālī. And here, all of the confusion caused by those *śaṅkā*s is destroyed. And there is not an inkling of *sphāra-rūpa udaya*, to again create." Ibid., verse 5.

257. "Saṁhārakālī is *bhāva-saṁhāra rūpī kālī*, whatever object we see, it destroys it. This is the Kālī who destroys objective differentiated-ness. Previously we said that Yamakālī digests [differentiated objectivity] and again throws it out. Now here, Saṁhārakālī destroys all differentiated objectiveness." Ibid., verse 5.

258. "Now a suspicion arises: when Saṁhārakālī has destroyed everything, why should there be Mṛtyukālī? But the texts says: No, even in this state of Saṁhārakālī there are still some traces remaining, because She goes on destroying and this entails some effort. It is not *pūrṇāhantā*, it is not a state of fullness of that destruction. There are still traces of impressions of I-ness (this-ness is digested in *ahaṁ* there)." Ibid., introduction to verse 6.

LJA TA04I (03:23)

6. Mṛtyukālī – *sthiti* (establishment) in *pramāṇa* (cognition).

संहार्योपाधिरेतस्याः स्वस्वभावो हि संविदः ।
निरुपाधिनि संशुद्धे संविद्रूपेऽस्तमीयते ॥ १५४ ॥

saṁhāryopādhiretasyāḥ svasvabhāvo hi saṁvidaḥ /
nirupādhini saṁśuddhe saṁvidrūpe'stamīyate //154//
(not recited in full)

This is the nature of consciousness that it creates again impressions of this [perception] that, "I have destroyed this universe." The impression still remains there, the impression of having destroyed this objective field. The impression is there that, "I have destroyed this objective field."[259]

JOHN: This is *sthiti.*

SCHOLAR: *Pramāṇa-sthiti.*

SWAMIJI: No, this is not *pramāṇa-sthiti*, this is but natural. But *pramāṇa-sthiti* [i.e., Mṛtyukālī] is that state of consciousness when that impression is also destroyed. That impression that, "I have destroyed this objective field", that impression also is destroyed in the pure state of consciousness, the pure state of Her consciousness (*nirupādhini saṁśuddhe*; *saṁśuddhe* means, pure; *nirupādhini* means, without any other adjustments).[260]

SCHOLAR: *Saṁśuddhe pramātrātmani.*

---

259. "So here, this objective world of differentiated-ness is actually without duality, *avabhāsitam*, and though it is without any duality, it shows duality." Ibid., verse 6.

260. "Mṛtyukālī is without any *upādhi-rahita*, it needs no crutches, because *svabhāvabhūta ahamtā*, it gets digested in itself without any effort. So it is called Mṛtyukālī–it is effortless. In the fifth Kālī, you still need some crutch because thisness is being digested in I-ness." Ibid.

SWAMIJI: *Pramātrātmani*. But it is not that *pramātā* (subject) in the subjective state. It is *pramātā* in the cognitive field. [Previously] there was *pramātā* in the objective field also.

This is nominated as Mṛtyukālī. The first was nominated as Saṁhārakālī. This is Mṛtyukālī because Mṛtyukālī is that state of consciousness which destroys the *mṛtyu* also (*mṛtyu* means, the destroyer of impressions).

SCHOLAR: *Mṛtyu*, literally, death.

SWAMIJI: Yes. Now he explains the *saṁhāra* in *pramāṇa*:

LJA TA04I (05:30)

7. Rudrakālī – *saṁhāra* (destruction) in *pramāṇa* (cognition).

विलापितेऽपि भावौघे कञ्चिद्भावं तदैव सा ।
आश्यानयेद्य एवास्ते शङ्कासंस्काररूपकः ॥१५५॥
शुभाशुभतया सोऽयं सोष्यते फलसम्पदम् ।

vilāpite'pi bhāvaughe kañcidbhāvaṁ tadaiva sā /
āśyānayedya evāste śaṅkāsaṁskārarūpakaḥ //155//
śubhāśubhatayā so'yaṁ soṣyate phalasampadam /

Here also, in this last state of, nearing the last state of, the cognitive field of consciousness, there also is the apprehension of being carried away from the reality of consciousness. *Vilāpite api bhāvaughe*, although that impression [that] this objective world is absolutely destroyed/swallowed, along with the impressions also, but *kañcit bhāvaṁ tadaiva sā āśyānayet*, again some object with which you have been attached previously, that object is coagulated again. That object is coagulated again.[261] This is the nature of *saṁvitti* (consciousness).

261. "What do you mean by 'coagulation'? When you understand that, 'I am the universe', your understanding is not coagulated. When you understand,

SCHOLAR: Coagulated.

SWAMIJI: Produced, it appears, but not all objects. In the previous, Yamakālī, all objects did appear, but here only one object appears with which you are totally attached.

SCHOLAR: Deepest impression.

SWAMIJI: Yes. That object appears again after destroying the impressions also.

JOHN: And that one object is left only.

SWAMIJI: Yes, one object. *Āśyānayet ya evāste śaṅkā saṁskāra*, that is *saṁskāra rūpa*, that is the embodiment of the impression of that object, and it again gets its life in appearance. *Śubhāśubhatayā so'yam soṣyate phala sampadam*, and that, too, carries you away from that God consciousness. That is also *śaṅkā* (doubt). *Śubhāśubhatayā*, it gives you pain and pleasure, good and bad [i.e., duality].

MARK D: As well as doubt.

SWAMIJI: Doubt, yes.

LJA TA04I (08:00)

पूर्वं हि भोगात्पश्चाद्वा शङ्केयं व्यवतिष्ठते ॥ १५६ ॥

pūrvaṁ hi bhogātpaścādvā śaṅkeyaṁ vyavatiṣṭhate //156//

This *śaṅkā* (this doubt) does not appear in the function of *bhoga* (enjoyment)[262], but before the function of *bhoga* and after the function of *bhoga*. Because the *bhoga* here is absolutely without doubt–here in this state of consciousness. In this state of consciousness, *bhoga* (enjoying), when you enjoy, when you taste *tzamin* or paneer or something else or anything [among] all the five senses, ...*

Because this is the world of the senses, the cognitive world is the world of the senses. The objective world was the world of objects. This is the world of the senses.

'I am somebody's wife, I have got two children', your understanding is coagulated, frozen in some limited cycle." Ibid., verse 7.

262. That is, while perceiving an object.

*...so when you are enjoying all these things, in the body of enjoyment, this doubt does not remain there. [This doubt appears] only in the beginning or in the end [of the enjoyment/perception].

SCHOLAR: "Should I do this?" or "Should I have done this?"

SWAMIJI: "Should I enjoy it or not? Oh, I have enjoyed it wrongly, I ought not to have enjoyed it." In the end also, this *śaṅkā* appears, and in the beginning also, this *śaṅkā* appears. And that *śaṅkā* (doubt) is only of one object, one particular object, not all objects. But here, there is one difference in this *śaṅkā*, in this *śaṅkā* there is one difference: although this *śaṅkā* will carry you away from God consciousness, it does not carry you away from God consciousness.

LJA TA04I (09:45)

अन्यदाऽश्यानितमपि तदैव द्रावयेदियम् ।

anyadāśyānitamapi tadaiva drāvayediyam / 157a

When this doubt appears there – "Should I enjoy this or not? I ought not to have enjoyed it" – in the end, this doubt remains only for one or two seconds, this doubt does not prevail for good. This doubt remains, it appears, only just like lightening, the lightening of this thunder. *Anyat āśyānitam api tadaiva drāvayediyam*, the next moment it is destroyed, this doubt is destroyed in this state of *saṁvitti* (consciousness).

LJA TA04I (10:38)

प्रायश्चित्तादिकर्मभ्यो ब्रह्महत्यादिकर्मवत् ॥ १५७ ॥

prāyaścittādikarmabhyo brahmahatyādikarmavat //157//

[For example], when some particular person commits some sin[263], and just after committing that sin he observes *prāyaścit* (penance), and

263. The example given in the text is the sin of killing a Brahmin.

after observing this penance, the fruit of the sin is removed, he does not become the victim of that fruit, *karma*. In the same way, this doubt is removed absolutely by its own self. This is the power of cognitive consciousness.

SCHOLAR: This is spontaneous manifestation of doubt and its removal.

SWAMIJI: Yes, doubt appears, and it is removed. So it is called Rudrakālī.

LJA TA04I (10:38)

रोधनाद्द्रावणाद्रूपमित्थं कलयते चितिः ।

rodhanāddrāvaṇādrūpam-itthaṁ kalayate citiḥ / 158a

Because there are two functions there simultaneously appearing: *rodhana* and *drāvaṇa*. *Rodhana* (coagulation) and the melting of that coagulated state – melting. Coagulated and again melting it away. *Rodhana* is coagulation. *Drāvaṇa* is to melt it. It is also nominated as Bhadrakālī.[264] *Bhedanāt drāvaṇāt rūpam*, give it differentiated form and carry it again in undifferentiated [form].

SCHOLAR: *Bhedasya drāvaṇāt.*

SWAMIJI: *Bhedasya drāvaṇāt*, differentiate it, and then get it sentenced in undifferentiated form. So, it is nominated in two ways, it has two names, this state of consciousness has two names: Rudrakālī or Bhadrakālī. You may nominate it as Rudrakālī, you may nominate it as Bhadrakālī.[265]

---

264. "*Drā* means, *drāvaṇa*, and *bha* means, *bhedana*, penetrating, when you drill it. To penetrate (*bhedana*) means, all these *rupas*, the *vikāsa* (expansion) of [those forms] – that is *bha* or *bhedana*. And *dra* means, *drāvaṇa*, those *vikāsas* (expansions) are again digested in Her own *svarūpa* (nature). It is why She is called Bhadrakālī." Ibid., verse 7.

265. "These *śaṅkās* (doubts), *malinya* (dross), *glāni* (aversion), *saṅkoca* (shrunkenness), they exist up to Sadāśiva-*dāśa*. So, Śrī Bhadrakālī is that *devī* who can destroy all these doubts in Herself. By Her grace, when a yogi gets *samāveśa* (absorbed)

JOHN: These Kālīs traveling in the cognitive field, ...

SWAMIJI: The cognitive field, yes.

JOHN: ... these are *bhedābheda* (differentiated and undifferentiated).

SWAMIJI: *Bhedābheda* is cognitive, yes.

JOHN: What is being perceived here? What is the content of perception? The senses are perceiving anything, taste, you said, perception, but there is no object of perception at this state.

SWAMIJI: But this is cognitive. You see, I will show you on Denise. When you look at Denise, you are diverted towards Denise with passion, and at that moment you become Denise. This is the field of the objective world. You are residing in the field of the objective world. When you look at Denise and at the same time know that, "I am John, I am not Denise", you don't give everything to Denise. In the objective field, you become Denise. In the objective field, you become the cheese yourself, you have melted in the cheese.

DEVOTEE: One with that.

SWAMIJI: You have become one with that. That is the objective world. That is the field of objectivity. The field of the cognitive [world] is when you know that, "I am John, she is Denise. We are two, we are not one." So you are a bit separated from Denise, are you not? This is the field of cognition. When you are absolutely away from objectivity, e.g., if you see Denise, you don't mind at all, you don't think of Denise at all, you are in your own nature, in your own real nature, that is the nature of *pramātṛ bhāva*, that is subjective, you remain in subjectivity.

---

in this state, all these *malinyas*, *śaṅkās*, *glaṅis*, and *saṅkocas*, when they rise, *yugapat anubhava karatā*, this yogi feels that they get destroyed immediately, and *sākṣātkāra karatā*, he [directly] sees that these are destroyed immediately (*anāyāsa* means, without any effort he goes to Bhadrakālī). This yogi sees Bhadrakālī and all his suspicions and doubts are destroyed. Previously, in Yamakālī, there were also doubts, but there the yogi had to use effort to remove them. In that state, if the yogis awareness is even slightly lessened, he falls asleep and comes out just like a worldly person. But here in the state of Bhadrakālī, all these *śaṅkās*, which rise in this yogi, without any effort those are destroyed immediately. This is the difference between the rise of doubts in Yamakālī and Bhadrakālī. Because *bhedana*, it penetrates those doubts like that drilling instrument, and *drāvaṇa*, it digest that doubt within itself." Ibid.

So this is the journey.

JOHN: So the journey is with the eyes ...

SWAMIJI: This journey is from objectivity to subjectivity. It will end in subjective consciousness.

JOHN: And that journey can take place just while you are perceiving anything.

SWAMIJI: And, at the same time, in the beginning also, you have to find out the reality of the ending reality.

JOHN: In the very beginning.

SWAMIJI: It is why it is called, it is all *anākhya cakra*.

SCHOLAR: (inaudible) nameless.

JOHN: Why, in this *sthiti* of cognitivity [viz., Mṛtyukālī], is this called the destruction of all objective impression?

SWAMIJI: It can't be *saṁhāra*. It can't be *saṁhāra* [of cognition], it is only *sthiti* [of cognition]. *Sthiti* means, establishment, when the cognitive field is established. When the cognitive field is destroyed, then there will be no possibility of the rising of doubts. So it is only *sthiti*. In the objective world, it took place in *anākhya*.[266]

SCHOLAR: So this is the stage of *pramāṇa-saṁhāra*, this Bhadrakālī.

SWAMIJI: Yes, *pramāṇa-saṁhāra*. It is not *anākhya*. It can't be *anākhya*. In the objective field, it was *anākhya* where the rising of doubts started. The rising of doubts started in *anākhya cakra* in the objective field. The rising of doubts started in *saṁhāra cakra* in the cognitive field. And this *saṁhāra cakra* is called, nominated as, Rudrakālī or Bhadrakālī. Both are ...

SCHOLAR: So here, this is only an instantaneous doubt, whereas in Yamakālī it would be...?

SWAMIJI: In Yamakālī, it is established doubt. In this Bhadrakālī or Rudrakālī, it is not established–it appears and is destroyed, it appears and is destroyed. There is only the bubbling of this doubt, only bubbling takes place. It bubbles out, and again down, destroyed. I have seen when one person was slaughtered in the railway [station], he was slaughtered (i.e., stabbed) by somebody. He had in his purse ten thousand rupees and it was taken by some thief, and he was slaughtered. And at that

266. Referring to Saṁhārakālī, the fourth state of Kālī, which is *anāhkyā* in *prameya bhāva* (the objective world).

time he was struggling [to live]. This was the state of Yamakālī, this was the state of Yamakālī.

SCHOLAR: Like that.

SWAMIJI: Like that. And afterwards, when he was lying dead, his body was moving like this (Swamiji demonstrates), because he was so young, his body was bubbling like this. Although there was no life in his body, but [still] it was bubbling. So this is the state of Bhadrakālī. There is no possibility of the rise of doubts, there are only impressions of doubts bubbling, because [they arise] from the impressions of the past. This takes place in this consciousness of the cognitive field in its state of *saṁhṛti*.

SCHOLAR: Of withdrawal.

SWAMIJI: Withdrawal, yes. This is all withdrawal, withdrawal to *anākhya*.

JOHN: Moving in, moving in, you are moving in through these twelve Kālīs, is it?

SWAMIJI: Yes. It is all withdrawal from objectivity to subjective consciousness, because it is *anākhya cakra*.

JOHN: So this is *nimīlanā*, moving in.

SWAMIJI: Yes, it is *nimīlanā*.

SCHOLAR: *Śakti cakra saṁdhāne viśva saṁhāra*.

SWAMIJI: Yes.

LJA TA04I (18:33)

तदपि द्रावयेदेव तदप्याश्यानयेदथ ॥ १५८ ॥

tadapi drāvayedeva tadapyāśyānayedatha //158//

Because in this *pramāṇa cakra*, in this field of cognition, *drāvaṇa* (melting) also takes place at the same time and *rodhana* (coagulation) also takes place, and the melting of cognition also takes place, both simultaneously.

Now he explains the state of *anākhya cakra* in the cognitive field.

LJA TA04I (19:03)

8. Mārtaṇḍakālī – *anākhya* (the gap[267]) in *pramāṇa* (cognition)

इत्थं भोग्येऽपि सम्भुक्ते सति तत्करणान्यपि ।
संहरन्ती कलयते द्वादशैवाहमात्मनि ॥ १५९ ॥

itthaṁ bhogye'pi sambhukte sati tatkaraṇānyapi /
saṁharantī kalayate dvādaśaivāhamātmani //159//

Now, this objective world is finished; *bhoge sambhukte*, this objective world is already *sambhukte*, swallowed, taken in. And the means of the objective world also are being destroyed here now – the means of the objective world. What are these means? The five senses…

SCHOLAR: The ten senses[268], *buddhi*, *māna*, *ahaṁkāra*.[269]

SWAMIJI: Yes. *Tat karaṇāni api dvādaśaiva*, these twelve organs also get entry in that *saṁvitti*, that state, the *saṁvitti* of I-consciousness.

SCHOLAR: So the whole cognitive field is dissolved here.

SWAMIJI: Dissolved into supreme voidness. You can't say [that it is] *pramātṛ bhāva* yet. Now he nominates these twelve organs:

LJA TA04I (20:25)

कर्मबुद्ध्यक्षवर्गो हि बुद्ध्यन्तो द्वादशात्मकः ।
प्रकाशकत्वात्सूर्यात्मा भिन्ने वस्तुनि जृम्भते ॥ १६० ॥

karmabuddhyakṣavargo hi buddhyanto dvādaśātmakaḥ /
prakāśakatvātsūryātmā bhinne vastuni jṛmbhate //160//

---

267. The *parasaṁvitti rūpa*, the supreme formation of consciousness.

268. The five *karmendriyas* (organs of action) and the five *jñānendriyas* (organs of knowledge).

269. Swamiji will clarify in verse 161 that *ahaṁkāra* (ego) is not included here among the "means of the objective world."

Karma buddhyakṣavargo hi, all these classes of senses regarding action and knowledge (so the senses of action and the senses of knowledge), *buddhyanta*, up to the *buddhi*, up to the intellect (the five senses of action, the five senses of knowledge, these are ten, and the mind and the intellect), so these twelve senses, *prakāśakatvāt sūryātmā*, because they give life to the perception of the universal field, perception in the universal field (the perception of the universal field is living only on these twelve organs), because it is *prakāśaka*[270], so it is *sūrya*, this is the field of *sūrya* (the sun).

SCHOLAR: *Pramāṇa* (cognition).

SWAMIJI: The objective field was the field of *soma* (the moon), the cognitive field is the field of *sūrya*, and the subjective field is the field of *agni* (fire). Why *ahaṁkāra* (ego) is not kept in this class? Why only the mind and the intellect are included with these organs?

SCHOLAR: But not the individuating factor, not *ahaṁkāra*.

SWAMIJI: Not *ahaṁkāra*. To that he explains in the 161 *śloka*:

LJA TA04I (22:13)

अहङ्कारस्तु करणमभिमानैकसाधनम् ।
अविच्छिन्नपरामर्शी लीयते तेन तत्र सः ॥ १६१ ॥

ahaṅkārastu karaṇam-abhimānaikasādhanam /
avicchinnaparāmarśī līyate tena tatra saḥ //161//
(not recited)

Ahaṅkārastu karaṇam, although *ahaṁkāra* is also a means of the senses, but it is *abhimānaika sādhanam*[271] and it is *avicchinna parāmarśa*.[272] It is *abhimāna*, it has got an ego, and it is *avicchinna parāmarśa*. It is not *avacchinna parāmarśa*, it has not the *parāmarśa* (perception) of *avacchinna*, it is not a specific or particular *parāmarśa*.

270. Making apparent or manifest.

271. Lit., a procurer (*sādhanam*) of pride or arrogance (*abhimāna*).

272. Lit., uninterrupted or continual (*avacchinna*) perception or experience (*parāmarśa*).

For instance, I perceive this, I see, I taste, I smell. This is *avacchinna parāmarśa*. But 'I', the one who says, "I see", 'I' is *avicchinna parāmarśa*. That *avicchinna parāmarśa* is explained in this way that, he who sees, the same person tastes, the same person touches, the same person.... So 'I' is pervading in each and every sense.

SCHOLAR: Nonspecific.

SWAMIJI: Nonspecific. That is *avicchinna parāmarśa*.

DEVOTEE: *Avicchinna* is *vyāpaka* (all-pervading).

SWAMIJI: It pervades all the senses – this 'I' (*abhimāna*, *ahaṁkāra*). So, *līyate tena tatra saḥ*, the twelvefold *cakra*s of the cognitive world are dissolved in that *ahaṁ*, *ahaṁ bhāva*. How? How it is *avicchinna parāmarśa*, he explains it in the next *śloka*:

LJA TA04I (23:53)

यथाहि खङ्गपाशादेः करणस्य विभेदिनः ।
अभेदिनि स्वहस्तादौ लयस्तद्वदयं विधिः ॥१६२॥

yathā hi khaṅgapāśādeḥ karaṇasya vibhedinaḥ /
abhedini svahastādau layastadvadayaṁ vidhiḥ //162//[273]

Just like *khaḍga pāśādeḥ*, when you have to tie somebody with a rope or you have to cut somebody's head, ...*

SCHOLAR: You want to hang them up or kill them.

SWAMIJI: Or hang them up.

*... *khaḍga pāśādeḥ*, *karaṇasya vibhedinaḥ*, all these means are separately existing outside, but this hand is only one means, which sometimes takes a *khaḍga* (a sword), sometimes takes/holds a rope, sometimes holds... the *karaṇa* (the means), the hand, is only one, one means. *Abhedini svahastādau layaḥ*, all these means are sentenced to one means, that one hand. In the same way, all these cognitive senses rest in one ego (*ahaṁkāra*, *abhimāna*, that 'I').

---

273. Swamiji recites "*khaḍga*" instead of the published "*khaṅga*", both of which translate as "sword".

LJA TA04I (25:03)

तेनेन्द्रियौघमार्तण्डमण्डलं कलयेत्स्वयम् ।
संविद्देवी स्वतन्त्रत्वात्कल्पितेऽहङ्कृतात्मनि ॥ १६३ ॥

tenendriyaughamārtaṇḍa-maṇḍalaṁ kalayetsvayam /
saṁviddevī svatantratvāt-kalpite'haṅkṛtātmani //163//

So, *indriyaugha mārtaṇḍa maṇḍalam*, this is the *mārtaṇḍa maṇḍala*, these are, in the real sense, these twelve senses are twelve suns.

SCHOLAR: Twelve rays of the sun?

SWAMIJI: Why "rays"? Twelve suns. In our tradition, there are twelve suns; *dvādaśaiva sūrya*, there are twelve suns. That is *mārtaṇḍa maṇḍala.*

SCHOLAR: Sun-*maṇḍala*.

SWAMIJI: Have you not gone through that eight *āhnika* [of the *Tantrāloka*]? There you will see, there you will find *mārtaṇḍa maṇḍala*, there is the association of all the suns, who is to be deputed on which and which date to rise in this universe. There is a *bhatak* of *mārtaṇḍa*s. There is a *bhatak* of moons.

SCHOLAR: *Bhatak*?

SWAMIJI: *Bhatak* means, an assembly, gathering. As these drivers [have an] association, [there are] so many drivers. One driver is deputed, "Oh, you have to go to…today you are deputed to go on this route." So, these suns are also deputed on various routes. That is *mārtaṇḍa maṇḍala. Mārtaṇḍa maṇḍala* is the field of the cognitive world, the cognitive senses. The cognitive senses are also the field of *mārtaṇḍa* (suns). *Indriyaugha mārtaṇḍa maṇḍalam*, so this is *indriya*, all these twelve organs, senses, are *mārtaṇḍa maṇḍala*, the class of suns. *Kalayet svayam saṁviddevī*, this *saṁvit devī*, this God consciousness, this *devī*, *kalayet* (*kalayet* means, *saṁharet*), destroys, swallows [this twelvefold *maṇḍala*] in *kalpita ahaṁkṛtātmani*, in the state of the limited ego, in the state of limited egoism (that is *ahaṁkāra*). So, in *ahaṁkāra* it is destroyed. Only *ahaṁkāra* remains there.

SCHOLAR: *Svatantratvāt. Svatantratvāt kalpite*?

SWAMIJI: No. *Saṁvid devī kalayet…kalayeti.*

JOHN: The state of *ahaṁkāra* only, is this *pralayākala*?

SWAMIJI: No, this is not *pralayākala*, this won't go to that. No, you can't adjust that state with this. This is a supreme state.

SCHOLAR: This is moving into *anākhya*. This is a *śāktopāya* realization.

SWAMIJI: This is moving into *anākhya*. This *anākhya cakra*, yes, this is *śāktopāya*, throughout *śāktopāya*. So, this state of consciousness, this state of the energy of consciousness, is called, is nominated as Mārtaṇḍakālī. It is Mārtaṇḍakālī because it swallows all these *mārtaṇḍa*s, all these suns of cognition.[274]

LJA TA04I (28:30)

एवं प्रमाणंशभक्षणप्रवणं देवीचतुष्टयं निरूपितम्

evaṁ pramāṇaṁśabhakṣaṇapravaṇaṁ devīcatuṣṭayaṁ nirūpitam (commentary)

So these four *devīs*, four Kālīs, are explained, which were residing, which were bent upon destroying the world of *pramāṇa*, the cognitive world.

इदानीं प्रमात्रंशाचर्वणाचतुरं देवीचतुष्टयं निरूपयति

idānīṁ pramātraṁśacarvaṇācaturaṁ devīcatuṣṭayam nirūpayati (commentary)

274. "Like a *pataṅga* (a moth) destroys itself in the flame, in the same way, all these twelve *indriya varga*s are destroyed in this flame of consciousness. They sacrifice their *prāṇa* on this flame and they end their *svarūpa* (nature) for all time. Here, the *pramāṇa daśa* (the cognitive cycle) is being drawn into *pramātṛ daśa* (the subjective cycle). Cognitive awareness is drawn into subjective awareness. This is the rising of *mita-pramātā* to *parā pramātā* (limited I-consciousness into universal consciousness)." *Shri Kramanya-pradīpikā*, verse 8 (LJA archive).

Now he explains the next four Kālīs, which are bent upon destroying and swallowing the state of *pramātṛ bhāva* also.

SCHOLAR: The knower.

LJA TA04I (29:11)

9. Paramārkakālī – *sṛṣṭi* (creation) in *pramātṛ* (subjectivity)

SWAMIJI:

स एव परमादित्यः पूर्णकल्पस्त्रयोदशः ।
करणत्वात्प्रयात्येव कर्तरि प्रलयं स्फुटम् ॥ १६४॥

sa eva paramādityaḥ pūrṇakalpastrayodaśaḥ /
karaṇatvātprayātyeva kartari pralayaṁ sphuṭam //164//

That *paramāditya*, that supreme *āditya* (sun), which has gobbled, which has dissolved, all these twelve suns, …*

Who has dissolved these twelve suns?

SCHOLAR: *Ahaṁkāra.*

SWAMIJI: *Ahaṁkāra.* That *ahaṁkāra* is himself *paramāditya*, the supreme sun.

*… that supreme sun who has dissolved in his own nature these twelve suns of cognition, *pūrṇa kalpas trayodaśaḥ*, he is full because of the twelve suns, the twelve suns are existing in him, *trayodaśa*, and he is the thirteenth sun (*trayodaśa*, the thirteenth sun). *Karaṇatvāt*, as long as it is admitted that *ahaṁkāra* is also one means of the organs, *ahaṁkāra*, …*

SCHOLAR: Individuated.

SWAMIJI: Because, [for example], "I am going to Amirakadal." You can't say, "Going to Amirakadal." You say, "I am going to Amirakadal." So 'I' is there. So 'I' is the thirteenth sun.

*… and that thirteenth sun, *karaṇatvāt*, because of being/existing in the organic field, *prayātyeva kartari pralayaṁ sphuṭam*, he gets entry in *kartā*, he gets entry in…

SCHOLAR: Agent.
SWAMIJI: Agent.
SCHOLAR: The means are dissolved in the agent, the hand and…
SWAMIJI: Yes.

LJA TA04I (30:51)

कर्ता च द्विविधः प्रोक्तः कल्पिताकल्पितात्मकः ।
कल्पितो देहबुद्ध्यादिव्यवच्छेदेन चर्चितः ॥१६५॥
कालाग्निरुद्रसञ्ज्ञास्य शास्त्रेषु परिभाषिता ।
कालो व्यवच्छित्तद्युक्तो वह्निर्भोक्ता यतः स्मृतः ॥१६६॥
संसाराक्लृप्तिक्लृप्तिभ्यां रोधनाद्द्रावणात्प्रभुः ।
अनिवृत्तपशूभावस्तत्राहङ्कृत्प्रलीयते ॥१६७॥

kartā ca dvividhaḥ proktaḥ kalpitākalpitātmakaḥ /
kalpito dehabuddhyādi-vyavacchedena carcitaḥ //165//
kālāgnirudrasañjñāsya śāstreṣu paribhāṣitā /
kālo vyavacchittadyukto vahnirbhoktā yataḥ smṛtaḥ //166//
saṁsārāklṛptiklṛptibhyāṁ rodhanāddrāvaṇātprabhuḥ /
anivṛttapaśūbhāvas-tatrāhaṅkṛtpralīyate //167//

Now he explains in which *kartā*, in which doer, this 'I' (*ahaṁkāra*) gets entry. *Kartā ca dvividhaḥ*, doers are said to be in two ways. Doers, agents, are explained in two ways. One agent is *kalpita*. *Kalpita* is …

MARK D: Formed, fashioned.

SWAMIJI: … formed, and another agent is not formed (*akalpita*) – *kalpita akalpitātmakaḥ*. *Kalpito*, that formed agent is *deha buddhyādi vyavacchedena carcitaḥ*, the formed agent is always connected with the organs of the senses – the formed agent. The natural agent is not attached to the senses. The natural agent is only residing in the state of *pramātṛ bhāva*.

SCHOLAR: The knower.

SWAMIJI: The formed agent, that is, the manufactured agent, formed, which is formed, which is not the real agent, that unreal agent is attached to the organic field. As long as I am perceiving that, "I am doing this", "I am eating", "I am drinking", "I am sleeping", "I am going", "I am walking", "I am enjoying", "I am sad", "I am…", all this, as long as this kind of perception takes place, this is the agency of that formed agent (*kalpita*). As long as I say "I", no one else – not doing, not going, not enjoying, not sad, not blissful – as long as there is [just] "I", that is the real agent, that is *pūrṇa pramātṛ bhāva*, the real state of *pramātṛ bhāva*. The unreal state, the formed state of *pramātṛ bhāva* is that *pramātṛ bhāva* who is attached with the senses.

SCHOLAR: To something specific.

SWAMIJI: Yes. *Kalpito, kalpita pramātṛ bhāva*, the formed agent, is *deha buddhyādi vyavacchedena carcitaḥ*, he is said to be adjusted with the organic field of the senses of cognition and the senses of action. *Kālāgnirudra sañjñāsya śāstreṣu paribhāṣitā* (verse 166), in our *śāstras* (scriptures), he is nominated as *kālāgnirudra*, he is named as *kālāgnirudra*. Who?

BRUCE P: The formed agent.

SWAMIJI: The formed agent, *mita pramātṛ*. But now he explains in his own verse what is *kālāgnirudra*, what is the meaning of *kālāgnirudra*. *Kāla*, *agni*, and *rudra*, these are three words combined in one word. *Kālo vyavacchid* (*kāla* means, time), time is that which gives you limitation. When you have come in the clutches of time, you have come in the clutches of limitation. When you are above time, then you have no such limitation. So *kāla* is always *vyavacchid*, that produces limitation.[275] *Tadyukto bhoktā*, with limitation, the enjoyer who resides with limitation, is *agni* (fire) – the enjoyer.

SCHOLAR: Who is connected, who is associated, with this limitation.

SWAMIJI: Who is connected with this limitation, who is associated with this limitation is *agni* (fire). *Saṁsāra klṛpta aklṛptibhyāṁ* (verse 167), because it produces worldly objects and it withdraws worldly objects. For instance, you have created *saṁsāra*. What *saṁsāra* have you created?

JOHN: *Saṁsāra* of my….

---

275. *Vyavacchid* is also defined as "separation", "distinction".

SWAMIJI: *Saṁsāra* of Abdul Rashid, all these agencies, that factory, Denise, Shanna, Swamiji, all these–this is your *saṁsāra*. *Saṁsāra aklṛpta-*, when you withdraw the other *saṁsāra*, you withdraw the *saṁsāra* of Bhagavan Das, you withdraw the *saṁsāra* of Rajanī, you withdraw the *saṁsāra* of…you have withdrawn that, you have owned only your own gathering in yourself, so this is [the function of] *rudra*. *Klṛpta aklṛptibhyāṁ*, he creates and withdraws (withdraws at some parts).

SCHOLAR: Discriminates.

SWAMIJI: Discriminates. *Saṁsāra aklṛptiklṛptibhyāṁ rodhanāt drāvaṇāt*, so you coagulate, …*

Where do you coagulate?

JOHN: Where do I coagulate in terms of…?

SWAMIJI: Yes.

*… you coagulate only in Abdul Rashid, in me, and in all these, and in Ishber, and Swamiji, and Denise, Shanna, you are coagulated there, and in other districts …

DEVOTEE: In other fields.

SWAMIJI: … you have destroyed that coagulation, you are not coagulated there. So you are a *rudra*. So, *kālāgnirudra* means, limited *pramātṛ*, that *pramātā* (subject) who is existing, who is living, in the limited scale. *Saṁsāra aklṛptiklṛptibhyāṁ rodhanāt drāvaṇāt prabhuḥ*, he is *prabhuḥ* (a lord), he is *samarthaḥ*, he is capable, of *rodhana* and *drāvaṇa*, he is capable of coagulating and destroying coagulation; coagulating on one side and destroying in other ways. *Anivṛtta paśū bhāva*, but his *paśu bhāva*, the state of limitation, is not destroyed. The state of his limitation is not destroyed, and in that state of *pramātṛ bhāva*, this *ahaṁkāra* gets entry, this *ahaṁkāra* is destroyed, *tatra* (there), not in *para pramātṛ bhāva*.[276]

---

276. "So, previously these *indriya*s along with mind and intellect were dissolved in Martaṇḍakālī, and here, this *ahaṁkāra*, or limited I-consciousness, which is the holder of all those *indriya*s, is being dissolved. It is why, in this state, even the traces of these *viṣaya*s (senses) do not remain. That *pramātṛ prakāśa*, the light of subjectivity, which is *nirvikalpa rūpatayā prakāśamāna*, without any thought, is illuminated here. So Abhinavagupta has described this stage as *kālāgnirudra*. Even though it is the state of *parimita pramātṛ saṁvitti* (limited subject), but he has

SCHOLAR: The ego is dissolved in the limited knower.

SWAMIJI: Yes, the limited ego.[277] So this is called Paramārkakālī. Paramārkakālī because Paramārkakālī is...*ārka* were twelve, the suns were twelve. *Paramārka* means, the thirteenth [sun], *ahaṁkāra*. And that Paramārkakālī means, that state who destroys that thirteenth *ahaṁkāra*, the thirteenth sun. So it is called Paramārkakālī. And this Paramārkakālī is residing in the *kālāgnirudra* state, in the state of *kālāgnirudra*, in the state of the limited *pramātṛ*.

SCHOLAR: So this is *pramātṛ sṛṣṭi*, the first creation of subjectivity without cognitivity and...

SWAMIJI: Yes, this is *pramātṛ sṛṣṭi*, yes. *Pramātā* (the subject) is being created, yes.[278]

LJA TA04I (39:03)

Evaṁ pramātṛgataṁ sṛṣṭisvarūpamabhidhāya sthiti-svarūpamapy-āha (comm.), now he explains the *sthiti* of *pramātṛ bhāva*.

SCHOLAR: Establishment.

SWAMIJI:

LJA TA04I (39:11)

---

called it *kālāgnirudra*. The reader should not take this *avasthā* (state) as *viṣayopa-dhi*; this state has no *viṣaya upādhi*, no impressions of the world of external senses. There is some traces of *paśu bhāva* (limitedness), but this state of subjectivity is vastly different from that state of the limited *jīva*. It is like the difference between *ākāśa* (heaven) and *pātāla* (hell)." *Shri Kramanya-pradīpikā* verse 9 (LJA archive).

277. "In this Paramārkakālī, *astodita dvādaśa bhānu bhāji*, the twelve suns (*indriyas*) rise and set. *Praśānta-dhāmni*, it dissolves these in its own *svarūpa* (nature) which is totally *śānta* (appeased). *Bharga-śikhā*, the flames of the sunshine of *paramāditya* (this *ahaṁkāra*, ego) are dissolved in their own light." Ibid.

278. "Even though the next Kālī after Paramārkakālī is called Kālāgnirudrakālī, one must understand that this is the state of *kālāgnirudra*, and the holder of this state is Kālāgnirudrakālī Herself." Ibid.

10. Kālāgnirudrakālī – *sthiti* (establishment) in *pramātṛ* (subjectivity).

सोऽपि कल्पितवृत्तित्वाद्विश्वाभेदैकशालिनि ।
विकासिनि महाकाले लीयतेऽहमिदम्मये ॥ १६८ ॥

so'pi kalpitavṛttitvād-viśvābhedaikaśālini /
vikāsini mahākāle līyate'hamidammaye //168//

And that, too, *so'pi kalpita vṛttitvāt*, that *pramātṛ*, that state of *pramātṛ*, because of its *kalpita bhāva*, because of its limitation, being a resident of the limited state, ...*

SCHOLAR: In the field of effects.

SWAMIJI: Yes.

*... *viśvābhedaikaśālini vikāsini mahākāle*, Mahākāla[279], the state of Mahākāla, which is *viśva abhedaika śālini*, where this whole universe is found established in the undifferentiated state (*viśva abhedaika śālini*), *vikāsini*, and it is effulgent ...

SCHOLAR: In expansion.

SWAMIJI: ... expanded – and that is Mahākāla – *līyate*, and in that Mahākāla state, this *mita pramātṛ* also *līyate*, is being destroyed. In which *pramātṛ bhāva*? *Ahaṁ idam maye*, where there is the perception of 'I' and 'this'; "I am this" and "this is I" – *ahaṁ idam maye.*

SCHOLAR: Identity there. Like Sadāśiva?

SWAMIJI: Just like Sadāśiva *bhāva*. And this state of Kālī is nominated as Kālāgnirudrakālī, because *kālāgnirudra* is also destroyed. Who was *kālāgnirudra*?

SCHOLAR: *Kalpita pramātṛ bhāva.*

SWAMIJI: *Kalpita pramātā* (the limited subject). That *kālāgnirudra* is also destroyed here. So this [destruction of] *kālāgnirudra* is the *sthiti* of *pramātṛ bhāva*.

SCHOLAR: So, in the creation of *pramātṛ bhāva*, the limited subject shines for a moment.

---

279. The Lord of time.

SWAMIJI: First, yes.[280]

SCHOLAR: And in its establishment (*sthiti*), that is dissolved…

SWAMIJI: Dissolved.

SCHOLAR: … in unlimited subjectivity.

SWAMIJI: Limited subjectivity is dissolved in unlimited subjectivity.

SCHOLAR: *Pūrṇāhantā.*

SWAMIJI: *Pūrṇāhantā.* Not exact *pūrṇāhantā*, only where there is *idam-ahaṁ bhāva*, not only *ahaṁ bhāva.*

SCHOLAR: Sadāśiva state. *Amṛta bhāva.*

SWAMIJI: Not *ahaṁ bhāva.* [Here it is] *ahaṁ-idam bhāva*, where you perceive the universe in 'I' and where you perceive 'I' in the universe. That is *ahaṁ-idam bhāva.* That is Īśvara *bhāva* or Sadāśiva *bhāva* (state), both can come in that.[281] Now, *saṁhāra svarūpa* and *anākhya svarūpa* will be explained next time, because they are very tasteful (laughs).

SCHOLAR: So we only have *pramātṛ saṁhāra* and *pramātṛ anākhya* to go.

SWAMIJI: Yes, *pramātṛ saṁhāra* and *anākhya*, one lesson. Because I have to speak something more from my mind for this. *Bas*?

LJA TA04I (42:02) end
LJA TA04J (00:00) start

280. In Paramārkakālī.

281. "This *bhairava rūpī kāla*, *sṛjati* (manifests) *jagat* (this universe) right from Brahmā to an insect, *icchāvaśena*, by Her uninterrupted *icchā* (will), which is *anargala* (an unimpeded flow). It means that a yogi who attains this state of *pramātṛ rūpī*, *teja-sthāna*, he manifests *pañca-kṛtya-kāritva-pada*, these fivefold acts of *sṛṣṭi*, *sthiti*, *saṁhāra*, *tirodhana*, and *anūgraha*, just like Paramaśiva. These fivefold acts become his own *svabhāva* (nature). It is why it is also said in the *Śiva Sūtras* that this yogi becomes 'just like Śiva'. Here, in this state, that previous *kālāgnirudra*, who was the *mita pramātā*, becomes *para pramātṛ saṁvitti*, he merges into *para pramātṛ saṁvitti*, his limited I-consciousness merges into I-God consciousness. This means, She destroys the *deha pramātṛ*, *prāṇa pramātṛ*, *puryaṣṭaka pramātṛ*; the three states of I-consciousness on waking, dreaming, and sleep are merged in this supreme light of Kālāgnirudrakālī. Here, *deha*, *prāṇa*, *puryaṣṭaka*, etcetera, refers to that which is *anātma*, anything other than the *ātma* or pure state of Self." Ibid., verse 10.

Evaṁ pramātṛgataṁ sthiti-svarūpam-abhidhāya saṁhāra-svarūpam-apyāha (comm.), the *sthiti* in *pramātṛ* he has already explained. Now he explains here the destructive state of *pramātṛ bhāva*.

LJA TA04J (00:20)

11. Mahākālakālī – *saṁhāra* (destruction) in *pramātṛ* (subjectivity).

एतस्यां स्वात्मसंवित्ताविदं सर्वमहं विभुः ।
इति प्रविकसद्रूपा संवित्तिरवभासते ॥ १६९ ॥
ततोऽन्तः स्थितसर्वात्मभावभोगोपरागिणी ।
परिपूर्णापि संवित्तिरकुले धाम्नि लीयते ॥ १७० ॥

etasyāṁ svātmasaṁvittāv-idaṁ sarvamahaṁ vibhuḥ /
iti pravikasadrūpā saṁvittiravabhāsate //169//
tato'ntaḥsthitasarvātma-bhāvabhogoparāgiṇī /
paripūrṇāpi saṁvittir-akule dhāmni līyate //170//

In this supreme Self-consciousness of Mahākāla–Mahākāla is that state of *pramātṛ bhāva* in which state this limited state of *pramātṛ bhāva* has completely dissolved/disappeared–in this supreme Self of Mahākāla (*para pramātṛ bhāva*), *etasyām svātma saṁvittau*, which is one's own consciousness, there you find the perceiving state that, "I am all" or "This is all, this is not other than myself–I am all (*idam sarvam ahaṁ*)."

SCHOLAR: *Vibhuḥ*.

SWAMIJI: *Vibhuḥ* means, all-pervading. The all-pervading Self is 'I' that is everywhere. *Iti pravikasadrūpā saṁvittir avabhāsate*, and in this way, *pravikasadrūpā*, only the effulgent supreme consciousness shines (the effulgent supreme consciousness, *pravika sadrūpā saṁvittir avabhāsate*).

SCHOLAR: So this is the state of Sadāśiva.

SWAMIJI: This is the state of *para pramātṛ bhāva*. Why take Sadāśiva? Who told you that it is Sadāśiva?

SCHOLAR: I didn't. No one told me. I was asking.

SWAMIJI: This is the state of *para pramātṛ bhāva*, and this *para pramātṛ bhāva* is also a hindrance to that state of *pramātṛ bhāva* where the perceiving of *pramātṛ bhāva* also does not exist. As long as this perception exists that, "I am this universe", this [means] there is some deficiency there. When it becomes your nature, then there is no place for this perceiving also. Then you are what you are. So this state of *para pramātṛ bhāva* is to be withdrawn in some supreme state of consciousness.

SCHOLAR: So, in the previous [state], which was *pramātṛ sthiti*, you said that this covered both Īśvara and Sadāśiva.

SWAMIJI: Yes.

SCHOLAR: This now is *para pramātṛ bhāva* being dissolved, so this is the state of Sadāśiva being dissolved.

SWAMIJI: No, Sadāśiva is also the same, Sadāśiva is also *para pramātṛ bhāva*, Śuddhavidyā is also *para pramātṛ bhāva*. The beginning of the *para pramātṛ bhāva* (state) begins from Śuddhavidyā and ends in Śadāśiva. So, Sadāśiva, Īśvara, and Śuddhavidyā are one, in one state. That is the span of *para pramātṛ bhāva*. And that *para pramātṛ bhāva* is also being dissolved in some supreme consciousness.

Tato antaḥ sthita sarvātma bhāva-bhogoparāgiṇī paripūrṇāpi saṁvitti (verse 170), although this state of consciousness is already filled with the fullness of Her nature (*bhāva-bhogopa-rāgiṇī paripūrṇāpi*, although She is filled with Her fullness of consciousness), *bhāva bhogoparāgiṇī*, because by tasting the nectar of all the objective world, objective consciousness, universal objects, all universal objects shine there in one-ness, ...*

SCHOLAR: Within Her nature – *antaḥ sthita*.

SWAMIJI: Within Her nature, yes.

*... although She is filled with that fullness of Her consciousness, still She dissolves and disappears in *akula dhāma*, She gets full entry in the state of *akula*.[282] *Akula* is that supreme state where there is no perceiving; perception also does not exist differentiatedly. Perception is there as your own nature, not to confirm, there is no confirmation. There [in the previous state], He confirmed.

---

282. The abode (*dhama*) of undifferentiated totality (*akula*).

SCHOLAR: Sadāśiva–"*sarvamidam ahaṁ*".

SWAMIJI: "*Sarvamidam ahaṁ.*"[283]

SCHOLAR: So this previous state, in 169, what dissolves into *akula dhāma* is, in fact, the Sadāśiva state.

SWAMIJI: Yes, the Sadāśiva state, yes. And this state of Kālī is nominated as Mahākālakālī. Mahākāla is also destroyed or withdrawn in one's own nature–Mahākāla. So it is nominated as Mahākālakālī.[284]

---

283. "I am everything."

284. "In this *avasthā* of *kāla-kalanā ka ullaṁghana karatā āvastha*, a yogi crosses the boundary of time and space and enters into *samanā pada* (*samanā* is the eleventh state in the twelve states of sound; *a-u-ṁ-bindu-ardhacandra-nāda-nādānta-niroḍhīka-śakti-vyāpinī-samanā* and *unmanā*). Here, there is no *kāla kālana*, there is no time, it is pure *śūnya* (void), so it is called Mahākālakālī, and She is above time. So this yogi becomes *akālakalita*, he who is not touched by time, who is above the sphere of time. *Kāla* here means both time and formation, and *akāla* means it is beyond time and beyond *pūrṇa-rūpena*, the formation of fullness. Here, the lord of time, Māhākāla, has lost his authority, and the yogi in this state feels as if centuries are passing *kṣaṇa tulya*, in an instant. *Na sadā*, it is neither always, *na tadā*, nor is it particular time, *na caikadeti*, not simultaneous time either. *Sā yatra na kāladhīrbhavet*, it cannot be calculated. *Tadidaṁ bhavadīya darśanaṁ*, that is your *darśana* (vision). Which *darśana* is that? *Na nityam*, that is not *nitya* (eternal), *na ca kathyate'nyathā*, nor is it not eternal. The *buddhi* (intellect) of this yogi becomes like that. [According to Utpaladeva], in the real sense, that is the sign of experiencing your nature, this is the only sign of experiencing your nature, *tadidaṁ bhavadīya darśanam yatra*, in which nature, in which experience, there is no time. Up to the previous state of Kālāgnirudrakālī, there is still some semblance of being in the body, but in this state, even that faint impression is gone. When the yogi enters this state, he experiences the *vyāpinī parameśvarī, sarva-sarvaṁ-rūpatā prakāśamāna*, the light of that all-pervading *prakāśa* which is beyond space and time. *Prakāśa-pūrṇa-rūpa*, that formation which is of the fullness of *prakāśa* is *naktaṁ* (dissolved) along with *digkhecarī cakra-gañena sākam*, all these goddesses, Brahmī, etcetera, the *dik-khecarī*s. He feels that *alaṁ-grāsa-bhairava-ātmaka-sthiti ka anubhava svyaṁ hi karane lagatā*, everything has been *alaṁgrāsa* (digested in one gulp) in the state of *bhairavātmaka*. *Mahābhūtalaye*, all the *mahābhūta*s are dissolved, *hṛdaya-rūpī śmaśāna*, in the heart of this *śmaśāna* (crematory) Kālī. All *saṁskāra*s (impressions) of the objective world (*samasta bhāva*

Now, the state of *saṁhāra* in *pramātṛ bhāva* is already explained. Now, he explains the *anākhya* of *pramātṛ bhāva*.

LJA TA04J (06:23)

12. Mahābhairavacaṇḍaugraghorakālī – *anākhya* (the gap[285]) in *pramātṛ* (subjectivity).

प्रमातृवर्गो मानौघः प्रमाश्च बहुधा स्थिताः ।
मेयौघ इति यत्सर्वमत्र चिन्मात्रमेव तत् ॥ १७१ ॥

pramātṛvargo mānaughaḥ pramāśca bahudhā sthitāḥ /
meyaugha iti yatsarvam-atra cinmātrameva tat //171//

After residing in the *akula* state of supreme *para pramātṛ bhāva*, where *para pramātṛ bhāva* also is not confirmed separately, where the state of *para pramātṛ bhāva* has taken its natural way, natural state – not confirmation, confirmation is over – *pramātṛ vargaḥ*, in this state, all the classes of *pramātṛ bhāva*, and all the classes of *māna* (*pramāṇa*), all the classes of *pramiti*, and all the classes of *prameya* (that is, the objective world, the cognitive world, and the subjective world, and the supreme subjective world),…*

---

varga, the whole objective world of impressions), *niḥsaṁskāra rūpa praśamana*, is uprooted here in this *avasthā* (state) and only consciousness in the form of Bhairava remains. So it is the *alaṁgrāsa* of *bhairavātmaka sthiti*. But there is one unique thing about this state of *saṁhāra* or destruction in the cycle of *pramātṛ daśa*, the subjective cycle, where Mahākālakālī is functioning. *Apane svabhāvabhūta akula-dhāma*, She wants to go into Her own natural state of *akula dhāma*, which has no *kula*. She is always bent upon and eager to enter into that *akula dhāma* because it is Her own *svarūpa* (nature)." *Shri Kramanya-pradīpikā*, verse 11 (LJA archive)." See Appendix 17 of *Tantrāloka Vol. One*, p. 405, "*The praṇava mantra auṁ* (*oṁ*)".

285. The *parasaṁvitti rūpa*, the supreme formation of consciousness.

The supreme subjective world is *pramiti*, the supreme subjective world where there is no reflection of *prameya bhāva*, when there is no perception of the objective world in that state. When there is the impression of objectivity in knowledge, in the state of the knower, that is *pramātṛ bhāva*. When there is no impression, impression also is vanished, that is *pramiti bhāva*.

SCHOLAR: Why does he use the plural–*pramāśca bahudhā sthitāḥ*?

SWAMIJI: In each and every state, because *bahudhāḥ* means, in all these states, in all these eleven Kālīs.

SCHOLAR: But he says "*pramāḥ*" here, he uses the plural.

SWAMIJI: Yes.

SCHOLAR: But if *pramiti* is beyond the subject, the object, and the means of knowledge, how is it divided?

SWAMIJI: But there are so many *anākhya cakra*s there you will find. The *anākhya cakra*s you have been explained in *prameya*, in *pramāṇa*, and in *pramātṛ bhāva*, so it is *bahuvacana*, so it is plural.

SCHOLAR: So he is not using "*pramāḥ*" here in the ordinary sense in Sanskrit as to mean the act of knowledge–*pramāḥ*.

SWAMIJI: No, that is not…it is only *bahudhāḥ sthitāḥ pramāḥ*, in various ways of consciousness of objectivity, cognitivity, subjectivity you find *pramiti bhāva* everywhere.

SCHOLAR: *Pramiti bhāva*s.

SWAMIJI: Yes, *pramiti bhāva*s–plural.

*… and all these elevenfold states of consciousness, *sarvam atra cinmātrameva tat*, are perceived as one with Her own nature here in this state of supreme consciousness of *anākhya cakra* in *pramātṛ bhāva*.

LJA TA04J (09:30)

इयतीं रूपवैचित्रीमाश्रयन्त्याः स्वसंविदः ।

iyatīṁ rūpavaicitrīm-āśrayantyāḥ svasaṁvidaḥ /

Although one's own consciousness has held all these states of consciousness, …

स्वाच्छन्द्यमनपेक्षं यत्सा परा परमेश्वरी ॥ १७२ ॥

svācchandyamanapekṣaṁ yatsā parā parameśvarī //172//

... but where there is *anapekṣaṁ svācchandyam* (*anapekṣaṁ svācchandyam* means, that *svātantrya* which has no concern with any dependence), unconditioned freedom, ...*

DEVOTEE: *Kaḥ pratyaya*?

SWAMIJI: This is the twelfth Kālī. Eleven Kālīs, the state of eleven Kālīs.

*... so it is nominated as Mahā-bhairava-caṇḍa-ugra-ghora-kālī. Mahābhairava will take... you go to the commentary of Jayaratha:

LJA TA04J (09:42)

Prameya prakriya (comm.), just to make it clear, make clear this situation of supreme Kālī, just to make it clear: *pramātṛ padena mahābhairava caṇḍasya*, as *pramātṛ bhāva* is also dissolved in this state, so the "Mahābhairava"–*śabda* (the word) is adjusted to it–"Mahābhairava". Mahābhairava means, supreme Bhairava, the supreme state of Bhairava where all objectivity and cognitivity is taken in. That is Mahābhairava *bhāva*. And *meya padena caṇḍa śabdasya*, and *meya-bhāva*, the objective state is also taken in this state. *Caṇḍa-śabdasya, caṇḍa* means, fierce or violent, violent for consciousness; *meya caṇḍa śabdasya*, fierce or violent for one's own consciousness. One's own consciousness is terrified in the objective field, so this [objective field] is nominated as "*caṇḍa*"; *meya*, *prameya*, *prameya bhāva* is nominated as "*caṇḍa*", fearful for consciousness, sweet for the objective world. It is sweet for the objective world and fearful for consciousness. And *pramā padena ugra śabdasya*, *pramiti bhāva* will be adjusted with "*ugra*"-*śabda* (*ugra* is "terrific"). [*Pramiti bhāva*] is terrific for the world and soft for your consciousness. *Pramiti bhāva* is terrific, terrifying, for the world. *Meya bhāva* (objectivity) terrifies consciousness. *Meya bhāva* withdraws you from consciousness whereas *pramiti bhāva* sentences you towards consciousness. *Pramiti bhāva* is fearful for the objective world whereas *prameya bhāva* is fearful for the subjective world. This is the difference between *meya* and *pramiti*.

Māna padena ghora śabdasya, and *pramāṇa* is hideous; "*ghora*"-*śabda*, "*ghora*" is adjusted with *pramāṇa*, the cognitive world. The cognitive world is supposed to be hideous for both states because it is a standstill situation of consciousness–*pramāṇa*. *Pramāṇa* is a standstill situation. It can carry you up and it can carry you down also. So it is nominated as "*ghora*". So, all these words have been adjusted in this state of supreme consciousness, so this supreme state of consciousness is called as Mahābhairava-caṇḍa-ugra-ghora-kālī. So all these words have come in this state.

[*Nanu*] *kiṁ nāmāsyāḥ asya paratvam* (comm.), what is the supremacy of this state of consciousness? To that he says:

LJA TA04J (14:02)

इमाः प्रागुक्तकलनास्तद्विजृम्भोच्यते यतः ।

imāḥ prāguktakalanās-tadvijṛmbhocyate yataḥ /*173a*

As all these *kalanās*, all these states of consciousness, all these eleven states of consciousness, are *tat vijṛmbha*, only the expansion of the effulgent light of this consciousness, all these drives of consciousness, ...*

You can say "drives" of consciousness?

SCHOLAR: Impulses?

SWAMIJI: *... drives of consciousness from *prameya gata sṛṣṭi* to *pramātṛ gata saṁhāra*[286], all these drives are ...*

What have you translated it?

DEVOTEES: Impulses.

SWAMIJI: *... all these drives or impulses of consciousness are nothing but the expansion of the supreme consciousness, nothing else.[287]

286. From creation in objectivity to destruction in subjectivity.

287. "This *anākhya daśa* is *sphuṭatama*, absolutely clear, vivid. When this *para-pramātṛ-rūpī*, *camatkṛti*, *sampūrṇa avasthā*, expands, She gives *janma* (life) to all these *daśa*s (cycles). She creates them and She digests them in Herself. *Unkī āśraya-sthāna*, and it becomes the resting place, it is the resting place of all these

Now it won't be out of place to mention here that Abhinavagupta explained this thing in his commentary of the *Krama Stotra*–Abhinavagupta himself. Turn to page 192. These are his words that are quoted by Jayaratha, the commentator.

LJA TA04J (15:32)

"*Yathaika śrīmān vīravaraḥ* ...", this is very important to this subject because we must know what was the order of *guru-śiṣya-krama*[288] of Abhinavagupta in this section of the *kramanāya*, in this Kālī section. In the order of the Kālīs, who was his guru in this section? Because he had been initiated by so many gurus of so many orders of Śaivism.

JOHN: So this isn't coming out of the Kula system at all. This is Krama.

SWAMIJI: This is the Krama System, yes. This is called the Krama System. In the Krama System, he was also initiated–Abhinavagupta. And these are his own words which are quoted by Jayaratha in his commentary.

---

previous *daśas* of *pramātā*, *pramāṇa*, and *prameya*. All these *devīs* (Sṛṣṭikālī, Raktakālī, etcetera), *udaya*, they rise there and they fall there. It is the resting place of everything. When all these *devīs* rise in this state, it is called *parā-devī-pūrṇa-rūpā*, the fullness of form of that supreme *devī*. When everything is created in Her, She is *parā-devī-pūrṇa-rūpā*. And when they are dissolved, it is called *durghaṭa saṁpādanātmikā māheśvarī kṛśarūpā*. It is called *māheśvarī kṛśarūpā* because it does that which is *durghaṭa-saṁpādana*, which cannot be done by anybody (*durghaṭa* means, that which nobody can accomplish). That is *ānātmikā māheśvarī, kṛśarūpā* (*kṛśā* means, that blade of this which is so minute, it is nothing; which is *anoraniyan*, it is the minutest of the minutest). At the same time, She is both *pūrṇa-rūpā* and *māheśvarī kṛśa-rūpā*. And this is *anākhya cakra*." *Shri Kramanya-pradīpikā*, verse 12 (LJA archive).

288. The succession of gurus and disciples.

The Lineage of Masters of the Krama System

LJA TA04J (16:24)

yathaikaḥ śrīmān vīravaraḥ sugṛhītanāmadheyo
'govindarājābhidhānaḥ' 'śrībhānukābhidhāno'
dvitīyaḥ śrīmān 'erakasamākhyaḥ' tṛtīyaḥ (commentary)[289]

These were the three great masters of the Krama System: *vīravaraḥ*, the supreme hero in this section was *sugṛhīta-nāmadheya*, who was *sugṛhīta-nāmadheya*, who had nominated himself by himself, Govindarāja.

SCHOLAR: *Sugṛhīta* means ...

SWAMIJI: Well-held.

SCHOLAR: ... of blessed name.

SWAMIJI: Yes, blessed name.

SCHOLAR: *Sugṛhītanām*. Not "*svagṛhīta*.

SWAMIJI: No, it is not "*svagṛhīta*". [It is] "*sugṛhīta*". Govindarāja was his name. That was the one and the foremost master of this Krama System – Govindarāja. The second was Bhānuka; Bhānuka was the second master of this system. And the third master was Erakanātha.

LJA TA04J (17:35)

samamevopadeśaṁ pīṭheśvarībhya uttarapīṭhalabdhopadeśāt
śrīśivānandanāthāllabda-anugrahābhyaḥ 'śrīkeyurvatī
śrīmadanikā-śrīkalyāṇikābhyaḥ prāpnuvantaḥ /
(commentary, not recited)[290]

These three masters were initiated *samameva* (*samameva* means, collectively) by three supreme ladies of this section, three supreme

289. KSTS *Tantrāloka* vol. 3, p. 192, lines 4–8.

290. Ibid., lines 9–10.

devīs, and those were nominated Keyūravatī, Madanikā, and Kalyānikā. Keyūravatī was the first *devī*, Madanikā was the second lady, and Kalyānikā was the third lady. And these three ladies had initiated these three masters collectively, not respectively.

SCHOLAR: Not separately.

DEVOTEE: At the same time.

SWAMIJI: The three ladies had initiated all of these three collectively. So, all these three ladies were masters of each master. Do you understand?

SCHOLAR: Yes.

SWAMIJI: They were not separately mastered.

JOHN: Three ladies for one master, three ladies for one, they ...

SWAMIJI: Yes, three ladies. *Samamevopadeśam*, that is the meaning of *samameva upadeśam*. And these three ladies had been initiated by the supreme founder of this Krama System, who was nominated Śivānanda. Śivānanda was the supreme founder, the originator of the Krama System.

SCHOLAR: Is this same as Jñānanetrānanda, Jñāna-netrānātha? Because all these Krama texts say that Jñāna-netrānanda is the revealer of the Krama System.

SWAMIJI: Yes, it might be so. Śivānandanātha and Avatārakanātha, he is nominated as Avatārakanātha.

SCHOLAR: Avatārakanātha is Jñānanetranātha.

SWAMIJI: Yes, Avatārakanātha is Śivānandanātha, no one else.

SCHOLAR: So then, Śivānanda and Jñānanetra are the same person.

SWAMIJI: Same person, one person. Jñānanetra *pada* is also Śivānandanātha, and Śivānandanātha is also Avatārakanātha. These are his three names. He is the originator of the Krama System. He has been the originator of the Krama System. And Śivanandanātha, Avatārakanātha or Jñānanetranātha had initiated these three ladies first in this Krama System. And these three ladies collectively initiated those three masters.

SCHOLAR: So this *Kālikā Stotra* is by Jñānanetra.

SWAMIJI: Yes, Jñānanetra – the *Kālikā Stotra*.[291]

291. *Kālikā Stotra* is a devotional hymn to the twelve Kālīs that was often recited by Swamiji and his devotees.

SCHOLAR: But others say it is by Śivanandanātha. So you say he's the same.

SWAMIJI: Yes, the same person. So Govindarāja, Bhānuka, and Eraka were initiated collectively by these three *devīs*. Now these are the words of Abhinavagupta. You have to believe them.

SCHOLAR: These were the words of Jayaratha.

SWAMIJI: No, these are the words of Abhinavagupta. Jayaratha has quoted from the *Kramakeli* his words.

SCHOLAR: But …

SWAMIJI: No, turn the leaf.

SCHOLAR: Yes, but there he is only referring to these twelve Kālīs.

SWAMIJI: Yes, yes.

SCHOLAR: *Yato atrāsya …*

SWAMIJI: Yes.

SCHOLAR: Surely these are Jayaratha's words.

SWAMIJI:

LJA TA04J (21:08)

yato atrāsya "śrīgovindarāja-śrībhānukādikrameṇa"
bahuśākhāmevaṁ gurupadeśaḥ samastīti,
yo'dyāpi mahātmanāṁ mahāguruṇāṁ hṛdayapathe śataśaḥ
pariposphurīti, yaduktaṁ tatraivānena (commentary)[292]

Anena abhinavagupta padena, these are Abhinavagupta's words, so these are …

SCHOLAR: Correct.

SWAMIJI: … correct.

LJA TA04J (21:36)

292. KSTS *Tantrāloka* vol. 3, p. 191, last line, to p. 192, line 4.

And:

sa cedaṁ rahasyaṁ śrīsomānandābhidhānāya gurave saṁcāryāṁ babhūva (commentary)[293]

And then Govindarāja, the first master of this Krama System, initiated this secret of the Krama Order to another master who was Somānanda. Not the Somānanda of Utpaladeva, this Somānanda is someone else. *Dvitīyo'pi evamevāste* (comm.), and Bhānuka, the second master, also initiated other masters to get it expanded in this universe – this Krama System.

LJA TA04J (22:28)

śrīmadujjaṭodbhaṭṭādinānāguruparipāṭīsaṁtatiḥ (commentary)[294]

Then Bhānuka had initiated Śrīmat Ujjaṭanātha, and Ujjaṭanātha had initiated Udbhaṭṭanātha, and so on, and then it came successively in the brain of Abhinavagupta in the end. So Abhinavagupta had three successive masters of this Krama System. One line of Govindarāja and the second line of Bhānuka. The successive masters from Bhānuka and the successive masters of Govindarāja were the successive masters of Abhinavagupta in the end. Not Erakanātha; Erakanātha didn't initiate anybody. He only went showing powers to people. So Erakanātha did no good to the public – Erakanātha, the third master. You know?

SCHOLAR: Does it say here that he showed powers?

SWAMIJI: Yes, yes.

LJA TA04J (23:47)

"*śrīmānerakastu*" *siddhyai prāyatata* (commentary)[295]

---

293. KSTS *Tantrāloka* vol. 3, p. 192, line 14.

294. Ibid., line 17.

295. KSTS *Tantrāloka* vol. 3, p. 193, line 1.

He only attempted to obtain powers, yogic powers, in the Krama System. And then he repented afterwards, then he repented afterwards, "Why I didn't take the path of my other two brothers, Govindarāja and Bhānuka?" Govindarāja and Bhānuka were the successive masters of Abhinavagupta. So this was to be told.

LJA TA04J (24:23)

SCHOLAR: So when he says at the bottom of page 192, *yat prasādāsāditamahima*-(comm.) …

SWAMIJI: … *mahimabhirasmābhiretat pradarśitam*, …

SCHOLAR: … *asmābhir* …

SWAMIJI: … *asmābhir abhinavagupta padaiḥ.*

SCHOLAR: It is not Jayaratha.

SWAMIJI: No, it is [Abhinavagupta's] words, these are his words. *Bas*, up to this. You know which are the words of Abhinavagupta? From "*yathaika śrīmān*", from here, "*yathaika śrīmān*", after leaving three lines aside, from "*yathaika*", these are Abhinavagupta's words, and ending [with] "*tāvatprasārayaṁllokān-anugṛhṇīyām iti*" on the second page.

JOHN: *Iti*, it ends with "*iti*".

SWAMIJI: Yes, up to this. From here to this are Abhinavagupta's words [that Jayaratha] has quoted. So this is jewelry in the *Tantrāloka*.[296]

LJA TA04J (25:35)

---

296. Jayaratha's commentary includes the following verse from Abhinavagupta's lost work, the *Kramakeli*:

श्रीमत्सदाशिवपदेऽपि महोग्रकाली भीमोत्कटभ्रकुटिरेष्यति भङ्गभूमिः ।
इत्याकलय्य परमां स्थितिमेत्यकाल संकर्षिणीं भगवतीं हठतोऽधितिष्ठत् ॥

śrīmatsadāśivapade'pi mahograkālī
bhīmotkaṭabhrukuṭireṣyati bhaṅgabhūmiḥ |
ityākalayya paramāṁ sthitimetya kāla-
saṅkarṣiṇī bhagavatīṁ haṭhato'dhitiṣṭhet ||

Kālī, even while in the glorious state of Sadāśiva, becoming extremely terrifying and forceful, attains the ultimate state of dissolution. The aspirant experiencing this transcendental Kālī should forcefully enter into and attain that state of Kālī.

Now he explains the meaning of "Kālī", what actually is meant by the "Kālī" word.

क्षेपो ज्ञानं च सङ्ख्यानं गतिर्नाद इति क्रमात् ॥ १७३ ॥

kṣepo jñānaṁ ca saṅkhyānaṁ gatirnāda iti kramāt //173//

These are the [five] meanings of Kālī: *kṣepa*, *jñāna*, *saṅkhyāna*, *gati*, and *nāda*. *Kṣepa* means, throwing. This "Kālī"-*śabda* (word) has been produced by the verbal root "*kal*". The verbal root "*kal*" is meant for "throwing", for "knowing", for "counting" or "fixing", for "going" or "resorting", or "sounding" or "shouting". These are the meanings derived from this "*kal*" verbal root from which "Kālī" has been made – the "Kālī"-*śabda*. *Kṣepo* – it is Abhinavagupta, he says – *kṣepa* is this first meaning, "throwing". Kālī is that who throws out. Kālī is that who knows (*jñānam*). Kālī is that who counts or fixes (*saṅkhyāna*). *Gatir*, Kālī is that who goes or resorts.[297]

SCHOLAR: *Gati jñānarthe*?

SWAMIJI: *Jñānarthe*, yes. But *jñānam* he has done. *Nāda*, and Kālī is that who sounds or shouts. Now he explains these five ways of the meanings of "Kālī" in his own words, in his own technical words – Abhinavagupta:

LJA TA04J (27:33)

स्वात्मनो भेदनं क्षेपो भेदितस्याविकल्पनम् ।
ज्ञानं विकल्पः सङ्ख्यानमन्यतो व्यतिभेदनात् ॥ १७४ ॥

297. *Gati* literally means, movement.

svātmano bhedanaṁ kṣepo bheditasyāvikalpanam /
jñānaṁ vikalpaḥ saṅkhyānam-anyato vyatibhedanāt //174//
(not recited)

Svātmano bhedanaṁ kṣepaḥ, "throwing", the first way of explaining this Kālī is "throwing". What is "throwing"? What is meant by "throwing"? "Throwing" means, *svātmano bhedanam*, throwing out from one's own consciousness – outside, the world. Getting it out from His own nature in the outside world, that is "throwing", that is the action of Kālī. *Bheditasya āvikalpanam jñānaṁ vikalpaḥ*, and *bheditasya*, "knowing", what is "knowing"? "Knowing" is, already it is thrown out of your consciousness, but to know that it is one with consciousness – the outside also. When you know that outside also, in the outside world also, this whole universe is one with your own consciousness, that is knowing, that is *jñānam*. So this is *vikalpa*.[298] *Vikalpa* means, "This is a jug, not a sheet"; *idamittham na anyatam*, "This is [a pair of] specks, not any other thing." So this is *vikalpa*. *Vikalpa* is *saṅkhyānaṁ*, counting, this is counting. This also is the functioning of Kālī. She counts also. "Counts" is [to] differentiate, distinguish. [Kālī] distinguishes between one [object and] another object; *anyato vyatibhedanāt saṅkhyānam vikalpaḥ*, from one object She differentiates the other object. That is *saṅkhyāna* (counting), that is the way of Kālī. And "*gatiḥ*", what is the "*gatiḥ*"? "*Gatiḥ*" is:

LJA TA04J (29:24)

गतिः स्वरूपारोहित्वं प्रतिबिम्बवदेव यत् ।

gatiḥ svarūpārohitvaṁ pratibimbavadeva yat /

298. Usually translated as "thought", here *vikalpa* means, alternation, variation, manifoldness, difference in perception.

Just to see that the whole universe is reflected in one's own consciousness, this is the *gatiḥ*, this is the "going", this is the journey of consciousness, and this journey of consciousness is functioned by Kālī.

"*Nāda*", what is "*nāda*"?

LJA TA04J (29:43)

नादः स्वात्मपरामर्शशेषता तद्विलोपनात् ॥ १७५ ॥

nādaḥ svātmaparāmarśa-śeṣatā tadvilopanāt //175//

Nāda is "shouting" or "announcing", announcing in this universe that, "There is nothing else than my own consciousness." That is *nāda*. That is also functioned by Kālī.

The next *śloka*:

इति पञ्चविधामेनां कलनां कुर्वती परा ।
देवी काली तथा कालकर्षिणी चेति कथ्यते ॥ १७६ ॥

iti pañcavidhāmenāṁ kalanāṁ kurvatī parā /
devī kālī tathā kālakarṣiṇī ceti kathyate //176//

So in this way, this supreme consciousness, the supreme *svātantrya śakti* of consciousness, the supreme energy of consciousness, functions these five states and is thus called "Kālī" and "Kālakarṣiṇī". And is nominated as "Kālī", this supreme energy of consciousness is nominated as "Kālī" or "Kālakarṣiṇī". Kālī means, that which resides in the sphere of time. Kālakarṣiṇī, although She resides in the sphere of time, She is above sphere of time – Kālakarṣiṇī. She is nominated as Kālī and Kālakarṣiṇī also. She is not only Kālī, She is Kālakarṣiṇī also. She can't be only Kālī. Kālī means, that [being] who resides in the state of time. She is above time also – Kālakarṣiṇī.

SCHOLAR: *Bheditasyā vikalpanam jñānam.*[299]
SWAMIJI: Yes.

LJA TA04J (31:25)

मातृसद्भावसञ्ज्ञास्यास्तेनोक्ता यत्प्रमातृषु ।
एतावदन्तसंवित्तौ प्रमातृत्वं स्फुटीभवेत् ॥ १७७॥
वामेश्वरीतिशब्देन प्रोक्ता श्रीनिशिसञ्चरे ।

mātṛsadbhāvasañjñāsyāstenoktā yatpramātṛṣu /
etāvadantasaṁvittau pramātṛtvaṁ sphuṭībhavet //177//
vāmeśvarīti śabdena proktā śrīniśisañcare /

In this state of supreme Kālī, in all the seven states of subjectivity (*yat pramātṛṣu*, in all the seven states of subjective states), ...*

You know the seven subjective states? *Sakala*, *pralayākala*, *vijñānākala*, *mantra pramātā* (Śuddhavidyā), *mantreśvara pramātā* (Īśvara), *mantra maheśvara pramātā* (Sadāśiva), and Śiva *pramātā*–these are the seven states of *pramātṛs* (perceivers).[300]

*... in these seven states of *pramātṛ*s, as She only shines in these seven states, so She is nominated as Mātṛsadbhāva. Mātṛsadbhāva, the life of *pramātṛ*, the life of these seven subjective energies, She is the life of these seven subjective energies, because *etāvadanta-saṁvittau pramātṛtvaṁ sphuṭī bhavet*, the supreme God consciousness is clarified in these seven states. In these seven states of subjectivity, the supreme God consciousness, the supreme energy of God consciousness, is clarified, is vividly found.

Vāmeśvarīti śabdena proktā śrīniśisañcare, in the *Niśāṭana Tantra*, She is nominated as Vāmeśvarī because She is *vāmā*, She walks in a crooked way, in an order-less way. So She is nominated as Vāmeśvarī.

SCHOLAR: *Saṁsāraviparītācāratvāt.*

---

299. From verse 174.

300. See *Kashmir Shaivism–The Secret Supreme*, chapters 8 and 9.

SWAMIJI: *Saṁsāra-viparītācāra.*[301] So, it means that She goes in the objective world (*vamati*), and at the same time She is residing in the subjective world. See, it is *vāmācāra.*[302]

LJA TA04J (33:51)

इत्थं द्वादशधा संवित्तिष्ठन्ती विश्वमातृषु ॥ १७८॥
एकैवेति न कोऽप्यस्याः क्रमस्य नियमः क्वचित् ।

ittham dvādaśadhā saṁvit-tiṣṭhantī viśvamātṛṣu //178//
ekaiveti na ko'pyasyāḥ kramasya niyamaḥ kvacit /

So this way, this energy of supreme consciousness is found in each and every *pramātṛ*, in each and every state of *pramātṛ bhāva*, or in all these seven states of the *pramātṛ bhāva*s, in twelve ways, in twelvefold ways. But although She resides in each and every *pramātṛ* in twelvefold ways, She is one (*ekaiva*). *Na ko'pi asyāḥ kramasya niyamaḥ kvacit*, these successive states that She has held, She has observed, She has owned, these successive twelve states that She has observed and owned, there is no proof for that. She is only one. Only one God consciousness is traveling in these successive twelve states.

301. She walks contrary (*viparīta*) to *saṁsāra.*
302. "*Saṁsāra*, this universal existence, is *vāmācāra*, it is just the vomiting of God consciousness outside. This is the vomiting of that supreme monistic state. Vāmeśvarī is the chief cycle of energies that hold, that governs and rules these other four energies [that govern the universe]–*khecarī*, *gocarī*, *dikcarī*, and *bhūcarī*." *Spanda Kārikā* and *Spanda Sandoha*, p. 211.

LJA TA04J (34:55)

क्रमाभावान्न युगपत्तदभावात् क्रमोऽपि न ॥ १७९ ॥
क्रमाक्रमकथातीतं संवित्तत्त्वं सुनिर्मलम्

kramābhāvānna yugapat-tadabhāvāt-kramo'pi na //179//
kramākramakathātītaṁ saṁvit-tattvaṁ sunirmalam
(not recited)

Kramābhāvāt na yugapat, so there is no *krama* (succession). When there is no succession, there is no simultaneous way of being. *Tadabhāvāt*, when there is no simultaneous way of being, *tat-abhāvāt kramo'pi na*, there is no succession. So, She is residing beyond the successive way and the non-successive way. *Kramākramakathātītaṁ saṁvit-tattvaṁ sunirmalam*, and She is absolutely pure consciousness.[303]

There ends the explanation of the twelve Kālīs. Now, *mantra vīrya* will be explained on Tuesday.

LJA TA04J (35:36)

303. "For instance, there is one blind person. A big elephant is put before him and he touches his tail. He does not know the remaining portion of the body of the elephant. He thinks that the elephant is just like a rope. Another blind person touches his legs and he thinks it is just like a log. This is the successive way. The simultaneous way is for those who are not blind. They see what is what, that the elephant is like this. They see the full shape of the elephant. That is beyond succession. That [blind person's perception] is succession and that, too, is correct. You cannot deny that it is like a rope. It is like a rope partly, it is like a log partly, it is just like a mount partly; when he touches his body, he thinks that it is a mountain, just like mount, like that. So in the successive way also, it is correct, and in the [way of] non-succession, simultaneously, [it is correct]. Those who are really realizing in the correct way, they also are correct, and those who are realizing partly, they are also correct. But one must think that *saṁvit tattva*, the essence of God consciousness is very pure, so pure that it can be anything." *Wisdom in Kashmir Shaivism*, verse 17 (LJA archives).

तदस्याः संविदो देव्या यत्र क्वापि प्रवर्तनम् ॥ १८० ॥
तत्र तादात्म्ययोगेन पूजा पूर्णैव वर्तते ।

tadasyāḥ saṁvido devyā yatra kvāpi pravartanam //180//
tatra tādātmyayogena pūjā pūrṇaiva vartate /

Tad (thus), *asyāḥ saṁvido devyā yatra kvāpi pravartanam*, wherever this energy of consciousness moves, just at that very moment, just at that very point, real worship is being conducted, real worship, because you are completely united with God consciousness at that time (*tādātmya yogena pūjā pūrṇaiva vartate*). So, wherever your consciousness moves (it may move to the five senses, it may move to God consciousness), God consciousness is prevailing everywhere, and this is, in the real sense, *pūjā* (worship). Worship is not *āvāhana visarjana*. [That] is not real *pūjā*.

JOHN: What is *āvāhanam visarjana*?

SWAMIJI: Just to put an idol in front of you and call that Consciousness [to enter] in that idol, and then worship it with flowers, *dhūpa*, *dīpa*, and incense, and then ask that idol to go (that is *visarjana*). This kind of *pūjā* is not a real *pūjā*. Real *pūjā* is, wherever your consciousness moves (it may move to the five senses or pleasures or the daily routine of life), there you will find the real *pūjā* existing because your individual consciousness is totally united with God consciousness there–if you have developed awareness, not otherwise.

Parāmarśa svabhāvatvād…next:

LJA TA04J (37:52)

परामर्शस्वभावत्वादेतस्या यः स्वयं ध्वनिः ॥ १८१ ॥
सदोदितः स एवोक्तः परमं हृदयं महत् ।

parāmarśasvabhāvatvād etasyā yaḥ svayaṁ dhvaniḥ //181//
sadoditaḥ sa evoktaḥ paramaṁ hṛdayaṁ mahat /

Etasyā yaḥ svayaṁ dhvaniḥ, that *svayam dhvani*, the automatic and eternal flow of *ahaṁ parāmarśa* (Self-awareness), which takes place because of the nature of this energy of consciousness, is said to be the supreme center of God consciousness (that is *paramaṁ hṛdayam*; *mahat*, supreme, *paramaṁ*, and the topmost, *hṛdayaṁ*, center of the heart). That is God consciousness–*ahaṁ parāmarśa.*

SCHOLAR: *Ahaṁ parāmarśa svabhāvatvāt.*

SWAMIJI: Because the nature is *ahaṁ parāmarśa* there. This *ahaṁ parāmarśa*, this universal consciousness of 'I', I-consciousness:

LJA TA04J (38:56)

हृदये स्वविमर्शोऽसौ द्राविताशेषविश्वकः ॥ १८२ ॥
भावग्रहादिपर्यन्तभावी सामान्यसञ्ज्ञकः ।
स्पन्दः स कथ्यते शास्त्रे स्वात्मन्युच्छलनात्मकः ॥ १८३ ॥

hṛdaye svavimarśo'sau drāvitāśeṣaviśvakaḥ //182//
bhāvagrahādiparyanta-bhāvī sāmānyasañjñakaḥ /
spandaḥ sa kathyate śāstre svātmanyucchalanātmakaḥ //183//

This is not nominated only as *ahaṁ parāmarśa* (it is not only "I-consciousness"), it is nominated in other names, too, and those names are "*spanda*", etcetera. It is nominated as "*spanda*" also in the *Spanda śāstra*. In the *Spanda śāstra*, it is said to be as *spanda*, internal movement.

JOHN: This I-consciousness? This *ahaṁ parāmarśa*?

SWAMIJI: Yes. When this I-consciousness, after having dissolved all differentiated *drāvitāśeṣa viśvakaḥ*, all differentiated perceptions (*drāvita aśeṣa viśvakaḥ*; *aśeṣa viśvakaḥ* means, all differentiated perceptions, when they are dissolved in that I-consciousness), and is one with that heart (*hṛdaye*, in that heart), right from the very rise of objective perceptions (*bhāva graha adiparyanta*; *bhāva graha adi*, right from the rise of differentiated perceptions of objective perceptions) up to the end of those perceptions (*ādi paryanta bhāvī*), and it is *sāmānya sañjñakaḥ*, this *ahaṁ* shines in sameness irrespective of differentiated states. *Spandaḥ sa kathyate śāstre*, this *ahaṁ* is then nominated as "*spanda*" because *svātmanyucchalana-ātmakaḥ*, because this *spanda*, this movement, does not come from inside to outside. It begins from inside, it rises from inside, and resides in inside. *Svātmani ucchalanātmaka*, it is a movement in your nature, it is not a movement in an outer agency.

SCHOLAR: This is *visarga*.

SWAMIJI: Yes, it is *visarga* in your own nature, in your own Self. The verbal root of this [word] *spanda* is *spadyacalane*; the verbal root of this, wherefrom this *spanda* word has come out, the verbal root of it is "*spadi*", the *spadi*-root. *Spadi* is *kiñcit calane*, it is "some movement within", it is not movement without. You know "without"? Outside.

LJA TA04J (41:47)

किञ्चिच्चलनमेतावदनन्यस्फुरणं हि यत् ।
ऊर्मिरेषा विबोधाब्धेर्न संविदनया विना ॥ १८४ ॥

kiñciccalanametāvad-ananyasphuraṇaṁ hi yat /
ūrmireṣā vibodhābdher-na saṁvidanayā vinā //184//
(not recited)

Kiñcit calanam etāvad, and that movement is *ananya sphuraṇam*, glittering or throbbing, not in [an] other agency, but in one's own nature – [that] is meant by *kiñcit calana*. *Kiñcit calana* is "throbbing in one's own self"; or "glittering and shining in one's own self" is called *spanda*, is called *kiñcit calana*. *Ūrmireṣā vibodhābdhe*, it is just like *ūrmi* (waves or tides) in the ocean of consciousness. You see, the tides in the ocean are not separate from the ocean, they are not other than the ocean. These numberless tides that come out from the ocean are one with the ocean. In the same way, the numberless tides of *spanda* (movements) that rise from that ocean of consciousness are one with that ocean of consciousness.

SCHOLAR: The *viśeṣa* (differentiated) *spanda* and *sāmānya* (undifferentiated) *spanda* are …

SWAMIJI: But it is *sāmānya spanda* [here].

SCHOLAR: But these *viśeṣa spanda*s are all …

SWAMIJI: *Viśeṣa spanda* are tides.

SCHOLAR: Its *parispanda.*

SWAMIJI: But *sāmānya spanda* is one, that is, *ahaṁ*. Because *na saṁvit anayā vinā*, without this [*spanda*], *saṁvit* cannot exist, consciousness cannot exist without movement. It is not stable consciousness as you find in the theory of Vedānta, because [according to Vedānta] it is one-pointedness, no movement of any kind is said to be the real existence of the Lord. But from our point of view, that is not the real existence of the Lord. The real existence of Lord is move always, It is in movement. And that movement is within, that movement is not outside. Because *saṁvit*, this consciousness, cannot remain without movement, without tides. This universe cannot remain without consciousness and consciousness cannot remain without the universe. The universe and consciousness are one.

SCHOLAR: Double reflection (*sampati kāra*).

SWAMIJI: Yes, double reflection. Because:

LJA TA04J (44:11)

निस्तरङ्गतरङ्गादिवृत्तिरेव हि सिन्धुता ।

nistaraṅgata-raṅgādi-vṛttireva hi sindhutā /185a

The mode of the ocean, the state of the ocean, is only being possessive of tides and not [being] possessive of tides.

SCHOLAR: So [Abhinavagupta] says: *tena bodhamahā-sindhor ullāsinyaḥ svaśaktayaḥ…*

SWAMIJI: …*svaśaktayaḥ āśrayantyūrmaya eva svātma-saṁghaṭṭa-citratām* (TĀ 3.102), this is the real state of an ocean; an ocean is always with tides and always without tides.

JOHN: At the same time?

SWAMIJI: From one point of view, with tides. From another point of view, without tides.

JOHN: Like *visarga*, the same. Is that the same analogy?

SWAMIJI: Yes.[304] Now he puts this subject briefly in its conclusion:

LJA TA04J (45:07)

सारमेतत्समस्तस्य यच्चित्सारं जडं जगत् ॥ १८५ ॥
तदधीनप्रतिष्ठत्वात्तत्सारं हृदयं महत् ।

sārametatsamastasya yaccitsāraṁ jaḍaṁ jagat //185//
tadadhīnapratiṣṭhatvāt-tatsāraṁ hṛdayaṁ mahat /

This state of I-consciousness is the essence of all, *jaḍa* (inanimate) and *cetana* (animate). You call it "innate" or…?

JOHN: Animate and inanimate.

SWAMIJI: The "paralyzed world" or the "non-paralyzed world" I would call it (laughs). This is the paralyzed world, that which is not in movement (*jaḍa*). And the non-paralyzed world is that which is in movement (*cetana*).

SCHOLAR: *Sthagita* and *nasthagita*.

SWAMIJI: Yes. *Jaḍa* and *cetana*. *Sārametat samastasya yat citsāraṁ*,

---

304. "So, *bodha mahāsindhor*, from the ocean of that conscious Being, *ullāsinyaḥ svaśaktayaḥ*, all His energies get rise. *Āśrayantyūrmaya eva svātmasaṁghaṭṭac-itratām*, and they create–they don't create any other state of being–they create only His being, the being of Lord Śiva, just like the ocean with many tides, numberless tides. The ocean is always included with tides. Without tides, the ocean is no ocean. Whenever there is an ocean, there are tides. *Svātma saṁghaṭṭa citratām*, this is the clashing of Lord Śiva [with Himself] that tides take place." *Tantrāloka* 3.102 (LJA archive).

this state of I-consciousness is the essence of all these two formations of the world, paralyzed and non-paralyzed. Because *yat citsāraṁ jaḍam jagat*, because by the grace of this I-consciousness, this *jaḍa-jagat*, this paralyzed world, has come into life, come into existence. What is this in a nose or in a face or in eyes? It is paralyzed, already paralyzed, but although it is paralyzed, it is in life because of that *cit*, because of that I-consciousness. I-consciousness is filled and injected in that and it is filled with life. *Tat adhīna pratiṣṭhatvāt tatsāraṁ hṛdayam mahat*, because the *pratiṣṭhā* (the existence) of this universe is dependent on that I-consciousness–*tat adhīna pratiṣṭhatvāt. Tatsāraṁ hṛdayam mahat*, so the supreme center of the heart, the supreme center of the heart of I-consciousness, is the essence of this whole universe.

SCHOLAR: So this is this *mantra vīrya* ...

SWAMIJI: This is *mantra vīrya*.[305]

SCHOLAR: ... in the context of *pūjā* and *śāktopāya*.

SWAMIJI: Yes. Now he adjusts this in two ways of sacred *mantras*, and then he will adjust it in conclusion in one. For instance, this I-consciousness, in the real sense, is *ahaṁ*, but as far as we recite '*ahaṁ*', '*ahaṁ*' is the rise from '*a*' through '*ha*' and resting in '*aṁ*' (*anusvāra*)–that is '*ahaṁ*'. This is the rise, what is called *sṛṣṭi sāra*, this is the rise of I-consciousness in a creative way. And there is the rise of I-consciousness in a destructive way, too. There is the rise of I-consciousness in a destructive way and in a creative way also. When the rise of I-consciousness takes place in a creative way, then it becomes '*ahaṁ*'–it rises from '*a*', travels in '*ha*', and ends in *anusvāra* ('*aṁ*'). And when this I-consciousness rises in a destructive way, then it rises from '*ma*', travels in '*ha*', and ends in '*a*'. The [destructive] journey is complete in '*a*'. So it is vice versa. You rise up and you rise down also. You rise within and you rise without also. It is not rise and fall as Vedāntists hold that rise is only when you get entry in your God consciousness, fall is only when you are thrown outside God consciousness in the universal objective world (that is the fall from their point of view). But going in and coming out, in both ways it is a rise from our point of view. From the Śaiva point of view, it is a rise. You can rise outside, you can rise inside, [it is] one and the same thing.

305. Lit., the power or life (*vīrya*) of *mantra*.

And '*ahaṁ*' is represented by the '*sauḥ*'-*mantra*. '*Ma-ha-a*' is represented by the *piṇḍanātha mantra*. *Piṇḍanātha mantra* is represented by the *mantra*… what *mantra*?

SCHOLAR: '*R-kṣ-kh-e-ṁ*'.

SWAMIJI: No. '*Ma-ha-a*.' And *parā bīja*, '*sauḥ*', is represented by the *mantra*, '*ahaṁ*'. That is what he describes now, explains:

LJA TA04J (50:12)

तथा हि सदिदं ब्रह्ममूलं मायाण्डसञ्ज्ञितम् ॥ १८६ ॥
इच्छाज्ञानक्रियारोहं विना नैव सदुच्यते ।
तच्छक्तित्रितयारोहाद्भैरवीये चिदात्मनि ॥ १८७ ॥
विसृज्यते हि तत्तस्माद्बहिरवाथ विसृज्यते ।

tathā hi sadidaṁ brahmā-mūlaṁ māyāṇḍasañjñitam //186//
icchājñānakriyārohaṁ vinā naiva saducyate /
tacchaktitritayārohād-bhairavīye cidātmani //187//
visṛjyate hi tattasmād-bahirvātha visṛjyate /

Now he takes first '*sauḥ*' (*para bīja*), the explanation of *para bīja*, in hand–*para bīja*, not *piṇḍanātha*.

Sat idaṁ brahmā mūlam māyāṇḍa sañjñitam, this *brahmāṇḍa*, this oval[306] of Brahmā, the oval of *prakṛti*, and the oval of *māyā*, these three ovals, these big ovals, big circles, oval-shaped circles of the universe,…*

SCHOLAR: Circles. An oval is shaped like that, like an egg.

SWAMIJI: Yes, it is egg-shaped, it is an egg-shaped circle. *Brahmāṇḍa* is an egg-shaped circle, *prakṛtyaṇḍa* is also an egg-shaped circle, and *māyāṇḍa* is also an egg-shaped circle–these three great circles of the universe.

*… and this whole universe is existing in these three great circles,

306. *Aṇḍa* literally means, egg.

oval-shaped circles. *Brahmāṇḍa* is gross, and subtle is *prakṛtyaṇḍa*, and the subtlest is *māyāṇḍa*. In *brahmāṇḍa*, from earth (from *pṛthivī*) up to *prakṛti*, excluding *prakṛti* (*prakṛti* is excluded there in this first oval-shaped circle), from earth to *ahaṁkāra*, from the earth element to the element of *ahaṁkāra*, all those elements exist in the oval-shaped circle of Brahmā, that is *brahmāṇḍa*.[307] And in *prakṛti*, [only] *prakṛti* resides in *prakṛti*; *prakṛti*, only one element, resides in *prakṛti*.[308] And in *māyā*, from *puruṣa* to *māyā*, these elements reside; in the oval-shaped circle of *māyā*, these seven elements reside.[309] All these thirty-one elements reside in these three oval-shaped circles, that is, *brahmāṇḍa*, *prakṛtyaṇḍa*, and *māyāṇḍa*. This group of thirty-one elements is said to be *sat*[310], is represented by the word '*sa*', the letter '*sa*'. And this '*sa*', *icchā jñāna kriyāroham vinā naiva saducyate* (verse 187), it cannot exist, it cannot [come into] its existence, unless it has risen in the three actions of Lord Śiva: *icchā śakti*, *jñāna śakti*, and *kriyā śakti*. Unless it has risen in those three actions of Lord Śiva, the three energies of Lord Śiva–*icchā* (will), knowledge, and action–this existence of the *sat*-world won't exist, won't remain. So, *icchā jñāna kriyāroham vinā naiva sat ucyate*, this *sat* won't exist without, unless it is rested, it rests ...

SCHOLAR: Grounded?

SWAMIJI: ... it is grounded, in *icchā śakti*, *jñāna śakti*, and *kriyā śakti*. *Icchā śakti*, and *jñāna śakti*, and *kriyā śakti* is represented by the letter '*au*'. This *sat* is represented by the letter '*sa*'. '*Sa*' is the outside [world], this-ness. And '*au*' is cognitive consciousness. This-consciousness ('*sa*') cannot exist without cognitive consciousness ('*au*'). And that cognitive consciousness ('*au*') cannot exist without creative and destructive consciousness. Creative and destructive consciousness is conducted by Lord Śiva Himself–creative and destructive consciousness–and that is *visarga* ('*aḥ*'). The same is explained here: *Tat śakti tritayārohāt*, when this *sat* has risen in these threefold energies of Lord

---

307. Also known as *pṛthvyaṇḍa*.

308. Some other texts indicate that *brahmāṇḍa* contains only one element of *pṛthivī* (earth), and *prakṛtyaṇḍa* contains twenty-three elements, from *jala* (water) up to *prakṛti*.

309. *Puruṣa*, the five *kañcukas* (coverings), and *māyā*.

310. Lit., existent, being.

Śiva (*icchā, jñāna*, and *kriyā*), *bhairavīye cidātmani visṛjyate*, then it is said that it is created inside the consciousness of Bhairava; *bahirvātha visṛjyate*, it is created inside the consciousness of Bhairava and it is created outside *in* the consciousness of Bhairava. Both ways they exist in the consciousness of Bhairava–outside and inside also. This is the reality of *visarga*. And this, in total conclusion, is represented by *parā bīja*, that is, '*sauḥ*'. And this '*sauḥ*' is represented by the creative energy of Lord Śiva, the creative I-consciousness of Lord Śiva. The creative I-consciousness of Lord Śiva is represented by '*ahaṁ*'.

LJA TA04J (56:26)

Now he will explain what is the destructive I-consciousness of Lord Śiva, because Lord Śiva is not represented only in a creative way, he is destructive, too, at the same time. So he will explain the next time the destructive way of God consciousness. The destructive way of God consciousness will be explained in the explanation of *piṇḍanātha*. And *piṇḍanātha*, in conclusion, will be '*ma-ha-a*'. And '*sauḥ*' (*parā bīja*), in conclusion, will be '*ahaṁ*'.

SCHOLAR: Now this '*sauḥ*', which is *mahā sṛṣṭi*, is in a way back to front.

SWAMIJI: Yes.

SCHOLAR: You would expect it to be '*ha-au-sa*', that way around.

SWAMIJI: Huh?

SCHOLAR: Because you've said that it is *sṛṣṭi krama*[311] here, ...

SWAMIJI: Yes.

SCHOLAR: ... one would expect that it would be first *visarga* ('*aḥ*'), then *au-kāra*, and then the objective field ('*sa*'), but it comes the other way around.

SWAMIJI: It is creative because it cannot be creative without *visarga* in the end. *Visarga* must be in the end. You can't keep *visarga* in the beginning because it is creative. So *visarga* is to be kept in the end of this experience of I-consciousness of *parā bīja*. So, it rises from '*a*' and ends in '*a*'. The *visarga* is a rise from '*a*' and ending in '*a*'. It is why he has explained: *bhairavīye cidātmani hi visṛjyate, tat tat tasmāt*

311. The process of creation.

bahirvātha visṛjyate, it is created in Bhairava-*cidātmā* in the inside, and it is created in Bhairava-*cidātmā* outside, too.[312]

SCHOLAR: So, from point of view of *saṁvit krama*, that *visarga* is experienced actually in the first moment in this *kāma tattva*.[313]

SWAMIJI: Yes.

SCHOLAR: So it really appears in its fullness at the end there.

SWAMIJI: Yes.

SCHOLAR: So you have also the form of *parā bīja* (‘*sauḥ*’) with *visarga*.

SWAMIJI: Yes, that is quite true. *Bas*, this will be done today because this is very tough, you must try to understand it.

LJA TA04J (59:03) end.
LJA TA04K (00:00) start.

Now, there is one important point to note first before we explain this *parā bīja*, *piṇḍanātha*, and *ahaṁ*. In fact, this *parā bīja* and the *piṇḍanātha mantra* is the commentary of ‘*ahaṁ*’. *Parā bīja* is also the expansion of ‘*ahaṁ*’, and *piṇḍanātha* is also the expansion of ‘*ahaṁ*’, but the difference is only [that] *parā bīja* is the creative movement of consciousness, this is creative (*sṛṣṭi pradhāna*), whereas *piṇḍanātha* is the destructive movement, the withdrawal movement. It is not destructive, you can't say [“destructive”]. It is the withdrawing way of consciousness, how you withdraw from outside to inner consciousness.[314]

SCHOLAR: The movement of *saṁhāra kuṇḍalinī*.

SWAMIJI: No, *saṁhāra kuṇḍalinī* is found in both. It is only the two aspects of *krama mudrā*.[315] Because as soon as *krama mudrā* takes place, you find in *samādhi*, when you are established in *samādhi*,

---

312. The consciousness (*cidātmā*) of Bhairava.

313. In desire, in will, in the energy of will.

314. “It does not destroy the state of God consciousness. It is only the destructive way of His being.” *Tantrāloka* 5.60 (LJA archive).

315. The automatic process of *krama mudrā* is the rapid osscilation between *nimīlanā* and *unmīlanā samādhi*. “One movement of *anākhya* is towards *nimīlanā*, and another movement that descends from *caturāra cakra* is *unmīlanā*.” (*Interviews*) See *Kashmir Shaivism–The Secret Supreme*, 16.114 and 17.120. See also *Self-Realization in Kashmir Shaivism*, 5.114.

just after two seconds of experiencing this *samādhi*, you come out, your breath comes out. Till then, in *samādhi* there is no breathing movement. Then breath comes out for one second, and the coming out, the process of coming out in *samādhi*, is '*sauḥ*', is *parā bīja*. And the process of going again inside is *piṇḍanātha*. So, the process of going out is '*ahaṁ*', is the essence of '*ahaṁ*', and going back again is '*ma-ha-a*' – '*ma*', '*ha*', and '*a*', the reverse [of '*ahaṁ*'].

LJA TA04K (02:07)

तथा हि सदिदं ब्रह्ममूलं मायाण्डसञ्ज्ञितम् ॥ १८६ ॥
इच्छाज्ञानक्रियारोहं विना नैव सदुच्यते ।

tathā hi sadidaṁ brahmā-mūlaṁ māyāṇḍasañjñitam //186//
icchājñānakriyārohaṁ vinā naiva saducyate /

Although these threefold egg-shaped universal states (*brahmāṇḍa*, *prakṛtyaṇḍa*, and *māyāṇḍa*), in which thirty-one elements exist from earth to *māyā tattva*, from the element earth to *māyā tattva*, it is nominated in our Śaivism as *sat* (existent) because it is existing outwardly (in the outward state it exists, all these thirty-one elements from *pṛthivī* to *māyā*), but this existence (*sat*) will never come in these thirty-one elements unless they are risen in the threefold energies of Lord Śiva (*icchā*, *jñāna*, and *kriyā*). And that *icchā*, *jñāna*, and *kriyā* is *triśūla*, it represents the *triśūla bīja* ('*au*').

SCHOLAR: *Sphuṭatama kriyā*.

SWAMIJI: Yes, *sphuṭatama kriyā*. Not *asphuṭa*, *sphuṭa*, or *sphuṭatara*. It is *sphuṭatama kriyā*.[316] *Icchā jñāna kriyā rohaṁ vinā naiva saducyate*, unless it has risen on that *icchā*, *jñāna*, and *kriyā* (these threefold energies, collective threefold energies, that is, '*au*'), it does not exist, its existence is nowhere to be seen. So:

---

316. "*Asphuṭa* is not vivid ('*e*'), *sphuṭa* is vivid ('*ai*'), *sphuṭatāra* is more vivid ('*o*'), *sphuṭatama* is most vivid ('*au*'). The energy of action is placed forth by these four vowels." *Parātrīśikā Vivaraṇa* (LJA archive).

LJA TA04K (03:46)

तच्छक्तित्रितयारोहाद्भैरवीये चिदात्मनि ॥ १८७ ॥
विसृज्यते हि तत्तस्माद्बहिरवाथ विसृज्यते ।

tacchaktitritayārohād-bhairavīye cidātmani //187//
visṛjyate hi tattasmād-bahirvātha visṛjyate /

So, these thirty-one elements as *sat*, by ascending on the threefold energies of Śiva, when they ascend, …*

SCHOLAR: They are grounded in that.

SWAMIJI: They are grounded.

*… are created in the state of Bhairava–*are* created in the state of Bhairava (that is *bhairavīye cidātmani dhāmani*, Bhairava which is filled with consciousness)–and are created outside also *in* Bhairava. They are created in Bhairava and they are created outside Bhairava–and in Bhairava, at the same time, in Bhairava. Outside also does not exist without Bhairava's state. So, there is no difference between outside and inside. They are created inside first and then outside. But where? In the basis of Bhairava. This is …

SCHOLAR: Bhairavī.

SWAMIJI: … this is the state of '*sauḥ*' (*parā bīja*), and this is the state of '*ahaṁ*'. And this is partly the state of *krama mudrā*, one part of *krama mudrā*–coming out. Because from *samādhi*, you come out first, you do not [go] in. You are already inside there, [so] you come out first and then you go again inside. It is why he has put first *parā bīja*, not *piṇḍanātha*.

Evaṁ sadrūpataivaiṣāṁ … next, 188:

LJA TA04K (05:39)

एवं सद्रूपतैवैषां सतां शक्तित्रयात्मताम् ॥ १८८ ॥
विसर्गं परबोधेन समाक्षिप्यैव वर्तते ।

evaṁ sadrūpataivaiṣāṁ satāṁ śaktitrayātmatām //188//
visargaṁ parabodhena samākṣipyaiva vartate /

This way, *sad rūpataiva eṣāṁ*, these threefold *aṇḍa*s, so the universal existence of these three *aṇḍa*s, oval-shaped worlds, exist only after taking hold of the threefold energies and *visarga*. Unless they take hold of threefold energies and *visarga*, they don't exist. So *brahmāṇḍa*, *prakṛtyaṇḍa*, and *māyāṇḍa* [are] pervaded by the *mantra*, '*sa*'.

Brahmāṇḍa sārṇenāṇḍatr-... there is one reference of the *Mālinīvijaya Tantra* here:

LJA TA04K (06:37)

शार्णेनाण्डत्रयं व्याप्तं त्रिशूलेन चतुर्थकम् ।
सर्वातीतं विसर्गेण पराया व्याप्तिरिष्यते ॥

sārṇenāṇḍatrayaṁ vyāptaṁ triśūlena caturthakam /
sarvātītaṁ visargeṇa parāyā vyāptiriṣyate //[317]

This is the omnipresence of the *parā bīja*, '*sauḥ*', in which there are three letters: '*sa*', '*au*', and *visarga* ('*aḥ*'): *sārṇena aṇḍa trayam vyāptam*, by the *mantra*, '*sa*' (*sārṇena*, by the *mantra*, '*sa*'), *āṇḍatrayam vyāptam*, these three *aṇḍa*s, these three circles (*brahmāṇḍa*, *prakṛtyaṇḍa*, and *māyāṇḍa*) [are] pervaded by '*sa*'. The fourth *aṇḍa* (that is, *śaktyaṇḍa*) is pervaded by the *mantra*, '*au*'. And the transcendental Lord Śiva is pervaded by *visarga* ('*aḥ*'). So this is the *vyāpti*, this is the omnipresence, of *parā bīja* explained in Śaivism, in the *Mālinīvijaya Tantra*.

Now the explanation of *parā bīja* is over. Now, he explains *piṇḍanātha* because *piṇḍanātha* is also adjusted with this flow.

317. Jayaratha quotes *Mālinīvijaya Tantra* 4.25.

LJA TA04K (07:48)

तत्सदेव बहीरूपं प्राग्बोधाग्निविलापितम् ॥ १८९ ॥
अन्तर्नदत्परामर्शशेषीभूतं ततोऽप्यलम् ।
खात्मत्वमेव सम्प्राप्तं शक्तित्रितयगोचरात् ॥ १९० ॥
वेदनात्मकतामेत्य संहारात्मनि लीयते ।

tatsadeva bahīrūpaṁ prāgbodhāgnivilāpitam //189//
antarnadatparāmarśa-śeṣībhūtaṁ tato'pyalam /
khātmatvameva samprāptaṁ śaktitritayagocarāt //190//
vedanātmakatāmetya saṁhārātmani līyate /

Tatsateva, when this outward universe is at first dissolved in the fire of consciousness (*tat sat eva bahīrūpaṁ*, this outward universe which is existing, it is first *prāk bodhāgni vilāpitam*, at first it is dissolved, melted, in the fire of consciousness), when there is the representation of fire, it means this is indicated [by] the first letter of *piṇḍanātha*.[318] The first letter of *piṇḍanātha* is '*ra*' ('*ra*' is the indicator of fire in our system). So this is '*ra*' that represents this state of consciousness, transcendental consciousness. When *tat sat eva*, when that existing universe, threefold universe, is at first (*prāk*, at first) *bodhāgni vilāpitam*, melted in *bodhāgni*, melted in the fire of consciousness, so this is the state of '*ra*'. Then it takes another position of that being. This is the first: *tatsadeva bahīrūpaṁ prāg bodhāgni vilāpitam*, this is the first letter, the explanation of the first letter, '*ra*'. Then the explanation of the second letter:

318. '*Ma-ha-a*' is the *bījākṣara akṣara* of *piṇḍanātha*, which is formed by separate letters with vowels. '*R-kṣ-kh-e-ṁ*' is the *piṇḍa akṣara* of *piṇḍanātha*, which is a conglomeration of letters without vowels.

LJA TA04K (09:35)

antarnadatparāmarśa-śeṣībhūtaṁ tato'pyalam /
khātmatvameva samprāptaṁ śaktitritayagocarāt //190//
vedanātmakatāmetya saṁhārātmani līyate /
(repeated)

Then this universe, *antarnadat parāmarśa śeṣībhūtaṁ*, then this universe is found as vibrating inside the state of supreme consciousness, I-consciousness (*antarnadat parāmarśa śeṣībhūtaṁ*), and this is '*kṣa*', this is represented by the letter '*kṣa*' in *piṇḍanātha*–the next letter.

SCHOLAR: *Śeṣībhūtam, tanmātra rūpam.*

SWAMIJI: *Śeṣībhūtam, bas...*

SCHOLAR: Nothing but that.

SWAMIJI: ... diluted by... *tadeva bhūtam, tādātmya bhāvam āptam–śeṣībhūtam.* And then (*tato api*, and then) there is another movement afterwards: *tato api alam khātmatvameva saṁprāptam*, this I-consciousness ('*ahaṁ*') is leveled to the extreme point of '*ahaṁ*'. After that also, this universe is seen as melted in nothingness (*śūnya*). That is *khātmatvam eva samprāptam*, it exists in absolute voidness, this universe, while getting inside, withdrawing. This is the movement of withdrawal ('*kha*'). Then *śakti tritaya gocarāt vedana-ātmakatāmetya saṁhārātmani līyate*, then it takes rise in the threefold energies (*icchā, jñāna*, and *kriyā*). That is the *asphuṭa* (not vivid) *kriyā śakti*. This is *trikoṇa* ('*e*').[319] This is not '*au*', this is not [*tri*]*śūlabīja*.

SCHOLAR: This is *saṁhāra krama*.

SWAMIJI: This is *saṁhāra krama* (destructive course). There also you find the threefold energies (*icchā, jñāna*, and *kriyā*). *Śakti tritaya gocarāt*, when it has risen on these threefold energies (*icchā, jñāna*, and *kriyā*), then *vedanātmakatām*, then it has risen, that is indicated by the letter '*e*' in *piṇḍanātha*. *Vedanātmakatāmetya saṁhārātmani līyate*, and then this voidness also of the universe is mounted in the surface of the threefold energies, and by coming to that extent, it takes the position of only a supreme vacuum, that is, the subjective and

319. The letter '*e*' is pronounced as 'a' in English.

the destructive state of consciousness. That is supreme *para pramātṛ bhāva*[320], that is '*aṁ*', that is indicated by '*aṁ*'.

So these five states of Being are indicated by these five letters. The first letter is '*r*' with *halanta* (not with '*a*', *r-halanta*), the next letter is '*kṣ*', the third letter is '*kh*', the fourth letter is *trikoṇa* ('*e*'), and the fifth letter is '*ṁ*'. '*R-kṣ-kh-e-ṁ*' is indicated by *piṇḍanātha*. And there is another *śloka* [in the commentary].

SCHOLAR: *Śivanabhasi.*

SWAMIJI: Yes, *śivanabhasi*, because it refers to *piṇḍanātha.*

LJA TA04K (13:03)

शिवनभसि विगलिताक्षः कौण्डिल्युन्मेषविकसितानन्दः ।
प्रज्वलितसकलरन्ध्रः कामिन्या हृदयकुहुरमधिरूढः ॥
योगी शून्य इवास्ते तस्य स्वयमेव योगिनीहृदयम् ।
हृदयनभोमण्डलगं समुच्चरत्यनलकोटिशतदीप्तम् ॥

śivanabhasi vigalitākṣaḥ kauṇḍilyunmeṣavikasitānandaḥ /
prajvalitasakalarandhraḥ kāminyā hṛdayakuhuramadhirūḍhaḥ //
yogī śūnya ivāste tasya svayameva yoginīhṛdayam /
hṛdayanabhomaṇḍalagaṁ samuccaratyanalakoṭiśatadīptam //[321]

Śivanabhasi vigalitākṣaḥ, when you say *śivanabhasi vigalitākṣaḥ*, when a yogi's all objective and cognitive senses (*akṣa*; *akṣa* does not mean only the senses, [it means] all objective senses and cognitive senses, *akṣa* means all objective and cognitive senses), ...*

SCHOLAR: This is like in *kanda cakra.*[322]

SWAMIJI: Yes.

SCHOLAR: His *ahaṁkāra* is not working.

---

320. The state of supreme subjectivity.

321. These verses of an unknown Krama source are quoted in Jayaratha's commentary.

322. A subtle *cakra* below the navel.

SWAMIJI: *Ahaṁkāra* is not working.

*... when a yogi's all objective and cognitive senses, *vigalitākṣaḥ*, are dissolved in the ether of Śiva (*śivanabhasi*, in the ether of Śiva, when all objective and cognitive senses are dissolved, get dissolution), this is '*ra*', this is indicated by the letter '*ra*' of *piṇḍanātha–śivanabhasi vigalitākṣaḥ*.

It was an important *śloka*, so I have to explain it, otherwise you can't understand it and you can't adjust this *śloka* with this *piṇḍanātha*.

Kauṇḍilyunmeṣa vikasitānandaḥ, and when his transcendental bliss, *vikasitānanda*, is expanded (*vikasita ānanda*), by the rise of *saṁhāra kuṇḍalinī*, ...*

This is the rise of *saṁhāra kuṇḍalinī*, because it is the withdrawal state. It is *saṁhāra kuṇḍalinī*.

SCHOLAR: This is *viṣa tattva* here.

SWAMIJI: Yes, it is like that, but this is the simultaneous state of both movements. *Samāveśa* (absorption), this is the real *samāveśa* of Śiva. One movement is an outside movement, the next movement is an internal movement, and it is simultaneous. It works half a second [for] one movement and the second half a second [for] another movement. It does not work in succession, it works simultaneously. And it works not only once, not only twice, it works one thousand times, so that you get your consciousness of I-consciousness vibrated inside and outside simultaneously, and you find the existence of Lord Śiva everywhere. This is automatic. You have not to do it. It is not to be functioned. It functions automatically.[323]

*... *kauṇḍilyunmeṣa vikasitānandaḥ*, this is represented by '*kṣa*', the letter '*kṣa*'. This is the next movement in the withdrawal state. *Pra jvalitasakalarandhraḥ*–this is the third movement–*prajvalita sakala randhraḥ*, and when the voidness of his nature is lighted from all sides (*prajvalita sakala randhra*, this is lighted from all sides in a vacuum), this is represented by the letter, '*kha*'. *Kāminyā hṛdaya kuhuram adhirūḍhaḥ*, and when he is, the yogi is, established in the cavity of the heart of his beloved (*kāminyā hṛdaya kuhuram adhirūḍhaḥ*, the beloved there is no one else than the supreme energy of *parā śakti*), and that *parā śakti* is represented by the letter, '*e*'. So '*e*' has also been included

323. This is the automatic process of *krama mudrā*.

in this. Then *yogī śūnya evāste*, then at that occasion, the yogi is seated as if seated on complete voidness, that is '*aṁ*' (that is *anusvāra*). So the '*r-kṣ-kh-e-ṁ*' has come in this *śloka*.[324] Then, *tasya svayameva yoginī hṛdayam hṛdayanabhomaṇḍalagaṁ samuccaratyanalakoṭiśatadīptam*, then the heart (or the center of the *yoginī*, *yoginī hṛdayam*), which is existing in the orbit of the universal center and which is bright and shining like millions of shining fires (*anala koṭiśata dīptam*) appears in its fullness (*samuccarati*; *samuccarati* means, appears).

LJA TA04K (18:28)

इदं संहारहृदयं प्राच्यं सृष्टौ च हृन्मतम् ॥ १९१ ॥

idaṁ saṁhārahṛdayaṁ prācyaṁ sṛṣṭau ca hṛnmatam //191//

This state of *parāmarśa* (consciousness) is the essence in the destructive state of Being, while the previous, *prācyaṁ sṛṣṭau ca hṛt matam*, while the previous state is the essence in the creative state of Being.

LJA TA04K (18:51)

एतद्रूपपरामर्शमकृत्रिममनाबिलम् ।
अहमित्याहुरेषैव प्रकाशस्य प्रकाशता ॥ १९२ ॥

etadrūpaparāmarśam-akṛtrimamanābilam /
ahamityāhureṣaiva prakāśasya prakāśatā //192//

This formation of *parāmarśa*, this twofold formation of *parāmarśa*, which has been explained in '*sauḥ*' *bīja* and *piṇḍanātha*, ...*

'*Sauḥ*' *bīja* begins from *anuttara* ('*a*') and ends in *aṁ-kāra* (*anusvāra*) – '*ahaṁ*'. And *piṇḍanātha* begins from *ma-kāra* and ends

324. See Appendix 5, p. 391, for a detailed explanation of this *mantra* in terms of the letter, *śloka* and *kuṇḍalinī*.

in *a-kāra* (*'ma-ha-a'*)–this is *saṁhāra krama*, this is the destructive successive way, and that [*'sauḥ' bīja* or *'ahaṁ'*] is the creative successive way.

*... and this *rūpa* (this formation) of *parāmarśa*, this twofold formation of *parāmarśa*, is called *'ahaṁ'*, is explained as the state of *'ahaṁ'*, supreme I-consciousness, which is un-artificial and the clear state of transcendental-I (*anābilam*). *Eṣaiva prakāśasya prakāśyatā*, this is the light of all lights, this is the *prakāśa*, the life of all lights.

LJA TA04K (20:29)

एतद्वीर्यं हि सर्वेषां मन्त्राणां हृदयात्मकम् ।
विनानेन जडास्ते स्युर्जीवा इव विना हृदा ॥१९३॥

etadvīryaṁ hi sarveṣāṁ mantrāṇāṁ hṛdayātmakam /
vinānena jaḍāste syur-jīvā iva vinā hṛdā //193//
(not recited)

Etadvīryaṁ hi sarveṣāṁ mantrāṇāṁ, all *mantra*s get life from this *ahaṁ-parāmarśa*, and this is the supreme heart of all *mantras*. *Anena vinā*, without this, all these *mantra*s are *jaḍa*, all these *mantra*s are lifeless, as all individuals are lifeless without the universal transcendental heart. When there is not the transcendental heart existing in your heart (that transcendental heart is supreme I-consciousness), when supreme I-consciousness is not there, all *jīva*s are just like dead, lifeless. So this is the twofold *parāmarśa* of *'ahaṁ'* in the real sense. And the firstfold is found in *'sauḥ' parāmarśa* (*parā bīja*), and the second is found in *piṇḍanātha*. *Piṇḍanātha* is the heart of destruction and *'sauḥ'* is the heart of creation. In the creative way, *ahaṁ-parāmarśa* takes place in the formation of *'ahaṁ'*, and in the destructive way, *ahaṁ-parāmarśa* takes place in the formation of *'ma-ha-a'*.

Japyādi Vāstavam – Real Japa (Recitation)

LJA TA04K (22:05)

अकृत्रिमैतद्धृदयारूढो यत्किञ्चिदाचरेत् ।
प्राण्याद्वा मृशते वापि स सर्वोऽस्य जपो मतः ॥ १९४ ॥

akṛtrimaitaddhṛdayā-rūḍho yatkiñcidācaret /
prāṇyādvā mṛśate vāpi sa sarvo'sya japo mataḥ //194//

The one who is established in this un-artificial heart of supreme I-consciousness, the one who is fully established in the un-artificial heart of supreme consciousness, whatever he does in action, whatever he does in breathing, or whatever he does in his thought, *mṛśyate vāpi*, everything becomes the recitation of *japa*, everything becomes *japa* for him, he is doing *japa*. If he does his daily activities of life, if he is given to the daily activities of life, it is *japa* for him. Whatever [way] he breathes, he may breathe in *abhyāsa* (in meditation) or breathe in fighting with each other, that breathing becomes *japa* for him. He may think of God or he may think of some very degraded thoughts, any thought, *sa sarvo asya japo mataḥ*, that becomes *japa* for him.

akṛtrimaitaddhṛdayā-rūḍho yatkiñcidācaret /
prāṇyādvā mṛśate vāpi sa sarvo'sya japo mataḥ //194//
(repeated)

That becomes *japa* for him – everything! Now he explains the reality of *dhyāna* (meditation) for him:

LJA TA04K (24:08)

यदेव स्वेच्छया सृष्टिस्वाभाव्याद्बहिरन्तरा ।
निर्मीयते तदेवास्य ध्यानं स्यात्पारमार्थिकम् ॥१९५॥

yadeva svecchayā sṛṣṭi-svābhāvyādbahirantarā /
nirmīyate tadevāsya dhyānaṁ syātpāramārthikam //195//

Yadeva (whatever) *svecchayā*, according to the nature of his fivefold actions, *sṛṣṭi svābhāvyāt ...**

Sṛṣṭi svābhāvyāt means, because he does *sṛṣṭi* (he creates), he protects, he destroys, he conceals and reveals (*pīḍana* is concealing) – *sṛṣṭi*, *sthiti*, *saṁhāra*, *pīḍana* and *anugraha*.

*... whatever he does according to this nature of action, this nature of fivefold actions, *bahir antarā*, whatever he does externally or internally, whatever he creates externally or internally – [internally] in the formation of pleasure, pain, joy, sorrow; externally in pots, jugs, everything, [all] external objects – in the world of external objects and in the world of internal objects, ...*

Do you know what are internal objects? Pleasure, pain, etcetera.

JOHN: Blue, sensations.

SWAMIJI: Not blue. Blue is external.[325]

*... *tadevāsya dhyānam syāt*, that is, in the real sense, the meditation center for him. The meditation center is not for him to meditate upon the formation of Lord Śiva or Brahmā or Viṣṇu or Nārāyaṇa or his master. The meditation center is anything, whatever he sees, whatever he does. He looks at a chair, that is the meditation center for him. He concentrates on a chair, it does not mean he concentrates on a chair, he concentrates on God consciousness. This is the way of meditation for him.

JOHN: In *śāktopāya*.

SWAMIJI: Yes, this is *śāktopāya*.

---

325. The color blue (*nīla*) is often cited in Kashmir Śaiva scripture to represent objective perception.

JOHN: What are these states of concealing and revealing for a *sādhaka*? I can understand those on the level of Lord Śiva, but for a *sādhaka*? I can understand creation, preservation, and destruction in terms of knowledge, but I ...

SWAMIJI: Concealing is when impressions remain. As long as impressions are there, it is the state of concealing. When those impressions also are destroyed, that is revealing.

SCHOLAR: But [John's] problem was why are the impressions there in *śāktopāya*. The others make perfect sense from the point of view of the movement of consciousness, but why in the awareness of the *śākta sādhaka* would there be the state of *pīḍana*?

SWAMIJI: Because it is the way of his meditation. He cannot travel in a direct [way].

JOHN: There is still some *vikalpana*.

SWAMIJI: There is some defect. As long as there is some defect, there is concealing, there are impressions.

JOHN: So his work is to remove this impression by ...

SWAMIJI: Yes.

JOHN: Is this what is meant by *vikalpa saṁskāra*?

SWAMIJI: *Vikalpa saṁskāra* also can remove.

SCHOLAR: But this describes the completed realization through *saṁvit cakrodaya*, does it not?

SWAMIJI: Yes.

SCHOLAR: So, in that case, all these five are at the same level.

SWAMIJI: They are at the same level when they are concealed and revealed also. When they are only concealed, not revealed, then they are not in one level.

SCHOLAR: So it will be wrong to say that, when he is referring to *pīḍana śakti* here, he is talking about the state in which the yogi's awareness is clouded.

SWAMIJI: Clouded, yes.

SCHOLAR: Surely he is just referring to the state in which his awareness is not clouded even though they are there.

SWAMIJI: No, it is the way of action, because concealing comes first and then revealing (revealing is the next state of his action).

SCHOLAR: *Bīja vilāpana.*[326]

SWAMIJI: *Bheda udghāṭana* and *bheda vilāpana.*[327] *Bheda udghāṭana* will take place first and *bheda vilāpana* will take place next.

JOHN: If there's no concealing, he wouldn't be in *śāktopāya.*

SWAMIJI: This is not that kind of concealing. It is an act in fivefold acts. It is the fourth act.

JOHN: But what is that act?

SWAMIJI: *Sṛṣṭi*, *sthiti*, *saṁhāra*, *pīḍana*, and *anugraha.*

JOHN: But how does he act in a concealing way – the *sādhaka*?

SWAMIJI: Just [to] hide it. They hide God consciousness. When God consciousness is hidden.

JOHN: He does that act.

SWAMIJI: He does that, yes.

SCHOLAR: This is his act. He is not acted upon here.

SWAMIJI: No (affirmative).

SCHOLAR: Right, that's the distinction.

SWAMIJI:

LJA TA04K (28:49)

निराकारे हि चिद्धाम्नि विश्वाकृतिमये सति ।
फलार्थिनां काचिदेव ध्येयत्वेनाकृतिः स्थिता ॥ १९६ ॥

nirākāre hi ciddhāmni viśvākṛtimaye sati /
phalārthināṁ kācideva dhyeyatvenākṛtiḥ sthitā //196//

As the state of consciousness is filled with universal forms (*viśvākṛti maye ciddhāmni*, *cid dhāmni*, the state of consciousness, when this *cid dhāmni*, the state of consciousness, is *viśvākṛti maye*, is filled with universal forms), ...*

326. The dissolving (*vilāpana*) of the seed (*bīja*).

327. The exposing (*udghāṭana*) of duality (*bheda*) and the dissolution (*vilāpana*) of duality (*bheda*).

Cid dhāma, the state of consciousness, is not the state where only one formation of Lord Śiva exists. This state of *cid dhāma* is that [state of consciousness] where universal formations are existing. Even the formation of a cow is existing there, the formation of a jug is existing there. It is why it is called *nirākāre*, it is formless. Formless means, filled with universal forms. Formless does not mean, which has no forms.

JOHN: Is this like the universal forms in Western philosophy, e.g., a universal chair (chair-ness) and table-ness, that kind of…?

SWAMIJI: No, it is not that. *Nirākāre* means, *nihita ākāra rahite*, he has translated – Jayaratha, the commentator – *nirākāre* does not mean, formless; *nirākāre* means, *nihita*, when there is not a particular state of formation.

SCHOLAR: Whatever appears, that is its appearing.

SWAMIJI: *… whatever formation takes place, that is the formation of Lord Śiva, and this is the real way of the existence of Lord Śiva, and this [perception] takes place only to those *sādhaka*s who have no particular thought of getting fruit, a particular fruit. *Phalārthināṁ*, but those who are bent upon attaining a particular fruit (*phalārthināṁ*), *kācidevadhyeyatvenākṛtiḥ*, for them, formation is limited, formation takes some particular way of being/existence. Those who want to create something, they have to think of Brahmā. Those who want to protect something, they have to think of Nārāyaṇa. Those who want to destroy somebody, they have to think of Lord Śiva.[328] But those who want to achieve the real state of I-consciousness, God consciousness, for them there is no bondage, they can concentrate on anything, any damn thing, and that is the concentration on Lord Śiva. Even this box, they can concentrate on this box, and the existence of Lord Śiva will appear to them. This binding is only for those who have got [a desire for] particular fruit, a particular way of gaining particular fruit. *Yathā hyabhedāt-pūrṇe'pi*… [Abhinavagupta] gives now *dṛṣṭānt*. What is "*dṛṣṭānt*"?

SCHOLAR: An example.

SWAMIJI: An example.

---

328. Referring to Lord Śiva as a part of the trinity of gods, not as the Absolute.

LJA TA04K (32:17)

यथा ह्यभेदात्पूर्णेऽपि भावे जलमुपाहरन् ।
अन्याकृत्यपहानेन घटमर्थयते रसात् ॥ १९७ ॥

yathā hyabhedātpūrṇe'pi bhāve jalamupāharan /
anyākṛtyapahānena ghaṭamarthayate rasāt //197//
(not recited in full)

Take one jug, it may be of earth (an earthen jug), it may be a golden jug, it may be a silver jug, whatever it is, it is a jug. *Abhedāt pūrṇe'pi bhāve*, this jug is made of silver, this jug is made of earth, or this jug is made of gold, but the person who has need for getting water from a spring, he does not think of [the material of] that jug, if it is gold, if it is silver, or if it is earthen. He wants a jug just that can contain water. He does not go to those other details of a jug. *Jalam upāharan*, that [person] who is in need of carrying water, *anya ākṛtyapahānena ghaṭam arthayate rasāt*, this is by nature [that] he thinks of a *ghaṭa*, he thinks of a jug; he does not think of a gold jug, he does not think of a silver jug, or he does not think of an earthen jug, he thinks of a jug only at that point.

LJA TA04K (33:52)

तथैव परमेशाननियतिप्रविजृम्भणात् ।
काचिदेवाकृतिः काञ्चित् सूते फलविकल्पनाम् ॥ १९८ ॥

tathaiva parameśāna-niyatipravijṛmbhaṇāt /
kācidevākṛtiḥ kāñcit sūte phalavikalpanām //198//

In the same way, *niyati vijṛmbhaṇāt*, by his restrained energy, by the restrained energy of Lord Śiva, *kācidevākṛti*, some particular formation is said to get you fruit, some particular fruit, for your desired objects, but the one who has no particular desire for any fruit, a particular fruit, for him there is no particular way of holding anything. He can hold a chair, he can hold this filtered water, he can hold this, he can hold a book – from a book he will get the same result. Who? The one who has no particular desire of holding, [but] only the desire of achieving I-consciousness. For him there is no particular way of thinking.

LJA TA04K (35:05)

यस्तु सम्पूर्णहृदयो न फलं नाम वाञ्छति ।
तस्य विश्वाकृतिर्देवी सा चावच्छेदवर्जनात् ॥ १९९ ॥

yastu sampūrṇahṛdayo na phalaṁ nāma vāñchati /
tasya viśvākṛtirdevī sā cāvacchedavarjanāt //199//

But the one who is *sampūrṇa hṛdaya*, whose heart is complete, whose heart has become fully filled with completion, *na phalaṁ nāma vāñchati*, and who has no particular desire of attaining fruit, particular fruit, *tasya viśvākṛtir devī*, for him, this consciousness, this energy of consciousness, is *viśvākṛti*, is filled with the formation of universality. He can concentrate on anything and achieve this object of attaining I-consciousness, *sā cāvacchedavarjanāt*, because there is no *avaccheda*, there is no limitation of his achieving; because he has to achieve I-consciousness, and that I-consciousness he will achieve from any object. So this is the real way of meditation.

Now the real way of position (*mudrā*) he explains in the next *śloka*:

LJA TA04K (36:28)

कुले योगिन उद्रिक्तभैरवीयपरासवात् ।
घूर्णितस्य स्थितिर्देहे मुद्रा या काचिदेव सा ॥ २०० ॥

kule yogina udrikta-bhairavīyaparāsavāt /
ghūrṇitasya sthitirdehe mudrā yā kācideva sā //200//

Kule yogina, the one who is a yogi already existing in a body (*kule* means, the body; in a body he who is *yogina*, a yogi; although existing in a body, he is a yogi), ...*

JOHN: Yogi means here, he who has already achieved union or who is seeking union?

SWAMIJI: Yes, he who is united with God consciousness. A yogi is that person who is united with God consciousness for always.

*... *udrikta bhairavīya parāsavāt*, when the supreme liquor, the supreme wine of Bhairava has risen to the supreme limit, the supreme highest limit, extreme limit of this *āsava*, this wine, the *āsava* (wine) of Bhairava, the wine of the state of Bhairava, ...*

JOHN: This "wine" means? "Wine" refers to ...

SWAMIJI: Union in Bhairava.

*... one who is united with Bhairava and is fully *ghūrṇitasya*, is fully intoxicated (*ghūrṇi tasya*) ...

JOHN: With His wine.

SWAMIJI: ... with the wine of Bhairava, the consciousness of Bhairava, *sthitir dehe mudrā yā kācideva sā*, his mere remaining in the body is the real position of yoga. *Mudrā* is not some particular position of the body as it is said [to be] in *khecarī mudrā*, or *karaṅkiṇī mudrā*, *krodhanī mudrā*, *cakitā mudrā*.[329] All these *mudrās* are useless there. *Mudrā* is meant only [as the position of] just remaining in the body with this intoxication, the intoxication held with this wine of Bhairava, the wine of the Bhairava state. So, he can remain like this, he can walk, he can go, he can talk, he can go to a movie, this is [all a] *mudrā* for him. He is established in the real *mudrā*. The real *mudrā* is not meant that you go in seclusion and remain on Mondays in one *āsana* (in one position) for twenty-four hours. That is not *mudrā* in the real sense. *Mudrā*, in the real sense is, going for a walk, talking, reading, laughing; whatever he does in this body is a *mudrā* for him, is the real position of yoga for him. But the only important point is that the wine of Bhairava must be there, must be filled there, and he must get intoxicated by that.

But what is the sacrificial fire for him, for such a yogi?

---

329. For an explanation of these *mudrās*, see *Vijñāna Bhairava–The Manual for Self-Realization*, *Dhāraṇā* 54, verse 77, p. 146.

LJA TA04K (40:06)

अन्तरिन्धनसम्भारमनपेक्ष्यैव नित्यशः ।
जाज्वलीत्यखिलाक्षौघप्रसृतोग्रशिखः शिखी ॥२०१॥
बोधाग्नौ तादृशे भावा विशन्तस्तस्य सन्महः ।
उद्रेचयन्तो गच्छन्ति होमकर्मनिमित्तताम् ॥२०२॥

antarindhanasambhāram-anapekṣyaiva nityaśaḥ /
jājvalītyakhilākṣaugha-prasṛtograśikhaḥ śikhī //201//
bodhāgnau tādṛśe bhāvā viśantastasya sanmahaḥ /
udrecayanto gacchanti homakarmanimittatām //202//

Antar indhana sambhāram anapekṣyaiva, this fire of God consciousness is *nityaśaḥ jājvalīti*, always gets inflamed, always is inflamed,…

"Inflamed" is correct?

DEVOTEE: Yes, correct.

SWAMIJI: …inflamed, but without *antar indhana sambhāram anapekṣyaiva*, without collecting firewood, etcetera, all those things [used for] fuel. Without collecting those fuels, but this fire of God consciousness, *jājvalīti*, [is inflamed]. And how? *Akhilākṣaugha prasṛtogra śikhaḥ śikhī*, and this fire has come out from each and every opening of his senses (his senses of action and his senses of cognition). The cognitive senses and the senses of action, that is the opening of this fire. This flame comes out from those senses of this yogi.

Bodhāgnau tādṛśe bhāvā (verse 202), in such a fire of consciousness, *bhāvā viśantaḥ*, all the objective world gets entry, all the objective world enters in that supreme fire of God consciousness, and *tasya sanmahaḥ udrecayanto gacchanti homa karma nimittatām*, and they enlighten the fire of his being,…

DEVOTEE: Intensify.

SWAMIJI: …intensify the fire of his being, and hence they become, they take the position of, *homa karma* (*havana*). This is the real reality of a *havana* (fire sacrifice). This is not the reality of *havana* as we did previously – "*svāhā*, *svāhā*, *svāhā*" for the whole day. It is useless.

LJA TA04K (42:41)

यं कञ्चित्परमेशानशक्तिपातपवित्रितम् ।
पुरोभाव्य स्वयं तिष्ठेदुक्तवद्दीक्षितस्तु सः ॥२०३॥

yaṁ kañcitparameśāna-śaktipātapavitritam /
purobhāvya svayaṁ tiṣṭhed-uktavaddīkṣitastu saḥ //203//

Now he explains how he initiates people. He does not initiate people by putting that spiritual *mantra* in [their] ear (*karṇa dīkṣa*). It is not that. *Yaṁ kañcit parameśāna śaktipāta vicitritam purobhāvya*, *yaṁ kañcit*, anybody…it does not mean he must have only a Brahmin [to initiate, that] he must have…

LJA TA04K (43:29)

न मे प्रियश्चतुर्वेदो मद्भक्तः श्वपचोऽपि वा ।
तस्मै देयं ततो ग्राह्यं स च पूज्यो यथा ह्यहम् ॥

na me priyaścaturvedo madbhaktaḥ śvapaco'pi vā /
tasmai deyaṁ tato grāhyaṁ sa ca pūjyo yathā hyahaṁ //[330]

He says, "*Na me priyaścaturvedo*, I don't like that Brahmin who has read the four *Veda*s–I don't like him". These are the sayings of Lord Śiva. "*Na me priyaḥ caturvedo*, *madbhaktaḥ*, but the one who is My devotee, [even though] he is an outcaste (*śvapaco'pi vā*), *tasmai deyaṁ tato grāhyaṁ*, he must be initiated, and you must get initiation from that person! *Sa ca pūjyo hi yathāhyahaṁ*, he is adorable as I am adorable–to the same level! He must be adored to the same level as people adore Me, Lord Śiva." These are His words.

SCHOLAR: But no one has heard this in India.

330. *Kulārṇava Tantra* 12.27, cited by Jayaratha's in his commentary.

DEVOTEES: (laughter)

SWAMIJI: Huh?

JOHN: Where does this come from, these words you've just quoted? They come from what? Some Tantra obviously.

SWAMIJI: Yes, it is Tantra.

JOHN: Do you know which Tantra that is?

SCHOLAR: Any Tantra.

SWAMIJI: Any Tantra (laughs). Why should you think of these particular things?

SCHOLAR: Every Tantra has …

JOHN: Every Tantra says that.

DEVOTEE: It has happened, an outcaste initiating people.

SCHOLAR: Yes, it happens.

SWAMIJI: *Yaṁ kañcit parameśāna śaktipāta pavitritam*, because he is purified by the *śaktipāta* of Lord Śiva, …*

JOHN: This person who is established in …

SWAMIJI: An outcaste, yes, because he has devotion. If he has devotion, he is purified by the flow of *śaktipāta* (grace) in him.

*… *purobhāvyet*, let him be seated before you, *svayam tiṣṭhet*, and go in your internal God consciousness yourself. *Uktavad dīkṣitastu*, but that internal God consciousness [of the master] will enter in his consciousness and he will become one with the master.

JOHN: So this person, then, this is any person who has been filled with the grace of God.

SWAMIJI: Any person! If [he is] Brahmin also.

JOHN: Yes, Brahmin, Kṣatriya, Śūdra, Cāṇḍāla, anyone.

SWAMIJI: Brahmin also, Śūdra, and an outcaste also. Yes, anyone.

JOHN: As long as he is filled with the grace by God …

SWAMIJI: There is no distinction of caste, creed, and color there.

JOHN: So then that person who has that grace of God, he sits before the person who has God consciousness, and that person goes inside and that automatically fills that person.

SWAMIJI: Yes. How?

LJA TA04K (42:08)

Bhujaṅgavad-garala-saṁkrāmaḥ (comm.), as this cobra, a poisonous cobra, when you sit before a poisonous cobra, that poison will get entry in you and you'll become filled with that poison at once, just in a glance.[331]

SCHOLAR: But if this person is without awareness, nothing will happen to them.

SWAMIJI: Which person?

SCHOLAR: The person that is placed in front [of the master].

SWAMIJI: No! If he does not have awareness, that does not matter. He must have devotion. He must have devotion, *bas*. Awareness does not count there.

SCHOLAR: But devotion and awareness are not two separate things.

SWAMIJI: Awareness will come, awareness will get transformed in his brain at once. There must be devotion, unconditional devotion, not devotion to receive something.

LJA TA04K (46:43)

जप्यादौ होमपर्यन्ते यद्यप्येकैककर्मणि ।
उदेति रूढिः परमा तथापीत्थं निरूपितम् ॥२०४॥

japyādau homaparyante yadyapyekaikakarmaṇi /
udeti rūḍhiḥ paramā tathāpīttham nirūpitam //204//

But what was the need of explaining all these ways of entering God consciousness? There was only one way needed: only the real way of recitation, or the real way of meditation, or the real way of a *havana*, or the real way of *mudrā*. Only one could purify, one could make you enter in God consciousness. What was the need of explaining in these various ways? For that, he explains:

---

331. "This is just like seeing a cobra, not from distance, but face-to-face. When you see a cobra and it bites you, you will be filled with the poison of that cobra. In the same way, when you observe a yogi who is established in the joy of *samādhi* and you understand that he is experiencing the joy of this *samādhi*, you will at once also relish the joy of this *samādhi*." *Shiva Sutras–The Supreme Awakening*, 1.18, p. 58.

Japyādau homaparyante, beginning from the real recitation of *mantra* and ending in the real *havana* (*homa*), *yadyapyekaika karmaṇi udeti rūḍhiḥ paramā*, although this supreme state of God consciousness rises from each and every act (even from *japa*, even from *dhyāna* or any meditation, or *havana*), *tathāpi ittham nirūpitam*, but we have variously explained these things this way as follows:

LJA TA04K (48:18)

यथाहि तत्र तत्राश्वः समनिम्नोन्नतादिषु ।
चित्रे देशे वाह्यमानो यातीच्छामात्रकल्पिताम् ॥२०५॥

yathā hi tatra tatrāśvaḥ samanimnonnatādiṣu /
citre deśe vāhyamāno yātīcchāmātrakalpitām //205//

Just as the unyielding horse, the horse who is not yielding, who is . . .

DEVOTEE: Undisciplined

SWAMIJI: Undisciplined. Unyielding. All horses are unyielding at first. You have to give them this kind of training so that they become yielding.

DEVOTEE: Unbroken, it is called unbroken.

SWAMIJI: Unbroken. *Yathāhi*, just as, *tatra tatra samanimna unnatādiṣu*, when an unyielding horse is whipped to run, whipped to run on leveled grounds, depressed grounds (depressed low grounds), and raised high grounds (uneven grounds), is whipped to run, *yāt īcchāmātra kalpitām*, then he runs smoothly on roadsides also. Otherwise, he won't run smoothly on roadsides. You have to train him to go down, to jump up on high level grounds, and smooth grounds also, and then he becomes yielding, then he can run smoothly without throwing you down on the ground. In the same way:

LJA TA04K (49:59)

तथा संविद्विचित्राभिः शान्तघोरतरादिभिः ।
भङ्गीभिरभितो द्वैतं त्याजिता भैरवायते ॥२०६॥

tathā saṁvidvicitrābhiḥ śāntaghoratarādibhiḥ /
bhaṅgībhirabhito dvaitaṁ tyājitā bhairavāyate //206//

In the same way, your consciousness is to be trained in each and every way of God consciousness. You have to train your God consciousness in *dhyāna* (meditation), you have to train your God consciousness in *japa*, in all these things, then your God consciousness will survive in each and every act of your daily life. This is the way.

Another example:

LJA TA04K (50:34)

यथा पुरःस्थे मुकुरे निजं वक्त्रं विभावयन् ।
भूयो भूयस्तदेकात्म वक्त्रं वेत्ति निजात्मनः ॥२०७॥

yathā puraḥsthe mukure nijaṁ vaktraṁ vibhāvayan /
bhūyo bhūyastadekātma vaktraṁ vetti nijātmanaḥ //207//

When you keep your mirror in front of you and you see your face, the reflection of your face in that mirror, once you have seen your reflection of your face in your mirror, that was all [there was to see]. Why do you [continue to] see it again and again? Why do you see it like this (Swamiji demonstrates)?

DEVOTEES: (laughter)

SWAMIJI: You see in each and every corner [for] understanding your face. You see like this (Swamiji demonstrates).

DEVOTEES: (laughter)

SWAMIJI: *Bhūyo bhūyaḥ tadekātma vaktraṁ vetti nijātmanaḥ*…this won't come in the tape, this won't be recorded.

DEVOTEES: (laughter)

SWAMIJI: *Bhūyo bhūyaḥ tadekātma vetti nijātmanaḥ*, but he always sees, he observes his face in each and every way. So, this is the way of understanding God consciousness. You have to understand God consciousness in each and every way!

LJA TA04K (51:39)

तथा विकल्पमुकुरे ध्यानपूजार्चनात्मनि ।
आत्मानं भैरवं पश्यन्नचिरात्तन्मयीभवेत् ॥ २०८ ॥

tathā vikalpamukure dhyānapūjārcanātmani /
ātmānaṁ bhairavaṁ paśyann-acirāttanmayībhavet //208//

In the same way, *vikalpa mukure*, in the mirror of your consciousness, you will feel when you observe God consciousness in *dhyāna*, when you observe your God consciousness in worship, and all *mudrā*, etcetera, meditation, *acirāt tanmayo bhavet*, you become one with God consciousness for eternity.

LJA TA04K (52:14)

तन्मयीभवनं नाम प्राप्तिः सानुत्तरात्मनि ।

tanmayībhavanaṁ nāma prāptiḥ sānuttarātmani /

Tanmayī bhava, becoming united with God consciousness is to realize the state of the highest transcendental Being.

पूर्णत्वस्य परा काष्ठा सेत्यत्र न फलान्तरम् ॥ २०९ ॥

pūrṇatvasya parā kāṣṭhā setyatra na phalāntaram //209//

This is the supreme state of fulfillment. There is no other fruit. Only this fruit comes there.

फलं सर्वमपूर्णत्वे तत्र तत्र प्रकल्पितम् ।
अकल्पिते हि पूर्णत्वे फलमन्यत्किमुच्यताम् ॥२१०॥

phalaṁ sarvamapūrṇatve tatra tatra prakalpitam /
akalpite hi pūrṇatve phalamanyatkimucyatām //210//

This particular fruit comes only from a particular way of thinking, a particular way of meditation. When you adopt a particular way meditation, a particular way of fruit will come to you. When you adopt every way of meditation, no fruit will come to you, only one fruit, that is, God consciousness. That is the real state of the reality of God consciousness.

LJA TA04K (53:57)

एष यागविधिः कोऽपि कस्यापि हृदि वर्तते ।
यस्य प्रसीदेच्चिच्चक्रं द्रागपश्चिमजन्मनः ॥२११॥

eṣa yāgavidhiḥ ko'pi kasyapi hṛdi vartate /
yasya prasīdecciccakraṁ drāgapaścimajanmanaḥ //211//

This way of worship (*eṣa yāgavidhiḥ*; *yāga* means there, worship), this way of worship is a unique way (*ko'pi*), and this way is observed and digested by some unique soul. Whom? *Yasya prasīdet cit cakram drāk apaścima janmanaḥ*, to whom this wheel of consciousness is *prasīdet*, has become clear (*prasīdet* (*prasādo*) *nirmalī bhāva*, whose wheel of consciousness has become clear), …*

JOHN: The "wheel of consciousness" means?

SWAMIJI: The wheel of consciousness.

JOHN: Twelve Kālīs.

SWAMIJI: All the the twelve Kālīs are the wheel of consciousness.

*…and it has become clear, not in a successive way, [but] *drāk*, in an instant, instantaneously. Because when it is clear perfectly, it is clear instantaneously. It does not become clear successively. Successively it is never clarified.

JOHN: So then the movement is up to one point, then (snap) at that one point clarity comes.

SWAMIJI: Only in one instant, in one instant it is cleared. In two instants it is not cleared.

SCHOLAR: There is only the appearance of succession, *akramākramam* there, in this rise of the twelve Kālīs.

SWAMIJI: It is appearance, is not succession.

SCHOLAR: It is not real succession, not disjunction.

SWAMIJI: It is why all the states are called *anākhya cakra*. And *apaścima janmanaḥ*, it is cleared only to that person who has not the following of rebirths, repeated births and deaths.

DEVOTEE: *Drāk*…?

SWAMIJI: *Drāk* means, instantaneously. *Apaścima janmanaḥ* means, he who has no following…

JOHN: Who is not going to have any more.

SWAMIJI: …any more rebirths and re-deaths.

LJA TA04K (55:53)

अत्र यागे गतो रूढिं कैवल्यमधिगच्छति ।
लोकैरालोक्यमानो हि देहबन्धविधौ स्थितः ॥२१२॥

atra yāge gato rūḍhiṁ kaivalyamadhigacchati /
lokairālokyamāno hi dehabandhavidhau sthitaḥ //212//

In this supreme state of worship, the one who is established fully (*gato rūḍhim*) absolutely attains the real liberation, the real supreme liberation. *Lokair ālokyamāno*, though by other people he is observed as entangled in the daily way of worldly life – he does gardening, he does everything, he quarrels, he fights, he is angry, he is sad, he is sick, he is hale, he goes to a doctor. Although people see him in this position, but he is perfectly liberated.

JOHN: How do you translate "*kaivalyam*", I mean, from the Śaivite…?

SWAMIJI: *Kaivalyam* is "perfect liberation"; *kaivalyam* is "perfect liberation". *Adhigacchati*, he attains that perfect liberation.

JOHN: It means, absolute oneness?

SWAMIJI: Absolute oneness in that supreme God consciousness.

SCHOLAR: No second.

JOHN: No second.

SWAMIJI: *Bas.*

LJA TA04K (57:15)

अत्र नाथः समाचारं पटलेऽष्टादशेऽभ्यधात् ।

atra nāthaḥ samācāraṁ paṭale'ṣṭādaśe'bhyadhāt /

In this state, he who has reached this highest state, Lord Śiva has explained his way of doing and thinking in the eighteenth chapter of the *Mālinīvijaya Tantra*–how he thinks, how he acts.

JOHN: For this person. But this person is established in *śāktopāya.*

SWAMIJI: Yes, he is established in *śāktopāya*, and he will now say how he thinks, how he observes, what is pure for him, what is impure for him, what is good for him, what is bad for him.

JOHN: So this is not just *śāktopāya*, this is also *śāmbhavopāya*. I mean, this is completion, so it is not limited to *śāktopāya*. This is not *śāktopāya* completion.

SWAMIJI: Yes, complete *śāktopāya* means, *śāmbhavopāya.*

SCHOLAR: Like complete *āṇavopāya* means the same?

SWAMIJI: And complete *āṇavopāya* means, *śāmbhavopāya.*

SCHOLAR: *Śāmbhavāvasthā.*

SWAMIJI: Yes, *śāmbhavāvasthā.*[332] *Nātra śuddhirna cāśuddhir*, there is no pure, there is no impure. Now it is to be explained–*atra*, *atra* (now).

JOHN: So there is no *samāveśa* (absorption) except for *śāmbhava samāveśa*. Is that true? I mean, really, in the real sense?

SWAMIJI: Yes.

LJA TA04K (58:44) end
LJA TA04L (00:00) start

332. The state (*avasthā*) of Śiva (*śāmbhava*).

In this connection, Lord Śiva has explained the rules and regulations of this kind of *sādhaka* in the eighteenth chapter of the *Mālinīvijaya Tantra*. That [paragraph] of the eighteenth chapter he reads first, then he will give its commentary. These *śloka*s are from that book, from the *Mālinīvijaya Tantra*.[333] These are not his own.

नात्र शुद्धिर्न चाशुद्धिर्न भक्ष्यादिविचारणम् ॥२१३॥
न द्वैतं नापि चाद्वैतं लिङ्गपूजादिकं न च ।
न चापि तत्परित्यागो निष्परिग्रहतापि वा ॥२१४॥
सपरिग्रहता वापि जटाभस्मादिसङ्ग्रहः ।
तत्त्यागो न व्रतादीनां चरणाचरणं च यत् ॥२१५॥
क्षेत्रादिसम्प्रवेशश्च समयादिप्रपालनम् ।
परस्वरूपलिङ्गादि नामगोत्रादिकं च यत् ॥२१६॥
नास्मिन्विधीयते किञ्चिन्न चापि प्रतिषिध्यते ।
विहितं सर्वमेवात्र प्रतिषिद्धमथापि च ॥२१७॥
किं त्वेतदत्र देवेशि नियमेन विधीयते ।
तत्त्वे चेतः स्थिरीकार्यं सुप्रसन्नेन योगिना ॥२१८॥
तच्च यस्य यथैव स्यात्स तथैव समाचरेत् ।
तत्त्वे निश्चलचित्तस्तु भुञ्जानो विषयानपि ॥२१९॥
न संस्पृश्येत दोषैः स पद्मपत्रमिवाम्भसा ।

333. The following verses on *vidhi* (rules and regulations) are from *Mālinīvijaya Tantra* 18.74–82.

विषापहारिमन्त्रादिसन्नद्धो भक्षयन्नपि ॥२२०॥
विषं न मुह्यते तेन तद्वद्योगी महामतिः ।

nātra śuddhirna cāśuddhirna bhakṣyādivicāraṇam //213//
na dvaitaṁ nāpi cādvaitaṁ liṅgapūjādikaṁ na ca /
na cāpi tatparityāgo niṣparigrahatāpi vā //214//
saparigrahatā vāpi jaṭābhasmādisaṅgrahaḥ /
tattyāgo na vratādīnāṁ caraṇācaraṇaṁ ca yat //215//
kṣetrādisampraveśaśca samayādiprapālanam /
parasvarūpaliṅgādi nāmagotrādikaṁ ca yat //216//
nāsminvidhīyate kiñcinna cāpi pratiṣidhyate /
vihitaṁ sarvamevātra pratiṣiddhamathāpi ca //217//
kiṁ tvetadatra deveśi niyamena vidhīyate /
tattve cetaḥ sthirīkāryaṁ suprasannena yoginā //218//
tacca yasya yathaiva syātsa tathaiva samācaret /
tattve niścalacittastu bhuñjāno viṣayānapi //219//
na saṁspṛśyeta doṣaiḥ sa padmapatramivāmbhasā /
viṣāpahārimantrādi-sannaddho bhakṣayannapi //220//
viṣaṁ na muhyate tena tadvadyogī mahāmatiḥ /

This is the end of this chapter from the *Mālinīvijaya Tantra*. Now my explanation, then Abhinavagupta's explanation on these *śloka*s will be explained.

Nātra śuddhir na cāśuddhiḥ, in this state, in this stage, when you achieve this topmost stage, there, there is nothing pure nor impure–*na ca śuddhir na ca aśuddhiḥ. Na bhakṣyādi vicāraṇam*, there is nothing eatable or not eatable; you can eat anything, you can avoid eating anything; you can avoid eating that which is not proper, you can eat that which is not proper. *Na ca bhakṣyādi vicāraṇam*, this kind of distinction does not take place there. *Na dvaitaṁ nāpi cādvaitaṁ* (verse 214), this is not a monistic way of being (this is not a monistic way), nor this is a dualistic way. Because when you say, "This is the monistic thought of our system", then the dualistic thought is excluded. Nothing is excluded, nothing is included. *Liṅga pūjādikaṁ na ca*, when you adore this idol worship, idol worship also you may do or you may not do, there is no restriction for that. *Na cāpi tat parityāga*, to abandon idol worship, worshiping those idols altogether, is not explained there. You can do idol worship, you can not do idol worship. Whatever you like, you can do (*na cāpi tatparityāgo*). *Niṣparigrahatāpi vā*[334], or idol worship, if you do idol worship daily in the morning of Lord Śiva's *liṅga*, when you have time you should worship that *liṅga*, when you have no time you should not worship, you should not die for that worshipping [of] that *liṅga*. That is *niṣparigrahatā*. *Niṣparigrahatā*, that, "I have to do this and then I will do other things of my daily routine of life." You should not be a victim to that idol worship.

DENISE: Mandatory.

SWAMIJI: Yes.

LJA TA04L (04:54)

Saparigrahatā vāpi jaṭābhasmādi saṅgraha (verse 215), or *saparigrahatā*. *Saparigrahatā* means, [acceptance]. There are two words related in the *Mālinīvijaya Tantra*: *niṣparigrahatā* and *saparigrahatā*. *Niṣparigrahatā* means, totally given to that worship, you can't live without worshipping that idol of Lord Śiva, you will die for that if you have not worshipped him. *Saparigrahatā* means, side-by-side: on the sidelines you can worship, on the sidelines you cannot worship, you may not worship, it does not matter. *Jaṭābhasmādi saṅgrahaḥ*, you can keep *jaṭā* (long hair) or you can apply that ash, what those Śaivites do in South [India]. They apply those ashes on their face, on arms, on legs, on body, or grow those *jaṭā*s (matted hair) on their heads. You can do that if you like [or] you may not do that. It is not necessary ...

SCHOLAR: It is not the point.

SWAMIJI: It is not the point, it is not the point to be understood. *Tattyāgo na vratādīnāṁ caraṇācaraṇam ca yat*, observing fasts or abandoning observing fasts, it is one and the same thing. You may observe fasts, you may not observe fasts, what then? *Kṣetrādi sampraveśaśca* (verse 216), now, entering in sacred shrines is said in Śaivism, in Southern Śaivism, in dualistic Śaivism, that entering in sacred shrines, taking a dip in a bath there in the spring, purifies your

334. Or non-acceptance.

mind, body and soul. But that is not the point. You may enter in that shrine, not bathe at all, and come back [home]. You may enter a shrine, not do any worship to Kheer Bhāvanī[335], and return [home]. What then? It is all the same for such a yogi.

Para svarūpa liṅgādi nāmagotrādikaṁ ca yat, and this point is also discussed in Śaivism that your name must be nominated by your master only and from your own order, not from other orders of Śaivites. *Para svarūpa*, not *para svarūpa* and not *para liṅga*; *svasvarūpa* and *svaliṅga*, your name should be [given] by your master from your own order, not from other orders of this thought. And the *liṅga* (*liṅga* means, clothes), for instance, ...

SCHOLAR: *Veṣābharaṇādi*

SWAMIJI: *Veṣābharaṇa*.

JOHN: What does that mean? Certain apparel, certain ways of beads and *mala*s, etcetera, etcetera.

SWAMIJI: *Pheren*[336] or beads and all, yes. That also you should do according to *your* orders. But this, too, is not necessary for such a yogi. You can do from other orders also [or] you can not do at all. You can wear pants and a sweater and a hat and a bush shirt, that is all.

Nāsmin vidhīyate kiñcit na cāpi pratiṣidhyate (verse 217), in this state of realization, there is nothing right, nothing wrong, nothing is to be done, nothing is to be abandoned. *Vihitam sarvamevātra*, everything is allowed. Whatever you do, that is allowed. *Prati-ṣiddham*, whatever you do [can be] discarded; you may own these signs of a *sādhaka* or you may disown these signs, it does not matter. Only one thing matters here in this state: *kiṁ tvedatra deveśi niyamena vidhīyate* (verse 218), this is an absolute *niyama*, this is a rule. What is that rule? *Tattve cetaḥ sthirīkāryaṁ*, you have to fix your mind on that supreme state of God consciousness. Fix your mind on that supreme state of God consciousness, and that fixing [of your] mind may occur by making love with a woman, or going to the cinema (going to the pictures), or doing meditation in a secluded corner. If it happens, if this one-pointedness occurs by that action, do that action. That action is necessary! You should take

335. A temple in Srinagar dedicated to the goddess, Kheer Bhavanī, which sits atop a sacred spring.

336. A traditional Kashmiri gown or overcoat.

that action by which action your mind will be focused on that supreme state of God consciousness. This is necessary. Absolute truth.

LJA TA04L (10:32)

Suprasannena yoginā, tat ca yasya yathaiva syāt, and that one-pointedness is observed in any way; in which[ever] way this one-pointedness is attained, you should do that, you should tread on that way. *Tattve niścala cittastu*, when your mind is absolutely established in that God consciousness, in the center of that God consciousness, *bhuñjāno viṣayānapi*, although you eat poisons also, …*

SCHOLAR: *Viṣayāna*.

SWAMIJI: This is poisonous, these are all poisonous things for *sādhaka*s: the *viṣaya*s (*śabda*, *sparśa*, *rūpa*, *rasa*, and *gandha*). Because by concentrating on those songs (*śabda*), by concentrating on *sparśa* (touch), by *rūpa* (forms), by *rasa* (taste), by *gandha* (smell), your attention is diverted from that God consciousness towards the outward objective world. So it is a poisonous thing.

*… but the one who has focused his mind in that God consciousness, it does not matter to him, he can enjoy the five senses absolutely. *Na spṛśyeta doṣaiḥ sa* (verse 220), all those defects that come out, that creep, that leak out, from enjoying these five senses, they do not appear to him, because *padma-patramivām bhasā*, he is just like a lotus in water, just like a lotus leaf in mud – that mud does not touch that lotus leaf. *Viṣāpahāri mantrādi sannaddho bhakṣayannapi viṣaṁ na muhyate*, when, for instance, there is a poison, there is a jug of poison, and by eating that poison one dies simultaneously, at once, instantaneously, and when you *abhimantra* (*abhimantra* means, when you purify that poison by some sacred *mantra*s that are described in all Tantras, in the *Svacchanda Tantra* mainly), *viṣayāpahāri mantrādi sannaddhaḥ*, that *viṣam*, *bhakṣayannapi*, although you take that poison, *na muhyate*, that poison won't affect you at all. In the same way, this yogi who has reached that topmost point of God consciousness, to him nothing happens, no wrong, no bad affect comes in appearance by enjoying these five senses. Here ends the chapter of the *Mālinīvijaya Tantra*.

LJA TA04L (14:11)

Etacca bahukṣodakṣamatvena vaiṣamyāt svayameva vyācaṣṭe (comm.), but Abhinavagupta commentates [upon] this himself in his verses, word-by-word. Because *bahukṣodakṣamatvena*, there may be some misunderstanding also in understanding what it really means. These words have come out from the lips of Lord Śiva, and so they must be commented upon properly, in the true sense, and that commentary is done by Abhinavagupta in the true sense for these words. Now there is the first word, "*nātra śuddhir na cāśuddhiḥ*, there is nothing pure and nothing impure." Now he commentates [upon] that word first:

LJA TA04L (14:59)

अशुद्धं हि कथं नाम देहाद्यं पाञ्चभौतिकम् ॥२२१॥

aśuddhaṁ hi kathaṁ nāma dehādyaṁ pāñcabhautikam //221//

For instance, take when a man dies. If you keep that body in warm weather, in hot weather for two hours, a dead body, what will happen to that?

SCHOLAR: It swells and smells, it gets dirty.

SWAMIJI: The dirtiest thing, it will appear to you the dirtiest thing possible in this world. But that dirtiest thing is *deha*, your body. Actually it is dirty. But is it impure? How can it be impure? *Aśuddhaṁ hi kathaṁ nāma dehādyaṁ pāñcabhautikam*, this *deha* (this body), which is made by five elements, how can it be impure? How can you call it impure? Because *prakā-*… he gives the cause:

LJA TA04L (16:03)

प्रकाशतातिरिक्ते किं शुध्यशुद्धी हि वस्तुनः ।

prakāśatātirikte kiṁ śuddhyaśuddhī hi vastunaḥ /

Vastunaḥ śuddhyaśuddhī, purity and impurity of something – for instance, this body – purity and impurity of this body, is this purity and impurity of the body separate from God consciousness? Is it separated from God consciousness? If it is separated from God consciousness, then it is impure. If it is not separated, if this body is not separated from the state of God consciousness, how can it be impure? How can you call it impure? If it smells bad, what then? You can't say it is impure because it is existing in the state of God consciousness. Because *vastunaḥ śuddhyaśuddhī*, the purity and impurity, the conception of pureness and impureness of something, is not *prakāśatā atirikte*, is not separate from God consciousness. If it is not separate from God consciousness, how can it be impure? So this body is absolutely pure if it is dead or alive.

SCHOLAR: It's neither pure nor impure.

SWAMIJI: In other words, it is neither pure nor impure.

SCHOLAR: It just appears.

SWAMIJI: Now you want to purify your body. Because it is impure, you purify it with water, with incense, with scents, with perfume, with soap, with hot water, with a tub-bath, you do all these arrangements to purify this body.

LJA TA04L (18:05)

अशुद्धस्य च भावस्य शुद्धिः स्यात्तादृशैव किम् ॥२२२॥
अन्योन्याश्रयवैयर्थ्यानवस्था इत्थमत्र हि ।

aśuddhasya ca bhāvasya śuddhiḥ syāttādṛśaiva kim //222//
anyonyāśrayavaiyarthyā-navasthā itthamatra hi /

If this *bhāva*, this body, is impure, it is not pure, and you have to make it pure by perfumes, by tub-baths, by all these things, but this body is made of five elements (earth, water, fire, *vāyu*, and *ākāśa*, these five elements), do you mean that this [body] will be purified with these very elements in other forms? Because you are going to purify this body with the same element, the same water, the same perfume of earth. Perfume has come out from earth, soap has come out from earth. So you want to purify earth with the same earth. Is it not madness (laughter)? This is absolutely madness! *Aśuddhasya ca bhāvasya śuddhiḥ syāt tādṛśaiva kim*, if your notion is that it will be purified by the same element in another formation, then *anyonyāśraya* and *vaiyarthya* and *anavasthā*, these defects are creeping in there. *Anyonyāśrya* means, you will help me and I will help you–it is *anyonyāśraya* (mutual dependence). And *vaiyarthya* is …

SCHOLAR: Redundancy, pointlessness.

SWAMIJI: … pointlessness, there is no fun in it; *vaiyarthya* means, without any *artha*, without any object.[337] And *anavasthā*, *anavasthā* is…

SCHOLAR: Infinite regress.

SWAMIJI: … if you want to purify this body with water, what substance will purify this water first? You have to purify the water first, then. If you purify this water with heat, you'll warm it, what substance will purify this heat/fire? You have to search for another object for purifying. So this will be *anavasthā*. *Anavasthā* means, this will be a defect in a chain[-like form].

JOHN: Never ceasing.

SWAMIJI: Never cease.

SCHOLAR: Infinite regress.

SWAMIJI: Infinite regress. Infinite regress is *anavasthā*.

DEVOTEE: Infinite…?

SCHOLAR: … regress.

SWAMIJI: Infinite regress. And these three kinds of defects he explains now in the next *śloka*–Abhinavagupta.

LJA TA04L (21:22)

पृथिवी जलतः शुद्ध्येज्जलं धरणितस्तथा ॥२२३॥
अन्योन्याश्रयता सेयमशुद्धत्वेऽप्ययं क्रमः ।

pṛthivī jalataḥ śuddhyet-jalaṁ dharaṇitastathā //223//
anyonyāśrayatā seyam-aśuddhatve'pyayaṁ kramaḥ /

If *pṛthivī* (this earth) will get purified by water, if earth is purified by water, and *jalaṁ dharaṇita*, and water is purified by earth, if water

337. That is, without any purpose or aim.

is purified by earth and earth is purified by water, this is *anyonyāśraya*, this is mutual dependence, this is a defect. This logic is incorrect, this logic won't stand. So this is not the reality of getting purified. So *pṛthivī* cannot be purified by water and water cannot be purified by *pṛthivī* (by earth). This logic is incorrect logic–*aśuddhatve'pyayaṁ kramaḥ*. For instance:

LJA TA04L (22:21)

अशुद्धाज्जलतः शुध्येद्धरेति व्यर्थता भवेत् ॥२२४॥

aśuddhājjalataḥ śuddhyed-dhareti vyarthatā bhavet //224//
(not recited)

Aśuddhāt jalataḥ śuddhyet dharā, when you say that, "No, not pure, pure things are not needed; you can purify *pṛthivī*, you can purify some element of earth, with the impure element of water, it does not matter", it is *vyarthatā*.[338] If *pṛthivī* was already impure, water is already impure, and you want to purify this earth (this impure earth) with impure water, why not let the earth remain as impure as it was before? This is useless, this is a useless struggle to purify the impure thing with an impure [thing]. It is already impure. Let it be purified, let you conceive, let you perceive that this is already pure [although] it is impure. If an impure thing is pure, if an impure thing gets purity by an impure thing, why not let it remain as impure? It will be pure. This is logic. So this is *vyarthatā*, there creeps that *vyarthatā*. *Vyarthatā* means…what do you call *vyarthatā*?

SCHOLAR: Pointlessness, or without object, reasoning without purpose.

SWAMIJI: Object, yes.

338. Without any logical purpose.

LJA TA04L (24:02)

वायुतो वारिणो वायोस्तेजसस्तस्य वान्यतः ।

vāyuto vāriṇo vāyos-tejasastasya vānyataḥ /

Water will be purified by *vāyu* (air), *vāriṇo vāyu*, by water *vāyu* will be purified, *tejas*, and *teja* (fire) will be purified by *vāyu*, this is all a useless struggle for getting purified. So, in fact, there is nothing pure, nothing impure. Purity and impurity is all bogus, it is only the imagination of a man.

Now there is another section:

LJA TA04L (24:48)

बहुरूपादिका मन्त्राः पावनात्तेषु शुद्धता ॥२२५॥

bahurūpādikā mantrāḥ pāvanātteṣu śuddhatā //225//

"No, this is not the way of purifying", if you say, "This is not the way of purifying an impure thing", ...*

For instance, this body is impure, you want to get it purified, not by *jala*, water won't purify it, because water is also impure, and *agni* is also impure. So these elements won't purify this body. But what else is there that will purify this body? That is *mantra*.

*"... the *mantric* tradition of our Śaivism will purify it – by *mantra*s. If you recite *mantra*s, and this body will be touched by the hands while reciting *mantra*s, then it will get purified. By the *bahurūpa mantra*, by the *praṇava mantra*, by the *sauḥ mantra*, by the *piṇḍanātha mantra*, all these *mantra*s will purify because they are pure, they are actually pure. Those *mantra*s are actually pure, so these *mantra*s will purify this body." If you say that, this is also another point:

LJA TA04L (26:08)

मन्त्राः स्वभावतः शुद्धा यदि तेऽपि न किं तथा ।

mantrāḥ svabhāvataḥ śuddhā yadi te'pi na kiṁ tathā /

Who has purified these *mantras*? I want to know how you have come to this point that *mantra*s are pure and the body is impure. Who has purified *mantra*s and who has kept this body as impure? "*Svabhāvataḥ śuddhā*, this is the nature of *mantras*!" The answer for that question is, "The nature of *mantra*s is they are pure, and the nature of the body is that it is impure." If this is nature, if *mantra*s have the nature of being pure, *yadi te'pi na kiṁ tathā*, why the body is not also pure by nature? Who has concluded, who has come to this conclusion that *mantra*s are pure by nature and the body is impure by nature? Who has concluded it? How have you come to this conclusion?

SCHOLAR: That there is purity and impurity in the nature of things.

SWAMIJI: Why should you not agree that the body is also pure? Now the answer to this objection is:

LJA TA04L (27:25)

शिवात्मता तेषु शुद्धिर्यदि तत्रापि सा न किम् ॥२२६॥

śivātmatā teṣu śuddhir-yadi tatrāpi sā na kim //226//

"*Śivātmatā teṣu śuddhi*, no, *mantra*s have got the touch of God consciousness, *mantra*s have got the touch of God consciousness, whereas the body has not the touch of God consciousness, so the body is impure and the *mantra*s are pure." This is the answer for this question – *śivātmatā teṣu śuddhiḥ. Yadi tatrāpi sā na kim*, [but] who has inserted *śivātmatā* in *mantra*s and who has not inserted *śivātmatā* in the body? Will you tell me that? How has *śivātmatā* come to exist in *mantra*s and *śivātmatā* is not existing in the body? *Śivātmatā* means, the state of God consciousness. If the state of God consciousness is found in *mantra*s and the state of God consciousness is absent in the body, who has told you that? It is your own imagination. You say that *mantra*s are pure because there is, "*oṁ naphar hrīṁ*", "*oṁ namaḥ śivāya*", "*oṁ jai guru deva*", these words are pure, and "bloody fool", "rascal", and these words are impure. Who has told that?

DENISE: My mother.

DEVOTEES: (laughter)

SWAMIJI: "Bloody fool" and "rascal" are also in the same level if you get real entry in that state of God consciousness.

Śivātmatva-... now he again puts an objection for this point:

LJA TA04L (29:09)

शिवात्मत्वापरिज्ञानं न मन्त्रेषु धरादिवत् ।
ते तेन शुद्धा इति चेत्तज्ज्ञप्तिस्तर्हि शुद्धता ॥२२७॥

śivātmatvāparijñānaṁ na mantreṣu dharādivat /
te tena śuddhā iti cet-tajjñaptistarhi śuddhatā //227//

"*Śivātmatva*, no, I do not say that God consciousness is not existing in the body and God consciousness is existing in *mantra*s – I don't say that!" If you say this point, if you tell me that, "God consciousness is not existing in the body, and God consciousness is existing in *mantra*s, I don't say that, I say only this point that God consciousness is already existing in the body and in the same way in *mantra*s also – God consciousness – but recognizing God consciousness, the recognizing way of God consciousness, is not existing in the body, whereas in *mantra*s it is existing, so this is the point that [*mantra*] purifies this body."

Have you understood it? *Śivātmatva aparijñānaṁ*.

SCHOLAR: Non-recognition.

SWAMIJI: Non-recognition of God consciousness, the non-recognition of God consciousness is in the body, and the recognition of God consciousness is in *mantra*s, but God consciousness is existing in both ways, in both of these things. God consciousness is existing, but recognition is absent there. Where?

DENISE: In body.

SWAMIJI: In body, and in *mantra*s, the recognition is existing. So this is the important point in *mantras* that they purify this body–*śivātmatva aparijñānaṁ na mantreṣu dharādivat.*

Te tena śuddhā iti cet, if you say that, "By that recognition of God consciousness, they have become purified", then you must come to this conclusion that recognizing God consciousness is the purifier of everybody. If you recognize really/fully God consciousness, then everything is pure.

SCHOLAR: And if you don't, everything is impure.

SWAMIJI: If you don't, and if you take a full bath with mud, with water, with incense, soap, and wash your clothes with your own hands, don't give it to the washerman, and be purified in one corner, don't touch anybody, and *śivātmatā*, the recognition of God consciousness is not there, [then] you are absolutely the dirtiest fellow in this world. If God consciousness is there and you have the dirtiest clothes around your body, you are the purest person in this world! This is what the real thing exists in this system. *Tat jñaptistarhi śuddhatā*, then knowledge is *śuddhatā*; when you recognize that God consciousness, that is the purifier, that will purify.

Bas, this much we will do today.

In the previous *śloka* he has decided that, if the knowledge of God consciousness exists everywhere for a realized soul, then nothing is pure and nothing is impure–everything is pure.

LJA TA04L (33:17)

योगिनं प्रति सा चास्ति भावेष्विति विशुद्धता ।

yoginaṁ prati sā cāsti bhāveṣviti viśuddhatā /

Sā, the knowledge of God consciousness, for yogis, is found in the objective world also, so this objective world is also pure for him. For a yogi, the objective world is also pure because he observes God consciousness in the objective world also, not only in *mantras*.

Now he objects:

LJA TA04L (33:59)

ननु चोदनया शुध्यशुध्यादिकविनिश्चयः ॥ २२८॥

nanu codanayā śuddhya-śuddhyādikaviniścayaḥ //228//

The objection is: by the directing or inciting of *sāstras* (*codana*, the direction of *śāstras*, e.g., this is pure and this is impure, this you should do, this you should eat, this you should not eat),…

SCHOLAR: *Vidhi.*

SWAMIJI: *Vidhi.*

…this *codana* (inciting order) of the *śāstras*, by those inciting orders of *śāstras*, a firm conviction of impurity and purity exists. How do you say that impurity and purity does not exist? *Śāstras* say like that, that "This is pure" and "This is impure" – this is the order of *śāstra*. For instance:

LJA TA04L (34:52)

ऊर्ध्वं नाभेर्यानि खानि तानि मेध्यानि सर्वशः ।
यान्यधःस्थान्यमेध्यानि देहाच्चैव मलाश्च्युताः ॥

ūrdhvaṁ nābheryāni khāni tāni medhyāni sarvaśaḥ /
yānyadhaḥsthānyamedhyāni dehāccaiva malāścyutāḥ //[339]
(not recited in full)

Those limbs which are above the navel – in the body, those limbs which are above the navel – they are considered to be pure, and below the navel, all limbs are impure, always. This is the inciting order of the *śāstras*.

SCHOLAR: This is Manu, huh?[340]

SWAMIJI: This is Manu, yes. Manu was the …

339. Jayaratha cites *Manusmṛti* 5.132.

340. The author of India's original code of law, the *Manusmṛti*.

JOHN: … chief order-giver.
SWAMIJI: Yes.

LJA TA04L (35:24)

इत्थमस्तु तथाप्येषा चोदनैव शिवोदिता ।

itthamastu tathāpyeṣā codanaiva śivoditā / 229a

Let it be like that. [Although] Manu has said like that, that "This is pure" and "This is impure", but this *codana* (this inciting order) from Lord Śiva has come out like this that, "There is nothing pure and nothing impure." This is also an inciting order of Lord Śiva. If that is the inciting order of Manu, this is the inciting order of Lord Śiva that nothing is pure and nothing is impure, or everything is pure!

DENISE: Who was Manu?

SWAMIJI: Manu was the originator of rules and regulations of religion.

DENISE: He was a man?

SWAMIJI: Yes, a *ṛṣi* (seer).

LJA TA04L (36:12)

का स्यात्सतीति चेदेतदन्यत्र प्रवितानितम् ॥२२९॥

kā syātsatīti cedetad-anyatra pravitānitam //229//

Now, which inciting order is genuine? You can't distinguish that, you can't say that, that this is genuine, [that] the inciting order of Manu is genuine and the inciting order of Lord Śiva is not genuine – you can't say that. This is the inciting order of Śiva that everything is pure. You can't object in this respect.

JOHN: So Śiva has the preference in this, precedence in this case, or not? Are they on equal setting?

SWAMIJI: Now will see, we'll come to a conclusion.

LJA TA04L (37:03)

वेदवर्त्मानुवर्ती च प्रायेण सकलो जनः ।

vedavartmānuvartī ca prāyeṇa sakalo janaḥ /[341]

In fact, we have come to this conclusion that everybody acts according to the directions of the *Veda*s. So, whatever is other than the *Veda*, it is absurd. This is the objection.

SCHOLAR: A trick, *vañcanaiva.*

SWAMIJI: Yes. This is only a useless order. Only the order of the *Veda*s is genuine. This is what *vādi* (Vedāntins) says.

SCHOLAR: Mīmāṁsāka.

SWAMIJI: Other orders are only deceit.

वेदबाह्यस्तु यः कश्चिदागमो वञ्चनैव सा ।

vedabāhyastu yaḥ kaścid-āgamo vañcanaiva sā //

That *āgama*, that Śaivism, is only *vañcana*, only deceit, nothing comes out of it, there is nothing real [in it].

LJA TA04L (38:02)

वैदिक्या बाधितेयं चेद्विपरीतं न किं भवेत्

vaidikyā bādhiteyaṁ ced-viparītaṁ na kiṁ bhavet /

If you say that the order of the *Veda*s have subsided the order of Lord Śiva, why not say that the order of Lord Śiva will subside the order of the *Veda*s? Why not say on the contrary? If you say, "The *Veda*s

341. This verse of unknown origin is cited in Jayaratha's commentary.

have subsided the other orders", [then] I will say to that, "The orders of Śaivism has subsided all other orders." So you can't come to any conclusion in this respect. Now, if you believe that the operation [of refuting] takes place on both sides, [then]:

LJA TA04L (38:43)

सम्यक्चेन्मन्यसे बाधो विशिष्टविषयत्वतः ॥२३०॥
अपवादेन कर्तव्यः सामान्यविहिते विधौ ।

samyakcenmanyase bādho viśiṣṭaviṣayatvataḥ //230//
apavādena kartavyaḥ sāmānyavihite vidhau /

If you believe that the operation [of refuting] takes place on both sides in sameness, then you will have to come to this conclusion that the special rule [refutes] the general rule. For instance, there is a general rule [that Jayaratha] will say just now:

LJA TA04L (39:20)

चमसेनापः प्रणयेत् ।
गोदोहनेन पशुकामस्य प्रणयेत् ।
अष्टाश्रिर्यूपो भवति ।
वाजपेयस्य चतुरश्रः ।

camasenāpaḥ praṇayet /
godohanena paśukāmasya praṇayet /
aṣṭāśriryūpo bhavati /
vājapeyasya caturaśraḥ /

The water in a sacrificial fire must be kept in *camasa pātra*, a vessel used for drinking *soma rasa*. There is a special vessel made for taking *soma rasa* in that ritual fire. And it is ordered by the *Veda*s that in that *camasa pātra*, that special vessel, you must put water in that special vessel and purify that water in a special vessel, not in other vessels. This is a general order of the *Veda*s.

Godohanena paśukāmasya praṇayet, and that is [refuted] by this special rule. That was a general rule that you should purify water [in that special vessel]. *Godohanena paśukāmasya praṇayet*, but those who want to raise the number of cows in their houses, for those people, they should put water in that sacrificial fire in *godoha pātra*, a milk pail, you know, in which milk is kept. That you must wash and put water and purify water in that, in that sacrificial fire.

JOHN: For this particular…if you want to have cows.

SWAMIJI: This is special. That special rule has subsided the general rule.

DEVOTEE: *Paśu kāmasya praṇayet*?

SWAMIJI: *Paśu kāmasya*, that [person] who wants to raise the number of cows in his house. Again, there is [another] general rule and a special rule. The general rule is:

LJA TA04L (41:14)

Aṣṭāśriryūpo bhavati, in that sacrificial fire, you fix a post and that post must be *aṣṭāśrir*, with eight sides; an eight-sided posts must be fixed in that sacrificial fire. This is a general rule in the *Veda*s. And the special rule is: *vājapeyasya caturaśraḥ*, when a special *vājapeya* sort of sacrificial fire is produced, then you have to fix a post, only a four-sided post.

JOHN: What kind of fire is this?

SWAMIJI: This is *vājapeya yajña*. This is a *yajña* adopted in the *Veda*s. Generally you keep only eight-sided posts in each and every *havana*, in each and every *yajña*, but this *vājapeya yajña* is special, so for that *vājapeya yajña* you have to put only a four-sided post. So this general way, general rule, has been subsided by this special rule.

JOHN: There's no translation for this *vājapeya*.

SWAMIJI: No, *vājapeya* is the name of that *yajña*.[342] So, now we have come to this conclusion…the next *śloka*:

---

342. The drink of strength or of battle.

LJA TA04L (42:40)

शुध्यशुद्धी च सामान्यविहिते तत्त्वबोधिनि ॥२३१॥
पुंसि ते बाधिते एव तथा चात्रेति वर्णितम् ।

śuddhyaśuddhī ca sāmānya-vihite tattvabodhini //231//
puṁsi te bādhite eva tathā cātreti varṇitam /

So we have come to this conclusion that arranging order for purity and impurity is described in a general way of the *Vedas*. "This is pure" and "This is impure", this arranging order is described in the *Vedas* in a general way. But *tattva bodhinī puṁsi*, when you have realized God consciousness everywhere, then for that realized one, this directing order [of the *Vedas*] is suppressed by the special way of Śaivism. So, "This is pure" and "This is impure", this is a general rule of the *Vedas*, and this general rule is suppressed by the special rule of Śaivism.

SCHOLAR: It becomes a particular rule in relation to the Śaivite rule.

SWAMIJI: Yes. *Tathā cātreti varṇitam*, so this is already described in the *Mālinīvijaya Tantra*: *nātra śuddhir na cāśuddhiḥ*, there is no question of purity and impurity in the real sense.[343]

Again, another *śloka*:

LJA TA04L (43:58)

मृच्छैलधातुरत्नादिभवं लिङ्गं न पूजयेत् ।
यजेदाध्यात्मिकं लिङ्गं यत्र लीनं चराचरम् ॥

mṛcchailadhāturatnādi-bhavaṁ liṅgaṁ na pūjayet /
yajedādhyātmikaṁ liṅgaṁ yatra līnaṁ carācaram //[344]

343. See verse 213.

344. Jayaratha quotes *Mālinīvijaya Tantra* 18.2cd-3ab.

So one who is fully realized in the state of God consciousness should not worship an idol (*liṅgam*) made from earth, made from stone, or made from gold or silver, etcetera. He should not worship that idol. He should worship the internal idol, which pervades the whole universe. That idol should be worshipped, not these idols.[345] So, this is a general rule that you should worship an idol made from earth, stone, or gold, or silver, etcetera. This is a general rule. And a special rule is that you should not worship those idols, you should worship the internal idol. The internal idol, that is transcendental God consciousness, you should worship that. This is a special rule which has subsided that rule.

Now there is a doubt:

LJA TA04L (45:12)

नार्थवादादिशङ्का च वाक्ये माहेश्वरे भवेत् ॥२३२॥

nārthavādādiśaṅkā ca vākye māheśvare bhavet //232//

Why not say that it is *arthavāda*? There are two classes of orders. One is *arthavāda*, one is *vidhivāda*.[346] *Vidhi* is a general rule, e.g., that you should observe purity of body and mind. "You should observe purity of body and mind", this is *vidhivākya*. "The person who does not observe purity of body and the mind will be directed to hell, will be sentenced to hell, without any doubt", this rule is *arthavāda*, this rule is not real, this is just to make you follow the rule. *Arthavāda* has no basis, no correct basis. *Arthavāda* is also explained and put forth in the *Veda*s–*arthavāda*. You see, "If you serve your master, you will go to heaven. You must serve your master." This is *vidhivākya*. "If you don't serve your master, you will just ruin yourself", this is *arthavāda*. This is not correct. You won't ruin [yourself].

SCHOLAR: These are like scarecrows.

---

345. See commentary for verse 256.

346. The explanation of the meaning of any precept (*arthavāda*) and the precept itself (*vidhivāda*). *Arthavāda* is a statement that encourages or discourages a certain action in relation to *vidhivāda* (a particular rule).

SWAMIJI: Yes.
SCHOLAR: *Bāla vibhīṣikāḥ.*
SWAMIJI: *Bāla vibhīṣikāḥ.*[347] Now the next:

LJA TA04L (46:45)

अबुद्धिपूर्वं हि तथा संस्थिते सततं भवेत् ।
व्योमादिरूपे निगमे शङ्का मिथ्यार्थतां प्रति ॥२३३॥

abuddhipūrvaṁ hi tathā saṁsthite satataṁ bhavet /
vyomādirūpe nigame śaṅkā mithyārthatāṁ prati //233//

This apprehension of *arthavāda* rises only in the shallow teachings of the *Veda*s. Really, these teachings of the *Veda*s are shallow. You know "shallow"? Without any substance in it.

JOHN: Superficial.

SWAMIJI: Superficial, without any substance in it. The teachings of the *Veda*s are absolutely shallow teachings. It is why he has said, "*vyomādirūpe nigame*", it is *vyoma* (*vyoma* means, consisting of no substance there). And it is *abuddhi pūrvaṁ*, the ruling of the *Veda*s is meant only for those who are ignorant, not for those realized persons.

DEVOTEE: *Abuddhi pūrvam*?

SWAMIJI: *Abuddhi pūrvam.*

SCHOLAR: *Daṇḍa pūrvam.*

SWAMIJI: *Daṇḍa pūrvam*, yes.

JOHN: *Abuddhi pūrvaṁ* means, non-aware, people who have no awareness?

SWAMIJI: No awareness, no intellect.

SCHOLAR: These statements don't come about through awareness, but simply because they are there, like a stick (*daṇḍa*).

---

347. "These ways, established in the Tantras, are just for diverting ignorant boys from bad actions. You terrify these boys by saying that, 'If you do such and such actions, there is a ghost, he will eat you just now. Don't do this action.' This is *bāla vibhīṣikāḥ*." *Vijñāna Bhairava–The Manual for Self-Realization*, verse 13.

SWAMIJI: Yes. *Śaṅkā mithyārthatāṁ prati*, so there is doubt, there is possibility of the rise of doubt in the *Veda*s, but in Śaivism there is no possibility of the rise of doubts.

JOHN: Can I ask a question? This special rule that there is nothing pure and impure for that person who is in God consciousness, which overrules that specific general rule that there is purity and impurity, how does that affect those *sādhaka*s of Śaivism who aren't in God consciousness?

SWAMIJI: Who are not in God consciousness. But they must know the ending point. They must not become the victim of these small things on the path. On the path they should know that, "This is not the path. We have to reach that point where there is nothing pure and nothing impure."

SCHOLAR: So they only accept those rules which are given by their master for the realization of that point.

SWAMIJI: Yes, for the realization.

SCHOLAR: Otherwise, they are moving on some other path.

SWAMIJI: Yes.

LJA TA04L (48:55)

अनवच्छिन्नविज्ञानवैश्वरूप्यसुनिर्भरः ।
शास्त्रात्मना स्थितो देवो मिथ्यात्वं क्वापि नार्हति ॥२३४॥

anavacchinnavijñāna-vaiśvarūpyasunirbharaḥ /
śāstrātmanā sthito devo mithyātvaṁ kvāpi nārhati //234//

And on the contrary, in Śaivism, Lord Śiva has become the embodiment of the *śāstras*. *Anavacchinna*, it is in a chain, just like a chain[348], [in that] *vijñāna vaiśvarūpya sunirbharaḥ deva*, Lord Śiva has become the embodiment of *śāstra*s (*śāstrātmanā sthito devaḥ*), *mithyātvaṁ kvāpi nārhati*, who is universally complete in true transcendental knowledge. So the question of *arthavāda* does not arise there. There is

348. Lit., uninterrupted.

no *arthavāda*, it is only pure *vidhivākya* in Śaivism. In the *Vedas*, there are two ways of orders: one is *vidhi* and the other is *arthavāda*. But in Śaivism, there is only *vidhi* (direct order).

JOHN: What is this idea of a "chain" here? That he is the embodiment of the *śāstras* coming out?

SWAMIJI: Yes, the *śāstras* are the body of Lord Śiva. He is the embodiment of the *śāstras*, he has become the *śāstras* (*śāstrātmanā sthito deva*; *śāstra* means those *śāstras* of Śaivism).[349]

SCHOLAR: So, the actual words say that he is overflowing with the universality of unbroken awareness.

SWAMIJI: Yes. *Vaiśva rūpya sunirbharaḥ*.

LJA TA04L (50:30)

इच्छावान्भावरूपेण यथा तिष्ठासुरीश्वरः ।
तत्स्वरूपाभिधानेन तिष्ठासुः स तथा स्थितः ॥२३५॥

icchāvānbhāvarūpeṇa yathā tiṣṭhāsurīśvaraḥ /
tatsvarūpābhidhānena tiṣṭhāsuḥ sa tathā sthitaḥ //235//

Just as Lord Śiva has taken the formation of the objective world by his supreme independent will (*icchāvān*, by his supreme independent will, *īśvaraḥ*, Lord Śiva, has taken *bhāva rūpeṇa tiṣṭhāsu*, has taken the formation of the objective world), just as he has taken the formation of the objective world (that is, *prameya*), in the same way, he has taken the formation of the cognitive world (*pramāṇa* also), that is, *śāstra*. In the same way, just to explain the objective world, he has taken the formation of *vācaka jagat* (*vācaka jagat* is the world of sound, that is, the *śāstras*).

---

349. Therefore, Lord Śiva and His scriptures do not merit (*nārhati*) the accusation of falsehood (*mithyatvaṁ*) in any case (*kvāpi*).

LJA TA04L (51:26)

अर्थवादोऽपि यत्रान्यविध्यादिमुखमीक्षते ।
तत्रास्त्वसत्यः स्वातन्त्र्ये स एव तु विधायकः ॥२३६॥

arthavādo'pi yatrānya-vidhyādimukhamīkṣate /
tatrāstvasatyaḥ svātantrye sa eva tu vidhāyakaḥ //236//

Where the *arthavāda* consisting of praises and blaming exists for strengthening the directing orders of the *Veda*s...this is just to strengthen the order of the *Veda*s–this *arthavāda*. *Arthavāda* is meant just to strengthen the order of the *Veda*s. "You should serve your elders", this is a *vidhivākya* of the *Veda*s. "If you don't serve your elders, you will only ruin yourself", this is *arthavāda*. You won't actually ruin yourself, but this *arthavāda* is meant to strengthen...

DENISE: Enforce.

SWAMIJI: Yes.

SCHOLAR: So, *arthavāda* is also there in statements like, "He who desires heaven should sacrifice." That *svargakāma*[350] section is also *arthavāda*.

SWAMIJI: Yes, that is *arthavāda*.

SCHOLAR: *Yajyet* (worship) is *vidhivāda*.

SWAMIJI: *Yajyet* is *vidhivāda*.

SCHOLAR: But in Śaivism it says that in practice...

SWAMIJI: [In Śaivism] there is only *vidhivāda*, there is only *vidhi*, there is no *arthavāda*.

SCHOLAR: There is no limited *arthavāda*, only universal.

SWAMIJI: Yes. As this *arthavāda* exists only on the background of independent *vidhi*...for instance:

350. For those desirous of heaven.

बर्हिषि रजतं न देयम् ।

barhiṣi rajataṁ na deyam (commentary)

This is *vidhivākya*: "You must not throw silver on that grass, *kuśā* grass, in the sacrificial fire." When a sacrificial fire is adopted, this *kuśā* grass is also laid down in some special way. In some special way, *kuśā* grass is also laid down for purifying *mantra*s, and on [those] *kuśā* grass blades, you must not throw any coin of silver. This is *vidhivākya*. Now, for that the *arthavāda* is:

LJA TA04L (53:32)

शोऽरोदीद्यदरोदीत् तद्रुद्रस्य रुद्रत्वम् ।

so'rodīdyadarodīt tadrudrasya rudratvam (commentary)

He wept. Because he wept, then he was nominated as a Rudra. He wept. Rudra, when he appeared in this world, at that moment of appearing, he wept, he bitterly wept. As he wept, so he was nominated as Rudra (*rudra* means, he who weeps). He was called, he was nominated as, Rudra.

Now this is another *vidhivākya*:

बर्हिषि यो रजतं ददाति पुरास्य संवत्सराद्गृहे रोदनं भवति ।

barhiṣi yo rajataṁ dadāti purāsya saṁvatsarādgṛhe rodanaṁ bhavati (commentary)

So, on that *kuśā* grass, if you put, if you place, that silver, silver coin on that, then after one year or so, in his house there will be weeping. Weeping will begin in his house. So there will be some death, it means there will be some death after a year or so in his house. So you should not put silver on this grass because…another *arthavāda*:

LJA TA04L (55:03)

रुद्रो रुरोद तस्य यदस्रु अशीर्यत तद्रजतमभवत् ।

rudro ruroda tasya yad asru aśīryata tadrajatamabhavat
(commentary)

When Rudra wept–Rudra had wept in the beginning when he appeared in this universe–when he had wept, *tasya yad asru aśīryata*, those tears which fell from his eyes, they became silver. So, silver must not be put on this *kuśā* grass. If you put silver on *kuśā* grass, after a year or so there will be weeping in your house. So this is *arthavāda* and *vidhivākya* both. So it has no sense.

LJA TA04L (55:50)

विधिवाक्यान्तरे गच्छन्नङ्गभावमथापि वा ।
न निरर्थक एवायं सन्निधेर्गजडादिवत् ॥२३७॥

vidhivākyāntare gacchann-aṅgabhāvamathāpi vā /
na nirarthaka evāyaṁ sannidhergajaḍādivat //237//

So *ayaṁ*, this *arthavāda*, *vidhivākyāntare gacchann aṅga bhāvam*, if [it] has become the part and parcel of *vidhivākya* (*arthavāda* has become the part and the parcel of *vidhivākya* as we have already explained), *na nirarthaka*, this has some sense, this *arthavāda* has some sense there, because *sannidher gajaḍādivat*, but it will give another sense, not the sense you mean. For instance, '*ga*', '*ja*', and '*ḍa*', these three letters, '*ga*', '*ja*', and '*ḍa*'. If you put '*ga*' and '*ja*' [together], it means, *gaja* (elephant). If you put '*ja*' and '*ḍa*' [together], it means, *jaḍa* (without any consciousness, unconscious). So this will give some sense, but not to the point. So *arthavāda* gives some sense there in *vidhivākya*, but it is not to the point.

LJA TA04L (57:00)

स्वार्थप्रत्यायनं चास्य स्वसंवित्त्यैव भासते ।
तदपह्नवनं कर्तुं शक्यं विधिनिषेधयोः ॥२३८॥

svārthapratyāyanaṁ cāsya svasaṁvittyaiva bhāsate /
tadapahnavanaṁ kartuṁ śakyaṁ vidhiniṣedhayoḥ //238//

Arthavāda produces the confidence of its object by one's own experience. If one rejects this *arthavāda* forcibly, then you have to reject *vidhivāda* also. So there in the *Vedas*, *arthavāda* is essential, *arthavāda* must be there, because [otherwise] you can't understand then why we should not put silver on grass. *Arthavāda* will explain this, what is the background of this [directing order]. The background of this is, Rudra wept, when he wept and his tears became silver. So silver must not be put on *kuśā* grass, [otherwise] there will be weeping (laughs) within one year or so.

LJA TA04L (58:07)

युक्तश्चात्रास्ति वाक्येषु स्वसंविच्चाप्यबाधिता ।
या समग्रार्थमाणिक्यतत्त्वनिश्चयकारिणी ॥२३९॥

yuktiścātrāsti vākyeṣu svasaṁviccāpyabādhitā /
yā samagrārthamāṇikya-tattvaniścayakāriṇī //239//

Now there is *yukti* in our *vākya*s, in our *vidhivākya*; in the directing orders of Śaivism, there is *yukti*, there is sense. And not only sense, *svasaṁvit cāpyabādhitā*, your own experience also is there. This is filled with experience and sense, *yā samagrārtha māṇikya tattva niścayakāriṇī*, which will decide what is real and what is not real. For instance…next:

LJA TA04L (58:58)

मृतदेहेऽथ देहोत्थे या चाशुद्धिः प्रकीर्तिता ।

mṛtadehe'tha dehotthe yā cāśuddhiḥ prakīrtitā /240a

Mṛtadehe, when in a dead body, a dead body is considered to be impure, or *dehotthe*, any substance which has come out from the living body (any substance, for instance, tears, for instance, this mucus, and perspiration, and spit), anything that has come out from a living body, that is considered to be impure. That is considered to be impure and the dead body is considered to be impure. *Mṛta dehe* and *dehotthe*, from the living body, what has come out from the living body, *yā cāśuddhiḥ prakīrtitā*, is said that it is impure.

LJA TA04L (1:00:06)

अन्यत्र नेति बुध्यन्तामशुद्धं संविदश्च्युतम् ॥२४०॥

anyatra neti buddhyantām-aśuddhaṁ saṁvidaścyutam //240//
(not recited)

Anyatra na, in other orders of Śaivism, you will see there is nothing pure and nothing impure. They say this dead body is also pure and the substance which has come out from the living body is also pure. Śaivism has said that. When you ignore God consciousness, everything is impure.

SCHOLAR: That is *mṛta deha*. That is *dehotthe*.

SWAMIJI: That is…

JOHN: Impurity comes out from the ignorance of God consciousness.

SWAMIJI: Yes.

LJA TA04L (1:00:42) end
LJA TA04M (00:00) start

So, *saṁvittādātmyam*…from our point of view:

संवित्तदात्म्यमापन्नं सर्वं शुद्धमतः स्थितम् ।

saṁvittādātmyamāpannaṁ sarvaṁ śuddhamataḥ sthitam /

This whole universe, it may be dead or it may be living, as long as it is true that this [universe] is one with God consciousness, it is absolutely pure! Everything is pure! Nothing is impure! You should come to this conclusion in the end.

LJA TA04M (00:30)

श्रीमद्वीरावलौ चोक्तं शुध्यशुद्धिनिरूपणे ॥ २४१ ॥

śrīmadvīrāvalau coktaṁ śuddhyaśuddhinirūpaṇe //241//

In the *Virāvala Tantra* also it is said in the chapter where purity and impurity are discussed, it is said there. What is said there?

सर्वेषां वाहको जीवो नास्ति किञ्चिदजीवकम् ।

sarveṣāṁ vāhako jīvo nāsti kiñcidajīvakam /242a

Sarveṣāṁ vāhaka jīva, the carrier of everything, all universality, the carrier of universality is *jīva*, is life. *Nāsti kiñcit ajīvakam*, nothing is without life. If you mean, there is a dead body, it is filled with germs – is it not filled with germs? – and those germs are moving in absolute consciousness, [then] where lies the question of impurity? That is also pure.

सर्वेषां वाहको जीवो नास्ति किञ्चिदजीवकम् ।
यत्किञ्चिज्जीवरहितमशुद्धं तद्विजानत ॥२४२॥

sarveṣāṁ vāhako jīvo nāsti kiñcidajīvakam /
yatkiñcijjīvarahitam-aśuddhaṁ tadvijānata //242//

Yatkiñcit jīva rahitam, whatever is away from *jīva*, away from life, that is impure. As long as it is true that the whole universe is filled with life, it is pure, absolutely pure, nothing is impure.

तस्माद्यत्संविदो नातिदूरे तच्छुद्धिमावहेत् ।

tasmādyatsaṁvido nātidūre tacchuddhimāvahet /

So, the conclusion of this subject is, whatever is *saṁvido nātidūre*, whatever is one with God consciousness is pure.

अविकल्पेन भावेन मुनयोऽपि तथाभवन् ॥२४३॥

avikalpena bhāvena munayo'pi tathābhavan //243//

In ancient times, those *ṛṣi*s (seers) and *muni*s (saints) also adopted this state of God consciousness without any doubt.

ऋषिभिर्भक्षितं पूर्वं गोमांसं च नरोद्भवम् ।

ṛṣibhirbhakṣitaṁ pūrvaṁ gomāṁsaṁ ca narodbhavam /[351]

---

351. A verse from the *Manusmṛti* quoted by Jayaratha's in his commentary.

Those *ṛṣi*s had eaten the flesh of cows, the flesh of men, and all other disgusting things. [That] which from our point of view are disgusting things, they took that without any doubt because they knew that God consciousness is everywhere.

LJA TA04M (03:21)

न चर्या भोगतः प्रोक्ता या ख्याता भीमरूपिणी ।
स्वचित्तप्रत्यवेक्षातः स्थिरं किं वा चलं मनः ॥

na caryā bhogataḥ proktā yā khyātā bhīmarūpiṇī /
svacittapratyavekṣātaḥ sthiraṁ kiṁ vā calaṁ manaḥ //[352]

This *caryā*, this act of Śaivism, is not described for taste, it is described just to understand and analyze your situation of God consciousness, if your God consciousness is exactly existing in your brain. If it is exactly existing, then there will be no doubt in taking anything absurd.

LJA TA04M (03:55)

लोकसंरक्षणार्थं तु तत्तत्त्वं तैः प्रगोपितम् ।

lokasaṁrakṣaṇārthaṁ tu tattattvaṁ taiḥ pragopitam /244a

Generally it is said for those highly elevated souls:

यद्द्रव्यं लोकविद्विष्टं यच्च शास्त्रबहिष्कृतम् ।
यज्जुगुप्स्यं च निन्द्यं च वीरैराहार्यमेव तत् ॥

352. *Śrī Hevajra Mahātantrarājā*, chapter 2, verse 22, quoted by Jayaratha here and in the 29th *āhnika*, commentary for verse 102.

yaddravyaṁ lokavidviṣṭaṁ yacca śāstrabahiṣkṛtam /
yajjugupsyaṁ ca nindyaṁ ca vīrairāhāryameva tat //[353]
(not recited)

Yaddravyaṁ lokavidviṣṭam, that thing which is prohibited from all sides, from all orders, and *yat ca śāstra bahiṣkṛtam*, which is discarded by *śāstra*s, *yat jugupsyam*, which is absolutely *jugupsa* (*jugupsa* means, an absurd thing), *nindyaṁ*, and what is not praised by anybody, that you should perform, that way of religion you should perform–the realized soul.

DEVOTEE: Defy everything.

SWAMIJI: Yes.

JOHN: For the person in the highest…

SWAMIJI: Highest level, yes. But *lokasaṁrakṣaṇārtham tu tattattvaṁ taiḥ pragopitam*, but that secret of truth they have concealed in the public. They have kept it a secret to themselves only. Because just to give life to the rules and regulations of worldly people, they have not exposed that elevated thought to people.

JOHN: So this teaching even is a secret teaching, then, is it?

SWAMIJI: This teaching is a secret teaching.

LJA TA04M (05:26)

बहिः सत्स्वपि भावेषु शुध्यशुद्धी न नीलवत् ॥ २४४ ॥
प्रमातृधर्म एवायं चिदैक्यानैक्यवेदनात् ।

bahiḥ satsvapi bhāveṣu śuddhyaśuddhī na nīlavat //244//
pramātṛdharma evāyaṁ cidaikyānaikyavedanāt /

This differentiation of purity and impurity does not come from the objects. This differentiated perception, differentiated knowledge, of purity and impurity, that this is pure and this is impure, it does not come from the object itself.

353. A verse from an unknown source cited in Jayaratha's commentary for verse 243.

SCHOLAR: It is not externally existing like some color.

SWAMIJI: It is not externally existing in objects. Objects are not pure, objects are not impure, but we have perceived that way that this object is pure and this object is impure. Actually, *pramātṛ dharma evāyam*, this is the aspect of the handler of objects. This aspect, [that] this is pure and this is impure, this remains in the brain of the perceiver, not that [which is] perceived. That which is perceived, purity and impurity does not exist in that object. Purity and impurity, the perception of purity and impurity, exists in the brain of the perceiver. So if in the brain of an elevated perceiver, there is nothing right and nothing wrong, the objective world has nothing to do with that, the objective world is as good as it was before. We have injected this perception that this is pure and this is impure. When there is bread [given] from your hands, I'll perceive this is impure because it is from your hands. The bread has not told me, the bread has not declared that, "I am impure, don't take it!" Then who has declared?

DENISE: Your brain.

SWAMIJI: Your brain. So it is in your brain that this is pure and this is impure. So you must wash your brain from these misunderstood perceptions.

LJA TA04M (07:53)

यदि वा वस्तुधर्मोऽपि मात्रपेक्षानिबन्धनः ॥२४५॥
सौत्रामण्यां सुरा होतुः शुद्धान्यस्य विपर्ययः ।

yadi vā vastudharmo'pi mātrapekṣānibandhanaḥ //245//
sautrāmaṇyāṁ surā hotuḥ śuddhānyasya viparyayaḥ /

If this purity and impurity, the differentiation of purity and impurity, would be the aspect of the object, then…

There are two kinds of sacrifices: one is the Sautrāmaṇī sacrifice[354], one is another sacrifice (general sacrifices), when you offer these

354. A sacrifice in honor of Indra.

offerings in the fire. In Sautrāmaṇī (it is some special Sautrāmaṇī sacrifice), there you have to offer meat in the fire, there you have to offer whiskey in the fire, there you have to offer everything that is prohibited in the fire. And in other sacrifices, you have not to touch that [prohibited offering]. It is why it is said…

SCHOLAR: Sautrāmaṇī is a Vedic sacrifice.

SWAMIJI: Yes, it is a Vedic sacrifice. And *sautrāmaṇyam surām pibet*, it is essential that you have to drink wine before entering in the *yāga* (sacrifice) of Sautrāmaṇī, it is essential you have to take meat before entering in this *yāga* of Sautrāmaṇī. But it is prohibited in other sacrifices. So in the tradition of the *Veda*s also, one rule subsides another rule. One rule for the Sautrāmaṇī is separate, and other sacrifices are something else (there you have not to touch meat or whiskey or brandy). There, in the Sautrāmaṇī *yāga*:

शुराया अवघ्रणः कर्तव्यः ।

surāyā avaghrāṇaḥ kartavyaḥ (commentary)

You have not to taste it only, you have to smell it first with great reverence – in the Sautrāmaṇī *yāga*. What?

DENISE: The wine or whiskey.

SWAMIJI: The wine or whiskey.

LJA TA04M (10:10)

अनेन चोदनानां च स्ववाक्यैरपि बाधनम् ॥ २४६ ॥
क्वचित्सन्दर्शितं ब्रह्महत्याविधिनिषेधवत् ।

anena codanānāṁ ca svavākyairapi bādhanam //246//
kvacitsandarśitaṁ brahmā-hatyāvidhiniṣedhavat /

In this way, in these rules and the regulations of the *Veda*s also, in the body of the *Veda*s also, you find that some rules of the *Veda*s tell you that you should kill a Brahmin and offer the flesh of a Brahmin in a *havana*, in some particular *havana*:

ब्रह्मणो ब्रह्मण[मालभेत] ।

brahmaṇo brahmaṇa[*mālabheta*] (commentary)

And this is the action of a Brahmin. A Brahmin should kill a Brahmin to offer in that fire, a particular fire. It is in the *Veda*s. And in some *Veda*s:

ब्रह्मणो न हन्तव्यः ।

brahmaṇo na hantavyaḥ (commentary)

You must not injure in any way a Brahmin. A Brahmin must be respected all-around, it is said. So, in this body of the *Veda*s also, there are some rules and regulations which differ from each other. So there is nothing [substantial] in it in the real sense, it is all humbug, that this is to be done and this is not to be done.

Now, "*nātra śuddhir na ca aśuddhi*", that chapter of the *Mālinīvijaya* is over – the explanation of that stanza, "*nātra śuddhir na ca aśuddhi*, there is nothing pure, nothing impure."[355] "*Na bhakṣyādi vicāraṇam*" is next, the next word from the *Mālinīvijaya Tantra*:[356]

355. See verse 213 onwards.

356. "*Nātra śuddhir na cāśuddhir na bhakṣyādivicāraṇam*", *Mālinīvijaya Tantra*, 18.74.

LJA TA04M (11:59)

भक्ष्यादिविधयोऽप्येनं न्यायमाश्रित्य चर्चिताः ॥२४७॥

bhakṣyādividhayo'pyenaṁ nyāyamāśritya carcitāḥ //247//

This *bhakṣya* (food), what is to be eaten and what is not to be eaten, what is forbidden to take and what is not forbidden to take, in this way, [those] eatable things are also the same, they take the tradition of the same side, of the same thought. So there is nothing eatable, nothing not eatable. There is not a difference in eatable and not eatable. Pure things are eatable, impure things are not eatable from our point of view, but from [the realized soul's] point of view, you can eat anything.

LJA TA04M (12:51)

सर्वज्ञानोत्तरादौ च भाषते स्म महेश्वरः ।

sarvajñānottarādau ca bhāṣate sma maheśvaraḥ /

In the *Sarvajñāna Uttara Tantra* also, Maheśvara has explained the same thought. [Abhinavagupta] reads that chapter of the *Sarvajñānottara Tantra*:

नरर्षिदेवद्रुहिणविष्णुरुद्राद्युदीरितम् ॥२४८॥
उत्तरोत्तरवैशिष्ट्यात् पूर्वपूर्वप्रबाधकम् ।

nararṣidevadruhiṇa-viṣṇurudrādyudīritam //248//
uttarottaravaiśiṣṭyāt pūrvapūrvaprabādhakam /

That tradition which is fixed by ordinary human beings, that tradition which is fixed by *ṛṣi*s, that tradition which is fixed by *deva*s (gods), and that tradition which is fixed by Brahmā, Viṣṇu and Rudra, etcetera, *uttarottara vaiśiṣṭyāt pūrvapūrvaprabādhakam*, that [latter] tradition will subside [the former]. For instance, the tradition fixed by ordinary human beings will be subsided, suppressed, put down by the tradition of *ṛṣi*s, and the tradition of *ṛṣi*s will be suppressed by the tradition of the gods, and the tradition of the gods will be suppressed by the tradition of Brahmā, and the tradition of Brahmā will be suppressed by the tradition of Viṣṇu, and in the same way, the tradition of Viṣṇu will be subsided by the tradition fixed by Śiva.

SCHOLAR: Each one suppresses the preceding.

SWAMIJI: Yes. Because it is *uttarottara vaiśiṣṭyāt*, *viśiṣṭatā* (supremacy) lies in the latter, not in the former. For instance, the supreme way of tradition is of Lord Śiva, next to that is of Lord Viṣṇu, and Brahmā, and *devatā*, and *ṛṣi*s, and the human being. Why should we not suppress the *vākya* (sayings) of Śaivism by the *vākya* of Viṣṇu? What is the harm in that? To that he says:

LJA TA04M (15:11)

न शैवं वैष्णवैर्वाक्यैर्बाधनीयं कदाचन ॥२४९॥

na śaivaṁ vaiṣṇavairvākyair-bādhanīyaṁ kadācana //249//

The tradition fixed by Śaivites cannot be suppressed by the tradition fixed by Vaiṣṇavites.

वैष्णवं ब्रह्मसम्भूतैर्नेत्यादि परिचर्चयेत् ।

vaiṣṇavaṁ brahmasambhūtair-netyādi paricarcayet /
(not recited in full)

And the tradition of the Vaiṣṇavas cannot be suppressed by the tradition fixed by the followers of Brahmā. So, you should know this point also.

SCHOLAR: And the reason is that, from the point of view of human experience, that the level of *samādhi* attained is hierarchically graded as well.

SWAMIJI: Yes, that is quite true.
SCHOLAR: As explained before.
SWAMIJI:

LJA TA04M (15:59)

बाधते यो वैपरीत्यात्समूढः पापभाग्भवेत् ॥२५०॥

bādhate yo vaiparītyātsamūḍhaḥ pāpabhāgbhavet //250//

But the one who suppresses, on the contrary, for instance, he who suppresses the tradition of the Śaivites by the tradition of Viṣṇu (the Vaiṣṇavites), *sa mūḍhaḥ pāpa bhāgbhavet*, he is absolutely without a brain and he becomes the victim of sin. It is a sin to suppress the *vākya* of Śaivism by the *vākya* of the Vaiṣṇavites.
DEVOTEE: *Brahmasambhūta na vaiṣṇavaṁ.*
SWAMIJI: *Vaiṣṇavaṁ brahmasambhūtair na bādhanīyam.*

LJA TA04M (16:48)

तस्मान्मुख्यतया स्कन्द लोकधर्मान्न चाचरेत् ।

tasmānmukhyatayā skanda lokadharmānna cācaret /251a

"So, O Kumar" – this is the teaching taught by Lord Śiva to his son, Kumar – "O Kumar, *mukhyatayā*, in predominance, *lokadharmān na cācaret*, you must not go to in the depth of traditions. All traditions are baseless, they have no reality existing there."

LJA TA04M (17:26)

गर्भाधानादितः कृत्वा यावदुद्वाहमेव च ।
तावत्तु वैदिकं कर्म पश्चाच्छैवे ह्यनन्यभाक् ।
न मुख्यवृत्त्या वै स्कन्द लोकधर्मान्समाचरेत् ॥

garbhādānāditaḥ kṛtvā yāvadudvāhameva ca /
tavattu vaidikaṁ karma paścācchaive hyananyabhāk /
na mukhya vṛttyā vai skanda lokadharmānsamācaret //[357]
(not recited in full)

For instance, when you get birth, when you are born, from the time of your birth up to the time of your being married, all these traditions should be followed according to the *Veda*s. And after you are married, *paścāt śaive hi anya bhāk*, then you should get entry in Śaivism–after marriage. After marriage, all traditions are no traditions.

JOHN: Why do they make the distinction at that point–marriage? Why do they say here that the point of marriage is the point when you should shift?

SWAMIJI: Because marriage is also according to tradition, marriage also takes place according to tradition. In Śaivism, there is no marriage according to tradition. It is not said there, it is not told there [that] you should marry in a particular way.

SCHOLAR: Particular caste.

SWAMIJI: Particular caste, particular...along with these traditions. There you are free, you can marry with anybody. You have not to perform that *havana* that we perform at the time of marriage, or go to churches and take oaths [to] each other. There is no need of that in Śaivism. So these are rules and regulations of traditions up to marriage. When marriage is over, then you must get entry in Śaivism. So:

LJA TA04M (19:15)

अन्तः कौलो बहिः शैवो लोकाचारे तु वैदिकः ।
सारमादाय तिष्ठेत नारिकेलफलं यथा ॥

antaḥ kaulo bahiḥ śaivo lokācāre tu vaidikaḥ /
sāramādāya tiṣṭheta nārikelaphalaṁ yathā //[358]

357. A verse from an unknown source cited in Jayaratha's commentary.
358. A verse from an unknown source cited in Jayaratha's commentary.

Internally you should remain in the state of Śaivism (Kaula, Trika). *Bahiḥ śaiva*, externally you should remain as the follower of Lord Śiva, and when you are fixing the rules and regulations of the world, then you should become a Vaidika, then you should perform the traditions of the *Veda*s.

JOHN: This comes from where?

SWAMIJI: It is from our Tantras.

SCHOLAR: So, when he says "*bahiḥ śaiva*", he means, Śaiva in the sense of the form of rituals that are performed.

SWAMIJI: Rituals, yes. *Sāramādāya tiṣṭheta*, you must keep the essence, the real essence of Śaivism within yourself, you must not expose that to others, just like *nārikela phalaṁ yathā*, just like the coconut fruit–externally it is rough, internally it is filled with that juice of milk, sweet milk, and that sweet milk is Śaivism. External is that rough, that hairy substance, and that is Vedānta, those are traditions, rough traditions.

LJA TA04M (20:46)

नान्यशास्त्रसमुद्दिष्टं स्त्रोतस्युक्तं निजे चरेत् ॥२५१॥

nānyaśāstrasamuddiṣṭaṁ strotasyuktaṁ nije caret //251//

You must not mix the traditions of other traditions in your tradition. You must not mix other traditions in your own traditions. You must keep your tradition absolutely free from other traditions, the other mixture of traditions. Keep yourself absolutely free from all traditions.

JOHN: All traditions or other traditions?

SWAMIJI: Other traditions, all other traditions. [You should possess] only this tradition that [proclaims] there is no tradition. This is also one tradition. This is the supreme tradition that there is no tradition.

LJA TA04M (21:27)

यतो यद्यपि देवेन वेदाद्यपि निरूपितम् ।
तथापि किल सङ्कोचभावाभावविकल्पतः ॥२५२॥

yato yadyapi devena vedādyapi nirūpitam /
tathāpi kila saṅkoca-bhāvābhāvavikalpataḥ //252//

Although Lord Śiva has produced all these traditions, ...*

In fact, Lord Śiva is the producer of all these traditions–the tradition of the *Veda*s, the tradition of the Vaiṣṇavites, tradition of the Buddhists, all others.

*... because the chief producer of all these traditions is Lord Śiva, but these traditions have been put forth by Lord Śiva according to the ability of people. When he finds the ability of the people is absolutely elevated, he puts the tradition of Śaivism there. For those, he puts the tradition of Śaivism, which is no tradition.

LJA TA04M (22:26)

सङ्कोचतारतम्येन पाशवं ज्ञानमीरितम् ।
विकासतारतम्येन पतिज्ञानं तु बाधकम् ॥२५३॥

saṅkocatāratamyena pāśavaṁ jñānamīritam /
vikāsatāratamyena patijñānaṁ tu bādhakam //253//

By the succession of being shrunk by-and-by, in the succession of being shrunk, the shrinking succession, ...*

SCHOLAR: As one shrinks more and more, *pāśavaṁ jñānam*[359] emerges.

SWAMIJI: One is a shrinking succession, one is an expanding succession.

... for those who are treading on the path of shrinking succession, ...

For instance, "Oh, Denise has sat on my tablecloth–finished, my tablecloth is finished, I will have to wash it twenty times, then it will be purified." (laughs)

DEVOTEES: (laughter)

359. Beastly (or base) knowledge.

SWAMIJI: This is the tradition/path of being shrunk.

*… this tradition of this path is put forth by Lord Śiva for those who are shrunk already.

JOHN: And they become ever-more shrunk? Is this the idea? They become ever-more shrunk.

SWAMIJI: Huh?

JOHN: Through following this path, you become ever-more shrunk. Is that the idea?

SWAMIJI: Yes. By following [a shrunken path], you are always going [towards] shrinking and shrinking. This is the successive way of being shrunk.

JOHN: Shrinking *mokṣa*.

SWAMIJI: Shrinking. *Vikāsa tāratamyena patijñānaṁ tu bādhakam*, and the successive way of being expanded (in *vikāsa*), *patijñānam* (*patijñānam* means, the knowledge of *pati*[360]), the knowledge of Lord Śiva is put forth by Lord Śiva, which suppresses that shrinking way of succession.

Idaṁ dvaitam… now there is another word there in the *Mālinīvijaya Tantra*, that chapter: "*Na dvaitam nāpi cādvaitam*, there is nothing of duality, nothing of non-duality."

LJA TA04M (24:40)

इदं द्वैतमिदं नेति परस्परनिषेधतः ।
मायीयभेदक्लृप्तं तत्स्यादकाल्पनिके कथम् ॥ २५४ ॥

idaṁ dvaitamidaṁ neti parasparaniṣedhataḥ /
māyīyabhedaklṛptaṁ tat-syādakālpanike katham //254//

That which is un-artificial, that thought which is un-artificial, all-round un-artificial, in that thought, "This is the thought of dualism" [or] "This is the thought of monism", these things do not exist in that thought, because *māyīya bheda klṛptam*, [these ideas have] got life

360. The Lord.

from the illusive energy of Lord Śiva.

SCHOLAR: It is like *pāśava vedānta*, true and untrue.

SWAMIJI: *Pāśava vedānta*, yes.[361]

LJA TA04M (25:26)

उक्तं भर्गशिखायां च मृत्युकालकलादिकम् ।
द्वैताद्वैतविकल्पोत्थं ग्रसते कृतधीरिति ॥२५५॥

uktaṁ bhargaśikhāyāṁ ca mṛtyukālakalādikam /
dvaitādvaitavikalpotthaṁ grasate kṛtadhīriti //255//

Kṛtadhīr, the one whose intellect has become fully elevated (that is *kṛtadhī*, whose intellect has become fully elevated, that is, a Śaivite intellect), in the *Bhargaśikhā Śāstra* it is said that the possessor of that kind of intellect, *mṛtyu kālakalādikam*, death, the sphere of time, the sphere of actions, the sphere of dualism, the sphere of monistic thought, and all those traditions, *grasate*, he digests in his own nature, he dissolves. All these traditions are dissolved in that supreme intellectual being, supreme elevated intellectual being, because in the *Bhargaśikhā* it is said:

मृत्युं च कालं च कलाकलापं विकारजातं प्रतिपत्तिजालम् ।
ऐकात्म्यनानात्मवितर्कजातं तदा स सर्वं कवलीकरोति ॥

mṛtyuṁ ca kālaṁ ca kalākalāpaṁ vikārajātaṁ pratipattijālam /
aikātmyanānātmavitarkajātaṁ tadā sa sarvaṁ kavalīkaroti //[362]

361. Erroneous doctrine.

362. A verse from the *Bhargaśika Śāstra* cited in Jayaratha's commentary. See also *Shiva Sutras–The Supreme Awakening*, 1.6 commentary, p. 34.

At that point, when he comes to that point, when he achieves that supreme point of full elevation, then death, time, actions, and the changes of life, *pratipattijālam*, and differentiated perceptions, oneness and the absence of oneness, all are digested, all are dissolved in that state.

LJA TA04M (27:29)

Now, "*liṅga pūjādikaṁ ca na*"[363], this is explained now:

सिद्धान्ते लिङ्गपूजोक्ता विश्वाध्वमयताविदे ।
कुलादिषु निषिद्धासौ देहे विश्वात्मताविदे ॥२५६॥
इह सर्वात्मके कस्मात्तद्विधिप्रतिषेधने ।

siddhānte liṅgapūjoktā viśvādhvamayatāvide /
kulādiṣu niṣiddhāsau dehe viśvātmatāvide //256//
iha sarvātmake kasmāt-tadvidhipratiṣedhane /

Now *liṅga pūjā*, the worshipping of idols, idol worshipping. In Siddhāntamata[364], idol worshipping is said, idol worshipping is told, is said, to be performed.

SCHOLAR: Enjoined.

SWAMIJI: Yes. Why? *Viśvādhvamayatāvide*, that in this whole universe, everything can be an idol, can be Lord Śiva; *viśvādhva mayatāvide*, for knowing, for the knowledge that those idols are from this universe. Because it is universal, so that idol is universal. If you make an idol of stone, that [stone] is from this universe; if you make an idol from earth, that [earth] is from this universe.[365] So this idol worship is said in Siddhānta that it must be performed, that idol worshiping is

363. From the *Mālinīvijaya Tantra* as quoted previously in verse 214.

364. Dualistic Śaivism.

365. And is therefore one with Lord Śiva.

good. In the Kula *Śāstra* and the Kaula *Śāstra*, it is prohibited, that idol worshipping should not be done. Why? *Dehe viśvātmatāvide*, you must search [for] the right idol in your own body, you must search [for] the real idol which is existing in your own body, not in the universe. Don't go [looking for it] in the universe. See that [idol] in your own nature. So it is, in the Kaula *Śāstra*, it is prohibited–that idol worshipping.

Iha, in this Śaivism, in our Śaivism, [either path] is all-round best. *Kasmāt tat vidhi pratiṣedhane*, you may do [external] idol worshiping [or] you may do internal idol worshiping, well and good, everything is fine. In this Śaivism, everything is fine. You may do that, you may do this, you may do that, you may not do anything at all! Don't do idol worshipping, go and take rest for a full twenty-four hours, nothing will happen, it is all divine, because *sarvātmake*, it is *sarvātmaka*, it is universal, it is not only in the external universe and [that] in the internal body it is not existing, it is not so. *Kasmāt tat vidhi pratiṣedhane*, so there is no *vidhi* (injunction), no *niṣedha* (prohibition). In Siddhānta it is said:

LJA TA04M (30:33)

इष्टेन शिवलिङ्गेन विश्वं संतर्पितं भवेत् ।

iṣtena śivaliṅgena viśvaṁ saṁtarpitaṁ bhavet[366]

When you adopt the worship of an idol, idol worship, the whole universe is purified, the whole universe gets purification. This is said in the Siddhānta *Śāstra*. In Kaula *Śāstra* it is said:

यजेदाध्यात्मिकं लिङ्गं यत्र लीनं चराचरम् ॥

yajedādhyātmikaṁ liṅgaṁ yatra līnaṁ carāram //[367]

366. A verse from an unknown source cited in Jayaratha's commentary.

367. *Mālinīvijaya Tantra* 18.2cd-3ab, as quoted in the commentary for verse 231.

You must go and find out the internal idol that is living in the center of your heart, you must worship that (*yajet ādhyātmikaṁ liṅgam*), *yatra līnaṁ carācaram*, in which this whole universe exists.

SCHOLAR: *Atra liṅgaṁ sarvam iti liṅgam.*[368]

SWAMIJI: Yes.

LJA TA04M (31:17)

हृदयगुहागेहगतं सर्वज्ञं सर्वगं परित्यज्य ।
प्रणमति मितमतिरशिवं शिवाशयाश्मादिमश्लाघ्यम् ॥

hṛdayaguhāgehagataṁ sarvajñaṁ sarvagaṁ parityajya /
praṇamati mitamatiraśivaṁ śivāśayāśmādimaślāghyam //[369]

They have said this also: that *liṅga* which is situated in the cave of your heart, internal heart, that Śiva, that Śiva *liṅga*, who is omnipresent and all-pervading, leaving aside that worship, *mitamatir*, those who are ignorant people, they worship those external idols. They worship those external idols, which are already lifeless, they have no life. When you worship that [external] idol, it is lifeless, and *aślāghyam*, it is not worth worshipping. This is said by Kaulācāra.

Now, what is said by us? By us it is said, *na kvāpi gatvā*, you may go and perform [external] *liṅga* worship, you may go and perform the [worship of the] internal *liṅga* which is situated in the center of your heart, there is no difference in worshiping. He is [out] there also, he is inside also.

न क्वापि गत्वा हित्वा चा न किञ्चिदिदमेव ये ।
भव त्वद्धाम पश्यन्ति भव्यास्तेभ्यो नमो नमः ॥

---

368. Every idol resides in that internal idol.

369. A verse from an unknown source cited in Jayaratha's commentary.

na kvāpi gatvā hitvā cā na kiñcididameva ye[370] /
bhava tvaddhāma paśyanti bhavyāstebhyo namo namaḥ //[371]

They are actually fortunate people.

LJA TA04M (32:57)

नियमानुप्रवेशेन तादात्म्यप्रतिपत्तये ॥२५७॥
जटादि कौले त्यागोऽस्य सुखोपायोपदेशतः ।

niyamānupraveśena tādātmyapratipattaye //257//
jaṭādi kaule tyāgo'sya sukhopāyopadeśataḥ /

In some *śāstras* of Śaivism, it is said that you must perform the rules and regulations of the *śāstras*. That is, *ahiṁsā*, *satya*, *asteya*, *brahmacarya*, *aparigraha*, all these traditions you must perform just to get purification.

SCHOLAR: Moral rules – non-violence, not stealing, not hurting.

SWAMIJI: Moral rules, yes. *Niyamānu praveśena tādātmya pratipattaye*, because you get the ability for entering in that state of God consciousness then. So, just to avoid the attachment for the body, you have to [grow] *jaṭa*, you have to grow [matted] hair on your head, and you have to put *bhasma* (ashes) on your [body]. Those are also Śaivites. You have seen in Varanasi so many Śaivite *sadhus*. They have grown matted hair and they apply that [ash on their bodies]. It is just for attaining the non-attachment of the body. *Tat tyāgo asya sukhopāya-upadeśataḥ*, but in the Kaula *śāstra*, it is said, "No, these traditions should be totally avoided!" And in our Śaivism, you may do that or you may do nothing (laughs). You may grow hair on your head, well and good. You may shave it altogether, well and good. It is [such a] great thought.

---

370. Swamiji recites "*hi*" in place of the published "*ye*".

371. A verse from an unknown source cited in Jayaratha's commentary.

LJA TA04M (34:57)

व्रतचर्या च मन्त्रार्थतादात्म्यप्रतिपत्तये ॥२५८॥
तन्निषेधस्तु मन्त्रार्थसार्वात्म्यप्रतिपत्तये ।

vratacaryā ca mantrārtha-tādātmyapratipattaye //258//
tanniṣedhastu mantrārtha-sārvātmyapratipattaye /

Vratacaryā, performing *vrata*s (*vrata*s means, fasts and penances), *mantrārtha tādātmya pratipattaye*, it is said [to be performed] in Śaivism just to get the ability in attaining the oneness of *mantra* and *mantra devatā* (the lord of *mantra*). *Mantra* and *mantra devatā* become one by this *vrata*, by this penance, by adopting this penance, and *tapasya*, and all these traditions. *Tat niṣedhastu mantrārtha tādātmya pratipattaye*, but in Kaulamata, it is prohibited, these *vrata*s should to be totally avoided, no *vrata* should be performed, no penance should be performed, no fast should be performed. What is there in that? Nothing lies there. *Iha sarvātmake kasmāt tat pratiniṣedhāt*, in this, our own Śaivism, you can perform this *vrata*, well and good, [or] leave them altogether, well and good, because everything is divine (laughs).

LJA TA04M (36:36)

क्षेत्रपीठोपपीठेषु प्रवेशो विघ्नशान्तये ॥२५९॥
मन्त्राद्याराधकस्याथ तल्लाभायोपदिश्यते ।

kṣetrapīṭhopapīṭheṣu praveśo vighnaśāntaye //259//
mantrādyārādhakasyātha tallābhāyopadiśyate /

Kṣetra pīṭha upapīṭheṣu, there are four *pīṭha*s, four [sacred] places where our ancient masters initiated their disciples. There are four *pīṭha*s: Kāmarūpa *pīṭha*, Jālandhara *pīṭha*, Uḍḍiyāna *pīṭha*, and Pūrṇagiri *pīṭha*. These are four *pīṭha*s existing in India. These *pīṭha*s are meant as the thrones of masters, four sections of masters, and those four sections of masters would initiate, they were initiating people on those *pīṭha*s. There are *upa-pīṭha*s also for those less elevated masters, sub-centers of masters. There are not only four masters. Four masters are great masters existing in this India (Bharata *varśa*). Actually, these *pīṭha*s are in Bharata *varśa*, not in India only – Bharata *varśa* is the whole of the universe. And to get entry in those *pīṭha*s is just to subside all the *vighna*s (obstacles) in *sādhanā* (meditation). All obstacles in *sādhanā*s are washed off by entering in these *pīṭha*s before getting oneself initiated. *Mantrādyārādhakasyātha tat lābhāya upadiśyate*, because, for the *sādhaka*, he achieves the desired state swiftly.

SCHOLAR: *Yoginī saṁketasthāna.*[372]

SWAMIJI: Yes.

JOHN: By getting initiated in these *pīṭha*s.

SWAMIJI:

LJA TA04M (38:56)

क्षेत्रादिगमनाभावविधिस्तु स्वात्मनस्तथा ॥२६०॥
वैश्वरूप्येण पूर्णत्वं ज्ञातुमित्यपि वर्णितम् ।

kṣetrādigamanābhāva-vidhistu svātmanastathā //260//
vaiśvarūpyeṇa pūrṇatvaṁ jñātumityapi varṇitam /

But in Kaula, *kṣetrādi gamanābhāva vidhistu*, you should not get entry in those *pīṭha*s (shrines), absolutely avoid those *pīṭha*s, don't enter in these *pīṭha*s. It is only a bogus way of thinking that by getting entry in *pīṭha*s you will get rid of all those obstacles in *sādhanā*. *Vaiśva rūpyeṇa*, because this whole universe is owned by Lord Śiva himself, so you should not think of getting entry in those *pīṭha*s. *Iha sarvātmake kasmāt tat vipratiṣedhane* (verse 257), in this Śaivism, you can enter in those *pīṭha*s for getting initiated, you can disown those entries altogether, well and good – in Śaivism (laughs).

372. A sign (*saṁketasthāna*) of a *yoginī*.

SCHOLAR: But to accept those, to go to those lower things like *liṅga pūjā*, etcetera, is simply an act of concealment.

SWAMIJI: But "lower things" and "higher things", this remains only in illusion. How can [there] be a lower Śiva and a higher Śiva?

SCHOLAR: That's what I mean.

SWAMIJI: Can you explain who is lower Śiva and who is higher Śiva?

SCHOLAR: I didn't mean that. What I meant was that, when you hold the Trika point of view, then if you perform *liṅga pūjā*, you don't perform it as a Śaiva Siddhāntin performs it, with that feeling that Śiva is somewhere beyond the universe like a pot or …

SWAMIJI: You can feel like that also in Śaivism.

SCHOLAR: But if you really feel like that, then you are a Śaiva Siddhāntin, not a Trika Śaiva.

SWAMIJI: Actually, you don't feel like that because doing that or not doing that is the same for him.

SCHOLAR: But for a Śaiva Siddhāntin, it is not the same.

SWAMIJI: No (affirmative).

JOHN: A person would do that, a Trika Śaivite would do that, just to conceal himself, he'd do anything in this universe.

SWAMIJI: He can't be concealed. Actually he won't be concealed.

MARK D: But from another person's point of view.

SWAMIJI: Yes, from another person's …

SCHOLAR: So he might wear *jaṭa* even though there is no reason for a Trika Śaiva to wear such a hairstyle.

SWAMIJI: He can wear that also [or] he can discard that.

LJA TA04M (41:27)

There are Śaivites, there are Vedāntists, there are Buddhists. Actually, from my point of view, they are all Śaivites, they are situated in the Trika point of view.

SCHOLAR: But how can they be situated in the Trika point of view if their point of view is not that of Trika?

SWAMIJI: Universally, not individually.

SCHOLAR: Ah, yes.

SWAMIJI: Universally. "Universally" because you have given your life to *liṅga pūjā* [or] you have given your life to the absence of *liṅga pūjā*, so combining you two, this is Śaivism. If I combine you both …

SCHOLAR: But not from our point of view, only from the point of view of the person …

SWAMIJI: Not from the individual point of view, from the universal point of view. From the universal point of view, there is one. *Viśvātmayatāvidhi*, from the universal point of view, everybody is a Śaivite–from the universal point of view, not the individual point of view. Individual point of views differ.

SCHOLAR: But the danger of that point of view is that when you say everything is the same, then people follow paths of practice and awareness which are non-Śaivite, thinking, "Everything is the same, it makes no difference, I will continue to hold a completely bigoted and limited point of view because I have read in some book that actually they are all the same."

SWAMIJI: No, you must know that. There must be knowledge. Universal knowledge must come in your brain and then it is alright. If there is that …

SCHOLAR: Otherwise, hypocrisy.

SWAMIJI: If you are shrunk, then it is nothing.

DEVOTEE: Can we say other philosophies are shrinking and we are expanding?

SWAMIJI: From their point of view, those philosophies are shrinking; from our point of view, those philosophies are all …

DEVOTEE: … expanded.

SWAMIJI: Because actually Śaivism is living all-round, it is the living truth.

SCHOLAR: Only individuals are absent who know that (laughs).

SWAMIJI: Individuals, yes. Discard individuality and you are there.

JOHN: I remember one time one person told me, because he'd read somewhere that *nirvāṇa* and *saṁsāra* are the same, he said *nirvāṇa* and *saṁsāra* are the same, so there was no reason to do anything. And he believed this whole-heartedly [that] there was no reason to do *sādhanā* or any practice because he'd read somewhere that *nirvāṇa* and *saṁsāra* were the same, even though he did not understand that, he had understood that in his own way.

SWAMIJI: Yes, one must understand it fully, and then …

SCHOLAR: So that Absolute point of view has to be concealed to some extent. It has to be concealed …

SWAMIJI: Yes.

SCHOLAR: … because you talk about awareness, you talk about the unity of *nirvāṇa* and *saṁsāra*, but who will understand that except those who have given their life to that?

SWAMIJI: You have to conceal it. It is why *lokācārye tu vaidika*[373], you have to tell them, "You are right. Go on with this *liṅga pūjā*. This tradition is best for you."

DEVOTEE: Is it to be concealed by the master to the disciple also?

SWAMIJI: Because it is said:

LJA TA04M (44:57)

Yaḥ te kuryur na tat kuryāt, yad bhruyoḥ tad samāsa[374], whatever they do, you should not act according to their actions. They should act whatever is told by them to you. You should not follow their actions.

JOHN: Whose actions?

SWAMIJI: Master's actions. Whatever your master does is divine, [but] don't follow that.

SCHOLAR: So if your master touches an untouchable or something, you should not be upset.

SWAMIJI: No, that orthodox disciple should not be upset. He should do according to the orthodox ways of being. You should not think that, "Our master has fallen from his traditions, from his well-maintained tradition."

LJA TA04M (46:00)

Go to the text first:[375]

---

373. A line from an unknown verse as quoted by Jayaratha in his commentary for 4.24 and 4.250. The complete verse reads thus: *antaḥ kaulo bahiḥ śaivo lokācāre tu vaidikaḥ | sāramādāya tiṣṭheta nārikelaphalaṁ yathā ||*

374. Swamiji's recitation of this verse from an unknown source is somewhat inaudible.

375. Swamiji repeats the verses from the *Mālinīvijaya Tantra* that were just commentated upon by Abhinavagupta.

nātra śuddhirna cāśuddhirna bhakṣyādivicāraṇam //213//
na dvaitaṁ nāpi cādvaitaṁ liṅgapūjādikaṁ na ca /
na cāpi tatparityāgo niṣparigrahatāpi vā //214//
saparigrahatā vāpi jaṭābhasmādisaṅgrahaḥ /
tattyāgo na vratādīnāṁ caraṇācaraṇaṁ ca yat //215//
kṣetrādisampraveśaśca samayādiprapālanam /

To that point [of "*kṣetrādisampraveśaśca*"] he has explained. Now he explains "*samayādiprapālanam*", this stanza of the *Mālinīvijaya*:

LJA TA04M (46:31)

समयाचारसद्भावः पाल्यत्वेनोपदिश्यते ॥२६१॥
भेदप्राणतया तत्तत्त्यागात्तत्त्वविशुद्धये ।

samayācārasadbhāvaḥ pālyatvenopadiśyate //261//
bhedaprāṇatayā tattat-tyāgāttattvaviśuddhaye /

Samayācāra sadbhāvaḥ, the established rules and regulations of customs (that is *samaya*), *pālyatvenopadiśyate*, it is said that you should adopt that, you should have those established rules and regulations of customs, because *bheda prāṇatayā*, you have to differentiate what is right and what is wrong there. So for that, you have to establish the rules and regulations of customs. And *tat tat tyāgāt tattva viśuddhaye*, in that way, your nature of being will be purified and you will get realization. It is said in Siddhānta.

समयादिनिषेधस्तु मतशास्त्रेषु कथ्यते ॥२६२॥

samayādiniṣedhastu mataśāstreṣu kathyate //262//

But in the Mata *Śāstras*, it is prohibited, that there is no need to establish rules and regulations of customs. It is useless, so they are prohibited, these rules are prohibited. You should not be dependent to those rules and regulations of customs. It is said in the Mata *Śāstra*.[376]

निर्मर्यादं स्वसम्बोधं सम्पूर्णं बुद्ध्यतामिति ।

nirmaryādaṁ svasambodhaṁ sampūrṇaṁ buddhyatāmiti /

But in our system, in the system of Kaula *prakriyā* (the Kaula System or the Trika System), actually the reality of Self is all-round felt and no rules and regulations are found there.[377]

LJA TA04M (48:25)

परकीयमिदं रूपं ध्येयमेतत्तु मे निजम् ॥ २६३ ॥
ज्वालादिलिङ्गं चान्यस्य कपालादि तु मे निजम् ।

parakīyamidaṁ rūpaṁ dhyeyametattu me nijam //263//
jvālādiliṅgaṁ cānyasya kapālādi tu me nijam /

In Siddhānta it is said that, "*Parakīyam idam rūpam*, this [particular] formation to be worshipped is of others, is not our system, and the contemplation of this and that [particular] form of Lord Śiva is my own, and this way, other systems [of contemplation] are from other systems, it is not my own. I have to act according to my system." It is said in Siddhānta.

376. Also known as the *Matayāmala Tantra*.
377. "When *śaktipāta* is not so good, you become the follower of Siddhānta. When it is a little better, you become the follower of Vāma *marga* (path), and when it is more better, then you become the follower of Dakṣa, and then Mata, then Kula, and then Kaula, and in the end, when the *śaktipāta* is intense, then you become the follower of the Trika system. This is the way how *śaktipāta* takes place." *Tantrāloka* 13.300 (LJA archive).

JOHN: Siddhānta is Śaiva Siddhānta?

SWAMIJI: Śaiva Siddhānta, yes.[378] *Jvālādiliṅgaṁ cānyasya kapālādi tu me nijam*, Siddhānta says that *jvālādi liṅga* is to be worshipped; the *jvālā* (flame) *liṅga*, *mṛt* (earthen) *liṅga*, or a *liṅga* made of gold, etcetera, are to be worshipped in Siddhānta.

JOHN: This first *liṅga* is made of what?

SWAMIJI: *Jvālā*, flame. "*Kapālādi tu me nijam*, but this is not mine." Mata *Śāstra* says that, "*Kapālādi tu me nijam*, my own *liṅga* is my own *liṅga* existing in my own body (*ādhyātma liṅga*)." So there are variations in these rules and regulations.

आदिशब्दात्तपश्चर्यावेलातिथ्यादि कथ्यते ॥२६४॥

ādiśabdāttapaścaryā-velātithyādi kathyate //264//

By "etcetera" (*adi*), you must know that [the Siddhāntin believes], "*Tapasyā*, this kind of *tapasyā* is for me and this kind of *tapasyā* is not for me (this kind of penance); and this kind of action is for me and this kind of action is not for me; this kind of rules according to the real time, the rules of time, and the rules of *tithi*, the rules of day, [are for me]." The days are also fixed for worship in Siddhānta. Not only these.

LJA TA04M (50:43)

नाम शक्तिशिवाद्यन्तमेतस्य मम नान्यथा ।

nāma śaktiśivādyantam-etasya mama nānyathā /

And the follower of Siddhānta says that, "There are nominations also to be adopted according to our own system: *śakti śivādyantam*, for women, we put "Śakti" in the end; for men, we put "Śiva" in the end."

JOHN: In their names.

---

378. Also known as Southern Śaivism.

SWAMIJI: *Śikha śakti*... yes, names.

गोत्रं च गुरुसन्तानो मठिकाकुलशब्दितः ॥२६५॥

gotraṁ ca gurusantāno maṭhikākulaśabditaḥ //265//

And there is also *gotra*. *Gotra* is divided in two sections. *Gotra* means, *guru santāna*, the successive teachings of masters is *gotra*.

JOHN: Chain of masters?

SWAMIJI: Chain of masters. Successive teaching-chain of masters.

JOHN: This is *sampradāya*.[379] Is this *sampradāya*?

SWAMIJI: *Sampradāya*, yes. It is divided in two sections: *maṭhikā kula śabditaḥ*, one is called *maṭhikā* (school) and the other is called *kula* (family or community). A *maṭhikā* is where disciples reside with the master.

JOHN: That's external?

SWAMIJI: Yes, it's external.

JOHN: No, I mean, this external teaching as opposed to the internal of Kula or not? The secret is...

SWAMIJI: No, no.

JOHN: Not that kind of distinction.

SWAMIJI: It is an ordinary course.

JOHN: *Maṭhikā* is.

SWAMIJI: Yes, *maṭhikā* and *kula*.

JOHN: Both are ordinary.

SWAMIJI: Both.

LJA TA04M (52:19)

श्रीसन्ततिस्त्र्यम्बकाख्या तदर्धामर्दसञ्ज्ञिता ।
इत्थमर्धचतस्त्रोऽत्र मठिकाः शाङ्करे क्रमे ॥२६६॥

379. The line or tradition of masters.

śrīsantatistryambakākhyā tadardhāmardasañjñitā /
itthamardhacatasro'tra maṭhikāḥ śāṅkare krame //266//

In this Śaivism, in the successive teachings of Śaivism, there are three *maṭhikā*s and a half.

JOHN: Three? Oh yes, Tryambakanātha, yes.

SWAMIJI: Three *maṭhikā*s and a half. You have already been told that. Tryambaka, Āmardaka, and Śri Nātha, and a half, Ardhatryambakā (from Tryambaka's daughter). *Itthamardha-catasro'tra maṭhikāḥ śāṅkare krame.*

LJA TA04M (52:57)

युगक्रमेण कूर्माद्या मीनान्ता सिद्धसन्ततिः ।

yugakrameṇa kūrmādyā mīnāntā siddhasantatiḥ /267a

And according to the four *yuga*s (ages), there are also successive states of masters beginning from Kūrma, ending in Mīna.

SCHOLAR: Why does he say Kūrma when the lord of Kṛta *yuga* is Khagendranātha? *Khagendra kūrma meṣa…*

SWAMIJI: Khagendranātha is the chief, the first.

SCHOLAR: So why has he said "*kūrmādi*"? Is this strange? Never mind, it's not…

SWAMIJI: "*Kūrmādya*", it is "*kūrma adyaḥ*". *Kūrmādyaḥ* does not mean, Kūrma, etcetera.

SCHOLAR: Yes, yes.

SWAMIJI: [It means], the first of Kūrma.

SCHOLAR: *Kūrmādyaḥ mīnāntaḥ siddhasantatiḥ.*

SWAMIJI: *Kūrmādyāḥ* means, that which is before Kūrma. You go to the [commentary]: *kūrmanāthasya ādyaḥ kṛtayugāvatārakaḥ*, first is Kṛta *yuga*, next is Dvāpara *yuga*, third is Tretā *yuga*, and the fourth is Kali *yuga*. *Kṛta yuga avatārakaḥ* is Khagendranātha and so on. I think you will understand it. You must go through it and you will understand it in the twenty-ninth chapter of the *Tantrāloka*. In the twenty-ninth *āhnika* of the *Tantrāloka*, it is very well-explained there, and the nominations of all these *siddhas* and this Khagendranātha, etcetera.

In this system of Śaivism, there are six princes who were governing the kingdom of Kaula, Kaulamata. They were called princes, they were not saints, they were not called saints. They were actually saints, but they are called princes, six princes, because they were governing the whole kingdom of Kaulacāra. And the six princes are said to be *sādhikāra* six princes (authorized six princes), and there are non-authorized six princes also.

SCHOLAR: *Karmendriya* and *buddhindriya*.

SWAMIJI: No, not *karmendriya*. Princes, actually princes.

SCHOLAR: In the external sense, yes.

SWAMIJI: No. Why not go to those saints? There are *sādhikāra* six princes and *niradhikāra* six princes. The *sādhikāra* six princes are those who have got authority in the Kaula System and the *niradhikāra* six princes are who are not authorized in the Kaula System. They are actually residing in the state of the Kaula System, but they have no authority to initiate others, they are unauthorized there, they can't initiate people. And those who are authorized, they can initiate people. [They are] authorized because they are married, these six princes are married, and the other six princes are not married, they have stored all the semen in [their] brain.

JOHN: These other, these non-authorized…

SWAMIJI: Non-authorized.[380] They are not authorized because they want to observe *brahmacarya* (chastity). As they are to observe *brahmacarya*, so they have no authority in initiating people in the Kaula System. They are the unauthorized six princes. They are also divine in their own way.[381] *Sādhikāra* are authorized in initiating people. And these names of the six princes, the authorized six princes and the non-authorized six princes, are given in the twenty-ninth chapter of the *Tantrāloka*.

LJA TA04M (56:56) end

---

380. "If a lady is not there along with the master, the master has no authority to initiate." *Tantrāloka* 4 (additional audio, LJA archive).

381. "They are called *ūrdhvareta*s, as the master of Lord Kṛṣṇa was an *ūrdhvareta*–Durvasā. Lord Śiva has authority! He is *ūrdhvareta* also and *adhareta* also." *Tantrāloka* 4. Ibid.

LJA TA04N (00:00) start

आदिशब्देन च घरं पल्ली पीठोपपीठकम् ॥२६७॥
मुद्रा छुम्मेति तेषां च विधानं स्वपरस्थितम् ।

ādiśabdena ca gharaṁ pallī pīṭhopapīṭhakam //267//
mudrā chummeti teṣāṁ ca vidhānaṁ svaparasthitam /
(not recited)

["*Adi*" refers to *gharam* (houses), *pallī* (villages), *pīṭha* (centers), *upapītha* (sub-centers), *mudrā* (positions), and *chummā* (secret signs), and *vidhis* (rules) that][382] are also existing, *svaparasthitam*, in their own circle and in other circles also.

So, it is said in the Kula System:

तादात्म्यप्रतिपत्त्यै हि स्वं सन्तानं समाश्रयेत् ॥२६८॥

tādātmyapratipattyai hi svaṁ santānaṁ samāśrayet //268//

Just for getting complete entry in the oneness of God consciousness, you must not leave aside, you must hold, your own way of practice; you must hold your own way of practice, your own tradition of your masters, you must not touch any other section.

JOHN: This means what? That you do what your master tells you, *bas.*

DENISE: You don't do some other meditation.

SWAMIJI: Not some other meditation. Don't accept any order from outside your school.

382. Audio for the bracketed section is missing.

LJA TA04N (00:57)

भुञ्जीत पूजयेच्चक्रं परसन्तानिना नहि ।

bhuñjīta pūjayeccakraṁ parasantāninā nahi /

You must eat, you must worship, this *cakra* (this wheel) of your God consciousness, [of] your own, *parasantāninā nahi*, not from other sections.

एतच्च मतशास्त्रेषु निषिद्धं खण्डना यतः ॥२६९॥

etacca mataśāstreṣu niṣiddhaṁ khaṇḍanā yataḥ //269//

In the Mata *Śāstra* (in the Kaula *Śāstra*), it is *niṣiddha*, it is prohibited [to accept any order from outside of your school]. But what is there in that? You can go in other sections also. There is also the kingdom of God consciousness.

SCHOLAR: "*Pūjayet cakraṁ*" has a Kaula meaning as well here, not just the meaning you gave it. Is that right?

SWAMIJI: Not Kaula.

SCHOLAR: This *pūjayet cakra*, this refers to *cakra pūjā* as well.

SWAMIJI: Yes, *cakra pūjā* there also …

SCHOLAR: *Svasantāni vi cakra pūjayet.*

SWAMIJI: *Svaṁ santānaṁ samāśrayet bhuñjīta pūjayeccakraṁ, parasantāninā nahi*, not in other sections.

SCHOLAR: But this *cakraṁ* is not merely *saṁvit cakraṁ* here. It is *siddha yoginī cakraṁ*.

SWAMIJI: This is *yoginī cakraṁ. Etat ca mataśāstreṣu niṣiddham*, this is prohibited in the Mata *śāstra*. [But] you should not have such a shrunken mind that you should do only this, what is existing in your own way, because:

LJA TA04N (02:18)

एतच्च मतशास्त्रेषु निषिद्धं खण्डना यतः ॥२६९॥
अखण्डेऽपि परे तत्त्वे भेदेनानेन जायते ।

etacca mataśāstreṣu niṣiddhaṁ khaṇḍanā yataḥ //269//
akhaṇḍe'pi pare tattve bhedenānena jāyate /
(not recited in full)

Akhaṇḍa para tattva, the supreme state of God consciousness, which is all-round complete, it is shattered by the differentiated ways of rules and regulations, [by] the adoption of rules and regulations. You must not own these rules and regulations there. It will be shattered, that completion…

JOHN: This is in *śāktopāya*, moving in *śāktopāya*.

SWAMIJI: Not *śāktopāya*, this is Kaula.

SCHOLAR: Kaula, this is independent of *upāya*.

SWAMIJI:

LJA TA04N (02:54)

एवं क्षेत्रप्रवेशादि सन्ताननियमान्ततः ॥२७०॥
नास्मिन्विधीयते तद्धि साक्षान्नौपयिकं शिवे ।

evaṁ kṣetrapraveśādi santānaniyamāntataḥ //270//
nāsminvidhīyate taddhi sākṣānnaupayikaṁ śive /

So, *kṣetrādi praveśādi*, beginning from the rules and the regulations of entering in shrines, etcetera, or *santāna niyamāntataḥ*, and holding the ways and rules and regulations of your own ways of masters, *nāsmin vidhīyate taddhi*, it is not actually understood and it is not actually recognized there in that Kaula System, because it is not *aupayikam śive*, it is not the real way which will carry you to the state of God consciousness.

LJA TA04N (03:48)

न तस्य च निषेधो यन्न तत्तत्त्वस्य खण्डनम् ॥ २७१ ॥

na tasya ca niṣedho yanna tattattvasya khaṇḍanam //271//

But it is not prohibited also. You can do that if you reach to that state where nothing is to be done or nothing is undone.

SCHOLAR: He has written "*niṣodho*" here.

SWAMIJI: Yes, "*niṣedho*". How I read "*niṣedha*"?

SCHOLAR: Because you knew what it was (laughs).

SWAMIJI: Yes (laughs). *Na tasya ca niṣedho yat na tattattvasya khaṇḍanam*, and this will never be shattered, this state of God consciousness will never be shattered if you adopt limited rules and regulations or if you leave those aside.

SCHOLAR: So, from the Mata point of view, they are prohibited…

SWAMIJI: Yes.

SCHOLAR: …from point of view of the means, but from the Trika point of view, they may be adopted, hence they are introduced in the 29th [*āhnika*].

SWAMIJI: Yes, they may be adopted or they may not be adopted.

JOHN: And in the Kaula point of view, they are rejected.

SWAMIJI: They are rejected. In Kaula, they are rejected.

SCHOLAR: Kaula, Mata, Krama, etcetera.

SWAMIJI: [In] Kaula, Mata, they are rejected, and in Trika, they are not rejected also – you can have them [or] you cannot have them.

LJA TA04N (05:03)

विश्वात्मनो हि नाथस्य स्वस्मिन्रूपे विकल्पितौ ।
विधिर्निषेधो वा शक्तौ न स्वरूपस्य खण्डने ॥ २७२ ॥

viśvātmano hi nāthasya svasminrūpe vikalpitau /
vidhirniṣedho vā śaktau na svarūpasya khaṇḍane //272//

Because this Lord, Lord Śiva, who is *viśvātma*, who is universal, and when his universal state is *svasminrūpe vikalpitau*, is observed, then *vidhir niṣedho vā śaktau na svarūpasya khaṇḍane*, the adoption of these rules and regulations and the negation of these rules and regulations have no power there. You can adopt them, you can discard them.

Viśvātmano nāthasya svasminrūpe [is] *vikalpitau*. "*Vikalpitau*", it is *saptamī*.[383] *Vikalpitau satyām*[384], *vidhir niṣedho vā śaktau na svarūpasya khaṇḍane*, then *vidhi* (rules) and *niṣedha* (prohibitions) have no power. Have you understood?

SCHOLAR: Yes!

SWAMIJI: Now the only predominant and essential thing to be done, that he says in the next verse:

LJA TA04N (06:18)

परतत्त्वप्रवेशे तु यमेव निकटं यदा ।
उपायं वेत्ति स ग्राह्यस्तदा त्याज्योऽथ वा क्वचित् ॥२७३॥

paratattvapraveśe tu yameva nikaṭaṁ yadā /
upāyaṁ vetti sa grāhyas-tadā tyājyo'tha vā kvacit //273//

If you get entry, if you see, if you feel that you are entering in the supreme state of God consciousness through anything (for instance, by doing mischief with people, or by telling lies, or by [acting] in such a way which is prohibited by others), if you feel that by adopting those things you are going to enter in the state of God consciousness, [then] you must have it! Don't think of the sayings/observings of others. You must have it, you must own that, that way of action. It is predominant, it is essential that you must have that way–*sa grāhya. Tadā tyājyo'tha vā kvacit*, if you feel that by worshipping Lord Śiva in a corner, in a secluded state, in the mountains, in Himalayan caves, [if] by worshipping there you don't get entry, [then] you must leave that, it is

383. The seventh or locative case.

384. When true thought/observation is held.

prohibited for you. You must have that way [where even] if you do those vulgar things, and by those vulgar things you get entry, you feel that you are entering in God consciousness, [then] you must have it. This is the chief and the real way of acting – the rule.

JOHN: This is the real rule.

SWAMIJI:

LJA TA04N (08:05)

न यन्त्रणात्र कार्येति प्रोक्तं श्रीत्रिकशासने ।

na yantraṇātra kāryeti proktaṁ śrītrikaśāsane /

In the Trika *Śāstra*, it is said there is no *yantraṇā*, there is no restriction of any kind. The restriction is only there [that] you must get entry. If you get entry in God consciousness, well and good; if you don't get entry in God consciousness by telling the truth, by being honest to others, by uplifting those trodden-ones, if you don't get entry in God consciousness, [then] leave that. It is a sin for you to do that. If actually by doing sins and bad things, you get entry, you feel that you are entering in God consciousness, [then] have that.

LJA TA04N (08:49)

समता सर्वदेवानामोवल्लीमन्त्रवर्णयोः ॥२७४॥
आगमनां गतीनां च सर्वं शिवमयं यतः ।

samatā sarvadevānām-ovallīmantravarṇayoḥ //274//
āgamanāṁ gatīnāṁ ca sarvaṁ śivamayaṁ yataḥ /

Sameness in all gods, sameness in *ovallī*, sameness in *mantras*, sameness …*

JOHN: *Ovallī* is what?

SWAMIJI: *Ovallī* is where they have got the realization of God consciousness.

SCHOLAR: You mean this *ovallī*, this *jñāna santāna*[385] coming from each of these *rājaputras* (princes), this tradition coming from those and the names associated with them.

SWAMIJI: Yes, *jñāna santāna*.

*... and *mantra santāna* and *varṇā santāna*, and all Tantras, and all states which are achieved, in all these states, the feeling of oneness is Śiva, the feeling of oneness is the feeling of Lord Śiva. Lord Śiva is oneness. When you feel the sameness in each and every action of the Kaula System, the Siddhānta System, and the Mata System, that is Lord Śiva. No differentiation comes in the end. In the end, there is oneness.

LJA TA04N (10:08)

स ह्यखण्डितसद्भावं शिवतत्त्वं प्रपश्यति ॥२७५॥
यो ह्यखण्डितसद्भावमात्मतत्त्वं प्रपद्यते ।

sa hyakhaṇḍitasadbhāvaṁ śivatattvaṁ prapaśyati //275//
yo hyakhaṇḍitasadbhāvam-ātmatattvaṁ prakāśate /[386]

When by practicing on individual consciousness, ...*

Because unless you practice on individual consciousness, you can't get entry in universal God consciousness. Universal God consciousness is far away from our feeling.

*... *yaḥ akhaṇḍita sadbhāvam ātma tattvaṁ prāpadyate*, when your individual consciousness will be established, will get establishment in sameness of each and every action of this world, then that person is likely to enter in *akhaṇḍita sadbhāva śiva tattva*, that *pūrṇa* (full) Śiva *tattva* (element), he will get entry in that Śiva *tattva*.

385. Lineage (*santāna*) of knowledge (*jñāna*).

386. Swamiji says "*prakāśate*" in place of the published "*prāpadyate*". In his translation, however, he will say "*prāpadyate*".

LJA TA04N (11:05)

केतकीकुसुमसौरभे भृशं भृङ्ग एव रसिको न मक्षिका ।
भैरवीयपरमाद्वयार्चने कोऽपि रज्यति महेशचोदितः ॥ २७६ ॥

ketakīkusumasaurabhe bhṛśaṁ bhṛṅga eva rasiko na makṣikā /
bhairavīyaparamādvayārcane ko'pi rajyati maheśacoditaḥ //276//

Ketakī kusuma is a flower-plant of the *ketaka* plant. It has grown in our garden. You know *ketaka*?

DEVOTEE: Chrysanthemum.

JOHN: Chrysanthemum.

SWAMIJI: Yes. You know that?

JOHN: It's just getting ready to flower just now.

DEVOTEES: Autumn flower.

SWAMIJI: Yes. That is *ketakī kusuma*. It is filled with fragrance! And in that *kusuma*, in that flower-plant, who is authorized to suck the inscense (i.e., nectar) of that plant/flower? Only *bhṛṅga eva rasika*, a black bee only is *rasika lālāyita*[387], a black bee is the only authority in sucking the nectar of that plant.

SCHOLAR: The only connoisseur.

SWAMIJI: Connoisseur?

SCHOLAR: *Sahṛdaya*.

SWAMIJI: *Sahṛdaya*, yes.[388] *Na makṣikā*, a fly won't, a fly is not an authority in sucking the nectar of that flower. That flower, the nectar of that flower will be sucked only by the black bee. In the same way, *bhairavī paramādvayārcarne*, in the supreme and topmost monistic worship of Lord Śiva, only a few persons, a few fortunate persons are authorized to own that, own that worship, own that state of worship, who is *maheśa coditaḥ*, who is sentenced by Lord Śiva to that action.

---

387. Lit., drools (*lālāyita*) with delight (*rasika*).

388. Lit., "with heart".

LJA TA04N (13:16)

अस्मिंश्च यागे विश्रान्तिं कुर्वतां भवडम्बरः ।
हिमानीव महाग्रीष्मे स्वयमेव विलीयते ॥२७७॥

asmiṁśca yāge viśrāntiṁ kurvatāṁ bhavaḍambaraḥ /
himānīva mahāgrīṣme svayameva vilīyate //277//

In this supreme state of worship of Bhairava, the one who is established, the one who has taken full rest in that worship, for him, *bhava ḍambaraḥ svayam eva vilīyate*, the *ḍambara* (*ḍambara* means, the heaps, the masses), the masses of differentiated perceptions of the world, the worldly differentiated perceptions, melt away of their own accord, without any effort, just like *himānīva*, just like the heaps and the mountains of snow melt just in the entry of *grīṣma*, in the entry of summer.

अलं वातिप्रसङ्गेन भूयसातिप्रपञ्चिते ।

alaṁ vātiprasaṅgena bhūyasātiprapañcite /

Let us stop thinking on this subject [of] who is an authority on adopting this way of worship–let us stop that. You can't discriminate those people who are an authority on worshipping this way.

योग्योऽभिनवगुप्तोऽस्मिन्कोऽपि यागविधौ बुधः ॥२७८॥

yogyo'bhinavagupto'smin-ko'pi yāgavidhau budhaḥ //278//

Some unique realized Abhinavagupta is the only authority in adopting such a way of worship. [Abhinavagupta] says, "Abhinavagupta is the authority to adopt this *pūjā*."

Here ends the chapter.

LJA TA04N (15:06)

इत्यनुत्तरपदप्रविकासे शाक्तमौपयिकमद्य विविक्तम् ॥

ityanuttarapadapravikāse śāktamaupayikamadya viviktam //

So, this *śāktopāya* is *viviktam*, explained vividly, for getting entry, for getting the blooming of the supreme state of God consciousness today (*adya*, today). By "today" it seems that he composed an *āhnika* each day. Jayaratha, the commentator says [that Abhinavagupta] has said, "Today, today I have done this *āhnika*." It means he did it each day, one *āhnika* each day. The whole *Tantrāloka* he composed in thirty-seven days.

Here ends our lecture of today.

LJA TA04N (16:02)

Jai Guru Dev

Appendix

1. *Parāmarśa* (the state of 'awareness')

The literal meaning of *parāmarśa* is: seizing, affection, recollection, remembrance, consideration, inference (logic), conclusion (logic), reflection. *Para*: extreme. *Āmarśa*: similarity, contact, touching and nearness. *Parāmarśa* is variously described in Kashmir Shaivism as "direct experience", "direct perception", and "intense awareness". Simply stated, *parāmarśa* is *para* (extreme) awareness (*āmarśa*). Here, *parāmarśa* is not a static experience, but a dynamic pulsation (*spandana*) of awareness as explained by Swamiji in the following extracts:

> *Parāmarśa* is always in movement; *parāmarśa* is not only one-pointed. It is movement, not in one-pointedness, not in one thousand-pointedness, it is innumerable movements, innumerable times (*ananta*). This is what he says: *parāmarśo hi spandanātmaiva*, *parāmarśa* is always in *spandana*, in movement. It is the chain of movement. I would call it "chain of movement." It is not only sparks of movement. There is the possibility in sparks [that] there is a gap, [but] there is no gap [in *parāmarśa*]. It is movement in such a way that this movement is without any gap, and in this movement you feel as if there is no movement. It is only one movement, just like when you draw one line, this is the movement of these points.
> *Parātriśikā Laghu Vṛtti* (LJA archive).

> The conclusion of the third *āhnika* of the *Tantrāloka* is devoted to the subject of *ahaṁ parāmarśa*, which is defined as "supreme I-consciousness". To understand *ahaṁ parāmarśa*, one has to see how this word *ahaṁ* is divided into three parts: *a-ha-aṁ*.

> *anuttarādyā prasṛtirhāntā śaktisvarūpiṇī //*
> *pratyāhṛtāśeṣaviśvānuttare sā nilīyate /*
> (*Tantrāloka* 3.204–205a)

> Now he gives the conclusion of this *ahaṁ parāmarśa*: *Anuttarādyā prasṛti*, *ahaṁ parāmarśa* begins from the flowing out of creation.

Creation of what? Creation of your own nature. You have not to create any foreign matter. *Anuttarādyā prasṛti*, this flowing nature of His being, which begins from *a* and ends in *hāntā* (ends in *ha*)–and this *prasṛti* is in fact from *a* to *ha*–in conclusion this is the *prasṛti* of His energy. *Prasṛti* means, flowing out, *prasara*. This flowing out from *a* to *ha* is the flow of His energy, not anything else–*śakti svarūpiṇī*. And it is *pratyāhṛtāśeṣaviśva*, and it has digested this whole universe in Her own nature. When She has digested–this Śakti, this energy of Lord Śiva–has digested in Her own nature, in Her own being, this situation of the whole universe, *garbhikritānantaviśva*, and after having digested this whole differentiated world in Her own nature, *anuttare sā nilīyate*, in the end She absorbs Her nature inside Śiva again, in the end. And that is *aṁ*. So it is *ahaṁ*.[389] This is a very important point in our Śaivism.
Tantrāloka 3.204 commentary (LJA archive).

In the following extract, Swamiji explains how *ahaṁ parāmarśa* is also functioning on the individual level in everyday experience:

So, for instance, just take the individual way of experience for this *ahaṁ parāmarśa*. When you look at this pencil, just at the very beginning of looking towards the pencil–this is *ahaṁ*, this is the conducting way of *ahaṁ*, in the individual way for *sādhaka*s, for those who have to experience this *ahaṁ parāmarśa*–when your consciousness flows out to perceive this pencil, in the beginning your consciousness is established in *a*, when your consciousness travels up to the point of the pencil and it has not reached the point of pencil, this traveling span of space is the traveling from *a* to *ha*. And when you perceive [that] this is a pencil and you close your eyes [after confirming that], "Oh, this is a pencil," when you close your eyes, this is reality of *aṁ*. So, in each and every action of the universe, in worldly action also, you can realize this *aṁ*. You have to realize it. If you don't realize, you are kept away from Śaivite thought.
Tantrāloka, 3.204 (LJA archive).

---

389. This movement from *anuttara* (Śiva), to Śakti, to *aṁ* (Śiva) in the end.

2. Classes of Masters (verses 40–85)

Sāṁsiddhika master – through direct experience (*anubhava*) rises automatically without being dependent to *śāstra* and master. Discriminating transcendental logic (*tarka*) has risen in these masters automatically.

Mukta-śiva means, those Śiva's who have become liberated after being initiated by masters.

Anādisiddha-śiva is that Śiva who was never in ignorance, who is always in his own real nature.

Three classes of *Sāṁsiddhika* masters:

1. *Nirbhitti sāṁsiddhika* – rises without being dependent to a master or *śāstras*.
2. *Sahabhittiki sāṁsiddhika* – is dependent on masters and partly on *śāstras*.
3. *Bhittiḥ sāṁsiddhika* – is completely dependent on master and *śāstra*.

The *Sāṁsiddhika* master is also known as an *akalpita* master, i.e., "not manufactured" by other agencies, and there are three classes of *akalpita* masters.

1. *Akalpita kalpaka* – risen by the supreme way of understanding through *ātmabhāvanā* (on his own).
2. *Kalpita akalpaka* – risen through the grace of masters or *śāstras*.
3. *Kalpita* – depends upon the teaching of masters, but sometime, with some grace of Lord Śiva, some important points of *śāstras* he understands by himself.

3. *Prakṛti*

Right from heaven to this mortal world, you won't find such an individual existing who has not come in the grip of the three *guṇas* (lit., qualities). So, whoever is existing in this world or in the heavens are entangled in the cycle of three *guṇas*, the three *guṇas* which are born from *prakṛti*.

Bhagavad Gītā audio (LJA archive).

[*Prakṛti* is] the undifferentiated (*avyakta*, unmanifested) state of the three *guṇas*; *prakṛti* is the womb of three *guṇas*. In *prakṛti*, you can't see the three *guṇas*. So you have to agitate that…[and agitation is done by] Anantabhaṭṭāraka or Śrīkaṇṭhanātha…and that is the state of *guṇa tattva*, not *prakṛti tattva*. *Prakṛti tattva* is the unagitated state and *guṇa tattva* is the agitated state. It is why in Shaivism we have put another element of *guṇa tattva*. So *prakṛti* creates that *guṇa tattva*. But in *prakṛti*, *guṇa tattva* is not visible [because] it is mixed. *Prakṛti* is the mixture of three *guṇas*. [*Prakṛti* is] wherefrom the *guṇas* will come out. *Prakṛti* is the womb of the three *guṇas*.

Prakṛti is called "*sāmyavastha*", the equilibrium state of *sukha* (pleasure, *sāttvaguṇa*), *duḥkha* (pain, *rājoguṇa*), and *moha* (illusion, *tāmoguṇa*). And *prakṛti* is *karaṇa*, *prakṛti* is the cause, and the effect is *sukha*, *duḥkha*, and *moha*–pleasure, pain, and illusion (the unconscious state).

Prakṛti is an objective element. *Prakṛti* is to be enjoyed by the enjoyer. The enjoyer is *puruṣa* entangled with five subjective elements (the *kañcukas*).

Prakṛti is our nature, and that nature is limited by our intellect, which is the collection of *sāttvaguṇa*, *rājoguṇa*, and *tāmoguṇa*. *Prakṛti* is always wavering in the *guṇas*. Sometimes you are sad, sometimes you are joyous, sometimes you are giddy. That is *prakṛti*.

Prakṛti is always different for every person, each and every person.

Tantrāloka 9.215–223 (LJA archive).

These three tides of the three *guṇas* are, in the real sense, one with God consciousness.

Bhagavad Gītā audio (LJA archive).

Prakṛti is explained in the *śāstras* (scriptures) in two ways: *Aparā prakṛti*, which is said to be eightfold, is the combination of the five great elements, along with the mind, intellect, and ego. *Parā prakṛti* is that energy of being which governs and contains all the activities and conceptions of this universe.

Kashmir Shaivism–The Secret Supreme, 14.95.

…the five elements, mind, intellect, and ego. This is *aṣṭadhā*, the eightfold *prakṛti*. *Prakṛti* means, My *śakti*, but *apareyam*, this is *aparā* (gross).

And there is another one which is a subtle *śakti*. That is *parā prakṛti*, supreme *prakṛti*, supreme energy that is *svātantya śakti*, by which *svātantrya śakti* this whole universe is standing, is fixed. *Parā prakṛti* takes hold of the whole universe, whatever is and whatever is not existing.

Aparā prakṛti is just for the inferior scale. That is eightfold. The five elements, mind, intellect, and ego, this is called *aparā prakṛti*. And *parā prakṛti* is supreme, that is *svātantya śakti* by which this whole universe and I am also existing. That [*parā*] *śakti* is My personal property. And this *aparā śakti* is the property of Anantabhaṭṭāraka. He has to deal with that *śakti* according to the good *karma*s and the bad *karma*s of individual beings. And by that, he creates them, he protects them, and he destroys them. And this great *prakṛti*, which is *svātantrya śakti*, by that I conceal and reveal My nature to them.

Pidanā (concealing) and *anugraha* (revealing), I deal with that *svātantrya śakti*. The rest (creation, protection and destruction) is done according to your own *karma*s, and the operator is Anantabhaṭṭāraka.

This *aparā prakṛti* is held and understood by everybody – this inferior *prakṛti*. This *prakṛti* has created this universe and [has] protected and destroyed [it] from time to time. And the life of this *prakṛti* is separate, dwelling in My *parā prakṛti*. This is how the creation and these fivefold acts of this universe take place; the threefold acts by inferior *prakṛti* and the other twofold acts by supreme [*prakṛti*].

Bhagavad Gita in the Light of Kashmir Shaivism (with original video), Swami Lakshmanjoo, ed. John Hughes, (Lakshmanjoo Academy Book Series, Los Angeles, 2015), 7.5.

Prakṛti and *puruṣa* both are beginningless and endless. *Prakṛti* is endless and beginningless and *puruṣa* is endless and beginningless. Both are endless and beginningless, but *vikārāṁśca guṇāṁścaiva viddhi prakṛti saṁbhavān*, the three *guṇa*s and the *ghaṭa padādi*, all the objective world are produced by *prakṛti*. *Prakṛti* has produced these flowers; these houses, plants, motorcars, all other things, they are produced by *prakṛti*. And *prakṛti* has nothing to do with this production.

Prakṛti has made this for *puruṣa* to taste so that he will be entangled in the wheel of repeated births and deaths. *Prakṛti* is dumb, quiet – she is *jaḍa* (inert). She creates this for *puruṣa*. As soon as *puruṣa* gets awareness of *prakṛti* that, "*Prakṛti* is dancing on me", he becomes *mukta* (liberated) and he remains aloof from *prakṛti*. Then he enters into the state of Parabhairava and he is *jīvan mukta* (liberated while embodied).

As long as *prakṛti* is not aware that he knows me – Who? *Puruṣa* – she dances, she kicks him, she plays him, from one birth to another birth, from another birth to another birth, whatever she likes. But, as soon as he is aware of *prakṛti*, [that] "*Prakṛti* is playing with me", he becomes *jīvan mukta* at once.

Ibid., 13.20–21.

4. Twelve Kālīs in Kashmir Shaivism (verses 122–147)

The twelve Kālīs have their respective functions of creation (*sṛṣṭi*), protection (*sthiti*), destruction (*saṁhāra*), and *turya* (*anākhya*),[390] in the three states of objective (*prameya*), cognitive (*pramāṇa*), and subjective (*pramātṛ*) consciousness.

Four Kālīs in the objective cycle (*prameya*)

1. Sṛṣṭikālī: creation in the objective cycle
2. Raktakālī: protection in the objective cycle
3. Sthitināśakālī: destruction in the objective cycle
4. Yamakālī: *anākhya* in the objective cycle

Four Kālīs in the cognitive cycle (*pramāṇa*)

5. Saṁhārakālī: creation in the cognitive cycle
6. Mṛtyukālī: protection in the cognitive cycle
7. Bhadrakālī:[391] destruction in the cognitive cycle
8. Martāṇḍakālī: *anākhya* in the cognitive cycle

---

390. *Anākhya* means the gap between each of the cycles of objective, cognitive and subjective. Although related to the fourth state (*turya*), Swamiji says *anākhya* is more than *turya*.

391. Also nominated as Rudrakālī.

Four Kālīs in the subjective cycle (*pramātṛ*)

9. Paramārkakālī: creation in the subjective cycle
10. Kalāgnirudrakālī: protection in the subjective cycle
11. Mahākālakāl: destruction in the subjective cycle
12. Mahā-bhairava-ghora-caṇḍa-kālī:[392] *anākhya* in the subjective cycle.

What is the purpose of these twelve *kālī*s? The explanation of the twelvefold energies is the explanation of the kingdom of Trika – this is the kingdom of Trika *Śāstra*.

5. The *mantra* "*r-kṣ-kh-e-ṁ*" (verse 190)

शिवनभसि विगलिताक्षः कौण्डिल्युन्मेषविकसितानन्दः ।
प्रज्वलितसकलरन्ध्रः कामिन्या हृदयकुहुरमधिरूढः ॥
योगी शून्य इवास्ते तस्य स्वयमेव योगिनीहृदयम् ।
हृदयनभोमण्डलगं समुच्चरत्यनलकोटिशतदीप्तम् ॥

śivanabhasi vigalitākṣaḥ kauṇḍilyunmeṣavikasitānandaḥ /
prajvalitasakalarandhraḥ kāminyā hṛdayakuhuramadhirūḍhaḥ //
yogī śūnya ivāste tasya svayameva yoginīhṛdayam /
hṛdayanabhomaṇḍalagaṁ samuccaratyanalakoṭiśatadīptam //

392. Also nominated as Mahā-bhairava-ghora-ugra-caṇḍa-kālī.

Chart of mantra by parts	**Chart of śloka by parts**	**Chart of Kuṇḍalinī by parts**
When a yogi melts the objective world (*prameyā*) in the world of (*pramāṇa*) cognitive consciousness. This is indicated in the first *bīja mantra* of *piṇḍanātha* (*r*).	*śivanabhasi vigalitākṣaḥ* When all the *sādhaka*'s (aspirant's) organs are melted and vanished in the vacuum of God-consciousness (Lord Śiva).	When a yogi's *prāṇa* and *apāna* enter in *suṣumnā*, the central vein (*madhyadhām*) or *madhya nādī*.
pramāṇasya mita-pramatrī samāveśa This stage of Yoga is indicated in *piṇḍanātha's bīja mantra bīja* (*kṣ*)	*kuṇḍalinyunmeṣa vikasitānandaḥ* When *kuṇḍalinī* rises and the yogi experiences the highest bliss shining all-round with ecstasy and *ānandā*.	When *kuṇḍalinī*-(serpent-power) rises straight upwards from *mūladhārā* to *brahmarandrā*.
At this stage the limited *pramātṛ* (subject) gets entry in *para-pramātṛ bhāva*. This state of *samādhi* is indicated by the *bīja-mantra* of *piṇḍanātha* (*kh*).	*prajvalita sakala randhraḥ* When *ūrdhva kuṇḍalinī* is functioning and all the nine openings of organs are in their glamorous state.	When *ūrdhva kuṇḍalinī* blooms from *mūladhara* up to *brahmarandhra*, then all the yogis organs begin to bloom in God-consciousness, (*praveśa* and *prasarā*).
Kārmini is called *kriyā śakti*, and by this you have to notice the *svātantrya śakti* of Lord Śiva which is called "the mixed state of triple energies". This state is represented in *piṇḍanāthas bīja mantra* (*e*) also known as *yonibīja*.	*kāminyā hṛdaya-kuhuram-adhi-rūḍhaḥ etat traya samāveśaḥ śivo bhairava ucyate* *Tantrāloka* 3.173a When the energy of will, knowledge and action are mixed or united with each other. This is the *nirañjāna dhāma*. You will never come down from this state.	*ūrdhva kuṇḍalinyām saṅkoca-vikāsa-prādurbhāva* When a yogi gets entry in *ūrdhva kuṇḍalinī* then he experiences *vikāsā-saṁkocā*, expansion and contraction, simultaneously. This is the highest state of limited being united with unlimited Being.

Chart of mantra by parts	**Chart of śloka by parts**	**Chart of Kuṇḍalinī by parts**
avibhāga-vedan-ātmaka bindu-sattā This is the state of *bindu* (*ṁ*) which cannot be explained in words or by feeling, but only by becoming.	*yogi śūnya ivāste* In this state the yogi remains absorbed in nothingness. That is something which can neither be seen nor felt – the existence of consciousness.	*samadi vyutthānato saṁrasi-bhāvaḥ* This is that state of *kuṇḍalinī* where remaining in *samādhi* or in external worldly activities are absolutely undifferentiated.
piṇda-nātha-mantrasya kāla-saṁkarṣiṇi-dhāmatayā varṇam In conclusion: The *piṇḍanātha mantra* "*r-kṣ-kh-e-ṁ*" is that *mantra* of "*ma-ha-a*" which sentences the yogi to the state of God consciousness where time has no existence.	*tasya svayam eva yoginī hṛdayam, hṛdaya-nabho- maṇḍalagaṁ-samuccara-tyanala-koṭi-śata-diptam* To that heroic yogi, the real heart of yoginīs is experienced without any *sādhana* (practice); on the contrary it is experienced as the state which was already there. It was his real nature.	*jagadānanda daśāyāḥ prasphuṭi-bhāvaḥ* The state of *jagadānanda* is explained in *Tantrāloka* 5.51. This state of *jagadānada* is the cream of the *piṇḍanātha mantra.*

Bibliography

Published text of Lakshmanjoo Academy Book Series

Essence of the Supreme Reality, Abhinavagupta's Paramārthasāra, with the commentary of Yogarāja, original video recording (Lakshmanjoo Academy Book Series, Los Angeles, 2015).

Bhagavad Gita in the Light of Kashmir Shaivism (with original video), ed. John Hughes (Lakshmanjoo Academy Book Series, Los Angeles, 2015).

Festival of Devotion and Praise, Shivastotrāvali, Hymns to Shiva by Utpaladeva, ed. John Hughes (Lakshmanjoo Academy Book Series, Los Angeles, 2015).

Kashmir Shaivism, The Secret Supreme, ed. John Hughes (Lakshmanjoo Academy Book Series, Los Angeles, 2015).

Light on Tantra in Kashmir Shaivism, Abhinavagupta's Tantrāloka, Vol. One, chapter 1, ed. John Hughes (Lakshmanjoo Academy, Los Angeles, 2017).

Light on Tantra in Kashmir Shaivism, Abhinavagupta's Tantrāloka, Vol. Two, chapters 2 & 3, ed. John Hughes (Lakshmanjoo Academy, Los Angeles, 2019).

Self-Realization in Kashmir Shaivism, The Oral Teachings of Swami Lakshmanjoo, ed. John Hughes (State University of New York Press, Albany, 1995).

Shiva Sutras, The Supreme Awakening, ed. John Hughes (Lakshmanjoo Academy Book Series, Los Angeles, 2015).

Stava Cintāmaṇi of Bhaṭṭanārāyaṇa, ed. John Hughes (Lakshmanjoo Academy Book Series, Los Angeles, 2018).

The Mystery of Vibrationless Vibration in Kashmir Shaivism, Vasugupta's *Spanda Kārikā* and Kṣemarāja's *Spanda Sandoha*, ed. John Hughes (Lakshmanjoo Academy, Los Angeles, 2016).

Vijñāna Bhairava, The Manual for Self-Realization, ed. John Hughes (Lakshmanjoo Academy Book Series, Los Angeles, 2015).

Unpublished texts from the Lakshmanjoo Academy (LJA) archive

Bhagavad Gitartha Samgraha of Abhinavagupta, translation and commentary by Swami Lakshmanjoo (original audio recording, LJA archive, Los Angeles, 1978).

Interview on Kashmir Shaivism, Swami Lakshmanjoo with Scholars and John Hughes (original audio recordings, LJA archive, Los Angeles 1980).

Janmamaraṇavicāragranthaḥ, *Janma Maraṇa Vicāra of Bhaṭṭa Vāmadeva*, Swami Lakshmanjoo (original audio recording, LJA archive, Los Angeles, 1980).

Parātrīśikā Laghuvṛtti, with the commentary of Abhinavagupta, translation and commentary by Swami Lakshmanjoo (original audio recording, LJA archive, Los Angeles, 1982).

Parātrīśikā Vivaraṇa, with the commentary of Abhinavagupta, translation and commentary by Swami Lakshmanjoo (original audio recording, LJA archive, Los Angeles, 1982–85).

Shri Kramanaya Pradīpikā – Shining Light on the Twelve Kālīs, by Swami Lakshmanjoo (Hindi), 1958. English translation by Pranath Kaul, 2003 (LJA archive).

Stava Cintāmaṇi of Bhaṭṭanārāyaṇa, translation and commentary by Swami Lakshmanjoo (original audio recording, LJA archive, Los Angeles, 1980–81).

The Tantrāloka of Abhinavagupta, Chapters 2 to 18, translation and commentary by Swami Lakshmanjoo (original audio recording, LJA archive, Los Angeles, 1972–1981).

Vātūlanātha Sūtras of Anantaśaktipāda, translation and commentary by Swami Lakshmanjoo (original audio recordings, LJA archive, Los Angeles, 1979).

Wisdom in Kashmir Shaivism, selected verses by Swami Lakshmanjoo, (audio/video recordings, LJA archive, Nepal, 1988).

Works Cited

Brahmayāmala Tantra (*Picumata*), Volume 1. Collection Indologie (Early Tantra Series). Institut Français d'Indologie/ École française d'Extrême-Orient/Universität Hamburg.

Kiraṇa Tantra, Bhaṭṭa Rāmakaṇṭha's Commentary on the Kiraṇatantra. Vol. One: chapters 1–6, critical edition and annotated translation, Publications du Départment d'Indologie 86.1, Institut Français de Pondichéry, Pondichéry 1998.

Kulārṇava Tantra. A. Avalon, introd. Sanskrit text: *Tārā nātha Vidyāratna*. Madras: Ganesh & Co., 1965.

Mālinīvijayottara Tantram (*KSTS*), No. 37, Srinagar, 1922.

Matayāmala Tantra – Anonymous.

Niśātana Tantra (*Nisācāra Tantra*) – Anonymous.

Sarvajñānottara Tantra, Muktabodha Indological Research Institute, under the direction of Mark S. G. Dyczkowski, 2011.

Shri Hevajra Mahātantrarāja, Snellgrove, D.L., The Hevajra Tantra, A Critical Study, 2 vols, London, 1959.

Siddhayogīśvarīmata (*Siddha Tantra*), Asiatic Society of Bengal, Calcutta.

Svacchandatantra, with commentary by Kṣemarāja (*KSTS*), No. 31, 38, 44, 48, 51, 53, and 56, Srinagar/Bombay, 1921–35.

Tantrāloka of Abhinavagupta. Chapters 1–2. (*KSTS*) No. XXIII, vol. 1, Allahabad, 1918.

Tantrāloka of Abhinavagupta. Chapter 3. (*KSTS*) No. XXVIII, vol. 2, Bombay, 1921.

Tantrāloka of Abhinavagupta. Chapters 4–5. (*KSTS*) No. XXX, vol. 3, Bombay, 1921.

Tantrārajatantra. Lakṣhmana Shastri, ed. Delhi: Motilal Banarsidass, 1981.

Vājasanīya Tantra – Anonymous.

Vīrāvala (*Vīra*) *Tantra*, Muktabodha Indological Research Institute, under the direction of Mark S. G. Dyczkowski, 2011.

Yogasaṁcāra Tantra – Anonymous.

Index

A

Abhimāna 248, 249
Abhinavagupta 26, 28, 51, 56, 66, 71, 80, 85, 86, 91, 94, 100, 105, 116, 117, 126, 136, 137, 147, 155, 167, 171, 184, 194, 198, 211, 212, 216, 227, 228, 229, 255, 266, 269, 270, 271, 272, 281, 301, 317, 321, 323, 351, 368
Abhiṣeka 67, 81, 82, 108
Abhyāsa 143, 149, 152, 297
Ācārya 98, 99, 108
Adhama 37, 69
Āgama 226, 331
Agnīṣomau 206, 209
Ahaṁkāra 18, 247, 248, 249, 250, 252, 253, 255, 256, 285, 294
Ahiṁsā 131, 143, 144, 145, 362
Āhnika 1, 2, 4, 20, 22, 26, 51, 55, 60, 69, 80, 91, 92, 108, 167, 168, 211, 213, 250, 346, 373, 377, 383, 384
Aiśvarī 41
Akalpaka 386
Akalpita 77, 78, 79, 80, 81, 82, 83, 84, 85, 86, 87, 88, 95, 97, 106, 109, 110, 111, 116, 117, 118, 253, 386
Ākāra 301
Ākāśa 201, 256, 322
Akasmāt 71, 72, 73
Akula 260, 261, 262
Alaṁgrāsa 197, 261, 262
Āmantraṇa 179
Āmardaka 372
Amokṣa 36
Amṛta 124, 170, 184, 185, 187, 189, 191, 212, 213, 258
Aṁśa 38, 74
Amukhya 74
Anākhya 5, 175, 176, 177, 181, 187, 188, 215, 216, 217, 219, 220, 221, 222, 223, 224, 226, 227, 228, 231, 232, 233, 234, 236, 237, 245, 246, 251, 258, 262, 263, 265, 266, 287, 313, 389, 390
Ānanda 46, 47, 49, 124, 140, 204, 213, 294
Ānandacāri 204
Anantabhaṭṭāraka 52, 53, 54, 55, 387, 388
Anapekṣaṁ 264
Āṇavamala 50, 51
Anavasthā 128, 129, 323
Āṇavopāya 3, 5, 6, 8, 9, 15, 16, 19, 20, 25, 26, 27, 28, 29, 49, 133, 146, 159, 160, 223, 315
Anubhava 66, 72, 228, 243, 261, 386
Anugraha 74, 298, 300, 388
Anupāya 22, 28
Anuttara 296, 385
Anyonyāśraya 128, 129, 323, 324
Apāna 133, 231, 232, 233, 236, 391
Aparigraha 131, 362
Apohana 145
Aprasiddha 72
Ārcana 27, 29
Ardhatryambakā 372
Argapātra 27
Arka 186, 187, 214, 256
Arthāt 212
Arthavāda 335, 336, 337, 338, 339, 340, 341, 342
Arthavādo 339
Arthayate 302
Arthebhyaḥ 136
Arthebhyo 136
Artificial 4, 30, 154, 157, 296, 297, 358
Artificially 104
Asadgurau 55, 56, 60
Asaṁkhyāra 189
Āsana 130, 132, 141, 142, 144, 304
Āsanas 142, 143
Āsava 304
Ascend 289
Asmābhiḥ 41
Asphuṭa 4, 10, 12, 13, 15, 16, 18, 222, 288, 292
Aspirant 4, 9, 16, 98, 134, 146, 271, 391
Astamitā 138, 139
Aṣṭāṣṭaka 167
Asteya 131, 362
Aśuddhi 350
Āsyātām 39
Ātma 78, 79, 81, 86, 117, 258, 381
Ātmabhāvanā 82, 87, 386
Ātmakaḥ 13, 280
Attachment 36, 37, 44, 45, 131, 363
Automatic 52, 67, 68, 69, 70, 71, 72, 73, 74, 75, 90, 92, 279, 287, 294
Avaccheda 303

Avacchinna 248
Avadhāna 95
Āvāhana 278
Āveśa 42
Avicchinna 248, 249
Avikalpataḥ 96
B
Bahirmukhī 226, 227
Bahuvacana 263
Bāhya 25, 132, 224
Bāhyaḥ 28
Bāla 336
Bhairava 20, 42, 116, 117, 118, 134, 149, 171, 172, 173, 231, 233, 236, 237, 258, 261, 262, 264, 286, 287, 289, 304, 336, 382, 390, 391, 393
Bhairavī 289, 382
Bhakti 89, 90
Bhaṭṭāraka 52
Bhāvanā 19, 33, 34, 81, 82, 83, 86, 149, 150
Bheda 23, 24, 43, 118, 300, 358, 369
Bhīmacaryā 92
Bhoga 37, 50, 57, 58, 241
Bhuktataḥ 50, 52
Bhukti 57, 58
Bījākṣara 170, 291
Bindu 261, 392
Bodha 51, 132, 134, 163, 168, 282
Bodhāgni 291
Bodhinī 334
Brahmā 38, 58, 135, 169, 170, 171, 204, 219, 258, 284, 285, 288, 298, 301, 351, 352, 349
Brahmacāri 51, 204, 205
Brahmacarya 131, 362, 374
Brahmāṇḍa 53, 54, 190, 218, 284, 285, 288, 290
Brahmarandhra 134, 218, 391
Brahmātmakaṁ 206
Brahmayāmala 88, 95, 96, 97, 98, 99, 101
Buddhi 142, 166, 247, 248, 261
Buddhindriya 373
Buddhist 46, 48, 125, 128
Butchering 155
C
Caitanyamātma 118
Cakitā 304
Cakra 10, 11, 28, 66, 92, 167, 168, 170, 175, 186, 188, 189, 190, 191, 193, 194, 195, 200, 201, 202, 203, 204, 205, 206, 207, 216, 217, 218, 219, 221, 222, 224, 231, 235, 236, 245, 246, 251, 261, 263, 266, 287, 294, 313, 375
Cakrodaya 31, 168, 171, 217, 225, 299
Cakṣurmaṇḍale 179
Caṇḍa 264, 265, 390
Cāṇḍāla 307
Caṇḍikā 97, 98, 99
Caryākrama 192, 194, 209, 210
Caste 307, 354
Caturāra 188, 196, 287
Causality 72, 106
Cetana 282
Cetasā 126
Cidānanda 124
Cidātmā 287
Cidbhairava 42
Cintana 147, 152
Citta 46, 132, 133, 134
Codana 329, 330
Cognition 27, 174, 175, 178, 195, 201, 214, 216, 218, 220, 236, 238, 240, 244, 245, 246, 248, 251, 252, 254, 305
Concealing 298, 299, 300, 388
Contemplate 14, 15, 18, 19, 84
D
Dakṣiṇa 60
Daṇḍa 336
Darśana 34, 39, 76, 261
Death 104, 205, 240, 340, 358, 359
Deha 142, 143, 144, 146, 253, 254, 258, 321, 343
Deities 27, 39, 66, 165, 167
Destruction 5, 50, 51, 53, 54, 103, 176, 177, 188, 216, 220, 221, 222, 229, 230, 231, 234, 237, 238, 240, 245, 257, 259, 262, 265, 296, 299, 388, 389, 390
Deva 14, 327, 337, 338
Devī 97, 99, 221, 222, 225, 231, 243, 250, 266, 268, 274, 303
Devotion 89, 90, 91, 235, 307, 308
Dhāraṇā 8, 14, 15, 34, 130, 132, 135, 136, 137, 138, 139, 140, 142, 143, 146, 304
Dhyāna 3, 12, 34, 82, 83, 87, 95, 130, 132, 135, 136, 138, 139, 140, 142, 143, 146, 161, 297, 309, 310, 311
Dīkṣa 98, 102, 108, 306
Discriminate 64, 65, 383
Doṣa 100, 103, 127, 128, 129
Doubt 75, 96, 110, 184, 229, 233, 234, 235,

237, 241, 242, 243, 244, 245, 335, 337, 345, 346
Doubts 75, 117, 153, 232, 234, 237, 243, 244, 245, 246, 337
Down 10, 40, 42, 83, 85, 91, 99, 146, 171, 207, 215, 221, 233, 236, 245, 265, 283, 309, 340, 352, 391
Drāvaṇā 243
Dravya 101
Dreaming 149, 150, 163, 176, 258
Dualism 358
Durgā 97
Durvasā 374
Dvādaśa 134, 193, 194, 196, 199, 256
Dvaita 111, 112, 139, 152, 158
E
Equilibrium 206, 387
Erakanātha 267, 270
G
Ghora 42, 264, 265, 390
Ghoratarī 42
Ghūrṇi 304
Goddesses 67, 261
Golakas 179
Govindarāja 267, 269, 270, 271
Graha 280
Grāhya 139, 379
Guhya 202, 204, 206, 207
Guhyacakrāṇyasau 201, 202
Guru 31, 66, 69, 75, 76, 77, 78, 79, 80, 81, 82, 83, 84, 87, 95, 101, 106, 109, 110, 111, 112, 115, 117, 118, 123, 147, 148, 266, 327, 371
H
Haṁsaḥ 209
Havan 26, 30, 67
Hiṁsā 143, 144, 145
Hṛdaya 261, 294, 295, 303, 391, 392
Hypocrisy 100, 366
I
Icchā 146, 258, 285, 286, 288, 292
Ignorance 57, 63, 68, 102, 112, 113, 121, 343, 386
Initiation 67, 68, 76, 77, 81, 82, 89, 93, 96, 97, 98, 102, 105, 106, 108, 112, 117, 124, 127, 306
Īśvara 47, 49, 54, 114, 131, 206, 258, 260, 275
J
Jagadānanda 182, 183, 392
Janmādhāra 206
Japa 93, 297
Jīva 114, 134, 135, 256, 344, 345
Jīvanmukti 26, 114
Jñāna 27, 89, 94, 95, 119, 138, 178, 187, 191, 225, 268, 272, 285, 286, 288, 292, 380
Jñānanetra 268
Jñānanetranātha 268
Jñānendriyas 194, 247
Jugupsa 347
Junction 2, 3, 4, 7
K
Kaivalyam 314
Kāla 149, 186, 187, 254, 258, 261, 271, 392
Kalādvādaśakātmaiva 174, 175
Kalāgnirudrakālī 390
Kalākalāpaṁ 359
Kālaṁ 50, 359
Kālikā 268
Kalpaka 75, 76, 78, 79, 80, 81, 82, 83, 84, 85, 86, 87, 95, 97, 106, 118, 386
Kalpita 31, 68, 75, 76, 106, 108, 109, 110, 111, 118, 250, 253, 254, 257, 386
Kalpitaḥ 108
Kalyānikā 268
Karaṇeśvarī 164, 231
Karaṅkiṇī 304
Kārmamala 50, 51
Karmendriya 373
Kaula 25, 29, 30, 31, 60, 101, 158, 223, 355, 360, 361, 363, 365, 369, 373, 374, 375, 376, 377, 380
Kaulacāra 373
Kaulācāra 361
Kevalaṁ 152
Keyūravatī 268
Khagendranātha 373
Khecarī 193, 276, 304
Kheer 319
Kleśa 46
Knower 47, 252, 253, 256, 263
Knowledge 27, 48, 49, 63, 64, 68, 69, 71, 72, 73, 86, 89, 93, 94, 95, 99, 100, 102, 105, 106, 107, 108, 109, 110, 112, 113, 117, 118, 119, 120, 122, 123, 124, 127, 128, 139, 147, 148, 176, 178, 187, 191, 194, 199, 225, 247, 248, 263, 285, 299, 328, 337, 347, 357, 360, 366, 380, 391
Known 53, 175, 176, 178, 188, 203, 219, 220, 285, 369, 370, 386, 391
Krama 25, 27, 30, 91, 110, 135, 148, 175, 196, 198, 202, 215, 216, 219, 228, 266, 277,

286, 287, 289, 292, 294, 296
Kramacatuṣṭayam 219
Kramakeli 216, 269, 271
Kramastotra 216
Kriyā 25, 199, 285, 286, 288, 292, 391
Kriyādīkṣā 76
Krodhanī 304
Kṛṣṇa 51, 181, 374
Kṣatriya 307
Kṣepaḥ 273
Kṣetra 364
Kula 29, 30, 31, 58, 60, 93, 157, 158, 178, 198, 262, 266, 360, 369, 371, 372, 374
Kuṇḍa 27, 196
Kuṇḍalinī 11, 19, 52, 112, 205, 207, 214, 215, 287, 294, 295, 391, 392
L
Laya 185
Liṅga 154, 157, 184, 185, 317, 318, 319, 359, 360, 361, 362, 365, 366, 367, 370
Liquor 101, 304
Lokānanda 162
Lokāprasiddho 72
M
Madanikā 268
Madbhaktaḥ 306
Madhyā 81, 82, 87
Mahābhairava 264
Mahākāla 257, 259, 261
Mahākālakālī 259, 261, 262
Maheśvaraḥ 351
Maithuna 101
Mālinīvijaya 34, 35, 36, 57, 71, 72, 100, 135, 136, 154, 290, 291, 315, 316, 317, 318, 320, 334, 350, 357, 359, 361, 368
Māṁsa 101
Manda 20, 81, 82, 87
Maṇḍala 11, 26, 27, 76, 90, 91, 93, 95, 179, 180, 181, 237, 250
Mantra 5, 15, 16, 19, 25, 31, 90, 92, 93, 95, 101, 102, 104, 161, 170, 206, 207, 226, 235, 262, 275, 277, 283, 284, 287, 290, 295, 306, 309, 325, 327, 363, 380, 390, 391, 392
Mantreśvara 206, 207, 275
Marriage 354
Martaṇḍakālī 255
Maṭhikā 371, 372
Mātṛsadbhāva 275
Māyā 23, 24, 44, 52, 53, 54, 56, 61, 62, 160, 186, 284, 285, 288
Māyāpāśa 56
Māyīya 358
Māyīyamala 50, 51
Meditation 19, 82, 90, 94, 149, 161, 226, 297, 298, 299, 303, 308, 309, 310, 311, 312, 319, 364, 375
Melāpa 90, 91, 92, 93
Mokṣa 37, 38, 45, 46, 47, 57, 58, 61, 134, 204, 357
Mokṣopāya 36
Moon 133, 174, 175, 185, 186, 187, 194, 233, 248
Mṛtyu 239, 240, 358
Mūḍha 40, 232
Mudrā 287, 289, 294, 303, 304, 308, 311, 374
Mukti 26, 57, 58, 204
N
Nāda 261, 272, 274
Navel 3, 294, 329
Netrānātha 268
Nimeṣonmeṣa 227
Nimīlanā 182, 207, 210, 221, 246, 287
Nirañjana 198, 199, 207, 230
Nirbhitti 73, 74, 75, 386
Nirmala 160
Nirvāṇa 48, 77, 367
Nirvikalpa 17, 18, 198, 225, 231, 255
Nistaraṅgata 281
Nityam 77, 261
Niyama 144, 146, 319
Niyati 36, 37, 302
O
Oṁ 7, 262, 327
Omnipresent 361
Ovallī 380
P
Pādāṅguṣṭha 218
Pāñcarātra 41, 44
Paramāditya 252, 256
Paramārka 256
Paramārkakālī 252, 256, 257, 390
Parāmarśa 13, 14, 21, 24, 62, 63, 130, 147, 148, 158, 160, 161, 163, 173, 174, 178, 248, 249, 278, 279, 292, 295, 296, 384, 385
Parāmarśamayī 21
Parāmarśasvarūpiṇī 173
Parameśvara 2
Parameśvarī 180, 232, 261
Pārampāra 25

Parāparā 133
Parāsavāt 304
Parāspadaṁ 62
Pārvatī 18, 25, 93, 96, 101, 155, 179, 180, 198
Pāśa 43
Paśu 194, 195, 201, 255, 256, 333
Paśū 255
Paśukāmasya 332, 333
Pāta 146, 212
Patañjali 34, 39, 130, 131
Pīḍana 186, 196, 200, 298, 299, 300
Piṇḍanātha 284, 286, 287, 288, 289, 291, 292, 293, 294, 296, 325, 391, 392
Pīṭha 364, 374
Prabuddhaḥ 233
Pradhāna 287
Prajñā 74, 117
Prakaraṇa 43, 85, 162
Prakāśa 186, 255, 261, 296
Prakriya 264
Prakṛti 45, 46, 53, 54, 114, 284, 285, 386, 387, 388, 389
Prakṛtyaṇḍa 53, 54, 284, 285, 288, 290
Pralaya 132, 133, 134
Pralayākala 47, 48, 49, 50, 51, 52, 140, 250, 251, 275
Pralīnaśaśibhāskare 232
Pramāṇa 5, 15, 174, 176, 177, 178, 181, 182, 186, 187, 189, 195, 199, 200, 201, 214, 216, 229, 231, 232, 236, 237, 238, 239, 240, 245, 246, 248, 251, 262, 263, 265, 266, 338, 389, 391
Pramāṇaṁśabhakṣaṇapravaṇaṁ 251
Pramātā 50, 51, 52, 54, 55, 124, 177, 181, 182, 225, 231, 239, 251, 255, 256, 257, 258, 266, 275
Pramātṛ 5, 51, 63, 163, 167, 171, 174, 175, 176, 177, 178, 181, 182, 183, 184, 186, 187, 189, 191, 193, 195, 197, 198, 201, 202, 203, 212, 214, 216, 220, 244, 247, 251, 252, 253, 254, 255, 256, 257, 258, 259, 260, 262, 263, 264, 265, 275, 276, 293, 348, 389, 390, 391
Prameya 5, 15, 175, 176, 177, 178, 181, 182, 183, 184, 186, 187, 189, 191, 195, 197, 199, 200, 208, 216, 225, 226, 229, 231, 232, 234, 237, 245, 262, 263, 264, 265, 266, 338, 389
Pramiti 174, 175, 181, 182, 186, 187, 189, 193, 220, 262, 263, 264
Prāṇa 133, 141, 142, 143, 205, 214, 215, 231, 232, 233, 236, 251, 258, 391
Praṇava 262, 325
prāṇāyāma 34, 130, 132, 134, 135, 136, 142, 143, 144, 154
Prāṇāyāma 34, 130
Prasaṅga 201, 202, 209
Prasara 212, 385
Prasiddhi 58
Pratiṣedha 157
Pratiṣṭhā 53, 283
Pratyabhijñā 179
Pratyāhāra 34, 130, 132, 135, 136, 137, 141
Priya 91, 92
Pṛthivī 53, 54, 285, 288, 323, 324
Pūjā 25, 27, 28, 31, 92, 154, 157, 169, 170, 171, 278, 283, 360, 365, 366, 367, 375, 383
Purāṇa 44
Pūrṇāhantā 258
Puruṣa 53, 54, 114, 285, 387, 388, 389
Putraka 98, 99, 108
R
Rāga 36, 37, 40, 44, 45
Rāgatattvaṁ 36, 45
Rahasya 194
Rakta 98
Raktādevī 99
Raktakālī 226, 227, 228, 229, 230, 266, 389
Randhra 294
Rañjanā 228
Rasa 124, 146, 159, 162, 164, 179, 185, 194, 196, 199, 230, 232, 320, 332, 333
Realization 84, 101, 112, 114, 115, 134 142, 149 159, 178, 192, 198, 215, 235, 251, 288 299, 304, 319, 336, 337, 369, 380, 393
Recognition 179, 327, 328
Rodhana 243, 246, 255
Ṛṣis 44, 345, 346, 351, 352
Rudra 28, 254, 255, 340, 341, 342, 351
Rudrakālī 240, 243, 245, 389
S
Śabda
Sadāśiva 51, 52, 54, 170, 206, 234, 243, 257, 258, 259, 260, 261, 271, 275
Sadbhāva 381
Sādhaka 52, 53, 54, 92, 97, 98, 99, 108, 146, 160, 162, 299, 300, 316, 319, 364
Sādhanā 364, 365, 367
Sadoditaḥ 279
Sahabhitti 75, 79, 80, 82, 83, 84, 85, 86, 87

Sahaja
Sahasrāra 189, 190, 205
Sahṛdaya 382
Sakala 275, 294, 391
Sākṣātkāra 16, 198
Śākta 146, 158, 299, 401
Śakti 51, 53, 54, 66, 74, 171, 197, 198, 203, 214, 246, 261, 274, 285, 292, 295, 299, 371, 385, 387, 388, 391
Śakticakra
Śaktipāta 59, 60, 63, 73, 74, 83, 124, 306, 307, 369
Śāktopāya 133, 144, 157, 159, 160, 164, 167, 190, 221, 223, 251, 283, 298, 299, 300, 315, 376, 383
Śaktyaṇḍa 53, 54, 290
Śālini 257
Samādhi 52, 92, 124, 130, 132, 135, 136, 139, 140, 141, 146, 162, 165, 182, 183, 205, 221, 234, 287, 288, 289, 308, 352, 391, 392
Sāmagrī 169
Sāmānya 236, 280, 281, 334
Samāveśa 199, 243, 294, 315, 391
Samayī 97, 98
Śāmbhava 119, 315
Śāmbhavāvasthā 315
Śāmbhavopāya 91, 133, 159, 167, 223, 315
Sambodha 90, 91, 93, 94
Sameness 208, 280, 332, 380, 381
Saṁghaṭṭa 119, 282
Saṁhāra 177, 216, 224, 229, 231, 232, 237, 238, 240, 245, 246, 258, 259, 262, 265, 287, 292, 294, 296, 298, 300, 389
Saṁhārakālī 237, 238, 240, 245, 389
Sāmīpya
Saṁkalpya 235
Sāṁkhya 55, 62, 114
Saṁkocā 391
Sampradāya 371
Sampūrṇa 265, 303
Saṁsāra 254, 255, 276
Sāṁsiddhika 65, 66, 69, 70, 73, 74, 75, 76, 77, 78, 79, 80, 82, 83, 84, 85, 86, 87, 101, 106, 111, 112, 113, 115, 118, 386
Saṁskāra 64, 94, 116, 129, 138, 199, 241, 299
Saṁviddevī 250
Saṁvit 132, 140, 168, 171, 175, 178, 203, 217, 221, 224, 225, 250, 276, 277, 281, 287, 299, 376
Saṁyogāt 135, 184
Sannyāsi 58
Sanskrit 112, 122, 263, 395
Santoṣa 131
Śarīram 134
Sarvātmaka 158, 360
Śāstra 60, 61, 64, 65, 66, 67, 69, 71, 72, 74, 76, 77, 78, 80, 81, 84, 85, 87, 100, 110, 117, 118, 119, 120, 122, 123, 174, 223, 279, 329, 338, 347, 358, 359, 360, 361, 363, 369, 370, 375, 376, 379, 386, 390
Śāstrajña 174
Śāstras 58, 64, 65, 66, 67, 70, 71, 72, 73, 74, 77, 78, 79, 80, 81, 85, 86, 87, 100, 101, 106, 108, 110, 111, 112, 116, 117, 118, 119, 121, 122, 123, 127, 128, 155, 174, 254, 329, 337, 338, 347, 362, 369, 386, 387
Sattarka 56, 66
Satya 53, 131
Śauca 131
Sauḥ 284, 286, 287, 288, 289, 290, 296, 325
Sāyujya
Semen 196, 202, 373
Sex 101, 105, 125, 169, 190, 191, 209, 213, 217
Siddha 65, 70, 88, 92, 105, 111, 113, 116, 195, 199, 376, 395
Siddhi 93, 94, 96, 204
Śiṣya 98, 266
Śivanabhasi 293, 294, 390, 391
Śivānanda 268
Śivānandanātha 268
Śivaśaktyātmakaṁ 197
Śivatattvaṁ 380
Skull 134, 218
Smṛta 79
Soma 175, 181, 182, 184, 185, 186, 187, 189, 190, 191, 192, 194, 195, 196, 201, 206, 208, 209, 210, 212, 248, 332, 333
Somānanda 270
Soul 158, 205, 236, 312, 319, 328, 347, 351
Spanda 161, 162, 193, 203, 220, 232, 233, 235, 236, 276, 279, 280, 281, 393
Sparśa 159, 164, 169, 179, 194, 320
Sphuṭa 222, 288
Sphuṭatama 222, 265, 288
Sphuṭatara 222, 288
Sphuṭībhāva
Śrībrahmayāmale 88
Śrīgovindarāja 269
Śrīpūrvaśāstre 57, 154
Śrotre 217

Sṛṣṭi 176, 177, 180, 187, 215, 216, 217, 219, 220, 224, 225, 228, 229, 230, 231, 232, 237, 238, 252, 256, 258, 265, 283, 286, 287, 298, 300, 389
Sṛṣṭikālī 225, 226, 227, 229, 230, 234, 266, 389
Sthāna 232, 258, 265
Sthiti 229, 245
Sthitināśa 231
Sthitināśakālī 229, 230, 231, 232, 389
Śuddhavidyā 51, 53, 54, 55, 57, 63, 64, 70, 71, 73, 75, 106, 111, 160, 161, 163, 206, 207, 208, 260, 275
Sukham 162
Śukra 196
Śūlabīja 292
Śūnya 177, 231, 261, 292, 293, 295, 390, 392
Sūrya 174, 175, 201, 248, 250
Sūryātmā 248
Suṣumnā 134, 236, 391
Suṣupti 52, 236
Sūtra 162
Svacchanda 61, 103, 320
Svacchandaśāstre 61
Svādhyāya 131
Svapna 83, 87, 149, 150
Svarūpa 122, 139, 231, 232, 243, 251, 256, 258, 262, 319
Svatantra 122, 171
Svātantrya 51, 144, 145, 173, 197, 203, 224, 264, 274, 388, 391
Svātantryavāda 144
Svātma 259, 282
Svātmaparāmarśa 274
T
Tanmayī 311
Tantra 57, 65, 71, 88, 91, 95, 96, 97, 98, 99, 100, 101, 103, 104, 105, 118, 132, 133, 135, 136, 137, 144, 154, 163, 167, 170, 178, 179, 192, 205, 275, 290, 291, 306, 307, 315, 316, 317, 318, 320, 334, 344, 350, 351, 357, 359, 361, 368, 369, 393, 395
Tantrāloka 52, 56, 58, 79, 91, 98, 100, 108, 114, 116, 133, 135, 137, 144, 167, 170, 171, 175, 183, 192, 196, 197, 198, 199, 200, 205, 211, 213, 216, 226, 250, 262, 267, 269, 270, 272, 282, 287, 369, 373, 374, 383, 384, 385, 386, 387, 391, 392, 393, 394, 395
Tantric 105
Tapas 90, 131, 132
Tapasyā 370
Tarka 64, 129, 130, 132, 136, 141, 142, 144, 152, 153, 154, 386
Tattva 51, 52, 53, 54, 94, 95, 170, 199, 203, 207, 214, 231, 277, 287, 288, 294, 334, 342, 369, 376, 381, 387
Time 52, 55, 60, 74, 80, 93, 99, 113, 114, 116, 117, 124, 145, 146, 148, 149, 151, 160, 164, 175, 186, 187, 188, 215, 217, 244, 245, 246, 251, 254, 257, 258, 261, 266, 268, 274, 276, 278, 282, 286, 289, 318, 354, 358, 359, 367, 371, 388, 392
Tīvra 81
Trika 58, 60, 62, 64, 157, 158, 223, 355, 365, 366, 369, 377, 379, 390
Trikoṇa 292, 293
Triśūla 288
Tryambakanātha 372
Turya 175, 176, 205, 216, 236, 389
Turyātīta 205
U
Uccāra 207
Ugra 264, 265, 390
Universal 53, 58, 65, 71, 109, 132, 134, 135, 166, 168, 170, 173, 191, 192, 193, 196, 203, 205, 208, 209, 248, 251, 260, 276, 279, 283, 288, 290, 295, 296, 300, 301, 339, 360, 366, 378, 381
Unmeṣa 52, 207, 227
Unmīlanā 165, 182, 202, 207, 209, 210, 221, 232, 287
Upalakṣaṇam 217
Upāsanā
Upāya 159, 376
Ūrdhvareta 374
Utkṛṣṭa 81, 82, 83
Utmost 77
Utpaladeva 261, 270, 393
Uttara 65, 351
V
Vācaka 338
Vaiṣṇava 60
Vākya 147, 352, 353
Vāmācāra 103, 276
Vāmeśvarī 193, 275
Vāñchati 303
Vāsanā 220
Vastudharmo 348
Vastunaḥ 321, 322

Vastuni 110, 149, 247
Vasudeva
Vasugupta 162, 193, 220, 235, 393
Vāyu 201, 322, 325
Vāyuto 325
Veda 331
Vedānta 56, 62, 224, 281, 355, 358
Vedāntists 283, 366
Vicāraṇam 317, 350
Viccheda
Vidhāna 97, 98
Vidhi 98, 157, 158, 316, 329, 335, 338, 339, 360, 378
Vidyā 53, 102
Vighnas 364
Vijñāna 51, 134, 149, 176, 177, 199, 304, 336, 337, 393
Vijñānākala 47, 48, 49, 51, 52, 54, 55, 275
Vikalpa 5, 2, 3, 6, 7, 8, 9, 10, 12, 13, 14, 17, 18, 19, 22, 27, 29, 31, 64, 129, 138, 160, 198, 199, 273, 299, 311
Vikāra 207
Vikāsa 243, 357, 391
Vilāpana 300
Vimala 171, 172
Vimarśa 147, 148
Vīra 88, 199
Vīrya 16, 25, 31, 217, 277, 278, 283
Visarga 23, 133, 280, 282, 285, 286, 287, 290
Viṣaya 256
Viśeṣa 281
Viṣṇu 46, 58, 135, 298, 351, 352, 353
Viśrānti 133
Viśva 24, 208, 218, 246, 257
Void 11, 139, 175, 177, 188, 261
Vowels 222, 223, 288, 291
Vrata 205, 363
Vyāpaka 249
Vyāpti 290
Vyāptiriṣyate 290
Vyavacchedena 253, 254
Vyoma 336
Vyomavameśvari 193
W
Wakefulness 149, 163
Whiskey 349
Wisdom 74, 89, 107, 233, 235, 277
Worship 4, 5, 25, 27, 29, 30, 31, 98, 101, 154, 157, 161, 169, 170, 171, 278, 311, 312, 313, 317, 318, 319, 335, 339, 360, 361, 362, 371, 375, 382, 383
Y
Yāga 198, 312, 349
Yama 130, 141, 144, 146, 232
Yamakālī 232, 233, 236, 237, 238, 241, 244, 245, 246, 389
Yamātmikā 234
Yasyonmeṣanimeṣābhyāṁ 203
Yoga 4, 5, 8, 31, 34, 39, 89, 93, 94, 112, 124, 129, 130, 131, 132, 136, 141, 149, 150, 154, 179, 304, 391
Yogāṅga 4, 31, 129, 130
Yoginī 18, 25, 80, 90, 91, 92, 93, 192, 199, 210, 214, 295, 364, 376, 392
Yoginībhūḥ 80, 210, 211, 214, 215
Yoginīhṛdayam 293, 390
Yoni 184
Yukti 342
Z
Zodiac 222, 223

Teachings of Swami Lakshmanjoo published by The Lakshmanjoo Academy

Bhagavad Gītā, In the Light of Kashmir Shaivism

Festival of Devotion & Praise, Hymns to Shiva
Shivastotrāvali by Utpaladeva

Vijñāna Bhairava, The Manual for Self-Realization

Shiva Sūtras, The Supreme Awakening

Kashmir Shaivism, The Secret Supreme

Self-Realization in Kashmir Shaivism,
The Oral Teachings of Swami Lakshmanjoo

Essence of the Supreme Reality,
Abhinavagupta's Paramārthasāra

The Mystery of Vibrationless-Vibration in Kashmir Shaivism,
Vasugupta's Spanda Kārikā & Kṣemarāja's Spanda Sandoha

The Magical Jewel of Devotion in Kashmir Shaivism
Bhaṭṭa Nārāyaṇa's Stava Cintāmaṇi

Light on Tantra of Kashmir Shaivism, Abhinavagupta's Tantrāloka
Chapter One - Volume One

Light on Tantra of Kashmir Shaivism, Abhinavagupta's Tantrāloka
Chapter Two and Three - Volume Two

Lakshmanjoo
ACADEMY

The teachings of Swami Lakshmanjoo are a response to the urgent need of our time: the transformation of consciousness and the evolution of a more enlightened humanity.

The Universal Shaiva Fellowship was established under Swamiji's direct inspiration, for the purpose of realizing Swamiji's vision of making Kashmir Shaivism available to the whole world. It was Swamiji's wish that his teachings be made available without the restriction of caste, creed, color or gender.

The Universal Shaiva Fellowship and the Lakshmanjoo Academy, along with the Kashmir Shaiva Institute (Ishwar Ashram Trust), India, have preserved Swamiji's original teachings and are progressively making these teachings available in book, audio and video formats.

This knowledge is extremely valuable and uplifting for all of humankind. It offers humanity a clear and certain vision in a time of uncertainty. It shows us the way home and gives us the means for the attainment of complete Self-Realization.

For information on Kashmir Shaivism or to support the work of The Universal Shaiva Fellowship and the Lakshmanjoo Academy and Kashmir Shaiva Institute (Ishwar Ashram Trust) visit the Lakshmanjoo Academy website or email us at info@LakshmanjooAcademy.org.

www.UniversalShaivaFellowship.org
www.LakshmanjooAcademy.org
www.IshwarAshramTrust.com

Instructions to download audio files

1. Go to https//:www.lakshmanjooacademy.org/tantra3-332

2. Fill out the email opt-in form to add your name to the Lakshmanjoo Academy email list.

3. When you click the button in the follow-up email to confirm your email subscription you will be directed to the audio page for your purchase.

   If you have any difficulties please contact us at: https//:www.lakshmanjooacademy.org/contact

www.ingramcontent.com/pod-product-compliance
Lightning Source LLC
Chambersburg PA
CBHW050309120526
44592CB00014B/1843
* 9 7 8 1 9 4 7 2 4 1 1 4 5 *